NEW TRENDS AND DEVELOPMENTS IN BIOMETRICS

Edited by **Jucheng Yang, Shan Juan Xie**

New Trends and Developments in Biometrics

http://dx.doi.org/10.5772/3420
Edited by Jucheng Yang, Shan Juan Xie

Contributors

Miroslav Bača, Petra Grd, Tomislav Fotak, Mohamad El-Abed, Christophe Charrier, Christophe Rosenberger, Homayoon Beigi, Joshua Abraham, Paul Kwan, Claude Roux, Chris Lennard, Christophe Champod, Aniesha Alford, Joseph Shelton, Joshua Adams, Derrick LeFlore, Michael Payne, Jonathan Turner, Vincent McLean, Robert Benson, Gerry Dozier, Kelvin Bryant, John Kelly, Francesco Beritelli, Andrea Spadaccini, Christian Rathgeb, Martin Drahansky, Stepan Mracek, Radim Dvorak, Jan Vana, Svetlana Yanushkevich, Vladimir Balakirsky, Jinfeng Yang, Jucheng Yang, Bon K. Sy, Arun P. Kumara Krishnan, Michal Dolezel, Jaroslav Urbanek, Tai-Hoon Kim, Eva Brezinova, Fen Miao, Ye LI, Cunzhang Cao, Shu-di Bao

Published by InTech

Janeza Trdine 9, 51000 Rijeka, Croatia

Publishing Process Manager Iva Lipovic
Typesetting InTech DTP Team
Cover InTech Design Team

Additional hard copies can be obtained from orders@intechopen.com

New Trends and Developments in Biometrics, Edited by Jucheng Yang, Shan Juan Xie
p. cm.
ISBN 978-953-51-0859-7

For EU product safety concerns:
IN TECH d.o.o., Prolaz Marije Krucifikse Kozulić 3, 51000 Rijeka, Croatia,
info@intechopen.com or visit our website at intechopen.com.

Meet the editors

Dr. Jucheng Yang is a special professor of Haihe Scholar in College of Computer Science and Information Engineering, Tianjin University of Science and Technology, Tianjin, China. He is a special professor of Tianjin City, too. He received his B.S. degree from South-Central University for Nationalities, China, and M.S. and Ph.D. degree from Chonbuk National University, Republic of Korea. He did his post-doc at the Advanced Graduate Education Center of Jeonbuk for Electronics and Information Technology-BK21 (AGEC-JEIT-BK21), Republic of Korea. He was a professor in Jiangxi University of Finance and Economics, China, and was a visiting fellow in the University of New South Wales, Australia. He has published over 50 papers in related international journals and conferences, and served as editor or review. He has applied nine Chinese patents and was awarded two Chinese patents of biometrics. His research interests include biometrics, image processing, pattern recognition and neural networks.

Dr. ShanJuan Xie received her B.S. degree from South-Central University for Nationalities, China, and M.S. and Ph.D. degree from Chonbuk National University, Republic of Korea. She is a post-doc at the Advanced Graduate Education Center of Jeonbuk for Electronics and Information Technology-BK21 (AGECJEIT-BK21), Republic of Korea. Her areas of interest are biometrics, pattern recognition, image processing, and machine learning, in which she has authored almost 30 papers in related international journals and conferences. She has served as reviewer of many conferences. She was awarded the best paper in the 4th Conference on Information and Communication Technology and two Chinese patents of biometrics.

Contents

Preface

In recent years, biometrics has developed rapidly with its worldwide applications for daily life. New trends and novel developments have been proposed to acquire and process many different biometric traits. The ignored challenges in the past and potential problems need to be thought together and deeply integrated.

The key objective of the book is to keep up with the new technologies on some recent theoretical development as well as new trends of applications in biometrics. The topics covered in this book reflect well both aspects of development. They include the new development in forensic speaker recognition, 3D and thermo face recognition, finger vein recognition, contact-less biometric system, hand geometry recognition, biometric performance evaluation, multi-biometric template protection, and novel subfields in the new challenge fields.

The book consists of 13 chapters. It is divided into four sections, namely, theory and method, performance evaluation, security and template protection, and other applications. Chapter 1 explores the latest techniques which are being deployed in the various branches of speaker recognition, and highlights the technical challenges that need to be overcome. Chapter 2 presents a novel biometric system based on 3D and thermo face recognition, including specify data acquisition, image processing and recognition algorithms. In Chapter 3, the author proposes a scattering removal method for finger-vein image restoration, which is based on a biological optical model which reasonably described the effects of skin scattering. Chapter 4 gives an overarching survey of existing principles of contact-based hand geometry systems and mentions trends in the contact-less systems. Chapter 5 introduces a new subfield, namely, Genetic and Evolutionary Biometrics (GECs), which shows how GECs can be hybridized with a well-known feature extraction technique needed for recognition, recognition accuracy, and computational complexity.

Section 2 is a collection of two chapters on performance evaluation. Chapter 6 analyzes the efficiently and reliably whether the state-of-the-art speaker recognition techniques can be employed in this context, as well as the limitations and their strengths to be improved to migrate from old-school manual or semi-automatic techniques to new, reliable and objective automatic methods. Chapter 7 presents the performance evaluation of biometric systems related to three aspects: data quality, usability, and security. Security as respect to the privacy of an individual is focused on emerging trends in this research fields.

Section 3 groups two methods for security and template protection. Chapter 8 gives an overarching analysis of existing problems that affect forensic speaker recognition. Chapter 9 provides a solution for the template security protection by multi-biometric fusion.

Finally, Section 4 groups a number of novel other biometric approaches or applications. In chapter 10, the author proposes a Likelihood Ratio model using morphometric and spatial analysis based on Support Vector Machine for matching both genuine and close imposter populations typically recovered from AFIS candidate lists. Chapter 11 describes the procedures of biometric solutions for securing body sensor network, including the entity identifiers generation scheme and relevant key distribution solution. Chapter 12 introduces a new, interesting and important research and development works in the skin diseased fingerprint recognition, especially the process of quality estimation of various diseased fingerprint images and the process of fingerprint enhancement. Chapter 13 proposes the algorithms for processing biometric data oriented to privacy protection and preservation of significant parameters.

The book was reviewed by editors Dr. Jucheng Yang and Dr. Shanjuan Xie. We deeply appreciate the efforts of our guest editors: Dr. Norman Poh, Dr. Loris Nanni, Dr. Dongsun Park and Dr. Sook Yoon, Dr. Qing Li, Ms. Congcong Xiong as well as a number of anonymous reviewers.

Dr. Jucheng Yang
Professor
Special Professor of Haihe Scholar
College of Computer Science and Information Engineering
Tianjin University of Science and Technology
Tianjin, China

Dr. Shanjuan Xie
Post-doc
Division of Electronics & Information engineering
Chonbuk National University
Jeonju, Jeonbuk
Republic of Korea

Section 1

Theory and Method

Chapter 1

Speaker Recognition: Advancements and Challenges

Homayoon Beigi

Additional information is available at the end of the chapter

http://dx.doi.org/10.5772/52023

1. Introduction

Speaker Recognition is a multi-disciplinary branch of biometrics that may be used for *identification*, *verification*, and *classification* of individual speakers, with the capability of *tracking*, *detection*, and *segmentation* by extension. Recently, a comprehensive book on all aspects of speaker recognition was published [1]. Therefore, here we are not concerned with details of the standard modeling which is and has been used for the recognition task. In contrast, we present a review of the most recent literature and briefly visit the latest techniques which are being deployed in the various branches of this technology.

Most of the works being reviewed here have been published in the last two years. Some of the topics, such as alternative features and modeling techniques, are general and apply to all branches of speaker recognition. Some of these general techniques, such as whispered speech, are related to the advanced treatment of special forms of audio which have not received ample attention in the past. Finally, we will follow by a look at advancements which apply to specific branches of speaker recognition [1], such as verification, identification, classification, and diarization.

This chapter is meant to complement the summary of speaker recognition, presented in [2], which provided an overview of the subject. It is also intended as an update on the methods described in [1]. In the next section, for the sake of completeness, a brief history of speaker recognition is presented, followed by sections on specific progress as stated above, for globally applicable treatment and methods, as well as techniques which are related to specific branches of speaker recognition.

2. A brief history

The topic of speaker recognition [1] has been under development since the mid-twentieth century. The earliest known papers on the subject, published in the 1950s [3, 4], were in search of finding personal traits of the speakers, by analyzing their speech, with some statistical underpinning. With the advent of early communication networks, *Pollack, et al.* [3] noted the need for speaker identification. Although, they employed human listeners to do the identification of individuals and studied the importance of the duration of speech and other facets that help in the recognition of a speaker. In most of the early activities, a text-dependent analysis was made, in order to simplify the task of identification. In 1959, not long after Pollack's analysis, *Shearme, et al.* [4] started comparing the formants of speech, in order to facilitate the identification process. However, still a human expert would do the analysis. This first incarnation of speaker recognition, namely using human expertise, has been used to date, in order to handle forensic speaker identification [5, 6]. This class of approaches have been improved and used in a variety of criminal and forensic analyses by legal experts. [7, 8]

Although it is always important to have a human expert available for important cases, such as those in forensic applications, the need for an automatic approach to speaker recognition was soon established. *Prunzansky, et al.* [9, 10] started by looking at an automatic statistical comparison of speakers using a text-dependent approach. This was done by analyzing a population of 10 speakers uttering several unique words. However, it is well understood that, at least for speaker identification, having a text-dependent analysis is not practical in the least [1]. Nevertheless, there are cases where there is some merit to having a text-dependent analysis done for the speaker verification problem. This is usually when there is limited computation resource and/or obtaining speech samples for longer than a couple of seconds is not feasible.

To date, still the most prevalent modeling techniques are the Gaussian mixture model (GMM) and support vector machine (SVM) approaches. Neural networks and other types of classifiers have also been used, although not in significant numbers. In the next two sections, we will briefly recap GMM and SVM approaches. See *Beigi* [1] for a detailed treatment of these and other classifiers.

2.1. Gaussian Mixture Model (GMM) recognizers

In a GMM recognition engine, the models are the parameters for collections of multi-variate normal density functions which describe the distribution of the features [1] for speakers' enrollment data. The best results have been shown on many occasions, and by many research projects, to have come from the use of Mel-Frequency Cepstral Coefficient (MFCC) features [1]. Although, later we will review other features which may perform better for certain special cases.

The *Gaussian mixture model* (*GMM*) is a model that expresses the probability density function of a random variable in terms of a weighted sum of its components, each of which is described by a *Gaussian* (*normal*) density function. In other words,

$$p(\mathbf{x}|\boldsymbol{\varphi}) = \sum_{\gamma=1}^{\Gamma} p(\mathbf{x}|\boldsymbol{\theta}_\gamma)P(\boldsymbol{\theta}_\gamma) \tag{1}$$

where the supervector of parameters, $\boldsymbol{\varphi}$, is defined as an augmented set of Γ vectors constituting the free parameters associated with the Γ mixture components, $\boldsymbol{\theta}_\gamma, \gamma \in \{1, 2, \cdots, \Gamma\}$ and the $\Gamma - 1$ mixture weights, $P(\theta = \boldsymbol{\theta}_\gamma), \gamma = \{1, 2, \cdots, \Gamma - 1\}$, which are the prior probabilities of each of these mixture models known as the *mixing distribution* [11].

The parameter vectors associated with each mixture component, in the case of the Gaussian mixture model, are the parameters of the normal density function,

$$\boldsymbol{\theta}_\gamma = \begin{bmatrix} \boldsymbol{\mu}_\gamma^T & \mathbf{u}^T(\boldsymbol{\Sigma}_\gamma) \end{bmatrix}^T \tag{2}$$

where the *unique parameters* vector is an invertible transformation that stacks all the free parameters of a matrix into vector form. For example, if $\boldsymbol{\Sigma}_\gamma$ is a full covariance matrix, then $\mathbf{u}(\boldsymbol{\Sigma}_\gamma)$ is the vector of the elements in the upper triangle of $\boldsymbol{\Sigma}_\gamma$ including the diagonal elements. On the other hand, if $\boldsymbol{\Sigma}_\gamma$ is a diagonal matrix, then,

$$(\mathbf{u}(\boldsymbol{\Sigma}_\gamma))_d \stackrel{\Delta}{=} (\boldsymbol{\Sigma}_\gamma)_{dd} \; \forall \, d \in \{1,2,\cdots,D\} \tag{3}$$

Therefore, we may always reconstruct $\boldsymbol{\Sigma}_\gamma$ from $\mathbf{u}_\gamma$ using the inverse transformation,

$$\boldsymbol{\Sigma}_\gamma = \mathbf{u}_\gamma{}^{-1} \tag{4}$$

The parameter vector for the mixture model may be constructed as follows,

$$\boldsymbol{\varphi} \stackrel{\Delta}{=} \left[\boldsymbol{\mu}_1^T \cdots \boldsymbol{\mu}_\Gamma^T \; \mathbf{u}_1^T \cdots \mathbf{u}_\Gamma^T \; p(\boldsymbol{\theta}_1) \cdots p(\boldsymbol{\theta}_{\Gamma-1})\right]^T \tag{5}$$

where only $(\Gamma - 1)$ mixture coefficients (prior probabilities), $p(\boldsymbol{\theta}_\gamma)$, are included in $\boldsymbol{\varphi}$, due to the constraint that

$$\sum_{\gamma=1}^{\Gamma} p(\boldsymbol{\varphi}_\gamma) = 1 \tag{6}$$

Thus the number of free parameters in the prior probabilities is only $\Gamma - 1$.

For a sequence of *independent and identically distributed* (*i.i.d.*) observations, $\{\mathbf{x}\}_1^N$, the log of likelihood of the sequence may be written as follows,

$$\begin{aligned}\ell(\boldsymbol{\varphi}|\{\mathbf{x}\}_1^N) &= \ln\left(\prod_{n=1}^{N} p(\mathbf{x}_n|\boldsymbol{\varphi})\right) \\ &= \sum_{n=1}^{N} \ln p(\mathbf{x}_n|\boldsymbol{\varphi})\end{aligned} \tag{7}$$

Assuming the mixture model, defined by Equation 1, the likelihood of the sequence, $\{\mathbf{x}\}_1^N$, may be written in terms of the mixture components,

$$\ell(\boldsymbol{\varphi}|\{\mathbf{x}\}_1^N) = \sum_{n=1}^{N} \ln\left(\sum_{\gamma=1}^{\Gamma} p(\mathbf{x}_n|\boldsymbol{\theta}_\gamma)P(\boldsymbol{\theta}_\gamma)\right) \tag{8}$$

Since maximizing Equation 8 requires the maximization of the logarithm of a sum, we can utilize the incomplete data approach that is used in the development of the *EM algorithm* to simplify the solution. *Beigi* [1] shows the derivation of the incomplete data equivalent of the maximization of Equation 8 using the *EM algorithm.*

Each multivariate distribution is represented by Equation 9.

$$p(\mathbf{x}|\boldsymbol{\theta}_\gamma) = \frac{1}{(2\pi)^{\frac{D}{2}} \left|\boldsymbol{\Sigma}_\gamma\right|^{\frac{1}{2}}} exp\left\{-\frac{1}{2}(\mathbf{x}-\boldsymbol{\mu}_\gamma)^T \boldsymbol{\Sigma}_\gamma^{-1}(\mathbf{x}-\boldsymbol{\mu}_\gamma)\right\} \tag{9}$$

where $\mathbf{x}$, $\boldsymbol{\mu}_\gamma \in \mathscr{R}^D$ and $\boldsymbol{\Sigma}_\gamma : \mathscr{R}^D \mapsto \mathscr{R}^D$.

In Equation 9, $\boldsymbol{\mu}_\gamma$ is the mean vector for cluster γ computed from the vectors in that cluster, where,

$$\boldsymbol{\mu}_\gamma \stackrel{\Delta}{=} \mathscr{E}\{\mathbf{x}\} \stackrel{\Delta}{=} \int_{-\infty}^{\infty} \mathbf{x}\, p(\mathbf{x}) d\mathbf{x} \tag{10}$$

The *sample mean* approximation for Equation 10 is,

$$\boldsymbol{\mu}_\gamma \approx \frac{1}{N} \sum_{i=1}^{N} \mathbf{x}_i \tag{11}$$

where N is the number of samples and $\mathbf{x}_i$ are the MFCC [1].

The *Covariance* matrix is defined as,

$$\boldsymbol{\Sigma}_\gamma \stackrel{\Delta}{=} \mathscr{E}\left\{(\mathbf{x} - \mathscr{E}\{\mathbf{x}\}) \left(\mathbf{x} - \mathscr{E}\{\mathbf{x}\}\right)^T\right\} = \mathscr{E}\left\{\mathbf{x}\mathbf{x}^T\right\} - \boldsymbol{\mu}_\gamma {\boldsymbol{\mu}_\gamma}^T \tag{12}$$

The diagonal elements of $\boldsymbol{\Sigma}_\gamma$ are the variances of the individual dimensions of $\mathbf{x}$. The off-diagonal elements are the covariances across the different dimensions.

The *unbiased estimate* of $\boldsymbol{\Sigma}_\gamma$, $\tilde{\boldsymbol{\Sigma}}_\gamma$, is given by the following,

$$\tilde{\boldsymbol{\Sigma}}_\gamma = \frac{1}{N-1}\left[\mathbf{S}_\gamma|_N - N(\boldsymbol{\mu}\boldsymbol{\mu}^T)\right] \tag{13}$$

where the *sample mean*, $\boldsymbol{\mu}_\gamma$, is given by Equation 11 and the *second order sum matrix (Scatter Matrix)*, $\mathbf{S}_\gamma|_N$, is given by,

$$\mathbf{S}_\gamma|_N \stackrel{\Delta}{=} \sum_{i=1}^{N} \mathbf{x}_i {\mathbf{x}_i}^T \tag{14}$$

Therefore, in a general GMM model, the above statistical parameters are computed and stored for the set of Gaussians along with the corresponding mixture coefficients, to represent each speaker. The features used by the recognizer are *Mel-Frequency Cepstral Coefficients* (*MFCC*). *Beigi* [1] describes details of such a **GMM**-based recognizer.

2.2. Support Vector Machine (SVM) recognizers

In general, *SVM* are formulated as *two-class* classifiers. Γ-class classification problems are usually reduced to Γ two-class problems [12], where the γth two-class problem compares the γth class with the rest of the classes combined. There are also other generalizations of the SVM formulation which are geared toward handling Γ-class problems directly. *Vapnik* has proposed such formulations in Section 10.10 of his book [12]. He also credits *M. Jaakkola* and *C. Watkins, et al.* for having proposed similar generalizations independently. For such generalizations, the constrained optimization problem becomes much more complex. For this reason, the approximation using a set of Γ two-class problems has been preferred in the literature. It has the characteristic that if a data point is accepted by the decision function of more than one class, then it is deemed as *not classified*. Furthermore, it is not classified if no decision function claims that data point to be in its class. This characteristic has both positive and negative connotations. It allows for better rejection of outliers, but then it may also be viewed as giving up on handling outliers.

In application to speaker recognition, experimental results have shown that *SVM* implementations of speaker recognition may perform similarly or sometimes even be slightly inferior to the less complex and less resource intensive *GMM* approaches. However, it has also been noted that systems which combine *GMM* and *SVM* approaches often enjoy a higher accuracy, suggesting that part of the information revealed by the two approaches may be complementary [13].

The problem of *overtraining* (*overfitting*) plagues many learning techniques, and it has been one of the driving factors for the development of support vector machines [1]. In the process of developing the concept of *capacity* and eventually SVM, *Vapnik* considered the generalization capacity of learning machines, especially *neural networks*. The main goal of support vector machines is to maximize the generalization capability of the learning algorithm, while keeping good performance on the training patterns. This is the basis for the *Vapnik-Chervonenkis theory* (*CV theory*) [12], which computes bounds on the risk, $R(o)$, according to the definition of the *VC dimension* and the *empirical risk* – see *Beigi* [1].

The multiclass classification problem is also quite important, since it is the basis for the speaker identification problem. In Section 10.10 of his book, *Vapnik* [12] proposed a simple approach where one class was compared to all other classes and then this is done for each class. This approach converts a Γ-class problem to Γ two-class problems. This is the most popular approach for handling multi-class SVM and has been dubbed the *one-against-all*[1] *approach* [1]. There is also, the *one-against-one approach* which transforms the problem into $\Gamma(\Gamma+1)/2$ two-class SVM problems. In Section 6.2.1 we will see more recent techniques for handling multi-class SVM.

3. Challenging audio

One of the most important challenges in speaker recognition stems from inconsistencies in the different types of audio and their quality. One such problem, which has been the focus of most research and publications in the field, is the problem of channel mismatch, in which the enrollment audio has been gathered using one apparatus and the test audio has been produced by a different channel. It is important to note that the sources of mismatch vary and are generally quite complicated. They could be any combination and usually are not limited to mismatch in the handset or recording apparatus, the network capacity and quality, noise conditions, illness related conditions, stress related conditions, transition between different media, etc. Some approaches involve normalization of some kind to either transform the data (raw or in the feature space) or to transform the model parameters. Chapter 18 of *Beigi* [1] discusses many different channel compensation techniques in order to resolve this issue. *Vogt, et al.* [14] provide a good coverage of methods for handling modeling mismatch.

One such problem is to obtain ample coverage for the different types of phonation in the training and enrollment phases, in order to have a better performance for situations when different phonation types are uttered. An example is the handling of whispered phonation which is, in general, very hard to collect and is not available under natural speech scenarios. Whisper is normally used by individuals who desire to have more privacy. This may happen under normal circumstances when the user is on a telephone and does not want others to either hear his/her conversation or does not wish to bother others in the

[1] Also known as one-against-rest.

vicinity, while interacting with the speaker recognition system. In Section 3.1, we will briefly review the different styles of phonation. Section 3.2 will then cover some work which has been done, in order to be able to handle whispered speech.

Another challenging issue with audio is to handle multiple speakers with possibly overlapping speech. The most difficult scenario would be the presence of multiple speakers on a single microphone, say a telephone handset, where each speaker is producing similar level of audio at the same time. This type of cross-talk is very hard to handle and indeed it is very difficult to identify the different speakers while they speak simultaneously. A somewhat simpler scenario is the one which generally happens in a conference setting, in a room, in which case, a far-field microphone (or microphone array) is capturing the audio. When multiple speakers speak in such a setting, there are some solutions which have worked out well in reducing the interference of other speakers, when focusing on the speech of a certain individual. In Section 3.4, we will review some work that has been done in this field.

3.1. Different styles of phonation

Phonation deals with the acoustic energy generated by the vocal folds at the larynx. The different kinds of phonation are *unvoiced*, *voiced*, and *whisper*.

Unvoiced phonation may be either in the form of *nil phonation* which corresponds to zero energy or *breath phonation* which is based on relaxed vocal folds passing a turbulent air stream.

Majority of voiced sounds are generated through *normal voiced* phonation which happens when the vocal folds are vibrating at a periodic rate and generate certain resonance in the upper chamber of the vocal tract. Another category of voiced phonation is called *laryngealization* (*creaky voice*). It is when the arytenoid cartilages fix the posterior portion of the vocal folds, only allowing the anterior part of the vocal folds to vibrate. Yet another type voiced phonation is a falsetto which is basically the un-natural creation of a high pitched voice by tightening the basic shape of the vocal folds to achieve a false high pitch.

In another view, the emotional condition of the speaker may affect his/her phonation. For example, speech under stress may manifest different phonetic qualities than that of, so-called, *neutral speech* [15]. Whispered speech also changes the general condition of phonation. It is thought that this does not affect unvoiced consonants as much. In Sections 3.2 and 3.3 we will briefly look at whispered speech and speech under stressful conditions.

3.2. Treatment of whispered speech

Whispered phonation happens when the speaker acts like generating a voiced phonation with the exception that the vocal folds are made more relaxed so that a greater flow of air can pass through them, generating more of a turbulent airstream compared to a voiced resonance. However, the vocal folds are not relaxed enough to generate an unvoiced phonation.

As early as the first known paper on speaker identification [3], the challenges of whispered speech were apparent. The general text-independent analysis of speaker characteristics relies mainly on the *normal voiced phonation* as the primary source of speaker-dependent information.[1] This is due to the high-energy periodic signal which is generated with rich resonance information. Normally, very little natural whisper data is available for training. However, in some languages, such as *Amerindian languages* [2] (e.g., *Comanche* [16] and *Tlingit* – spoken in Alaska) and some old languages, voiceless vocoids exist and carry independent meaning from their voiced counterparts [1].

An example of a whispered phone in English is the *egressive pulmonic whisper* [1] which is the sound that an [h] makes in the word, "home." However, any utterance may be produced by relaxing the vocal folds and generating a whispered version of the utterance. This partial relaxation of the vocal folds can significantly change the vocal characteristics of the speaker. Without ample data in whisper mode, it would be hard to identify the speaker.

Pollack, et al. [3] say that we need about three times as much speech samples for whispered speech in order to obtain an equivalent accuracy to that of normal speech. This assessment was made according to a comparison, done using human listeners and identical speech content, as well as an attempted equivalence in the recording volume levels.

Jin, et al. [17] deal with the insufficient amount of whisper data by creating two GMM models for each individual, assuming that ample data is available for the normal-speech mode for any target speaker. Then, in the test phase, they use the *frame-based score competition* (*FSC*) method, comparing each frame of audio to the two models for every speaker (normal and whispered) and only using the result for that frame, from the model which produces the higher score. Otherwise, they continue with the standard process of recognition.

Jin, et al. [17] conducted experiments on whispered speech when almost no whisper data was available for the enrollment phase. The experiments showed that noise greatly impacts recognition with whispered speech. Also, they concentrate on using a throat microphone which happens to be more robust in terms of noise, but it also picks up more resonance for whispered speech. In general, using the two-model approach with FSC, [17] show significant reduction in the error rate.

Fan, et al. [18] have looked into the differences between whisper and neutral speech. By neutral speech, they mean normal speech which is recorded in a modal (voiced) speech setting in a quiet recording studio. They use the fact that the unvoiced consonants are quite similar in the two types of speech and that most of the differences stem from the remaining phones. Using this, they separate whispered speech into two parts. The first part includes all the unvoiced consonants, and the second part includes the rest of the phones. Furthermore, they show better performance for unvoiced consonants in the whispered speech, when using *linear frequency cepstral coefficients* (*LFCC*) and *exponential frequency cepstral coefficients* (*EFCC*) – see Section 4.3. In contrast, the rest of the phones show better performance with MFCC features. Therefore, they detect *unvoiced consonants* and treat them using LFCC/EFCC features. They send the rest of the phones (e.g., voiced consonants, vowels, diphthongs, triphthongs, glides, liquids) through an MFCC-based system. Then they combine the scores from the two segments to make a speaker recognition decision.

The unvoiced consonant detection which is proposed by [18], uses two measures for determining the frames stemming from unvoiced consonants. For each frame, l, the energy of the frame in the lower part of the spectrum, $E_l^{(l)}$, and that of the higher part of the band, $E_l^{(h)}$, (for $f \leq 4000Hz$ and $4000Hz < f \leq 8000Hz$ respectively) are computed, along with the total energy of the frame, E_l, to be used for normalization. The relative energy of the lower frequency is then computed for each frame by Equation 15.

$$R_l = \frac{E_l^{(l)}}{E_l} \tag{15}$$

[2] Languages spoken by native inhabitants of the Americas.

It is assumed that most of spectral energy of unvoiced consonants is concentrated in the higher half of the frequency spectrum, compared to the rest of the phones. In addition, the Jeffreys' divergence [1] of the higher portion of the spectrum relative to the previous frame is computed using Equation 16.

$$\mathscr{D}_J(l \leftrightarrow l-1) = -P_{l-1}^{(h)} \log_2(P_l^{(h)}) - P_l^{(h)} \log_2(P_{l-1}^{(h)}) \tag{16}$$

where

$$P_l^{(h)} \triangleq \frac{E_l^{(h)}}{E_l} \tag{17}$$

Two separate thresholds may be set for R_l and $\mathscr{D}_J(l \leftrightarrow l-1)$, in order to detect unvoiced consonants from the rest of the phones.

3.3. Speech under stress

As noted earlier, the phonation undergoes certain changes when the speaker is under stressful conditions. *Bou-Ghazale, et al.* [15] have shown that this may effect the significance of certain frequency bands, making MFCC features miss certain nuances in the speech of the individual under stress. They propose a new frequency scale which it calls the *exponential-logarithmic* (*expo-log*) scale. In Section 4.3 we will describe this scale in more detail since it is also used by *Bou-Ghazale, et al.* [18] to handle the unvoiced consonants. On another note, although research has generally shown that cepstral coefficients derived from FFT are more robust for the handling of neutral speech [19], *Bou-Ghazale, et al.* [15] suggest that for speech, recorded under stressful conditions, cepstral coefficients derived from the linear predictive model [1] perform better.

3.4. Multiple sources of speech and far-field audio capture

This problem has been addressed in the presence of microphone arrays, to handle cases when sources are semi-stationary in a room, say in a conference environment. The main goal would amount to extracting the source(s) of interest from a set of many sources of audio and to reduce the interference from other sources in the process [20]. For instance, *Kumatani, et al.* [21] address the problem using the, so called, beamforming technique[20, 22] for two speakers speaking simultaneously in a room. They construct a generalized sidelobe canceler (GSC) for each source and adjusts the active weight vectors of the two GSCs to extract two speech signals with *minimum mutual information* [1] between the two. Of course, this makes a few essential assumptions which may not be true in most situations. The first assumption is that the number of speakers is known. The second assumption is that they are semi-stationary and sitting in different angles from the microphone array. *Kumatani, et al.* [21] show performance results on the far-field PASCAL speech separation challenge, by performing speech recognition trials.

One important part of the above task is to localize the speakers. *Takashima, et al.* [23] use an HMM-based approach to separate the acoustic transfer function so that they can separate the sources, using a single microphone. It is done by using an HMM model of the speech of each speaker to estimate the acoustic transfer function from each position in the room. They have experimented with up to 9 different source positions and have shown that their accuracy of localization decreases with increasing number of positions.

http://dx.doi.org/10.5772/52023

3.5. Channel mismatch

Many publications deal with the problem of channel mismatch, since it is the most important challenge in speaker recognition. Early approaches to the treatment of this problem concentrated on normalization of the features or the score. *Vogt, et al.* [14] present a good coverage of different normalization techniques. *Barras, et al.* [24] compare cepstral mean subtraction (CMS) and variance normalization, Feature Warping, T-Norm, Z-Norm and the cohort methods. Later approaches started by using techniques from factor analysis or discriminant analysis to transform features such that they convey the most information about speaker differences and least about channel differences. Most GMM techniques use some variation of *joint factor analysis* (*JFA*) [25]. An offshoot of JFA is the i-vector technique which does away with the channel part of the model and falls back toward a PCA approach [26]. See Section 5.1 for more on the i-vector approach.

SVM systems use techniques such as *nuisance attribute projection* (*NAP*) [27]. NAP [13] modifies the original *kernel*, used for a *support vector machine* (*SVM*) formulation, to one with the ability of telling specific channel information apart. The premise behind this approach is that by doing so, in both training and recognition stages, the system will not have the ability to distinguish channel specific information. This channel specific information is what is dubbed nuisance by *Solomonoff, et al.* [13]. *NAP* is a projection technique which assumes that most of the information related to the channel is stored in specific low-dimensional subspaces of the higher dimensional space to which the original features are mapped. Furthermore, these regions are assumed to be somewhat distinct from the regions which carry speaker information. This is quite similar to the idea of *joint factor analysis*. *Seo, et al.* [28] use the statistics of the eigenvalues of background speakers to come up with discriminative weight for each background speaker and to decide on the between class scatter matrix and the within-class scatter matrix.

Shanmugapriya, et al. [29] propose a *fuzzy wavelet network* (*FWN*) which is a neural network with a wavelet activation function (known as a *Wavenet*). A fuzzy neural network is used in this case, with the wavelet activation function. Unfortunately, [29] only provides results for the TIMIT database [1] which is a database acquired under a clean and controlled environment and is not very challenging.

Villalba, et al. [30] attempt to detect two types of low-tech spoofing attempts. The first one is the use of a far-field microphone to record the victim's speech and then to play it back into a telephone handset. The second type is the concatenation of segments of short recordings to build the input required for a text-dependent speaker verification system. The former is handled by using an SVM classifier for spoof and non-spoof segments trained based on some training data. The latter is detected by comparing the pitch and MFCC feature contours of the enrollment and test segments using dynamic time warping (DTW).

4. Alternative features

As seen in the past, most classic features used in speech and speaker recognition are based on LPC, LPCC, or MFCC. In Section 6.3 we see that *Dhanalakshmi, et al.* [19] report trying these three classic features and have shown that MFCC outperforms the other two. Also, *Beigi* [1] discusses many other features such as those generated by *wavelet filterbanks*, *instantaneous frequencies*, *EMD*, etc. In this section, we will discuss several new features, some of which are variations of cepstral coefficients with a different frequency scaling, such as *CFCC*, *LFCC*, *EFCC*, and *GFCC*. In Section 6.2 we will also see the *RMFCC* which was used to handle speaker identification for gaming applications. Other features are also discussed, which are more fundamentally different, such as *missing feature theory (MFT)*, and *local binary features*.

4.1. Multitaper MFCC features

Standard MFCC features are usually computed using a periodogram estimate of the spectrum, with a window function, such as the Hamming window. [1] MFCC features computed by this method portray a large variance. To reduce the variance, multitaper spectrum estimation techniques [31] have been used. They show lower bias and variance for the multitaper estimate of the spectrum. Although bias terms are generally small with the windowed periodogram estimate, the reduction in the variance, using multitaper estimation, seems to be significant.

A multitaper estimate of a spectrum is made by using the mean value of periodogram estimates of the spectrum using a set of orthogonal windows (known as tapers). The multitaper approach has been around since early 1980*s*. Examples of such taper estimates are *Thomson* [32], *Tukey's split cosine taper* [33], *sinusoidal taper* [34], and *peak matched estimates* [35]. However, their use in computing MFCC features seems to be new. In Section 5.1, we will see that they have been recently used in accordance with the i-vector formulation and have also shown promising results.

4.2. Cochlear Filter Cepstral Coefficients (CFCC)

Li, et al. [36] present results for speaker identification using *cochlear filter cepstral coefficients* (*CFCC*) based on an auditory transform [37] while trying to emulate natural cochlear signal processing. They maintain that the CFCC features outperform MFCC, PLP, and RASTA-PLP features [1] under conditions with very low signal to noise ratios. Figure 1 shows the block diagram of the CFCC feature extraction proposed by *Li, et al.* [36]. The *auditory transform* is a *wavelet transform* which was proposed by *Li, et al.* [37]. It may be implemented in the form of a filter bank, as it is usually done for the extraction of MFCC features [1]. Equations 18 and 19 show a generic wavelet transform associated with one such filter.

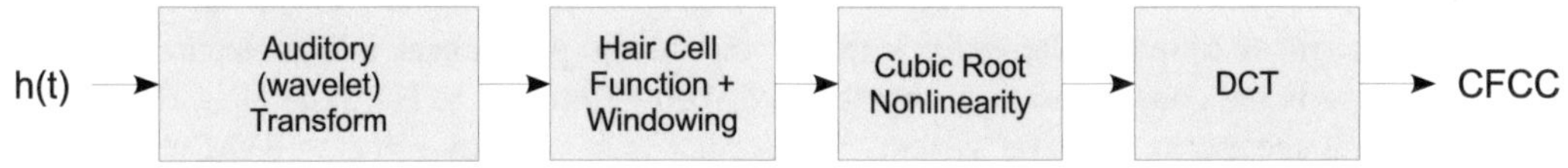

Figure 1. Block Diagram of Cochlear Filter Cepstral Coefficient (CFCC) Feature Extraction – proposed by *Li, et al.* [36]

$$T(a,b) = \int_{-\infty}^{\infty} h(t)\psi_{(a,b)}(t)dt \tag{18}$$

where

$$\psi_{(a,b)}(t) = \frac{1}{\sqrt{|a|}}\psi\left(\frac{t-b}{a}\right) \tag{19}$$

The *wavelet basis functions* [1], $\{\psi_{(a,b)}(t)\}$, are defined by *Li, et al.* [37], based on the *mother wavelet*, $\psi(t)$ (Equation 20), which mimics the cochlear impulse response function.

$$\psi(t) \triangleq t^{\alpha}\exp\left[-2\pi h_L \beta t\right]\cos\left[2\pi h_L t + \theta\right] \tag{20}$$

Each wavelet basis function,according to the scaling and translation parameters $a > 0$ and $b > 0$ is, therefore, given by Equation 21.

$$\Psi_{(a,b)}(t) = \frac{1}{\sqrt{|a|}}\left(\frac{t-b}{a}\right)^{\alpha}\exp\left[-2\pi h_L\beta\left(\frac{t-b}{a}\right)\right]\cos\left[2\pi h_L\left(\frac{t-b}{a}\right)+\theta\right] \tag{21}$$

In Equation 21, α and β are strictly positive parameters which define the shape and the bandwidth of the cochlear filter in the frequency domain. *Li, et al.* [36] determine them empirically for each filter in the filter bank. $u(t)$ is the units step (Heaviside) function defined by Equation 22.

$$u(t) \triangleq \begin{cases} 1 \ \forall\, t \geq 0 \\ 0 \ \forall\, t < 0 \end{cases} \tag{22}$$

4.3. Linear and Exponential Frequency Cepstral Coefficients (LFCC and EFCC)

Some experiments have shown that using *linear frequency cepstral coefficients* (LFCC) and *exponential frequency cepstral coefficients* (EFCC) for processing unvoiced consonants may produce better results for speaker recognition. For instance, *Fan, et al.* [18] use an unvoiced consonant detector to separate frames which contain such phones and to use LFCC and EFCC features for these frames (see Section 3.2). These features are then used to train up a GMM-based speaker recognition system. In turn, they send the remaining frames to a GMM-based recognizer using MFCC features. The two recognizers are treated as separate systems. At the recognition stage, the same segregation of frames is used and the scores of two recognition engines are combined to reach the final decision.

The EFCC scale was proposed by *Bou-Ghazale, et al.* [15] and later used by *Fan, et al.* [18]. This mapping is given by

$$E = (10^{\frac{f}{k}} - 1)c \quad \forall\ 0 \leq f \leq 8000Hz \tag{23}$$

where the two constants, c and k, are computed by solving Equations 24 and 25.

$$(10^{\frac{8000}{k}} - 1)c = 2595\log\left(1 + \frac{8000}{700}\right) \tag{24}$$

$$\{c,k\} = \min\left\{\left|(10^{\frac{4000}{k}} - 1) - \frac{4000}{k^2}c \times 10^{\frac{4000}{k}}\ln(10)\right|\right\} \tag{25}$$

Equation 24 comes from the requirement that the exponential and Mel scale functions should be equal at the Nyquist frequency and Equation 24 is the result of minimizing the absolute values of the partial derivatives of E in Equation 23 with respect to c and k for $f = 4000Hz$ [18]. The resulting c and k which would satisfy Equations 24 and 25 are computed by *Fan, et al.* [18] to be $c = 6375$ and $k = 50000$. Therefore, the exponential scale function is given by Equation 26.

$$E = 6375 \times (10^{\frac{f}{50000}} - 1) \tag{26}$$

Fan el al. [18] show better accuracy for unvoiced consonants, when EFCC is used over MFCC. However, it shows even better accuracy when LFCC is used for these frames!

4.4. Gammatone Frequency Cepstral Coefficients (GFCC)

Shao, et al. [38] use *gammatone frequency cepstral coefficients* (*GFCC*) as features, which are the products of a cochlear filter bank, based on psychophysical observations of the total auditory system. The Gammatone filter bank proposed by *Shao, et al.* [38] has 128 filters, centered from $50Hz$ to $8kHz$, at equal partitions on the *equivalent rectangular bandwidth* (ERB) [39, 40] scale (Equation 28)[3].

$$E_c = \frac{1000}{(24.7 \times 4.37)} \ln(4.37 \times 10^3 f + 1) \tag{27}$$

$$= 21.4 \log(4.37 \times 10^3 f + 1) \tag{28}$$

where f is the frequency in Hertz and E is the number of ERBs, in a similar fashion as Barks or Mels are defined [1]. The bandwidth, E_b, associated with each center frequency, f, is then given by Equation 29. Both f and E_b are in *Hertz (Hz)* [40].

$$E_b = 24.7(4.37 \times 10^3 f + 1) \tag{29}$$

The impulse response of each filter is given by Equation 30.

$$g(f,t) \triangleq \begin{cases} t^{(a-1)} e^{-2\pi bt} \cos(2\pi ft) & t \geq 0 \\ 0 & Otherwise \end{cases} \tag{30}$$

where t denotes the time and f is the center frequency of the filter of interest. a is the order of the filter and is taken to be $a = 4$ [38], and b is the filter bandwidth.

In addition, as it is done with other models such as MFCC, LPCC, and PLP, the magnitude also needs to be warped. *Shao, et al.* [38] base their magnitude warping on the method of cubic root warping (magnitude to loudness conversion) used in PLP [1].

The same group that published [38], followed by using a *computational auditory scene analysis* (CASA) front-end [43] to estimate a binary spectrographical mask to determine the useful part of the signal (see Section 4.5), based on *auditory scene analysis* (ASA) [44]. They claim great improvements in noisy environments, over standard speaker recognition approaches.

4.5. Missing Feature Theory (MFT)

Missing feature theory (MFT) tries to deal with bandlimited speech in the presence of non-stationary background noise. Such missing data techniques have been used in the speech community, mostly to handle applications of noisy speech recognition. *Vizinho, et al.* [45] describe such techniques by

---

[3] The ERB scale is similar to the Bark and Mel scales [1] and is computed by integrating an empirical differential equation proposed by *Moore and Glasberg* in *1983* [39] and then modified by them in *1990* [41]. It uses a set of rectangular filters to approximate human cochlear hearing and provides a more accurate approximation to the psychoacoustical scale (Bark scale) of *Zwicker* [42].

estimating the reliable regions of the spectrogram of speech and then using these reliable portions to perform speech recognition. They do this by estimating the noise spectrum and the SNR and by creating a mask that would remove the noisy part from the spectrogram. In a related approach, some feature selection methods use Bayesian estimation to estimate a spectrographic mask which would remove unwanted part of the spectrogram, therefore removing features which are attributed to the noisy part of the signal.

The goal of these techniques is to be able to handle non-stationary noise. *Seltzer, et al.* [46] propose one such Bayesian technique. This approach concentrates on extracting as much useful information from the noisy speech as it can, rather than trying to estimate the noise and to subtract it from the signal, as it is done by *Vizinho, et al.* [45]. However, there are many parameters which need to be optimized, making the process quite expensive, calling for suboptimal search. *Pullella, et al.* [47] have combined the two techniques of spectrographic mask estimation and dynamic feature selection to improve the accuracy of speaker recognition under noisy conditions. *Lim, et al.* [48] propose an optimal mask estimation and feature selection algorithm.

4.6. Local binary features (slice classifier)

The idea of statistical boosting is not new and was proposed by several researchers, starting with *Schapire* [49] in 1990. The *Adaboost algorithm* was introduced by *Freund, et al.* [50] in 1996 as one specific boosting algorithm. The idea behind statistical boosting is that a combination of weak classifiers may be combined to build a strong one.

Rodriguez [51] used the statistical boosting idea and several extensions of the Adaboost algorithm to introduce face detection and verification algorithms which would use features based on local differences between pixels in a 9×9 pixel grid, compared to the central pixel of the grid.

Inspired by [51], *Roy, et al.* [52] created local binary features according to the differences between the bands of the *discrete Fourier transform* (*DFT*) values to compare two models. One important claim of this classifier is that it is less prone to overfitting issues and that it performs better than conventional systems under low SNR values. The resulting features are binary because they are based on a threshold which categorizes the difference between different bands of the FFT to either 0 or 1. The classifier of [52] has a built-in discriminant nature, since it uses certain data as those coming from impostors, in contrast with the data which is generated by the target speaker. The labels of impostor versus target allow for this built-in discrimination. The authors of [52] call these features, *boosted binary features* (BBF). In a more recent paper [53], *Roy, et al.* refined their approach and renamed the method a *slice classifier*. They show similar results with this classifier, compared to the state of the art, but they explain that the method is less computationally intensive and is more suitable for use in mobile devices with limited resources.

5. Alternative speaker modeling

Classic modeling techniques for speaker recognition have used *Gaussian mixture models* (*GMM*), *support vector machines* (*SVM*), and *neural networks* [1]. In Section 6 we will see some other modeling techniques such as non-negative matrix factorization. Also, in Section 4, new modeling implementations were used in applying the new features presented in the section. Generally, most new modeling techniques use some transformation of the features in order to handle mismatch conditions, such as joint factor analysis (JFA), Nuisance attribute projection (NAP), and principal component analysis (PCA) techniques such as the i-vector implementation.[1] In the next few sections, we will briefly look at some recent developments in these and other techniques.

5.1. The i-vector model (total variability space)

Dehak, et al. [54] recombined the *channel variability space* in the JFA formulation [25] with the *speaker variability space*, since they discovered that there was considerable leakage from the speaker space into the channel space. The combined space produces a new projection (Equation 31) which resembles a PCA, rather than a factor analysis process.

$$\mathbf{y}_n = \boldsymbol{\mu} + \mathbf{V}\boldsymbol{\theta}_n \tag{31}$$

They called the new space *total variability space* and in their later works [55–57], they referred to the projections of feature vectors into this space, *i-vectors*. *Speaker factor coefficients* are related to the speaker coordinates, in which each speaker is represented as a point. This space is defined by the *Eigenvoice matrix*. These speaker factor vectors are relatively short, having in the order of about 300 elements [58], which makes them desirable for use with *support vector machines*, as the observed vector in the observation space ($\mathbf{x}$).

Generally, in order to use an i-vector approach, several recording sessions are needed from the same speaker, to be able to compute the within class covariance matrix in order to do within class covariance normalization (WCCN). Also, methods using *linear discriminant analysis* (*LDA*) along with WCCN [57] and recently, *probabilistic LDA* (*PLDA*) with WCCN [59–62] have also shown promising results.

Alam, et al. [63] examined the use of *multitaper MFCC features* (see Section 4.1) in conjunction with the i-vector formulation. They show improved performance using multitaper MFCC features, compared to standard MFCC features which have been computed using a *Hamming window* [1].

Glembek, et al. [26] provide simplifications to the formulation of the *i-vectors* to reduce the memory usage and to increase the speed of computing the vectors. *Glembek, et al.* [26] also explore linear transformations using principal component analysis (PCA) and Heteroscedastic Linear Discriminant Analysis[4] (HLDA) [64] to achieve orthogonality of the components of the Gaussian mixture.

5.2. Non-negative matrix factorization

In Section 6.3, we will see several implementations of extensions of non-negative matrix factorization [65, 66]. These techniques have been successfully applied to classification problems. More detail is give in Section 6.3.

5.3. Using multiple models

In Section 3.2 we briefly covered a few model combination and selection techniques that would use different specialized models to achieve better recognition rates. For example, *Fan, et al.* [18] used two different models to handle unvoiced consonants and the rest of the phones. Both models had similar form, but they used slightly different types of features (MFCC vs. EFCC/LFCC). Similar ideas will be discuss in this section.

---

[4] Also known as Heteroscedastic Discriminant Analysis (HDA) [64]

5.3.1. Frame-based score competition (FSC):

In Section 3.2 we discussed the fact that *Jin, et al.* [17] used two separate models, one based on the normal speech (neutral speech) model and the second one based on whisper data. Then, at the recognition stage, each frame is evaluated against the two models and the higher score is used. [17] Therefore, it is called a frame-based score competition (FSC) method.

5.3.2. SNR-Matched Recognition:

After performing voice activity detection (VAD), *Bartos, et al.* [67] estimate the signal to noise ratio (SNR) of that part of the signal which contains speech. This value is used to load models which have been created with data recorded under similar SNR conditions. Generally, the SNR is computed in *deciBels* given by Equations 32 and 33 – see [1] for more.

$$SNR = 10 \ \log_{10}\left(\frac{\mathscr{P}_s}{\mathscr{P}_n}\right) \tag{32}$$

$$= 20 \ \log_{10}\left(\frac{|H_s(\omega)|}{|H_n(\omega)|}\right) \tag{33}$$

Bartos, et al. [67] consider an SNR of 30dB or higher to be clean speech. An SNR of 30dB happens to be equivalent to the signal amplitude being about 30 times that of the noise. When the SNR is 0, the signal amplitude is roughly the same as the energy of the noise.

Of course, to evaluate the SNR from Equation 32 or 33, we would need to know the power or amplitude of the noise as well as the true signal. Since this is not possible, estimation techniques are used to come up with an instantaneous SNR and to average that value over the whole signal. *Bartos, et al.* [67] present such an algorithm.

Once the SNR of the speech signal is computed, it is categorized within a quantization of 4dB segments and then identification or verification is done using models which have been enrolled with similar SNR values. This, according to [67], allows for a lower equal error rate in case of speaker verification trials. In order to generate speaker models for different SNR levels (of 4dB steps), [67] degrades clean speech iteratively, using some additive noise, amplified by a constant gain associated with each 4db level of degradation.

6. Branch-specific progress

In this section, we will quickly review the latest developments for the main branches of speaker recognition as listed at the beginning of this chapter. Some of these have already been reviewed in the above sections. Most of the work on speaker recognition is performed on speaker verification. In the next section we will review some such systems.

6.1. Verification

As we mentioned in Section 4, *Roy, et al.* [52, 53] used the so-called boosted binary features (slice classifier) for speaker verification. Also, we reviewed several developments regarding the i-vector formulation in Section 5.1. The i-vector has basically been used for speaker verification. Many recent papers have dealt with aspects such as LDA, PLDA, and other discriminative aspects of the training.

Salman, et al. [68] use a neural network architecture with very deep number of layers to perform a greedy discriminative learning for the speaker verification problem. The *deep neural architecture (DNA)*, proposed by [68], uses two identical subnets, to process two MFCC feature vectors respectively, for providing discrimination results between two speakers. They show promising results using this network.

Sarkar, et al. [69] use multiple background models associated with different *vocal tract length (VTL)* [1] estimates for the speakers, using MAP [1] to derive these background models from a root background model. Once the best VTL-based background model for the training or test audio is computed, the transformation to get from that universal background model (UBM) to the root UBM is used to transform the features of the segment to those associated with the VTL of the root UBM. *Sarkar, et al.* [69] show that the results of this single UBM system is comparable to a multiple background model system.

6.2. Identification

In Section 5.3.2 we discussed new developments on SNR-matched recognition. The work of *Bartos, et al.* [67] was applied to improving speaker identification based on a matched SNR condition.

Bharathi, et al. [70] try to identify phonetic content for which specific speakers may be efficiently recognized. Using these speaker-specific phonemes, a special text is created to enhance the discrimination capability for the target speaker. The results are presented for the TIMIT database [1] which is a clean and controlled database and not very challenging. However, the idea seems to have merit.

Cai, et al. [71] use some of the features described in Section 4, such as MFCC and GFCC in order to identify the voice of signers from a monophonic recording of songs in the presence of sounds of music from several instruments.

Do, et al.[72] examine the speaker identification problem for identifying the person playing a computer game. The specific challenges are the fact that the recording is done through a far-field microphone (see Section 3.4) and that the audio is generally short, apparently based on the commands used for gaming. To handle the reverberation and background noise, *Do, et al.* [72] argue for the use of the, so-called, *reverse Mel frequency cepstral coefficients (RMFCC)*. They propose this set of features by reversing the triangular filters [1] used for computing the MFCC, such that the lower frequency filters have larger bandwidths and the higher frequency filters have smaller bandwidths. This is exactly the opposite of the filters being used for MFCC. They also use LPC and $F0$ (the fundamental frequency) as additional features.

In Section 3.2 we saw the treatment of speaker identification for whispered speech in some detail. Also, *Ghiurcau, et al.* [73] study the emotional state of speakers on the results of speaker identification. The study treats happiness, anger, fear, boredom, sadness, and neutral conditions; it shows that these emotions significantly affect identification results. Therefore, they [73] propose using emotion detection and having emotion-specific models. Once the emotion is identified, the proper model is used to identify the test speaker.

Liu, et al. [74] use the Hilbert Huang Transform to come up with new acoustic features. This is the use of intrinsic mode decomposition described in detail in [1].

In the next section, we will look at the multi-class SVM which is used to perform speaker identification.

6.2.1. Multi-Class SVM

In Section 2.2 we discussed the popular one-against-all technique for handling multi-class SVM. There have been other more recent techniques which have been proposed in the last few years. One such technique is due to *Platt, et al.* [75], who proposed the, so-called, *decision directed acyclic graph (DDAG)* which produces a classification node for each pair of classes, in a Γ-class problem. This leads to $\Gamma(\Gamma-1)/2$ classifiers and results in the creation of the *DAGSVM* algorithm [75].

Wang [76] presents a tree-based multi-class SVM which reduces the number of matches to the order of $\log(\Gamma)$. Although at the training phase, the number of SVM are similar to that of DDAG, namely, $\Gamma(\Gamma-1)/2$. This can significantly reduce the amount of computation for speaker identification.

6.3. Classification and diarization

Aside from the more prominent research on speaker verification and identification, audio source and gender classification are also quite important in most audio processing systems including speaker and speech recognition.

In many practical audio processing systems, it is important to determine the type of audio. For instance, consider a telephone-based system which includes a speech recognizer. Such recognition engines would produce spurious results if they were presented with non-speech, say music. These results may be detrimental to the operation of an automated process. This is also true for speaker identification and verification systems which expect to receive human speech. They may be confused if they are presented with music or other types of audio such as noise. For *text-independent speaker identification* systems, this may result in mis-identifying the audio as a viable choice in the database and resulting in dire consequences!

Similarly, some systems are only interested in processing music. An example is a music search system which would look for a specific music or one resembling the presented segment. These systems may be confused, if presented with human speech, uttered inadvertently, while only music is expected.

As an example, an important goal for audio source classification research is to develop filters which would tag a segment of audio as speech, music, noise, or silence [77]. Sometimes, we would also look into classifying the genre of audio or video such as movie, cartoon, news, advertisement, etc. [19].

The basic problem contains two separate parts. The first part is the segmentation of the audio stream into segments of similar content. This work has been under development for the past few decades with some good results [78–80].

The second part is the classification of each segment into relevant classes such as speech, music, or the rejection of the segment as silence or noise. Furthermore, when the audio type is *human speech*, it is desirable to do a further classification to determine the gender of the individual speaker. *Gender classification* [77] is helpful in choosing appropriate models for conducting better speech recognition, more accurate speaker verification, and reducing the computation load in large-scale speaker identification. For the speaker diarization problem, the identity of the speaker also needs to be recognized.

Dhanalakshmi, et al. [19] report developments in classifying the genre of audio, as stemming from different video sources, containing movies, cartoons, news, etc. *Beigi* [77] uses a *text* and *language independent* speaker recognition engine to achieve these goals by performing audio classification. The classification problem is posed by *Beigi* [77] as an identification problem among a series of speech, music, and noise models.

6.3.1. Age and Gender Classification

Another goal for classification is to be able to classify age groups. *Bocklet, et al.* [81] categorized the age of the individuals, in relation to their voice quality, into 4 categories (classes). These classes are given by Table 1. With the natural exception of the child group (13 years or younger), each group is further split into the two male and female genders, leading to 7 total age-gender classes.

Class Name	Age
Child	Age $\leq$ 13 years old
Young	14 years $\leq$ Age $\leq$ 19 years
Adult	20 years $\leq$ Age $\leq$ 64 years
Senior	65 years $\geq$ Age

Table 1. Age Categories According to Vocal Similarities – From [81]

Class Name	Age
Young	18 years $\leq$ Age $\leq$ 35 years
Adult	36 years $\leq$ Age $\leq$ 45 years
Senior	46 years $\leq$ Age $\leq$ 81 years

Table 2. Age Categories According to Vocal Similarities – From [82]

Bahari, et al. [82] use a slightly different definition of age groups, compared to those used by [81]. They use 3 age groups for each gender, not considering individuals who are less than 18 years old. These age categories are given in Table 2.

They use *weighted supervised non-negative matrix factorization* (*WSNMF*) to classify the age and gender of the individual. This technique combines *weighted non-negative matrix factorization* (*WNMF*) [83] and *supervised non-negative matrix factorization* (*SNMF*) [84] which are themselves extensions of *non-negative matrix factorization* (*NMF*) [65, 66]. NMF techniques have also been successfully used in other classification implementations such as that of the identification of musical instruments [85].

NMF distinguishes itself as a method which only allows additive components that are considered to be parts of the information contained in an entity. Due to their additive and positive nature, the components are considered to, each, be part of the information that builds up a description. In contrast, methods such as principal component analysis and vector quantization techniques are considered to be learning holistic information and hence are not considered to be parts-based [66]. According to the image recognition example presented by *Lee, et al.* [66], a PCA method such as Eigenfaces [86, 87] provide a distorted version of the whole face, whereas the NMF provides localized features that are related to the parts of each face.

Subsequent to applying WSNMF, according to the age and gender, *Bahari, et al.* [82] use a *general regression neural network* (*GRNN*) to estimate the age of the individual. *Bahari, et al.* [82] show a gender classification accuracy of about 96% and an average age classification accuracy of about 48%. Although it is dependent on the data being used, but an accuracy of 96% for the gender classification case is not necessarily a great result. It is hard to make a qualitative assessment without running the same algorithms under the same conditions and on exactly the same data. But *Beigi* [77] shows 98.1% accuracy for gender classification.

In [77], 700 male and 700 female speakers were selected, completely at random, from over 70,000 speakers. The speakers were non-native speakers of English, at a variety of proficiency levels, speaking freely. This introduced significantly higher number of pauses in each recording, as well as more than average number of humming sounds while the candidates would think about their speech. The segments were live responses of these non-native speakers to test questions in English, aimed at evaluating their linguistic proficiency.

Dhanalakshmi, et al. [19] also present a method based on an *auto-associative neural network* (*AANN*) for performing audio source classification. AANN is a special branch of feedforward neural networks which tries to learn the nonlinear principal components of a feature vector. The way this is accomplished is that the network consists of three layers, an input layer, an output layer of the same size, and a hidden layer with a smaller number of neurons. The input and output neurons generally have linear activation functions and the hidden (middle) layer has nonlinear functions.

In the training phase, the input and target output vectors are identical. This is done to allow for the system to learn the principal components that have built the patterns which most likely have built-in redundancies. Once such a network is trained, a feature vector undergoes a dimensional reduction and is then mapped back to the same dimensional space as the input space. If the training procedure is able to achieve a good reduction in the output error over the training samples and if the training samples are representative of the reality and span the operating conditions of the true system, the network can learn the essential information in the input signal. Autoassociative networks (AANN) have also been successfully used in speaker verification [88].

Class Name	Advertisement	Cartoon	Movie	News	Songs	Sports

Table 3. Audio Classification Categories used by [19]

Dhanalakshmi, et al. [19] use the audio classes represented in Table 3. It considers three different front-end processors for extracting features, used with two different modeling techniques. The features are LPC, LPCC, and MFCC features [1]. The models are Gaussian mixture models (GMM) and autoassociative neural networks (AANN) [1]. According to these experiments, *Dhanalakshmi, et al.* [19] show consistently higher classification accuracies with MFCC features over LPC and LPCC features. The comparison between AANN and GMM is somewhat inconclusive and both systems seem to portray similar results. Although, the accuracy of AANN with LPC and LPCC seems to be higher than that of GMM modeling, for the case when MFCC features are used, the difference seems somewhat insignificant. Especially, given the fact that GMM are simpler to implement than AANN and are less prone to problems such as encountering local minima, it makes sense to conclude that the combination of MFCC and GMM still provides the best results in audio classification. A combination of GMM with MFCC and performing Maximum a-Posteriori (MAP) adaptation provides very simple and considerable results for gender classification, as seen in [77].

6.3.2. Music Modeling

Beigi [77] classifies musical instruments along with noise and gender of speakers. Much in the same spirit as described in Section 6.3.1, [77] has made an effort to choose a variety of different instruments or sets of instruments to be able to cover most types of music. Table 4 shows these choices. A total of 14 different music models were trained to represent all music, with an attempt to cover different types of timbre [89].

An equal amount of music was chosen by *Beigi* [77] to create a balance in the quantity of data, reducing any bias toward speech or music. The music was downsampled from its original quality to $8kHz$, using 8-bit μ-Law amplitude encoding, in order to match the quality of speech. The 1400 segments of music were chosen at random from European style classical music, as well as jazz, Persian classical, Chinese classical, folk, and instructional performances. Most of the music samples were orchestral pieces, with some solos and duets present.

Although a very low quality audio, based on highly compressed telephony data (AAC compressed [1]), was used by *Beigi* [77], the system achieved a 1% error rate in discriminating between speech and music and a 1.9% error in determining the gender of individual speakers once the audio is tagged as speech.

Category	Model	Category	Model	Category	Model
Noise	Noise	Speech	Female	Speech	Male
Music	Accordion	Music	Bassoon	Music	Clarinet
Music	Clavier	Music	Gamelon	Music	Guzheng
Music	Guitar	Music	Oboe	Music	Orchestra
Music	Piano	Music	Pipa	Music	Tar
Music	Throat	Music	Violin		

Table 4. Audio Models used for Classification

Beigi [77] has shown that MAP adaptation techniques used with GMM models and MFCC features may be used successfully for the classification of audio into speech and music and to further classify the speech by the gender of the speaker and the music by the type of instrument being played.

7. Open problems

With all the new accomplishments in the last couple of years, covered here and many that did not make it to our list due to shortage of space, there is still a lot more work to be done. Although incremental improvements are made every day, in all branches of speaker recognition, still the channel and audio type mismatch seem to be the biggest hurdles in reaching perfect results in speaker recognition. It should be noted that perfect results are *asymptotes* and will probably never be reached. Inherently, as the size of the population in a speaker database grows, the intra-speaker variations exceed the inter-speaker variations. This is the main source of error for large-scale speaker identification, which is the holy grail of the different goals in speaker recognition. In fact, if large-scale speaker identification approaches acceptable results, most other branches of the field may be considered trivial. However, this is quite a complex problem and will definitely need a lot more time to be perfected, if it is indeed possible to do so. In the meanwhile, we seem to still be at infancy when it comes to large-scale identification.

Author details

Homayoon Beigi

President of Recognition Technologies, Inc. and an Adjunct Professor of Computer Science and Mechanical Engineering at Columbia University
Recognition Technologies, Inc., Yorktown Heights, New York, USA

References

[1] Homayoon Beigi. *Fundamentals of Speaker Recognition.* Springer, New York, 2011. ISBN: 978-0-387-77591-3.

[2] Homayoon Beigi. Speaker recognition. In Jucheng Yang, editor, *Biometrics*, pages 3–28. Intech Open Access Publisher, Croatia, 2011. ISBN: 978-953-307-618-8.

[3] I. Pollack, J. M. Pickett, and W.H. Sumby. On the identification of speakers by voice. *Journal of the Acoustical Society of America*, 26(3):403–406, May 1954.

[4] J. N. Shearme and J. N. Holmes. An experiment concerning the recognition of voices. *Language and Speech*, 2(3):123–131, 1959.

[5] Francis Nolan. *The Phonetic Bases of Speaker Recognition.* Cambridge University Press, New York, 1983. ISBN: 0-521-24486-2.

[6] Harry Hollien. *The Acoustics of Crime: The New Science of Forensic Phonetics (Applied Psycholinguistics and Communication Disorder).* Springer, Heidelberg, 1990.

[7] Harry Hollien. *Forensic Voice Identification.* Academic Press, San Diego, CA, USA, 2001.

[8] Amy Neustein and Hemant A. Patil. *Forensic Speakr Recognition – Law Enforcement and Counter-Terrorism.* Springer, Heidelberg, 2012.

[9] Sandra Pruzansky. Pattern matching procedure for automatic talker recognition. 35(3):354–358, Mar 1963.

[10] Sandra Pruzansky, Max. V. Mathews, and P.B. Britner. Talker-recognition procedure based on analysis of vaiance. 35(11):1877–, Apr 1963.

[11] Geoffrey J. McLachlan and David Peel. *Finite Mixture Models.* Wiley Series in Probability and Statistics. John Wiley & Sons, New York, 2nd edition, 2000. ISBN: 0-471-00626-2.

[12] Vladimir Naumovich Vapnik. *Statistical learning theory.* John Wiley, New York, 1998. ISBN: 0-471-03003-1.

[13] A. Solomonoff, W. Campbell, and C. Quillen. Channel compensation for svm speaker recognition. In *The Speaker and Language Recognition Workshop Odyssey 2004*, volume 1, pages 57–62, 2004.

[14] Robbie Vogt and Sridha Sridharan. Explicit modelling of session variability for speaker verification. *Computer Speech and Language*, 22(1):17–38, Jan. 2008.

[15] Sahar E. Bou-Ghazale and John H. L. Hansen. A comparative study of traditional and newly proposed features for recognition of speech under stress. *IEEE Transactions on Speech and Audio Processing*, 8(4):429–442, Jul 2002.

[16] Eliott D. Canonge. Voiceless vowels in comanche. *International Journal of American Linguistics*, 23(2):63–67, Apr 1957. Published by: The University of Chicago Press.

[17] Qin Jin, Szu-Chen Stan Jou, and T. Schultz. Whispering speaker identification. In *Multimedia and Expo, 2007 IEEE International Conference on*, pages 1027–1030, Jul 2007.

[18] Xing Fan and J.H.L. Hansen. Speaker identification within whispered speech audio streams. *Audio, Speech, and Language Processing, IEEE Transactions on*, 19(5):1408–1421, Jul 2011.

[19] P. Dhanalakshmi, S. Palanivel, and V. Ramalingam. Classification of audio signals using aann and gmm. *Applied Soft Computing*, 11(1):716 – 723, 2011.

[20] Lucas C. Parra and Christopher V. Alvino. Geometric source separation: merging convolutive source separation with geometric beamforming. *IEEE Transactions on Speech and Audio Processing*, 10(6):352–362, Sep 2002.

[21] K. Kumatani, U. Mayer, T. Gehrig, E. Stoimenov, and M. Wolfel. Minimum mutual information beamforming for simultaneous active speakers. In *IEEE Workshop on Automatic Speech Recognition and Understanding (ASRU)*, pages 71–76, Dec 2007.

[22] M. Lincoln. The multi-channel wall street journal audio visual corpus (mc-wsj-av): Specification and initial experiments. In *IEEE Workshop on Automatic Speech Recognition and Understanding (ASRU)*, pages 357–362, Nov 2005.

[23] R. Takashima, T. Takiguchi, and Y. Ariki. Hmm-based separation of acoustic transfer function for single-channel sound source localization. pages 2830–2833, Mar 2010.

[24] C. Barras and J.-L. Gauvain. Feature and score normalization for speaker verification of cellular data. In *Acoustics, Speech, and Signal Processing, 2003. Proceedings. (ICASSP '03). 2003 IEEE International Conference on*, volume 2, pages II–49–52, Apr 2003.

[25] P. Kenny. Joint factor analysis of speaker and session varaiability: Theory and algorithms. Technical report, CRIM, Jan 2006.

[26] Ondrej Glembek, Lukas Burget, Pavel Matejka, Martin Karafiat, and Patrick Kenny. Simplification and optimization of i-vector extraction. pages 4516–4519, May 2011.

[27] W.M. Campbell, D.E. Sturim, W. Shen, D.A. Reynolds, and J. Navratil. The mit-ll/ibm 2006 speaker recognition system: High-performance reduced-complexity recognition. In *Acoustics, Speech and Signal Processing, 2007. ICASSP 2007. IEEE International Conference on*, volume 4, pages IV–217–IV–220, Apr 2007.

[28] Hyunson Seo, Chi-Sang Jung, and Hong-Goo Kang. Robust session variability compensation for svm speaker verification. *Audio, Speech, and Language Processing, IEEE Transactions on*, 19(6):1631–1641, Aug 2011.

[29] P. Shanmugapriya and Y. Venkataramani. Implementation of speaker verification system using fuzzy wavelet network. In *Communications and Signal Processing (ICCSP), 2011 International Conference on*, pages 460–464, Feb 2011.

[30] J. Villalba and E. Lleida. Preventing replay attacks on speaker verification systems. In *Security Technology (ICCST), 2011 IEEE International Carnahan Conference on*, pages 1–8, Oct 2011.

[31] Johan Sandberg, Maria Hansson-Sandsten, Tomi Kinnunen, Rahim Saeidi Patrick Flandrin, , and Pierre Borgnat. Multitaper estimation of frequency-warped cepstra with application to speaker verification. *IEEE Signal Processing Letters*, 17(4):343–346, Apr 2010.

[32] David J. Thomson. Spectrum estimation and harmonic analysis. *Proceedings of the IEEE*, 70(9):1055–1096, Sep 1982.

[33] Kurt S. Riedel, Alexander Sidorenko, and David J. Thomson. Spectral estimation of plasma fluctuations. i. comparison of methods. *Physics of Plasma*, 1(3):485–500, 1994.

[34] Kurt S. Riedel. Minimum bias multiple taper spectral estimation. *IEEE Transactions on Signal Processing*, 43(1):188–195, Jan 1995.

[35] Maria Hansson and Göran Salomonsson. A multiple window method for estimation of peaked spectra. *IEEE Transactions on Signal Processing*, 45(3):778–781, Mar 1997.

[36] Qi Li and Yan Huang. An auditory-based feature extraction algorithm for robust speaker identification under mismatched conditions. *Audio, Speech, and Language Processing, IEEE Transactions on*, 19(6):1791–1801, Aug 2011.

[37] Qi Peter Li. An auditory-based transform for audio signal processing. In *IEEE Workshop on Applications of Signal Processing to audio and Acoustics*, pages 181–184, Oct 2009.

[38] Yang Shao and DeLiang Wang. Robust speaker identification using auditory features and computational auditory scene analysis. In *Acoustics, Speech and Signal Processing, 2008. ICASSP 2008. IEEE International Conference on*, pages 1589–1592, 2008.

[39] Brian C. J. Moore and Brian R. Glasberg. Suggested formulae for calculating auditory-filter bandwidths and excitation. *Journal of Aciystical Society of America*, 74(3):750–753, 1983.

[40] Brian C. J. Moore and Brian R. Glasberg. A revision of zwicker's loudness model. *Acta Acustica*, 82(2):335–345, Mar/Apr 1996.

[41] Brian R. Glasberg and Brian C. J. Moore. Derivation of auditory filter shapes from notched-noise data. *Hearing Research*, 47(1–2):103–138, 1990.

[42] E. Zwicker, G. Flottorp, and Stanley Smith Stevens. Critical band width in loudness summation. *Journal of the Acoustical Society of America*, 29(5):548–557, 1957.

[43] Xiaojia Zhao, Yang Shao, and DeLiang Wang. Robust speaker identification using a casa front-end. In *Acoustics, Speech and Signal Processing (ICASSP), 2011 IEEE International Conference on*, pages 5468–5471, May 2011.

[44] Albert S. Bergman. *Auditory Scene Analysis: The Perceptual Organization of Sound.* Bradford, 1994.

[45] A. Vizinho, P. Green, M. Cooke, and L. Josifovski. Missing data theory, spectral subtraction and signal-to-noise estimation for robust asr: An integrated study. In *Eurospeech 1999*, pages 2407–2410, Sep 1999.

[46] Michael L. Seltzer, Bhiksha Raj, and Richard M. Stern. A bayesian classifier for spectrographic mask estimation for missing feature speech recognition. *Speech Communication*, 43(4):379–393, 2004.

[47] D. Pullella, M. Kuhne, and R. Togneri. Robust speaker identification using combined feature selection and missing data recognition. In *Acoustics, Speech and Signal Processing, 2008. ICASSP 2008. IEEE International Conference on*, pages 4833–4836, 2008.

[48] Shin-Cheol Lim, Sei-Jin Jang, Soek-Pil Lee, and Moo Young Kim. Hard-mask missing feature theory for robust speaker recognition. *Consumer Electronics, IEEE Transactions on*, 57(3):1245–1250, Aug 2011.

[49] R. E. Schapire. The strength of weak learnability. *Machine Learning*, 5(2):197–227, 1990.

[50] Yoav Freund and Robert E. Schapire. Experiments with a new boosting algorithm. In *Proceedings of the Thirteenth International Conference on Machine Learning (ICML)*, pages 148–156, 1996.

[51] Yann Rodriguez. *Face Detection and Verification Using Local Binary Patterns.* Ecole Polytechnique Fédérale de Lausanne, 2006. PhD Thesis.

[52] Anindya Roy, Mathew Magimai-Doss, and Sébastien Marcel. Boosted binary features for noise-robust speaker verification. volume 6, pages 4442–4445, Mar 2010.

[53] A. Roy, M. M. Doss, and S. Marcel. A fast parts-based approach to speaker verification using boosted slice classifiers. *IEEE Transactions on Information Forensic and Security*, 7(1):241–254, 2012.

[54] Najim Dehak, Réda Dehak, Patrick Kenny, Niko Brummer, Pierre Ouellet, and Pierre Dumouchel. Support vector machines versus fast scoring in the low-dimensional total variability space for speaker verification. In *InterSpeech*, pages 1559–1562, Sep 2009.

[55] Najim Dehak, Reda Dehak, James Glass, Douglas Reynolds, and Patrick Kenny. Cosine similarity scoring without score normalization techniques. In *The Speaker and Language Recognition Workshop (Odyssey 2010)*, pages 15–19, Jun-Jul 2010.

[56] Mohammed Senoussaoui, Patrick Kenny, Najim Dehak, and Pierre Dumouchel. An i-vector extractor suitable for speaker recognition with both microphone and telephone speech. In *The Speaker and Language Recognition Workshop (Odyssey 2010)*, pages 28–33, June 2010.

[57] N. Dehak, P.J. Kenny, R. Dehak, P. Dumouchel, and P. Ouellet. Front-end factor analysis for speaker verification. *IEEE Transactions on Audio, Speech and Language Processing*, 19(4):788–798, May 2011.

[58] Najim Dehak, Patrick Kenny, Réda Dehak, O. Glembek, Pierre Dumouchel, L. Burget, V. Hubeika, and F. Castaldo. Support vector machines and joint factor analysis for speaker verification. pages 4237–4240, Apr 2009.

[59] M. Senoussaoui, P. Kenny, P. Dumouchel, and F. Castaldo. Well-calibrated heavy tailed bayesian speaker verification for microphone speech. In *Acoustics, Speech and Signal Processing (ICASSP), 2011 IEEE International Conference on*, pages 4824–4827, May 2011.

[60] L. Burget, O. Plchot, S. Cumani, O. Glembek, P. Matejka, and N. Briimmer. Discriminatively trained probabilistic linear discriminant analysis for speaker verification. In *Acoustics, Speech and Signal Processing (ICASSP), 2011 IEEE International Conference on*, pages 4832–4835, May 2011.

[61] S. Cumani, N. Brummer, L. Burget, and P. Laface. Fast discriminative speaker verification in the i-vector space. In *Acoustics, Speech and Signal Processing (ICASSP), 2011 IEEE International Conference on*, pages 4852–4855, May 2011.

[62] P. Matejka, O. Glembek, F. Castaldo, M.J. Alam, O. Plchot, P. Kenny, L. Burget, and J. Cernocky. Full-covariance ubm and heavy-tailed plda in i-vector speaker verification. In *Acoustics, Speech and Signal Processing (ICASSP), 2011 IEEE International Conference on*, pages 4828–4831, May 2011.

[63] M.J. Alam, T. Kinnunen, P. Kenny, P. Ouellet, and D. O'Shaughnessy. Multi-taper mfcc features for speaker verification using i-vectors. In *Automatic Speech Recognition and Understanding (ASRU), 2011 IEEE Workshop on*, pages 547–552, Dec 2011.

[64] Nagendra Kumar and Andreas G. Andreou. Heteroscedastic discriminant analysis and reduced rank hmms for improved speech recognition. *Speech Communication*, 26(4):283–297, 1998.

[65] D. D. Lee and H. S. Seung. Learning the parts of objects by nonnegative matrix factorization. *Nature*, 401(6755):788–791, 1999.

[66] Daniel D. Lee and H. Sebastian Seung. Algorithms for non-negative matrix factorization. *Advances in Neural Information Processing Systems*, 13:556–562, 2001.

[67] A.L. Bartos and D.J. Nelson. Enabling improved speaker recognition by voice quality estimation. In *Signals, Systems and Computers (ASILOMAR), 2011 Conference Record of the Forty Fifth Asilomar Conference on*, pages 595–599, Nov 2011.

[68] A. Salman and Ke Chen. Exploring speaker-specific characteristics with deep learning. In *Neural Networks (IJCNN), The 2011 International Joint Conference on*, pages 103–110, 2011.

[69] A.K. Sarkar and S. Umesh. Use of vtl-wise models in feature-mapping framework to achieve performance of multiple-background models in speaker verification. In *Acoustics, Speech and Signal Processing (ICASSP), 2011 IEEE International Conference on*, pages 4552–4555, May 2011.

[70] B. Bharathi, P. Vijayalakshmi, and T. Nagarajan. Speaker identification using utterances correspond to speaker-specific-text. In *Students' Technology Symposium (TechSym), 2011 IEEE*, pages 171–174, Jan 2011.

[71] Wei Cai, Qiang Li, and Xin Guan. Automatic singer identification based on auditory features. In *Natural Computation (ICNC), 2011 Seventh International Conference on*, volume 3, pages 1624–1628, Jul 2011.

[72] Hoang Do, I. Tashev, and A. Acero. A new speaker identification algorithm for gaming scenarios. In *Acoustics, Speech and Signal Processing (ICASSP), 2011 IEEE International Conference on*, pages 5436–5439, May 2011.

[73] M.V. Ghiurcau, C. Rusu, and J. Astola. A study of the effect of emotional state upon text-independent speaker identification. In *Acoustics, Speech and Signal Processing (ICASSP), 2011 IEEE International Conference on*, pages 4944–4947, May 2011.

[74] Jia-Wei Liu, Jia-Ching Wang, and Chang-Hong Lin. Speaker identification using hht spectrum features. In *Technologies and Applications of Artificial Intelligence (TAAI), 2011 International Conference on*, pages 145–148, Nov 2011.

[75] John C. Platt, Nello Cristianini, and John Shawe-Taylor. Large margin dags for multiclass classification. In S.A. Solla, T.K. Leen, and K.R. Müller, editors, *Advances in Neural Information processing Systems*. MIT Press, Boston, 2000.

[76] Yuguo Wang. A tree-based multi-class svm classifier for digital library document. In *International Conference on MultiMedia and Information Technology (MMIT)*, pages 15–18, Dec 2008.

[77] Homayoon Beigi. Audio source classification using speaker recognition techniques. World Wide Web, Feb 2011. Report No. RTI-20110201-01.

[78] Stephane H. Maes Homayoon S. M. Beigi. Speaker, channel and environment change detection. Technical Report, 1997.

[79] Homayoon S.M. Beigi and Stephane S. Maes. Speaker, channel and environment change detection. In *Proceedings of the World Congress on Automation (WAC1998)*, May 1998.

[80] Scott Shaobing Chen and Ponani S Gopalakrishnan. Speaker, environment and channel change detection and clustering via the bayesian inromation criterion. In *IBM Techical Report, T.J. Watson Research Center*, 1998.

[81] Tobia Bocklet, Andreas Maier, Josef G. Bauer, Felix Burkhardt, and Elmar Nöth. Age and gender recognition for telephone applications based on gmm supervectors and support vector machines. pages 1605–1608, Apr 2008.

[82] M.H. Bahari and H. Van Hamme. Speaker age estimation and gender detection based on supervised non-negative matrix factorization. In *Biometric Measurements and Systems for Security and Medical Applications (BIOMS), 2011 IEEE Workshop on*, pages 1–6, Sep 2011.

[83] N. Ho. *Nonnegative Martix Factorization Algorithms and Applications*. Université Catholique de Louvain, 2008. PhD Thesis.

[84] H. Van-Hamme. Hac-models: A novel approach to continuous speech recognition. In *Interspeech*, pages 2554–2557, Sep 2008.

[85] Emmanouil Benetos, Margarita Kotti, and Constantine Kotropoulos. Large scale musical instrument identification. In *Proceedings of the 4th Sound and Music Computing Conference*, pages 283–286, Jul 2007.

[86] M. Kirby and L. Sirovich. Application of the karhunen-loeve procedure for the characterization of human faces. *IEEE Transactions on Pattern Analysis and Machine Intelligence*, 12(1):103–108, Jan. 1990.

[87] M. Turk and A. Pentland. Eigenfaces for recognition. *Journal of Cognitive Neuroscience*, 3:71–86, 1991.

[88] S.P. Kishore and B. Yegnanarayana. Speaker verification: minimizing the channel effects using autoassociative neural network models. In *Acoustics, Speech, and Signal Processing, 2000. ICASSP '00. Proceedings. 2000 IEEE International Conference on*, volume 2, pages II1101–II1104, Jun 2000.

[89] Keith Dana Martin. *Sound-Source Recognition: A Theory and Computational Model*. Massachusetts Institute of Technology, Cambridge, MA, 1999. PhD Thesis.

Chapter 2

3D and Thermo-Face Fusion

Štěpán Mráček, Jan Váňa, Radim Dvořák,
Martin Drahanský and Svetlana Yanushkevich

Additional information is available at the end of the chapter

http://dx.doi.org/10.5772/3420

1. Introduction

Most biometric-based systems use a combination of various biometrics to improve reliability of decision. These systems are called multi-modal biometric systems. For example, they can include video, infrared, and audio data for identification of appearance (encompassing natural changes such as aging, and intentional ones, such as surgical changes), physiological characteristics (temperature, blood flow rate), and behavioral features (voice and gait) [1].

Biometric technologies, in a narrow sense, are tools and techniques for identification of humans, and in a wide sense, they can be used for detection of alert information, prior to, or together with, the identification. For example, biometric data such as temperature, blood pulse, pressure, and 3D topology of a face (natural or changed topology using various artificial implants, etc.) must be detected first at distance, while the captured face can be further used for identification. Detection of biometric features, which are ignored in identification, is useful in design of Physical Access Security Systems (PASS) [2][3]. In the PASS, the situational awareness data (including biometrics) is used at the first phase, and the available resources for identification of person (including biometrics) are utilized at the second phase.

Conceptually, a new generation of the biometric-based systems shall include a set of biometric-based assistants; each of them deals with uncertainty independently, and maximizes its contribution to a joint decision. In this design concept, the biometric system possesses such properties as modularity, reconfiguration, aggregation, distribution, parallelism, and mobility. Decision-making in such a system is based on the concept of fusion. In a complex system, the fusion is performed at several levels. In particular, the face biometrics is considered to be the three-fold source of information, as shown in Figure 1.

In this chapter, we consider two types of the biometric-based assistants, or modules, within a biometric system:

• A thermal, or infrared range assistant,

• A 3D visual range assistant.

We illustrate concept of fusion at the recognition component, which is a part of more complex decision-making level. Both methods are described in terms of data acquisition, image processing and recognition algorithms. The general facial recognition approach, based on the algorithmic fusion of the two methods, is presented, and its performance is evaluated on both 3D and thermal face databases.

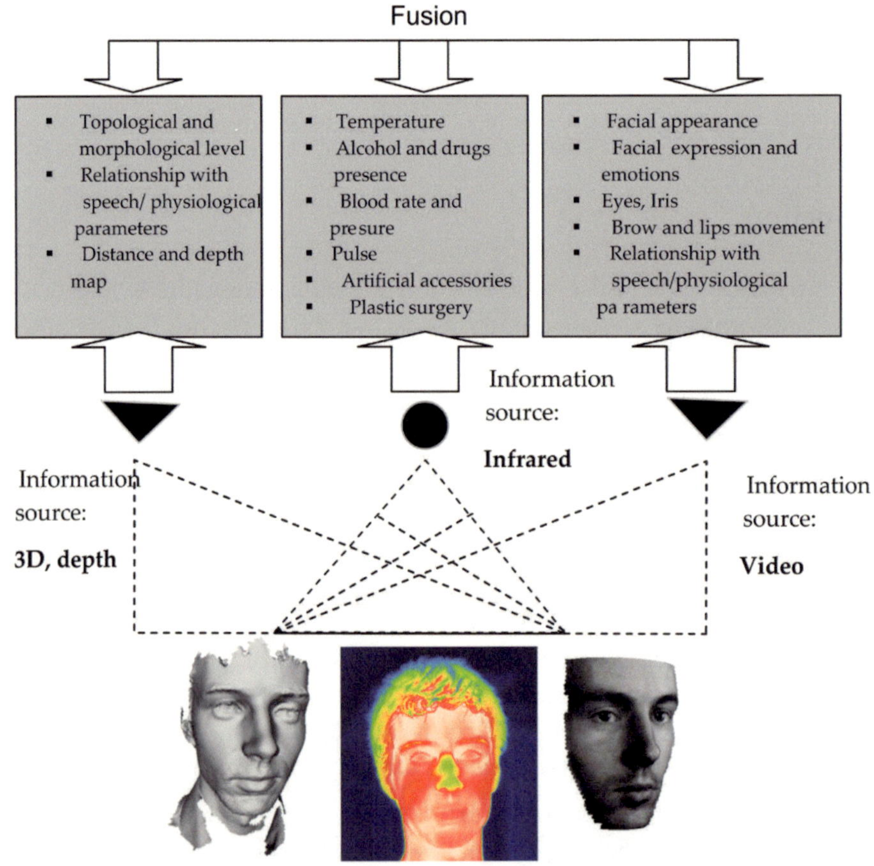

Figure 1. Thee sources of information in facial biometrics: a 3D face model (left), a thermal image (center) and a visual model with added texture (right).

Facial biometric, based on 3D data and infrared images, enchnace the classical face recognition. Adding depth information, as well as the information about the surface temperature, may reveal additional discriminative abilities, and thus improve recognition performance. Furthermore, it is much harder to forge a 3D, or thermal model, of the face.

The following sections provide an overview of how 3D and infrared facial biometrics work, and what is needed in terms of data acquisition and algorithms. The first section deals with the 3D face recognition. Thermal face recognition is described in the second section. Next, a general method for recognition, of both 3D and thermal images, is presented. The fusion on a decision (recognition score) level is investigated. Finally, the performance of the proposed fusion approach is evaluated on several existing databases.

2. Three dimensional face recognition

The three-dimensional (3D) face recognition is a natural extension of the classical two-dimensional approach. Contrary to 2D face recognition, additional possibilities for the recognition are available, due to the added dimension. Another advantage, for example, is a more robust system, in terms of pose variations. An overview of the advantages of the biometric system, based on a 3D face, is shown in Table 1.

Pose variation robustness	Due to the 3D form of the data, the face can be easily rotated into a predefined position.
Lighting condition robustness	Many 3D scanners work in infra-red spectra or emit their own light, for inappropriate lighting conditions do not affect recognition performance.
Out-of-the-box liveness detection	It is much more difficult to spoof fake data on a 3D sensor. While in 2D face recognition, simple systems may be fooled by a photograph or video, it is much more difficult to create an authentic 3D face model.

Table 1. Advantages of 3D face recognition.

The wide range of applications of 3D face recognition systems is limited by a high acquisition cost of special scanning devices. Moreover, a 3D face is targeted more at access control systems, rather than surveillance applications, due to the limited optimal distance range between the scanned subject and the sensor.

2.1. Acquisition of 3D data

Most facial 3D scanners use structured light in order to obtain the three-dimensional shape of a face. Structured light scanners project certain light pattern onto the object's surface, which is simultaneously captured by a camera from a different angle. The exact surface is then computed from the projected light pattern distortion, caused by the surface shape. The most commonly structured light pattern in 3D scanning devices consists of many narrow stripes lying side by side. Other methods, either using a different pattern, or one without the structured light, can be also used [4], however, they are not common in biometric systems.

The pattern can be projected using visible or infra-red light spectrum. An advantage to the infrared light is its non-disturbing effect on the user's eyes. On the other hand, it is more difficult to segment the image and distinguish between the neighboring stripes properly. Therefore, many methods of acquiring the 3D surface use a visible light and color camera. The description of the method, where many color stripes are used, is given in [5]. The authors use the De Bruijn sequence there (see Figure 2), which consists of seven colors, in order to minimize the misclassification between the projected lines and the lines in the image captured by the camera.

Figure 2. The De Bruijn color sequence [5].

The algorithm for surface reconstruction is composed of several steps. In the first step, two images are taken. In the first one ($IM_{pattern}$), the object is illuminated by structured light, whereas in the second one (IM_{clean}) unstructured light is used. Next, the projected light is extracted from the background by subtracting the two images:

$$IM_{extracted} = IM_{pattern} - IM_{clean} \tag{1}$$

The pattern in $IM_{extracted}$ is matched with the original pattern image. In the last step, the depth information of the points lying on the surface is calculated by the trigonometry principle. In order to calculate the exact depths properly, the precise position of the camera and projector, including their orientation, need to be known. It can be measured, or calculated by the calibration of both devices.

An example of a 3D scanner (commercial solution) is the Minolta Vivid Laser 3D scanner. The light reflected by the object is acquired by the CCD camera. Then, the final model is calculated, using the standard triangulation method. For instance, the scanner was used to collect models from the FRGC database [20].

Figure 3. The examples of an acquired 3D face models, using Artec 3D scanner.

Another example is the Artec 3D scanner [6] which has a flash bulb and camera. The bulb flashes a light pattern onto an object, and the CCD camera records the created image. The distortion pattern is then transferred to the 3D image, using Artec software. The advantage of the scanner is its ability to merge several models (pattern images) belonging to the same object. When models are taken from different angles, the overall surface model is significantly accurate, and possible gaps in the surface are minimized. On the other hand, the surface of facial hair, or shiny materials, such as glasses, is hard to reconstruct because of a highly distorted light pattern (see Figure 3).

2.2. 3D face preprocessing

A key part of every biometric system is the preprocessing of input data. In the 3D face field, this task involves primarily the alignment of the face into a predefined position. In this section, several possible approaches of the face alignment will be described. In order to fulfill such a task, the important landmarks are located first. Detecting the facial landmarks from three-dimensional data cannot be performed using the same algorithms as in the case of two-dimensional data. It is mainly because two-dimensional landmark detection is based on analyzing color space of the input face picture, which is not usually present in raw three-dimensional data. However, if the texture data is available, the following landmark detection methods, based on the pure 3D model, may be skipped.

The location of the tip the nose is a fundamental part of preprocessing in many three-dimensional facial recognition methods [7][8][9][15]. Segundo et al. [10] proposed an algorithm for nose tip localization, consisting of two stages. First, the y-coordinate is found, then an appropriate x-coordinate is assigned. To find the y-coordinate, two vertical y-projections of the face are computed – the profile and median curves. The profile curve is determined by the maximum depth value in each row, while the median curve is defined by the median depth value of every set of points with the same y-coordinate. A curve that represents the difference between the profile and median curves is created. A maximum of this difference curve along the y-axis is the y-coordinate of the nose. The x-coordinate of the nose tip is located as follows: along the horizontal line, that intersects the y-coordinate of the nose, the density of peak points is calculated; the point with the highest peak density is the final location of the nose tip (see Figure 4).

In order to classify the points on the surface as peaks, curvature analysis is performed. The curvature at that specific point denotes how much the surface diverges from being flat. The sign of the curvature k indicates the direction in which the unit tangent vector rotates as a function of the parameter along the curve. If the unit tangent rotates counterclockwise, then $k > 0$. Otherwise, $k < 0$.

To depart from 2D curve to 3D surface, two principal (always mutually orthogonal) curvatures k_1 and k_2 are calculated at each point. Using these principal curvatures, two important measures are deduced: Gaussian curvature K and mean curvature H [11]:

$$K = k_1 k_2 \tag{2}$$

$$H = (k_1 + k_2)/2 \tag{3}$$

Classification of the surface points based on signs of Gaussian and mean curvatures is presented in Table 2.

	$K < 0$	$K = 0$	$K > 0$
$H < 0$	saddle ridge	ridge	peak
$H = 0$	minimal	flat	(none)
$H > 0$	saddle valley	valley	Pit

Table 2. Classification of points on 3D surface, based on signs of Gaussian (K) and mean curvatures (H).

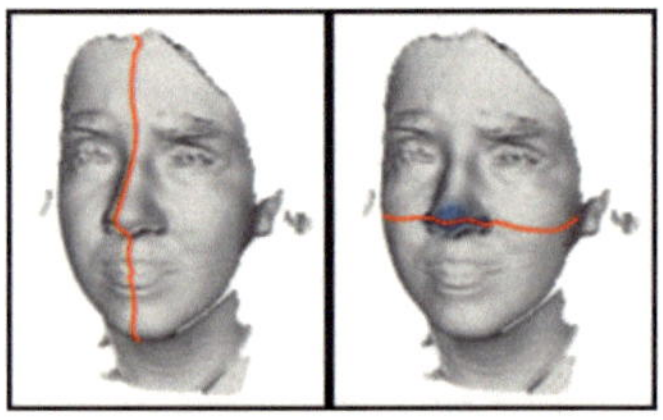

Figure 4. The vertical profile curve that is used to determine the y-coordinate of the nose. Once the y-coordinate is located, another horizontal curve is created. Along the new curve, the density of peak points is calculated and exact position of the nose tip is located.

2.3. Overview of methods

2.3.1. Adaptation of 2D face recognition methods

The majority of widespread face recognition methods are holistic projection methods. These methods take the input image consisting of r rows and c columns, and transform it to a column vector. Pixel intensities of the input image directly represent values of individual components in the resulting vector. Rows of the image are concatenated into one single column.

Projection methods

A common attribute of projection methods is the creation of the data distribution model, and a projection matrix, that transforms input vector $v \in \mathrm{R}^{r \cdot c}$ into some lower dimensional space. In this section, the following methods will be described:

- Principal component analysis (PCA)
- Linear discriminant analysis (LDA)
- Independent component analysis (ICA)

http://dx.doi.org/10.5772/3420

Principal component analysis (PCA) was first introduced by Karl Pearson and covers mathematical methods, which reduce the number of dimensions of a given multi-dimensional space. The dimensionality reduction is based on data distribution. The first principal component is the best way to describe the data in a minimum-squared-error sense. Other components describe as much of the remaining variability as possible.

The *eigenface* method is an example of PCA application. It is a holistic face recognition method, which takes grayscale photographs of people, normalized with respect to size and resolution. The images are then interpreted as vectors. The method was introduced by M. Turk and A. Pentland in 1991 [12].

Linear discriminant analysis (LDA), introduced by Ronald Aylmer Fisher, is an example of supervised learning. Class membership (data subject identity) is taken into account during learning. LDA seeks for vectors that provide the best discrimination between classes after the projection.

The *Fisherface* method is a combination of principal component analysis and linear discriminant analysis. PCA is used to compute the face subspace in which the variance is maximized, while LDA takes advantage of intra-class information. The method was introduced by Belhumeur et al. [13].

Another data projection method is *independent component analysis* (ICA). Contrary to PCA, which seeks for dimensions where data varies the most, ICA looks for the transformation of input data that maximizes non-gaussianity. A frequently used algorithm that computes independent components is the FastICA algorithm [14].

Using projection methods for a 3D face

The adaptation of projection methods for a 3D face is usually based on the transformation of input 3D scans into range-images [15]. Each vertex of a 3D model is projected to a plane, where the brightness of pixels corresponds to specific values of z-coordinates in the input scan. An example of an input range image, and its decomposition in PCA subspace, consisting of 5 eigenvectors, is in Figure 5. Projection coefficients form the resulting feature vector, directly.

The face recognition method proposed by Pan et al. [9] maps the face surface into a planar circle. At first, the nose tip is located and a region of interest (ROI) is chosen. The ROI is the sphere centered at the nose tip. After that, the face surface within the ROI is selected and mapped on the planar circle. The error function E that measures the distortion between the original surface and plane is used. The transformation to the planar circle is performed so that E is minimal. Heseltine [15] shows that the application of certain image processing techniques to the range image has a positive impact on recognition performance.

2.3.2. Recognition methods specific to 3D face

So far, the methods that have emerged as an extension of the classical 2D face recognition were mentioned. In this section, an overview of some purely 3D face recognition methods is provided.

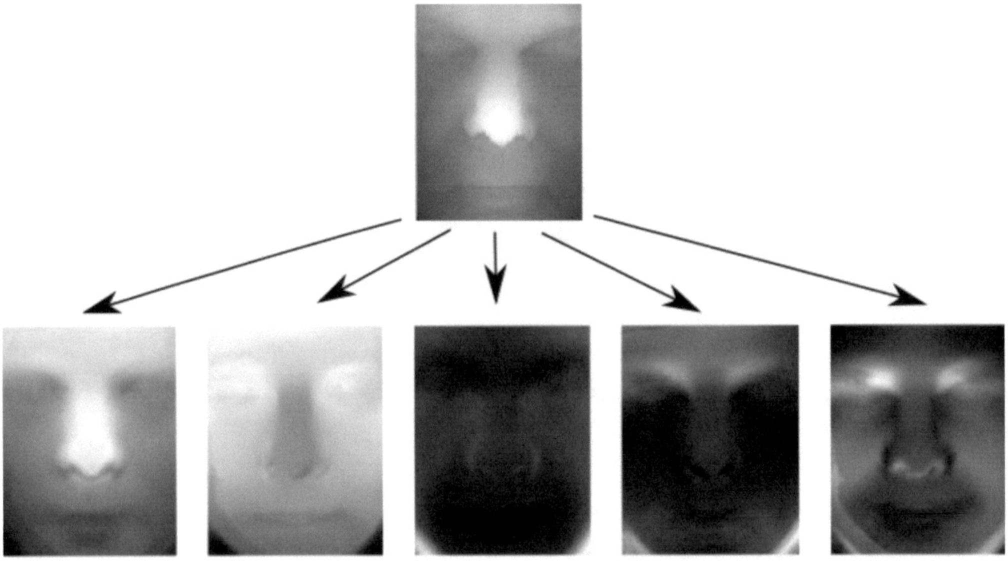

Figure 5. An input range image and its decomposition in PCA subspace consisting of 5 eigenvectors.

Direct comparison using the hybrid ICP algorithm

Lu et. al [7] proposed a method that compares a face scan to a 3D model stored in a database. The method consists of three stages. At first, landmarks are located. Lu uses the nose tip, the inside of one eye and the outside of the same eye. Localization is based on curvature analysis of the scanned face. These three points, obtained in the previous step, are used for coarse alignment with the 3D model, stored in the database. A rigid transformation of the three pairs of corresponding points is performed in the second step.

A fine registration process, the final step, uses the Iterative Closest Point (ICP) algorithm. The root mean square distance minimized by the ICP algorithm, is used as the comparison score.

Recognition using histogram-based features

The algorithm introduced by Zhou et al. [16] is able to deal with small variations caused by facial expressions, noisy data, and spikes on three-dimensional scans. After the localization of the nose, the face is aligned, such that the nose tip is situated in the origin of coordinates and the surface is converted to a range image. Afterwards, a rectangle area around the nose is selected (*region of interest*, ROI). The rectangle is divided into N equal stripes. Each stripe n contains S_n points. Maximal $Z_{n,max}$ and minimal $Z_{n,min}$ z-coordinates within each stripe are calculated and the z-coordinate space is divided into K equal width bins. With the use of the K bins, a histogram of z-coordinates of points forming the scan, is calculated in each stripe. This yields to a feature vector consisting of $N \cdot K$ components. An example of an input range image, and a graphical representation of the corresponding feature vector, is shown in Figure 6.

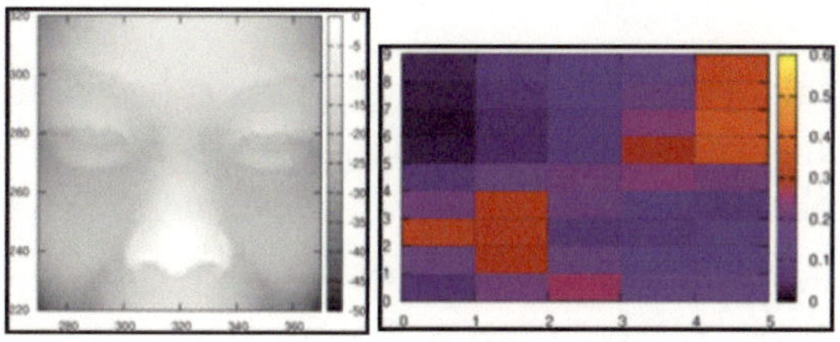

Figure 6. An input range image and its corresponding histogram template, using 9 stripes and 5 bins in each stripe.

Recognition based on facial curves

In recent years, a family of the 3D face recognition methods, which is based on the comparison of facial curves, has emerged. In these methods, the nose tip is located first. After that, a set of closed curves around the nose is created, and the features are extracted.

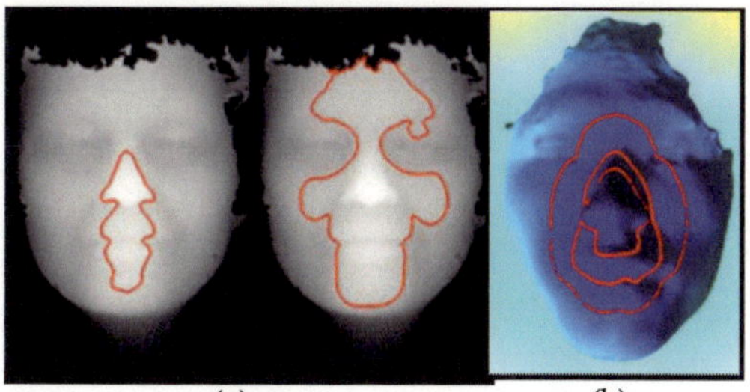

(a) (b)

Figure 7. Iso-depth (a) and iso-geodesic (b) curves on the face surface [15].

In [18], recognition based on iso-depth and iso-geodetic curves is proposed. The iso-depth curve is extracted from the intersection between the face surface and the parallel plane, perpendicular to the z-axis (see Figure 7(a)). The iso-geodesic curve is a set of all points on the surface that have the same geodesic distance from a given point (see Figure 7(b)). The geodesic distance between two points on the surface is a generalization of the term distance on a curved surface.

There is one very important attribute to a the iso-geodesic curve. Contrary to the iso-depth curves, from a given point, iso-geodesic curves are invariant to translation and rotation. This means that no pose normalization of the face is needed, in order to deploy a face recognition algorithm strictly based on iso-geodesic curves. However, precise localization of the nose-tip is still a crucial part of the recognition pipeline.

There are several shape descriptors used for feature extraction in [18]. A set of 5 simple shape descriptors (convexity, ratio of principal axes, compactness, circular variance, and elliptical variance) is provided. Moreover, the Euclidian distance between the curve center and points on the curve is sampled for 120 points on the surface and projected using LDA in order to reduce dimensionality of the feature vector. Three curves are extracted for each face.

The 3D face recognition algorithm proposed in [19] uses iso-geodetic stripes and the surface data are encoded in the form of a graph. The nodes of the graph are the extracted stripes and the directed edges are labeled with *3D Weighted Walkthroughs*. The walkthrough from point $a=(x_a, y_a)$ to $b=(x_b, y_b)$ is illustrated in Figure 8. It is a pair $\langle i, j\rangle$ that describes the sign of mutual positions projected on both axes. For example, if $x_a<x_b \wedge y_a>y_b$ holds, then $\langle i, j\rangle=\langle 1, -1\rangle$. For more information about the generalization of walkthroughs from points to a set of points and to 3D space, see [19].

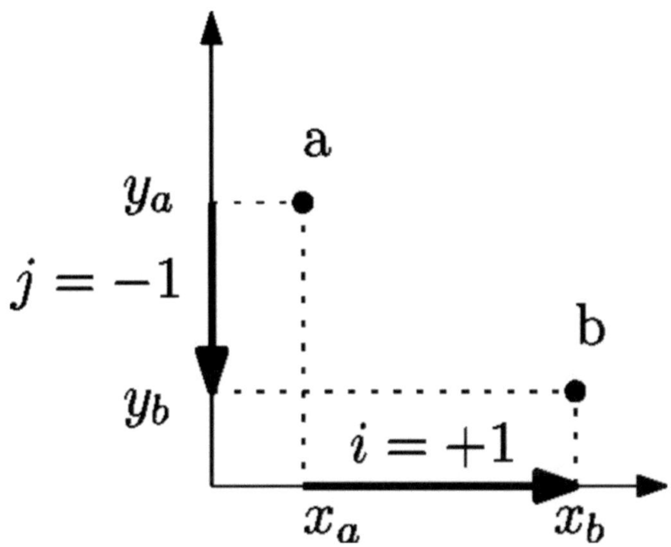

Figure 8. The walktrough $\langle i, j\rangle=\langle 1, -1\rangle$ from *atob*.

Recognition based on the anatomical features

Detection of important landmarks, described in section 2.2, may be extended to other points and curves on the face. The mutual positions of the detected points, distances between curves, their mutual correlations, and curvatures at specific points may be extracted. These numerical values directly form a feature vector, thus the distance between two faces may be instantly compared using an arbitrary distance function between these two feature vectors.

In [17], 8 facial landmarks and 4 curves were extracted from each input scan (see Figure 9) and form over sixty features. These features may be divided into four categories (see Table 3).

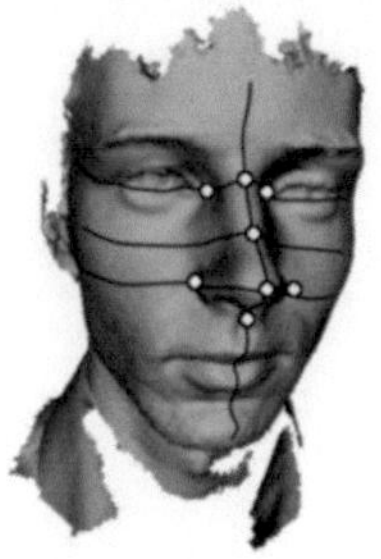

Figure 9. Detected facial landmarks (marked with white circles) and four facial curves: vertical *profile curve*, horizontal *eye curve*, horizontal *nose, or middle, curve* (that intersects the tip of the nose and horizontal curve lying directly between the eye and nose curves).

Category	Description	Number of features
Basic	Distances between selected landmarks	7
Profile curve	Utilization of several distances between the profile curve, extracted from input scan and the corresponding curve from the mean (average) face	4
Eyes curve	Distances between the eyes curve from an input scan and its corresponding eyes curve from the average face model	4
Nose curve	Distances between the nose curve from an input scan and the corresponding nose curve from the average face model	4
Middle curve	Distances between the middle curve from an input scan and the corresponding middle curve from the average face model	4
1st derivation of curves	Distances between the 1st derivation of facial curves and corresponding curves from the average face model	16
2nd derivation of curves	Distances between the 2nd derivation of facial curves and the corresponding curves from the average face model	16
Curvatures	Horizontal and vertical curvatures on selected facial landmarks	6
		Σ 61

Table 3. Categories of anatomical 3D face features.

A fundamental part of recognition, based on anatomical features, is the selection of feature vector components. This subset selection boosts components, with good discriminative ability, and decreases the influence of features with low discriminative ability. There are several possibilities on how to fulfill this task:

- Linear discriminant analysis. The input feature space consisting of 61 dimensions is linearly projected to a subspace, with fewer dimensions, such that the intra-class variability is reduced, and inter-class variability is maximized.
- Subset selection and weighting. For the selection and weighting based on the discriminative potential, see section 4.2.

2.3.3. State-of-the-art

The developed face recognition system should be compared with other current face recognition systems available on the market. In 2006, the National Institute of Standards and Technology in USA found the Face Recognition Vendor Test (FRVT) [20]. It has been the latest, thus far, in a series of large scale independent evaluations. Previous evaluations in the series were the FERET, FRVT 2000, and FRVT 2002. The primary goal of the FRVT 2006 was to measure progress of prototype systems/algorithms and commercial face recognition systems since FRVT 2002. FRVT 2006 evaluated performance on high resolution still images (5 to 6 mega-pixels) and 3D facial scans.

A comprehensive report of achieved results, and used evaluation methodology is described in [21]. The progress that was achieved during the last years is depicted in Figure 10. Results show achieved false rejection rate, at a false acceptance rate of 0.001, for the best face recognition algorithms. This means that, if we admit that 0.1% of impostors are falsely accepted as genuine persons, only 1% of genuine users are incorrectly rejected. The best 3D face recognition algorithm that has been evaluated in FRVT 2006 was Viisage, from the commercial portion of participating organizations [21].

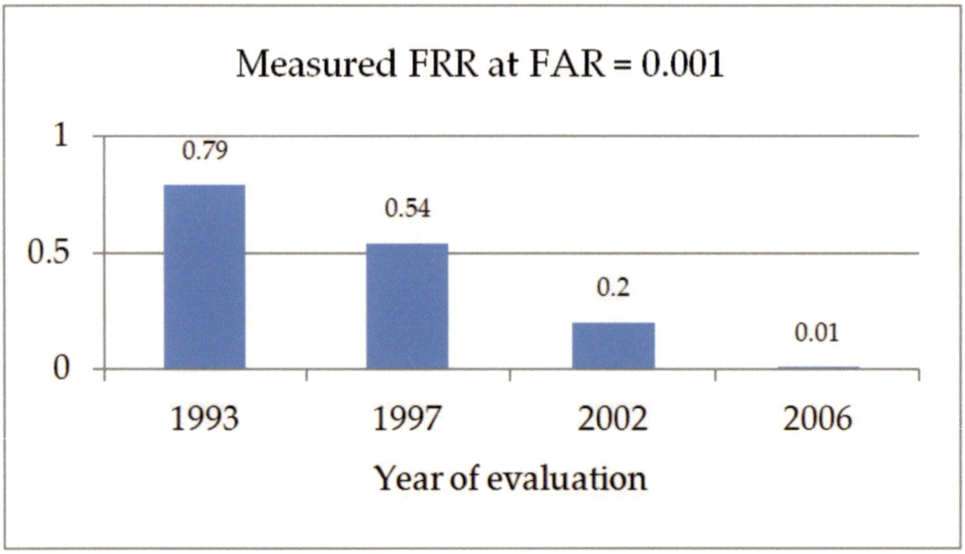

Figure 10. Reduction in error rate for state-of-the-art face recognition algorithms as documented through FERET, FRVT 2002, and FRVT 2006 evaluations.

http://dx.doi.org/10.5772/3420

The upcoming Face Recognition Vendor Test 2012 continues a series of evaluations for face recognition systems. The primary goal of the FRVT 2012 is to measure the advancement in the capabilities of prototype systems and algorithms from commercial and academic communities.

3. Thermal face recognition

Face recognition based on thermal images has minor importance in comparison to visible light spectrum recognition. Nevertheless, in applications such as the liveness detection or the fever scan, thermal face recognition is used as a standalone module, or as a part of a multi-modal biometric system.

Thermal images are remarkably invariant to light conditions. On the other hand, intra-class variability is very high. There are a lot of aspects that contribute to this negative property, such as different head poses, face expressions, changes of hair or facial hair, the environment temperature, current health conditions, and even emotions.

3.1. Thermal-face acquisition

Every object, whose temperature is not absolute zero, emits the so called "thermal radiation". Most of the thermal radiation is emitted in the range of 3 to 14 μm, not visible to the human eye. The radiation itself consists primarily of self-emitted radiation from vibrational and rotational quantum energy level transitions in molecules, and, secondarily, from reflection of radiation from other sources [26]. The intensity and the wavelength of the emitted energy from an object are influenced by its temperature. If the object is colder than 50°C, which is the case of temperatures of a human being, then its radiation lies completely in the IR spectrum.

3.1.1. Temperature measurements

The radiation properties of objects are usually described in relation to a perfect blackbody (the perfect emitter) [27]. The coefficient value lies between 0 and 1, where 0 means none and 1 means perfect emissivity. For instance, the emissivity of human skin is 0.92. The reflected radiations from an object are supposed to be much smaller than the emitted ones, therefore they are neglected during imaging.

Atmosphere is present between an object and a thermal camera, which influences the radiation due to absorption by gases and particles. The amount of attenuation depends heavily on the light wavelength. The atmosphere usually transmits visible light very well, however, fog, clouds, rain, and snow can distort the camera from seeing distant objects. The same principle applies to infrared radiation.

The so-called atmospheric windows (only little attenuation), which lie between 2 and 5 μm (the mid-wave window), and 7.5–13.5 μm (the long-wave window) have to be used for thermo-graphic measurement. Atmospheric attenuation prevents an object's total radiation from reaching the camera. The correction of the attenuation has to be done in order to get the true temperature, otherwise it will be dropping, with increasing distance.

3.1.2. Thermal detectors

Majority of IR cameras have a microbolometer type detector, mainly because of cost considerations. They respond to radiant energy in a way that causes a change of state in the bulk material (i.e., the bolometer effect) [27]. Generally, microbolometers do not require cooling, which allows for compact camera designs (see Figure 11) to be relatively low cost. Apart from lower sensitivity to radiation, another substantial disadvantage of such cameras is their relatively slow reaction time, with a delay of dozens of milliseconds. Nevertheless, such parameters are sufficient for biometric purposes.

Figure 11. FLIR ThermaCAM EX300[28].

For more demanding applications, quantum detectors can be used. They operate based on an intrinsic photoelectric effect [27]. The detectors can be very sensitive to the infrared radiation which is focused on them by cooling to cryogenic temperatures. They also react very quickly to changes in IR levels (i.e., temperatures), having a constant response time in the order of 1μs. However, their cost disqualifies their usage in biometric applications in these days.

3.2. Face and facial landmarks detection

Head detection in a visible spectrum is a very challenging task. There are many aspects making the detection difficult such as a non-homogenous background and various skin colors. Since the detection is necessary in the recognition process, much effort was invested in dealing with this problem. Nowadays, one of the most commonly used methods is based on the Viola-Jones detector, often combined with additional filtering, required for skin color model.

In contrast to the visible spectrum, detection of the skin on thermal images is easier. The skin temperature varies in a certain range. Moreover, skin temperature remarkably differs from the temperature of the environment. That is why techniques based on background and foreground separation are widely used. The first step of skin detection is usually based on a thresholding. A convenient threshold is in most scenarios computed using Otsu algorithm [34]. Binary images usually need more correction consisting of hole removal and contour smoothing [33]. Another approach detects the skin, using Bayesian segmentation [29].

The next step of detection is the localization of important facial landmarks such as the eyes, nose, mouth and brows. The Violla-Jones detector can be used to detect some of them. Friedrich and Yeshurn propose eye brow detection by analysis of local maxima in a vertical histogram (see Figure 12) [33].

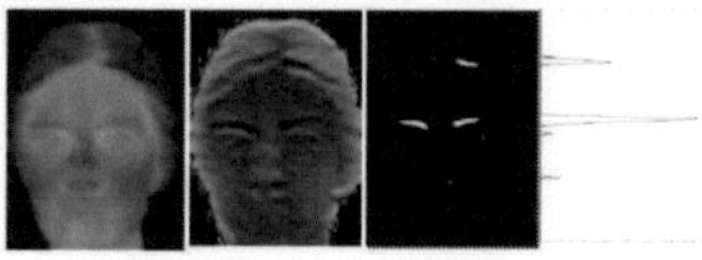

Figure 12. Eye brow detection by [33]: Original image (left), edges enhancement, binarized image and its vertical histogram - sum of intensities in each row (right).

3.3. Head normalization

If a comparison algorithm is performed on raw thermal face images, without any processing, we would get unacceptable results. This is becuase the thermal faces belong to biometrics with high intra-class variability. This makes thermal face recognition one of the most challenging methods, in terms of intra-class variability reducing, while keeping or increasing the inter-class variability of sensory data. The normalization phase of the recognition process tries to deal with all these aspects and decrease the intra-class variability as much as possible, while preserving the inter-class variability.

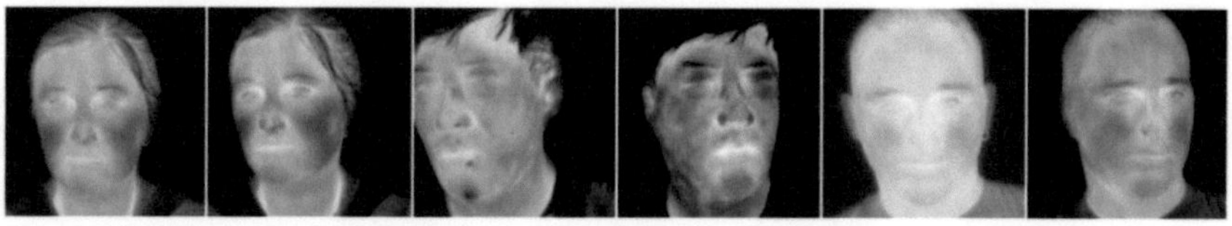

Figure 13. Thermal images of 3 different people. Output of all normalization methods is demonstrated by processing these raw images.

Proposed normalization consists of a pose, intensity and region of stability normalization. All normalization methods are described in the following sections and their output is visualized on the sample thermal images in Figure 13.

3.3.1. Pose normalization

Biometric systems based on face recognition do not strictly demand the head to be positioned in front of the camera. The task of pose (geometric) normalization is to transform the captured face to a default position (front view without any rotation). The fulfillment of this task is one of the biggest challenges for 2D face recognition technologies. It is obvious that a perfect solution cannot be achieved by 2D technology, however, the variance caused by different positions should be minimized as much as possible.

Geometric normalization often needs information about the position of some important points within the human face. These points are usually image coordinates of the eyes, nose and mouth. If they are located correctly, the image can be aligned to a default template.

2D affine transformation

Basic methods of geometric normalization are based on affine transformation, which is usually realized by transformation, using a matrix T. Each point $p=[x,\ y]$ of original image I is converted to homogenous coordinates $p_h=[x,\ y,\ 1]$. All these points are multiplied by the matrix T to get the new coordinates p'.

Methods of geometric normalization vary with the complexity of transformation matrix computation. The *general affine transformation* maps three different facial landmarks of the original image, I, to their expected positions within the default template. Transformation matrix coefficients are computed by solving a set of linear algebraic equations [23].

3D projection

Human heads have an irregular ellipsoid-like 3D shape, therefore, the 2D-warping method works well, when the head is scaled or rotated in the image plane. In the case of any other transformation, the normalized face is deformed (see Figure 15).

The proposed 3D-projection method works with an average 3D model of the human head. A 3D affine transformation, consisting of translation, rotation and scaling, can be applied to each vertex. The transformed model can be perspectively projected to a 2D plane afterwards. This process is well known from 3D computer graphics and visualization.

Model alignment, according to the image, I, is required. The goal is to find a transformation of the model whose orientation after the transformation will reveal each important facial landmark. The texture of the input image, I, is projected onto the aligned model. Then, the model is transformed (rotated and scaled) to its default position and finally, the texture from the model is re-projected onto the resulting image (see Figure 14).

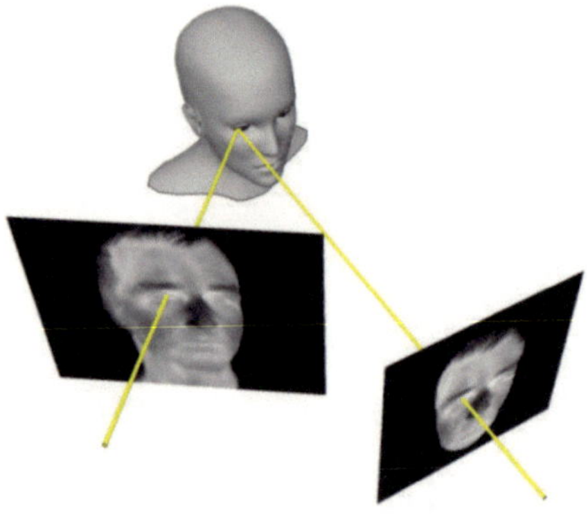

Figure 14. Visualization of the 3D projection method.

This kind of normalization considers the 3D shape of the human face. However, the static (unchangeable) model is the biggest drawback of this method. There are more advanced techniques that will solve this problem by using the *3D Morphable Face Model* [22].

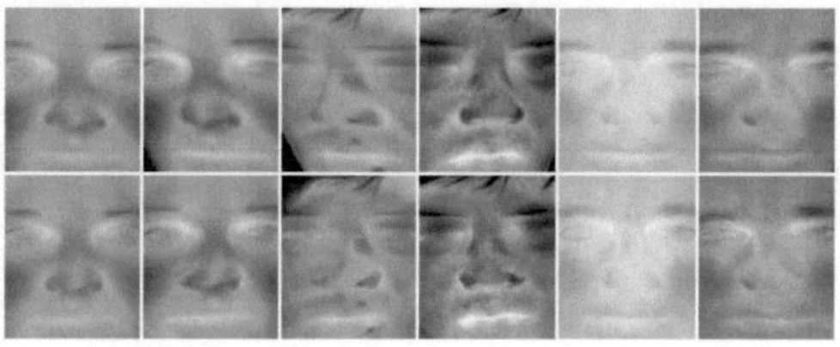

Figure 15. Pose normalization methods overview: 2D affine transformation (first row) and the 3D projection method (second row).

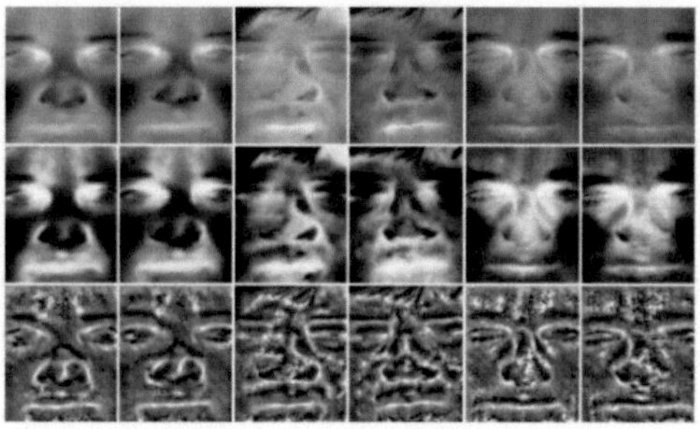

Figure 16. Intensity normalization methods overview: Min-max (first row), Global equalization (send row) and Local equalization (third row).

3.3.2. Intensity normalization

A comparison of thermal images in absolute scale does not usually lead to the best results. The absolute temperature of the human face varies with environmental temperature, physical activity and emotional state of the person. Some testing databases even do not even contain information on how to map pixel intensity to that temperature. Therefore, intensity normalization is necessary. It can be accomplished via global or local histogram equalization of noticeable facial regions (see Figure 16).

3.3.3. Region of stability normalization

The region of stability normalization takes into account the shape of a face, and a variability of temperature emission within different face parts. The output image of previous normalizations has a rectangular shape.

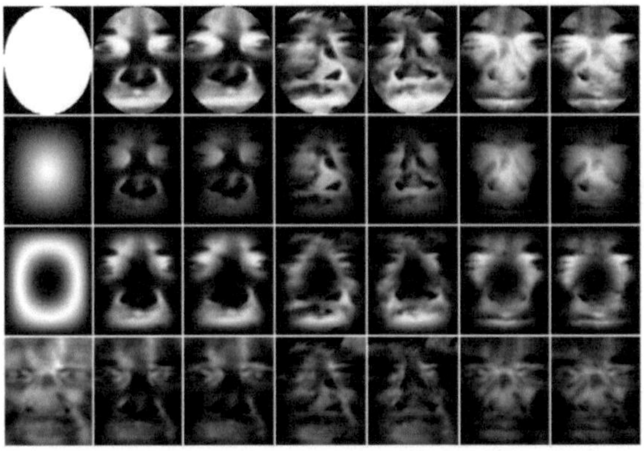

Figure 17. Overview of methods used for region of stability and the normalization. The masks (first column) and normalization responses are displayed for the following methods: Elliptical (top row), Smooth-Elliptical, Weighted-Smooth-Elliptical, Discriminative potential (bottom row).

The main purpose of this normalization is to mark an area where the most important face data are located, in terms of unique characteristics. This normalization is done by multiplying the original image by some mask (see Figure 17).

- Elliptical mask: The human face has an approximately elliptical shape. A Binary elliptical mask is therefore the simplest and most practical solution.

- Smooth-elliptical mask: The weighted mask does not have a step change on the edge between the expected face points and background points.

- Smooth-weighted-elliptical mask: Practical experiments show that the human nose is the most unstable feature, in terms of temperature emissivity. Therefore, the final mask has lower weight within the expected nasal area position.

- Discriminative potential mask: Another possibility to mark regions of stability is by training on part of a face´s database. A mask is obtained by the discriminative potential method described in section 4.2.

3.4. Feature extraction on thermal images

Several comparative studies of thermal face recognition approaches have been developed in recent years. The first recognition algorithms were appearance-based. These methods deal with the normalized image as a vector of numbers. The projected vector turns into a (low dimensionality) subspace, where the separation between impostors and genuines can be efficiently computed with higher accuracy. The commonly used methods are the PCA, LDA and ICA, which are described in more detail in section 4.2.

While appearance-based methods belong to the global-matching methods, there are local-matching methods, which compare only certain parts of an input image to achieve better performance. The LBP (*Local Binary Pattern*) method was primarily developed for texture description and recognition. Nevertheless, it was successfully used in visible and thermal face recognition [24]. It encodes the neighbors of a pixel, according to relative differences, and calculates a histogram of these codes in small areas. These histograms are then combined with a feature vector. Another comparative study [25] describes other local-matching methods such as the Gabor Jets, the SIFT (*Scale Invariant Feature Transform*), the SURF (*Speeded up Robust Features*) and the WLD (*Weber Linear*) descriptors.

A different approach extracts the vascular network from thermal images, which is supposed to be unique according to each individual. One of the prominent methods [29] extracts thermal minutia points (similar to fingerprints minutia) and compares two vascular networks subsequently (see Figure 18). In another approach, it is proposed to use a feature set for the thermo-face representation: the bifurcation points of the thermal pattern and geographical, and gravitational centers of the thermal face [30].

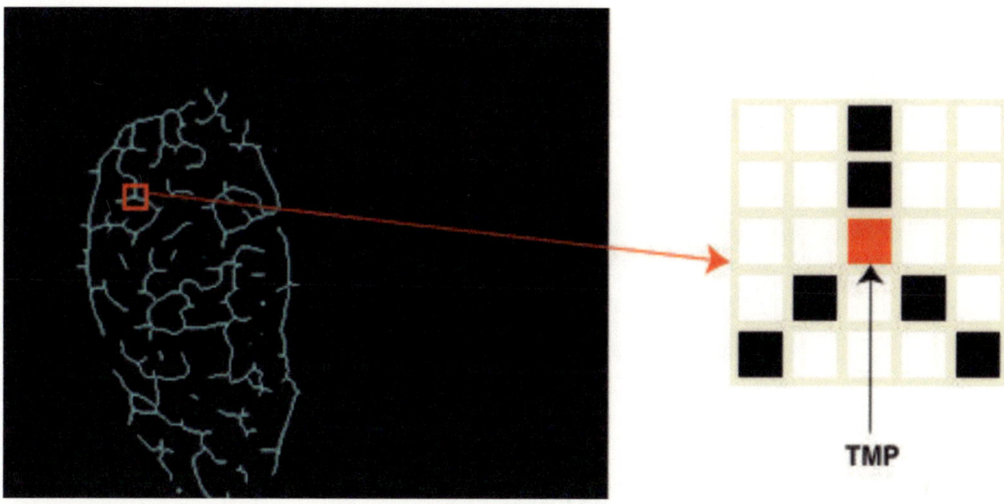

Figure 18. A thermal minutia point being extracted from a thinned vascular network[29].

4. Common processing parts for normalized, 3D, and thermal images

For both thermal and 3D face recognition, it is very difficult to select one method, out of numerous possibilities, which gives the best performance in each scenario. Choosing the best method is always limited to a certain or specific database (input data). In order to address this problem, multi-algorithmic biometric fusion can be used.

In the following sections, a general multi-algorithmic biometric system will be described. Both 3D face recognition and thermal facial recognition require a normalized image. Since many of these characteristics are similar, we do not distinguish between origins of the normalized image. This section describes generic algorithms of feature extraction, feature projection and comparison, which are being evaluated on normalized 3D, as well as thermal images.

4.1. Feature extraction of the normalized image

The feature extraction part takes the normalized image as input, and produces a feature vector as output. This feature vector is then processed in the feature projection part of the process.

Vectorization is the simplest method of feature extraction. The intensity values of the image $I = w \times h$ are concentrated to a single column vector. Performance of this extraction depends on the normalization method.

Since normalized images are not always convenient for direct vectorization, feature extraction with the use of the **bank of filters** has been presented in several works. The normalized image is convolved with a bank of 2D filters, which are generated, using some kernel function with different parameters (see Figure 19). Each response of the convolution forms a final feature vector.

The **Gabor filter bank** is one of the most popular filter banks [32]. We employed the **Laguerre-Gaussian filter bank** as well due to its good performance in the facial recognition field [31].

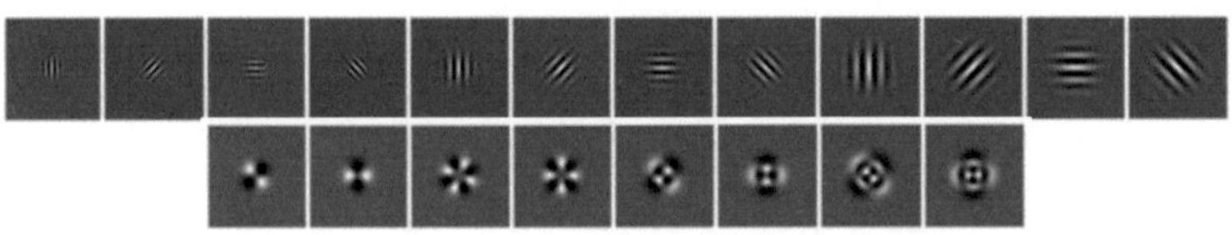

Figure 19. The Gabor (first row) and Laguere-Gaussian (second row) filter banks.

4.2. Feature vector projection and further processing

Statistical projection methods linearly transform the input feature vector from an input m-dimensional space into an n-dimensional space, where $n < m$. We utilize the following methods:

- Principal component analysis (PCA, Eigenfaces)
- PCA followed by linear discriminant analysis (LDA of PCA, Fisherfaces)
- PCA followed by independent component analysis (ICA of PCA)

Every projectional method has a common learning parameter, which defines how much variability of the input space is captured by the PCA. This parameter controls the dimensionality of the output projection space. Let k eigenvalues, computed during the PCA calculation, be denoted as $e_1, e_2, \ldots, e_k$, $(e_1 > e_2 > \ldots > e_k)$. These eigenvalues directly represent the variability in each output dimension. If we want to preserve only 98% of variability, then only the first l eigenvalues and its corresponding eigenvectors are selected, such that their sum forms only 98% of the $\sum_{j=1}^{k} e_j$.

There is an optional step to perform a per-feature z-score normalization after the projection, so that each vector fv is transformed into

$$fv' = \frac{fv - \bar{fv}}{\sigma}, \tag{4}$$

where $\bar{fv}$ is the mean vector and σ is the vector of standard deviations.

Optional processing, after the application of statistical projection methods, is the feature weighting. Suppose that we have a set FV of all pairs of feature vectors, v_j, and their corresponding class (subject) labels, id_j:

$$FV = \{(id_1, fv_1), (id_2, fv_2), \ldots, (id_n, fv_n)\} \tag{5}$$

The individual feature vector components, $v_{j1}, fv_{j2}, \ldots, fv_{jm}$, of the vector fv_j do not have the same discriminative ability. While some component may have positive contribution to the overall recognition performance, the other component may not. We have implemented and evaluated two possible feature evaluation techniques.

The first possible solution is the LDA application. The second option is to make an assumption that the good feature vector component has stable values across different scans of the same subjects, however, the mean value of a specific component across different subject differs to the greatest possible extent. Let the intra-class variability of the feature component i be denoted as $intra_i$, as it expresses the mean of standard deviations of all measured values for the same subjects. The inter-class variability of component i is denoted as $inter_i$, and expresses the standard deviation of means of measured values for the same subject. The resulting discriminative potential, therefore, can be expressed as follows:

$$discriminativepotential = inter_i - intra_i \tag{6}$$

4.3. Fusion using binary classifiers

The number of combinations for common feature extraction techniques and optional feature vector processing, yields a large set of possible recognition methods. For example, the Gabor filter bank, consisting of 12 kernels, may be convolved with an input image. The results of the convolution are concatenated into one large column vector, which is then processed with PCA, followed by LDA. Another example is an input image processed by the PCA. The individual features in the resulting feature vector, are multiplied by their corresponding normalized discriminative potential weight.

After the features are extracted, the feature vector is compared with the template from a biometric database, using some arbitrary distance function. If the distance is below a certain threshold, the person, whose features were extracted, is accepted as a genuine user. If we are using several different recognition algorithms, the simple threshold becomes a binary classification problem. The biometric system has to decide whether the resulting score vector $s = (s_1, s_2, \ldots, s_n)$ belongs to the genuine user or the impostor. An example of a general multimodal-biometric system employing a score-level fusion is in Figure 20, but the same approach may be applied to a multi-algorithmic system, where input is just one sample and more than one feature extraction and comparison method is applied.

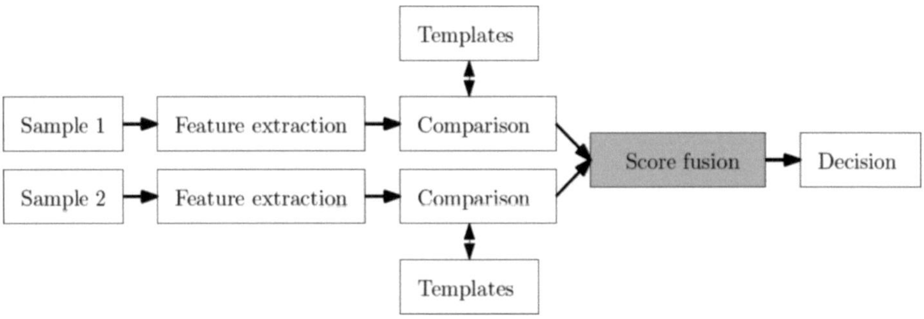

Figure 20. A generic multimodal biometric system using score-level fusion.

In order to compare and fuse scores that come from different methods, normalization, to a certain range, has to be performed. We use the following score normalization: the score values are linearly transformed so that the genuine mean (the score, obtained from comparing the same subjects) is 0, and the impostor mean (score, obtained from comparing different subjects) is 1. Note that individual scores may have negative values. This does not matter in the context of score-level fusion, since these values represent positions within the classification space, rather than distances between two feature vectors.

The theoretical background of general multimodal biometric fusion, especially the link between the correlation and variance of both impostor and genuine distribution between the employed recognition methods, is described in [35]. The advantage provided by score fusion relative to monomodal biometric systems is described in detail in [36].

In our fusion approach, we have implemented a classification using logistic regression [37], support vector machines (SVM), with linear and sigmoidal kernel [37], and linear discriminant analysis (LDA).

4.4. Experimental results

For evaluation of our fusion approach on ethermal images, we used the Equinox [38] and Notre-dame databases [39][40]. Equinox contains 243 scans of 74 subjects, while the Notre Dame database consists of 2,292 scans. Evaluation for 3D face recognition was performed on the "Spring 2004" part on the FRGC database [20], from which we have selected only subjects with more than 5 scans. This provided 1,830 3D scans in total.

The evaluation scenario was as follows. We divided each database into three equal parts. Different data subjects were present in each part. The first portion of the data was used for training of the projection methods. The second portion was intended for optional calculation of z-score normalization parameters, the feature weighting, and the fusion classification training. The final part was used for evaluation.

To ensure that the particular results of the employed methods are stable and reflect the real performance, the following cross-validation process was selected. The database was randomly divided into three parts, where all parts had an equal number of subjects. This random division, and subsequent evaluation was processed n times, where n depends on the size of the database. The Equinox database was cross-validated 10 times, while the Notre-dame database and FRGC were cross-validated 3 times. The performance of a particular method was reported as the mean value of the achieved equal error rates (EERs).

4.4.1. Evaluation on thermal images

For thermal face recognition the following techniques were fused:

- Local and global contrast enhancement,
- The Gabor and Laguerre filter banks,
- PCA and ICA projection,
- Weighting based on discriminative potential,
- Comparison using the cosine distance function.

From these techniques, 10 best different recognition methods were selected for final score-level fusion. Logistic regression was used for score fusion. The results are given in Table 4.

4.4.2. Evaluation on 3D face scans

For performance evaluation of the 3D face scans, the following recognition methods were used:

- Recognition, using anatomical features. The discriminative potential weighting was applied on the resulting feature vector, consisting of 61 features. The city-block (Manhattan, L_0) metric was employed.
- Recognition using histogram-based features. We use a division of the face into 10 rows and 6 columns. The individual feature vector components were weighted by their discriminative potential. Cosine metric is used for the distance measurement.
- Cross correlation of shape-index images[7], see Figure 21.
- Shape-index images projected by the PCA, weighting based on discriminative potential, and the cosine distance function.
- Shape-index images projected by the PCA followed by the ICA, weighting based on discriminative potential, and the cosine distance function.

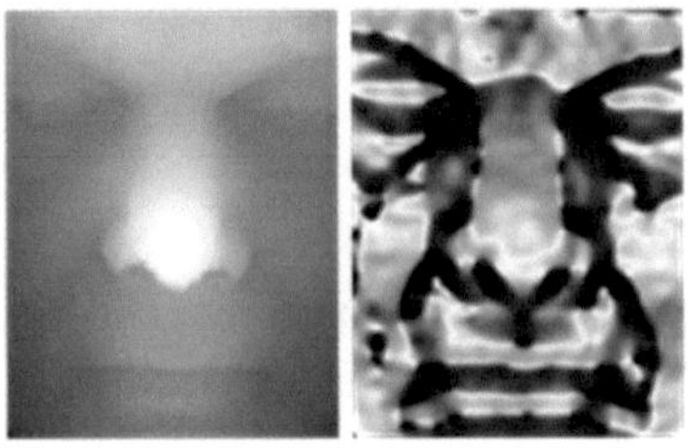

Figure 21. An original range image and shape index visualization.

The result of the algorithms evaluation using FRGC database is given in Table 4.

Database	Best single method name	Best single method EER	Fusion EER	Improvement
Equinox	Global contrast enhancement, no filter bank, ICA, cosine distance	2.28	1.06	53.51%
Notre-dame	Global contrast enhancement, no filter bank, PCA, cosine distance	6.70	5.99	10.60%
FRGC	Shape index, PCA, weighting using discriminative potential, cosine distance	4.06	3.88	4.43%

Table 4. Evaluation of fusion based on logistic regression. For every fusion test, all individual components of the resulting fusion method were evaluated separately. The best component was compared with overall fusion, and improvement was also reported. The numbers represent the achieved EER in %.

5. Conclusion

This chapter addressed a novel approach to biometric based-system design, viewed as design of a distributed network of multiple biometric modules, or assistants. The advances of multi-source biometric data are demonstrated using 3D and infrared facial biometrics. A particular task of such system, namely, identification, using fusion of these biometrics, is demonstrated. It is shown that reliability of the fusion-based decision increases. Specifically, 3D face models carry additional topological information, and, thus, are more robust, compared to 2D models. Thermal data brings additional information. By deploying the best face recognition techniques for both 3D and thermal domains, we showed, through experiments, that fusion increases the overall performace up to 50%.

It should be noted that the important components of the processing pipeline image processing and the correct feature selection greatly influence the decision-making (comparison). Also, choice of another way of fusion may influence the results.

The identification task, combined with advanced discriminative analysis of biometric data, such as temperature and its derivatives (blood flow rate, pressure etc.), constitute the basis for the higher-level decision-making support, called semantic biometrics [3]. Decision-making in semantic form is the basis for implementation in distributed security systems, PASS of the next generation. In this approach, the properties of linguistic averaging are efficiently utilized for smoothing temporal errors, including errors caused by insufficiency of information, at the local and global levels of biometric systems. The concept of semantics in biometrics is linked to various disciplines; in particular, to dialogue support systems, as well as to there commender systems.

Another extension of the concept of PASS is the Training PASS (T-PASS) that provides a training environment for the users of the system [41]. Such a system makes use of synthetic biometric data [42], automatically generated to "imitate" real data. For example, models can be generated from real acquired data, and can simulate age, accessories, and other attributes of the human face. Generation of synthetic faces, using 3D models that provide the attribute of convincing facial expressions, and thermal models which have a given emotional coloring, is a function of both the PASS (to support identification by analysis through synthesis, for instance, modeling of head rotation to improve recognition of faces acquired from video), and T-PASS (to provide virtual reality modeling for trainees).

Acknowledgement

This research has been realized under the support of the following grants: "Security-Oriented Research in Information Technology" – MSM0021630528 (CZ), "Information Technology in Biomedical Engineering" – GD102/09/H083 (CZ), "Advanced secured, reliable and adaptive IT" – FIT-S-11-1 (CZ), "The IT4Innovations Centre of Excellence" – IT4I-CZ 1.05/1.1.00/02.0070 (CZ) and NATO Collaborative Linkage Grant CBP.EAP.CLG 984 "Intelligent assistance systems: multisensor processing and reliability analysis".

Author details

Štěpán Mráček[1], Jan Váňa[1], Radim Dvořák[1], Martin Drahanský[1] and Svetlana Yanushkevich[2]

1 Faculty of Information Technology, Brno University of Technology, Czech Republic

2 University of Calgary, Canada

References

[1] Jain A. K., Nandakumar K., Uludag U., LuX. Multimodal biometrics: augmenting face with other cues, In: Face Processing: Advanced Modeling and Methods, Elsevier, 2006.

[2] Yanushkevich S. N., Stoica A., Shmerko V. P. Experience of design and prototyping of a multi-biometric early warning physical access control security system (PASS) and a training system (T-PASS), In: Proc. 32nd Annual IEEE Industrial Electronics Society Conference, Paris, pp. 2347-2352, 2006.

[3] Yanushkevich S. N., Shmerko V. P., Boulanov O. R., StoicaA. Decision making support in biometric-based physical access control systems: design concept, architecture, and applications, In book: N. Bourgoulis and L. Micheli-Tsanakou, K. Platantionis (Eds.), Biometrics: Theory, Methods and Applications, IEEE/Wiley Press, pp. 599-632, 2009.

[4] Peng T."Algorithms and Models for 3-D Shape Measurement Using Digital Fringe Projections", Ph.D. thesis, University of Maryland, 2006.

[5] Fechteler P., Eisert P., Rurainsky J. Fast and High Resolution 3D Face Scanning, In Proceedings of the 14th International Conference on Image Processing (ICIP2007), San Antonio, Texas, USA, 2007.

[6] Artec M™ 3D Scanner. ARTEC GROUP. Artec M™ – Artec 3D Scanners, http://www.artec3d.com/3d_scanners/artec-m (accessed 21 April 2012).

[7] Lu X., Colbry D. & Jain A. Three-Dimensional Model Based Face Recognition, in ICPR 04: Proceedings of the Pattern Recognition, 17th International Conference on Pattern Recognition, pp. 362-366, 2004.

[8] Mahoor, M. H. & Abdel-Mottaleb, M. Face recognition based on 3D ridge images obtained from range data, Pattern Recognition, vol. 42, no. 3, pp. 445-451, 2009.

[9] Pan G., Han S., Wu Z. & Wang Y. 3D Face Recognition using Mapped Depth Images, in 2005 IEEE Computer Society Conference on Computer Vision and Pattern Recognition (CVPR'05) - Workshops, vol. 3, p. 175, 2005.

[10] Segundo M., Queirolo C., Bellon O. & Silva L. Automatic 3D facial segmentation and landmark detection, in ICIAP '07 Proceedings of the 14th International Conference on Image Analysis and Processing, pp. 431-436, 2007.

[11] GrayA. The Gaussian and Mean Curvatures, in Modern Differential Geometry of Curves and Surfaces with Mathematica, pp. 373-380, 1997.

[12] Turk M. & Pentland A. Face recognition using eigen faces, in IEEE Computer Society Conference on Computer Vision and Pattern Recognition, vol. 591, no. 1, pp. 586-591, 1991.

[13] Belhumeur P., Hespanha J. & Kriegman D. Eigenfacesvs. Fisherfaces: Recognition Using Class Specific Linear Projection, IEEE Transactions on Pattern Analysis and Machine Intelligence, vol. 19, no. 7, pp. 711-720, 1997.

[14] Hyvärinen A. Fast and robust fixed-point algorithms for independent component analysis., IEEE transactions on neural networks / a publication of the IEEE Neural Networks Council, vol. 10, no. 3, pp. 626-34, 1999.

[15] Heseltine T., Pears N. & Austin J. Three-dimensional face recognition using combinations of surface feature map subspace components," Image and Vision Computing, vol. 26, no. 3, pp. 382-396, 2006.

[16] Zhou X., Seibert H. & BuschC. A 3D face recognition algorithm using histogram-based features, Eurographics 2008 Workshop on 3D Object Retrieval, pp. 65-71, 2008.

[17] Mráček Š., Busch C., Dvořák R. &Drahanský M. Inspired by Bertillon - Recognition Based on Anatomical Features from 3D Face Scans, in Proceedings of the 3rd International Workshop on Security and Communication Networks, pp. 53-58, 2011.

[18] Jahanbin S., Choi H., Liu Y. &Bovik A. C. Three Dimensional Face Recognition Using Iso-Geodesic and Iso-Depth Curves, in 2nd IEEE International Conference on Biometrics: Theory, Applications and Systems. 2008.

[19] Berretti S., Del Bimbo A. & Pala P. 3D Face Recognition Using iso-Geodesic Stripes. IEEE transactions on pattern analysis and machine intelligence, vol. 32, no. 12, pp. 2162-2177, 2010.

[20] Phillips P. J. et al. Overview of the Face Recognition Grand Challenge, in IEEE Computer Society Conference on Computer Vision and Pattern Recognition (CVPR'05), vol. 1, pp. 947-954, 2005.

[21] Phillips P. J. et al., FRVT 2006 and ICE 2006 large-scale experimental results, IEEE transactions on pattern analysis and machine intelligence, vol. 32, no. 5, pp. 831-46, 2010.

[22] Blanz V. Face Recognition based on a 3D Morphable Model, in Proc. of the 7th Int. Conference of Automatic Face and Gesture Recognition, pp. 617–622, 2006.

[23] Raton B. Affine Transformations. In Standard Mathematical Tables and Formulae, D. Zwillinger, pp. 265–266, 1995.

[24] Mendez H., San Martı´n C., Kittler J., Plasencia Y., Garcı´a E. Face recognition with LWIR imagery using local binary patterns, LNCS5558, pp. 327–336, 2009.

[25] Hermosilla G., Ruiz-del-Solar J., Verschae R., Correa M. A comparative study of thermal face recognition methods in unconstrained environments, Pattern Recognition, vol. 45, no. 7, pp. 2445-2459, 2012.

[26] Lloyd J. M. Thermal Imaging Systems, New York: Plenum Press. ISBN 0-306-30848-7, 1975.

[27] FLIR Systems. The Ultimate Infrared Handbook for R&D Professionals: A Resource Guide for Using Infrared in the Research and Development Industry, United Kingdom, 2012.

[28] FLIR Systems, ThermaCAM Reporter - user's manual, Professional Edition, Version 8.1, publ. No. 1558567, 2007.

[29] Buddharaju P., Pavlidis I. Multi-spectral face recognition - fusion of visual imagery with physiological information, in:R. I. Hammoud,B. R. Abidi, M. A. Abidi (Eds.),

Face Biometrics for Personal Identification: Multi-Sensory Multi-Modal Systems, Springer, pp.91–108, 2007.

[30] Cho S. Y., Wang L., Ong W. L. Thermal imprint feature analysis for face recognition, Industrial Electronics, ISIE2009, IEEE International Symposium on, pp.1875–1880, 2009.

[31] Jacovitti, G. & Neri, A. Multiscale image features analysis with circular harmonic wavelets,in Proceedings of SPIE, vol. 2569, pp. 363–374, 1995.

[32] Lee T. Image representation using 2D Gabor wavelets, IEEE Transactions on Pattern Analysis and Machine Intelligence, pp. 959–971, 1996.

[33] Friedrich G. & Yeshurun Y. Seeing People in the Dark: Face Recognition in Infrared Images, in BMCV '02 Proceedings of the Second International Workshop on Biologically Motivated Computer Vision, pp. 348–359. Springer-Verlag London, UK, 2002.

[34] Otsu N. A Threshold Selection Method from Gray-Level Histograms, IEEE Transactions on Systems, Man and Cybernetics, pages 62-66, 1979.

[35] Poh N. & Bengio S. How Do Correlation and Variance of Base-Experts Affect Fusion in Biometric Authentication Tasks? IEEE Transactions on Signal Processing, vol. 53, no. 11, pp. 4384-4396, 2005.

[36] Puente L., Poza M. J., Ruíz B. & Carrero D. Biometrical Fusion – Input Statistical Distribution, in Advanced Biometric Technologies, InTech, 2011, pp. 87-110, 2011.

[37] Bishop C. Pattern Recognition and Machine Learning, vol. 4, no. 4. Springer, p. 738, 2006.

[38] Equinox, Multimodal face database. http://www.equinoxsensors.com/products/HID.html, (accessed 3 May 2012).

[39] Chen X., Flynn P. & Bowyer K. Visible-light and infrared face recognition, ACM Workshop on Multimodal User Authentication, pp. 48-55, 2003.

[40] Flynn P., Bowyer K. & Phillips P. Assessment of time dependency in face recognition: An initial study, Lecture Notes in Computer Science, vol. 2688, pp. 44-51, 2003.

[41] Yanushkevich S. N., Stoica A. & Shmerko, V. P. Fundamentals of biometric-based training system design, In: S. N. Yanushkevich, P. Wang, S. Srihari, and M. Gavrilova, Eds., M. S. Nixon, Consulting Ed., Image Pattern Recognition: Synthesis and Analysis in Biometrics, World Scientific, 2006.

[42] Yanushkevich S. N., Stoica A., Shmerko V. Synthetic Biometrics, IEEE Computational Intelligence Magazine, Volume 2, Number 2, pp. 60-69, 2007.

[43] Wu S., Lin W., Xie S. Skin heat transfer model of facial thermograms and its application in face recognition. Pattern Recognition 41(8): 2718-2729, 2008.

[44] Lu Y., Yang J., Wu S., Fang Z. Normalization of Infrared Facial Images under Variant Ambient Temperatures, book chapter, Advanced Biometrics Technologies, Intech, Vienna, Austria, ISBN 978-953-307-487-0, 2011.

Chapter 3

Finger-Vein Image Restoration Based on a Biological Optical Model

Jinfeng Yang, Yihua Shi and Jucheng Yang

Additional information is available at the end of the chapter

http://dx.doi.org/10.5772/52104

1. Introduction

Finger-vein recognition, as a highly secure and convenient technique of personal identification, has been attracted much attention for years. In contrast to conventional appearance-based biometric traits such as face, fingerprint and palmprint, finger-vein patterns are hidden beneath the human skin and unnoticeable without the help of some specific viewing or imaging devices. This makes finger-vein trait resistant to steal or forgery, and thereby highly reliable for identity authentication.

Generally, in order to visualize finger-vein vessels inside the finger tissues, the near infrared (NIR) transillumination is often adopted in image acquisition system [1], as shown in Fig. 1. In this imaging manner, the image sensor placed under a finger is used to visualize the transmitted NIR lights, as shown in Fig. 1(a) and (b), here, Fig. 1(b) is a disassembled homemade imaging device. Then with the help of imaging software, the finger-vein images can be captured by the computer. Due to the interaction between NIR light and biological tissues, thus the captured images inevitably carry some important inner information of finger tissue. In blood vessels, the hemoglobin absorbs more NIR radiation than other substances in finger tissues [2], the intensity distribution of transmitted NIR rays therefore vary spatially in terms of the vessel distribution, and venous regions can cast darker "shadows" on imaging plane while the other tissues present a brighter background, as shown in Fig. 1(d). From Fig. 1(d), we can clearly see that, in a captured image, not all regions are useful for accuracy finger-vein recognition, so to eliminate some unwanted regions, a simple but effective method of region of interest (ROI) localization have been proposed in our previous work [5]. In Fig. 1(e), we list some ROI extraction results for illustration.

Unfortunately, the captured finger-vein images are always not good in quality due to lower cotrast such that the venous regions are not salient. This certainly makes finger-vein feature representation unreliable, and further impairs the accuracy of finger-vein recognition in

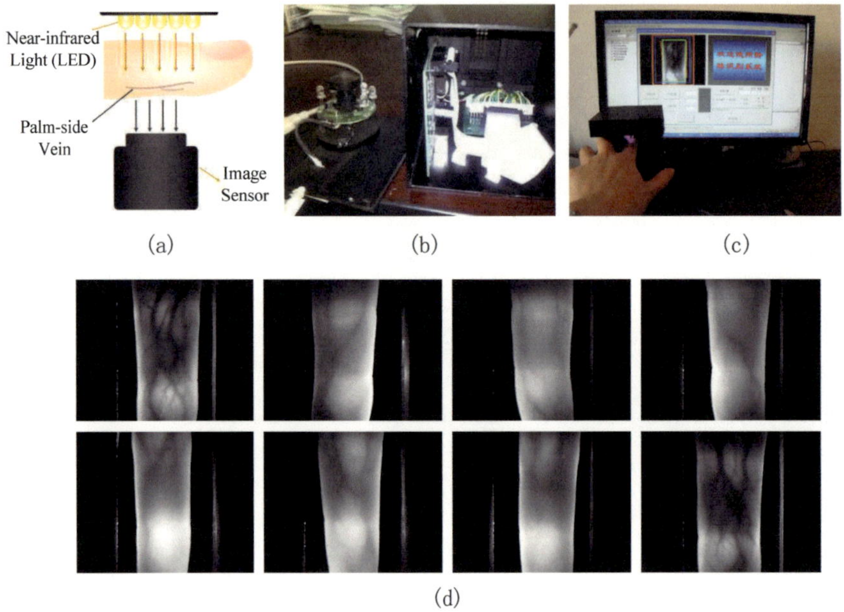

Figure 1. Finger-vein image acquisition. (a) NIR light transillumination. (b) A homemade finger-vein imaging device. (c) Our finger-vein image acquisition system. (d) Some captured finger-vein images.

practice. According to tissue optics, multiple light scattering predominates in lights that penetrate through the biological tissue layer [3] as the biological tissue is a kind of highly heterogeneous optical medium in imaging. Thus, the quality of finger-vein images is always not good because the scattering effects can greatly reduce the contrast between the venous and non-venous regions [4]. The basic concept of image degradation due to light scattering is illustrated in Fig. 3. If the incident light is not scattered in optical medium, a real shadow of an object must be casted on the imaging plane, as shown in Fig. 3(a), where the dark circle region represents the real shadow of an object. However, the object shadow is always blurred to a certain extent since light scattering is inevitable in real situations, as shown in Fig. 3(b). Hence, in practical scenario, the inherent advantage of finger-vein can not always be exploited effectively and reliably for finger-vein recognition due to the low contrast of venous regions. Therefore, to exploit the genuine characteristics in finger-vein images, the visibility of finger-vein patterns should be reliably improved in advance.

In this chapter, we first give an analysis of the intrinsic factors causing finger-vein image degradation, and then propose a simple but effective image restoration method based on scattering removal. To give a proper description of finger-vein image degradation, a biological optical model (BOM) specific to finger-vein imaging is proposed according to the principle of light propagation in biological tissues. Finally, based on BOM, the light scattering component is properly estimated and removed for finger-vein image restoration.

In the following sections, we first give a brief description of the related work in Section 2. Then, in Section 3 the traditional image dehazing model is presented, and the optical model used in this chapter is derived after discussing the difference and relationship between our model and the image dehazing model. In Section 4, the steps of scattering removal algorithm are detailed. For finger-vein image matching, the Phase-Only-Correlation measure is used in Section 5. The experimental results are reported in Section 6. Finally, in Section 7, we give some conclusions.

http://dx.doi.org/10.5772/52104

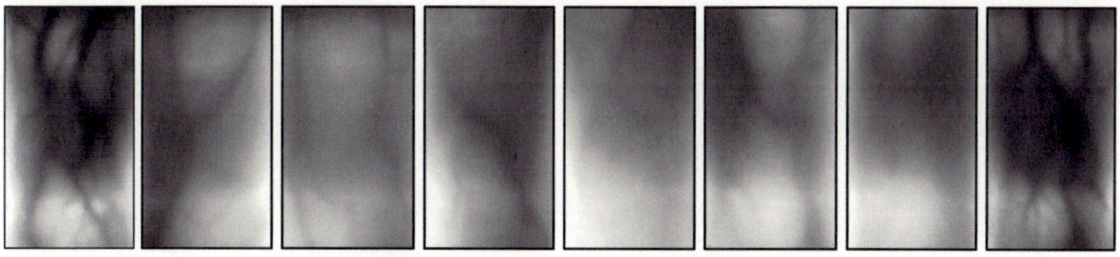

Figure 2. Finger-vein ROI extraction. Here the used ROI extraction method is proposed in [5].

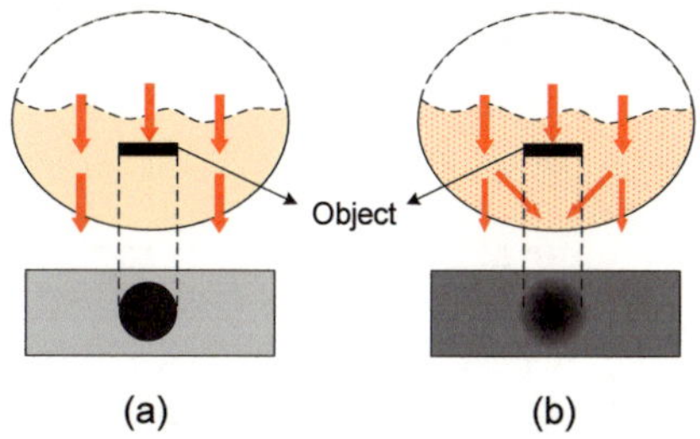

Figure 3. Image contrast reduction due to light scattering. (a) A real shadow as no light scattering. (b) The shadow is blurred due to light scattering.

2. Related work

Traditionally, many image enhancement methods have been proposed to improve the quality of vein images. Histogram equalization based algorithms were used to enhance the contrast between the venous and background regions in [6, 7]. Considering the variations of vein-coursing directions, different oriented filtering strategies were used to highlight the finger-vein texture. [8–11]. The retinex theory combined with the fuzzy was adopted to enhance the near-infrared vein images [12]. Pi *et al.* [13] used an edge-preserving filter and an elliptic high-pass filter together to denoise and enhance some small blurred finger veins. Gao *et al.* [14] combined the traditional high frequency emphasis filtering algorithm and the histogram equalization to sharpen the image contrast. Oh *et al.* [15] proposed a homomorphic filter incorporating morphological subband decomposition to enhance the dark blood vessels. Although these methods can respectively enhance vein images to some extent, their performances were considerably undesirable in practice since they all did not treat of the key issue of light scattering in degrading finger-vein images.

Strong scattering occurring in the biological tissue during vein imaging is the main reason causing contrast deterioration in finger-vein images [16]. Considering light transport in skin tissue, Lee and Park used an depth-dependent point spread function (D-PSF) to address the blurring issue in finger-vein imaging [29, 30]. This method is encouraging in finger-vein visibility improvement, however, D-PSF is derived for handling degraded issues in transcutaneous fluorescent imaging manner but not in transillumination manner [31]. Hence, the performance of D-PSF on light scattering suppression is still unsatisfying for finger-vein images since, in transillumination, light attenuation (absorption and scattering) arises not only from the skin but from other tissues of the finger, such as bone, muscles, and blood vessels [33]. Moreover, estimating biological parameters properly is also a difficult task for D-PSF based image debluring technique in practice. Therefore, for reliable finger-vein image contrast improvement, this chapter aims to find a proper way of scattering removal according to tissue optics, especially skin optics.

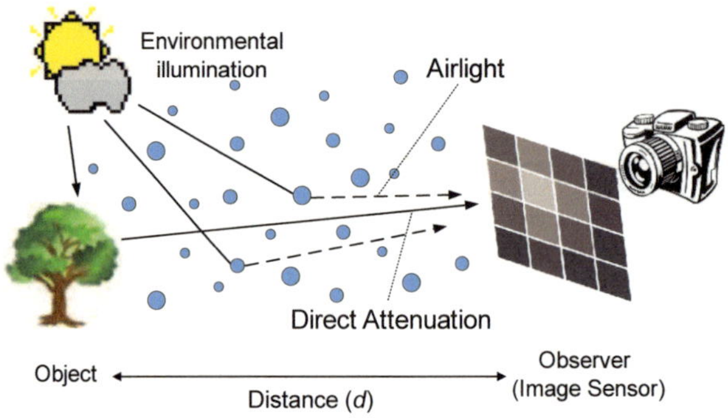

Figure 4. Light scattering in the atmospheric medium. Here, the environmental illumination is redundant for object imaging.

In computer vision, scattering removal has been a hot topic for reducing the atmospheric scattering effects on the images of outdoor scenes [17–21]. This technique often is termed as dehazing or de-weather, which is based on a physical model that describes the formation of hazing image. Inspired by image dehazing, we here propose an optical-model-based scattering removal algorithm for finger-vein image enhancement. The proposed optical model allows for the light propagation in finger-skin layer such that it is powerful in describing the effects of skin scattering on finger-vein images.

3. The optical model of atmospheric scattering

Light scattering is a physical phenomenon as light transports in turbid medium. In daily life, we are very familiar with light scattering, such as blue sky, fog and smoke. Therefore, the irradiance received by the camera is often attenuated due to medium absorption and scattering, which degrades the captured images and make them lose the contrast. Removing the scattering effect is certainly necessary for improving the scene visibility. In computer vision, the physical model widely used to image dehazing, also named Koschmieder model, is expressed as [22]

$$I_d = e^{-Kd} I_0 + (1 - e^{-Kd}) I_\infty. \tag{1}$$

This model provides a very simple but elegant description for two main effects of atmospheric scattering on the observed intensity I_d of an object at a distance d in a hazing or foggy day. Here, the intensity at close range (distance $d = 0$) I_0 is called the intrinsic intensity of the object, I_∞ is the intensity of environmental illumination (equivalent to an object at infinite distance), which is generally assumed to be globally constant, and K is the extinction coefficient of the atmosphere.

As illustrated in Fig. 4, the first effect of atmospheric scattering is called direct attenuation, and can be described by Beer–Lambert law, which results in an exponential attenuation of object intensity with the transmission distance through scattering media, i.e., the first term $e^{-Kd} I_0$ on the right side of Eq. (1). The second effect, referred to as airlight in Koschmieder theory of horizontal visibility, is caused by the suspended particles in haze or fog that scatter the environmental illumination toward the observer. The airlight acts as an additional radiation superimposed on the image of the object, whose intensity is related to the environmental illumination I_∞ and increases with pathlength d from the observer to the object, as described by the term $(1 - e^{-Kd}) I_\infty$.

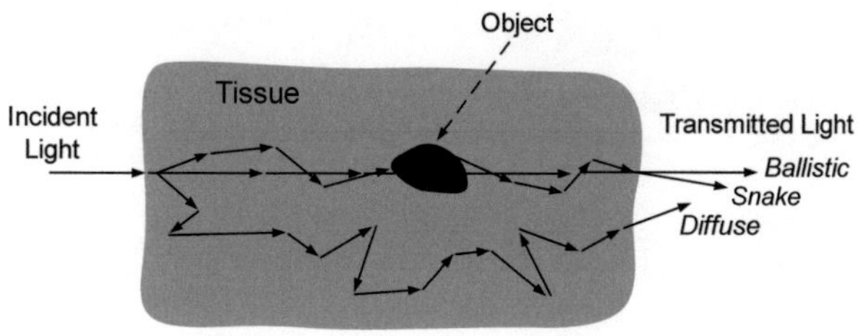

Figure 5. Light propagation through biological tissue. Here, multiple scattering is mainly caused by diffuse photons.

It is noticeable that, despite having not taken multiple scattering into account, the Koschmieder model is practicable for vision applications. In atmosphere, the distances between particles are usually large enough so that the particles can be viewed as independent scatterers, whose scattered intensities do not significantly interfere with each other, and thus the effect of multiple scattering is negligible [23]. Whereas, in the case of biological tissue, light propagation suffers a more complex process due to the complexity of tissue structure. Particularly, the scattering particles in biological tissue are so dense that the interaction of scattered intensities between neighboring particles cannot be ignored [24]. Hence, multiple scattering is said to be prevalent in the biological optical medium [1, 32–35].

From the biophotonic point of view, as the light propagates through a tissue, the transmitted light is composed of three components—the ballistic, the snake, and the diffuse photons [25], as shown in Fig. 5. Ballistic photons travel a straight, undeviated path in the medium. Snake photons experience some slight scattering events, but still propagate in the forward or near-forward direction. Diffuse photons undergo multiple scattering and emerge from random directions. Obviously, in transillumination imaging of objects embedded in the biological tissue, the ballistic photons with propagation direction preservation can form sharp shadows of objects on the imaging plane, whereas the multiple scattered diffuse photons can inevitably reduce the contrast of the shadows as well as giving rise to the unwanted, incoherent imaging background [26]. That is to say, the multiple scattering is the most unfavorable factor that contributes to diffuse photons and further leads to image blurring in optical transillumination imaging.

Based on the preceding analysis of image dehazing model and the associated knowledge about light propagation through biological tissue, we propose a simplified skin scattering model to characterize the effects of skin scattering on finger-vein imaging, as shown in Fig. 6. Before giving mathematical description of the proposed model, there are several points with respect to the optical model should be stated:

- In a real finger-vein imaging system, the objects to be visualized are palm-side vein vessels which are mostly interspersed within the inner layer of the finger skin (see Fig. 7(a)). So, for the sake of simplicity, only the skin layer is considered as a reference optical medium regardless of the atmosphere between skin surface and camera, whose scattering effect is very small and negligible here.
- Human skin is known to be an inhomogeneous, multilayered tissue containing epidermis, dermis and subcutaneous layer, as shown in Fig. 7(a). But at the molecular level, skin tissues are composed of a limited number of basic molecular species, and these molecules are composed of optically similar chemical units [3]. Moreover, the ensemble of light-skin interaction homogenizes the optical behavior of biological structures. Thus, the skin

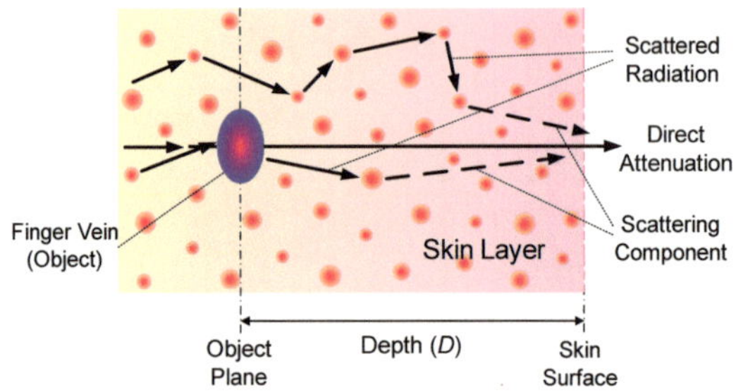

Figure 6. The simplified scattering model in human skin layer. Here, the light photons are divided into scattered and un-scattered groups.

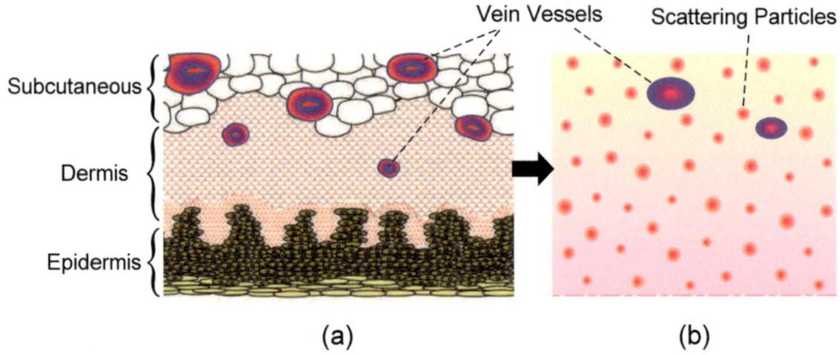

Figure 7. Skin layer modeling. (a) Cross-sectional view of human skin. (b) Simplified model of finger palm-side skin layer.

can be viewed as a medium with a random but homogeneous distribution of scattering particles over its thickness [27], as shown in Fig. 7(b), and then the scattering coefficient of the skin tissue here can be assumed to be locally constant for a given finger subject.

- Different from the image dehazing techniques, we need not consider the effect of environmental illumination as well as the airlight indeed. Nevertheless, due to light interaction occurs among biological scatterers, the scattered radiation from both the object and the background will be partially re-scattered towards the observer, which approximately amounts to environmental illumination for finger-vein imaging.

In view of these points, the radiant intensity observed at skin surface corresponding to the object with a certain depth in the skin can be simply decomposed into the direct attenuation component and the scattering component, as shown in Fig. 6. The former, representing the unscattered of ballistic photons, is a reduction of the original radiation over the traversing medium, which obeys the Beer–Lambert law [16, 36], while the latter represents the effect of snake and diffuse photons, which emerges randomly from the tissue surface. Especially, the proportion of scattered radiation enters into the direction of observer and interferes with the direct radiation of object, whose intensity increases with depth because a deeper object tends to suffer more influence of the scattered radiation.

For the direct attenuation component, its intensity on the imaging plane is mainly determined by the non-scattered light. So, assume that μ_1 and μ_2 denote the optical absorption and scattering coefficients, based on the Beer–Lambert law, we can obtain

$$I_{tr} = I_0 e^{-\mu D}, \tag{2}$$

where I_0 represents an finger-vein image free of degradation, D is the object depth in a biological medium, $\mu = \mu_1 + \mu_2$ is called transport attenuation coefficient, and I_{tr} denotes the transmitted intensity after absorption and scattering. Noticeably, due to the heterogeneity of skin tissue and the spatial randomness of vein distribution, both the transport attenuation coefficient μ and the depth D vary spatially in tissue medium, that is, $\mu = \mu(x,y)$ and $D = D(x,y)$. So, for a given biological tissue, we can define

$$T(x,y) = e^{\mu(x,y)D(x,y)}. \tag{3}$$

$T(x,y)$ is often called non-scattered transmission map [16], which describes the optical transmissivity of the given tissue medium.

For the scattering component, due to the randomicity of the scattered light, it can be regarded as the background illumination on the whole, and only a part of the background illumination can arrive at the imaging plane. For intuitively understanding this point, Fig. 8 gives a schematic illustration. In Fig. 8, s represents an original source in x-y coordinates, p is the observation of s on the imaging plane, H denotes a small column in the skin tissue corresponding to a beam from the object point s to a point p on the image plane (each pixel corresponds to a small column), the neighbor points $(s'_i, i = 1,2,\cdots,n)$ around s are viewed as the local background radiation sources, which would emit radiation and produce a scattering component along H.

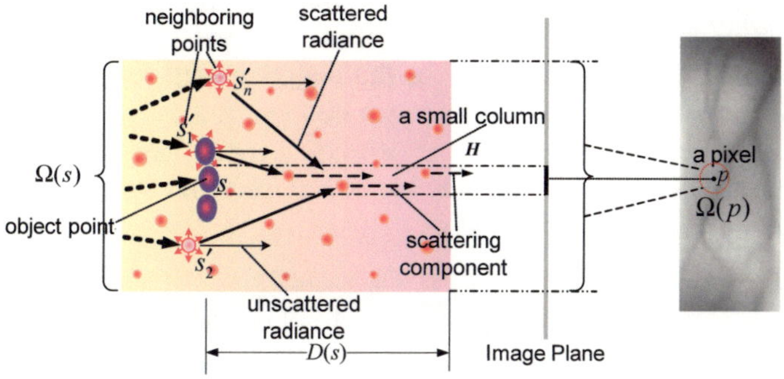

Figure 8. Schematic representation of the effect of scattered radiation and the finger-vein image degradation process. Here, both s and p respectively corresponds to any one point in x-y coordinates.

Accordingly, in a similar way of Koschmieder model, the proposed biological optical model (BOM) is defined as

$$I(p) = I_0(s)T(s) + (1 - T(s))I_r(s), \tag{4}$$

where $I_0(s)$ still represents the intrinsic intensity of the object, that is veins, to be visualized, $I_r(s)$ denotes the intensity of scattered radiation, and $I(p)$ is the observation of the vein object on the image plane. A key point needs to be noted that, different from the environmental illumination in atmosphere, $I_r(s)$ varies spatially because its value is associated to the intensities of the imaging background.

Let the original intensity of a neighbor point s'_i be $I_0(s'_i)$, then the direct transmitted radiation of this point, that is the unscattered radiation, should be $I_0(s'_i)T(s'_i)$. So, according to the energy conservation principle, the scattered radiation of this point should be $(1 - T(s_i'))I_0(s_i')$, where $D(s_i')$ is the depth of point s_i' in the skin layer. Thus, we can obtain the scattered radiation $I_r(s)$ in H. Since the scattering directions are random, $I_r(s)$ here is considered as an average of total radiation from overall neighbor points and can be rewritten as

$$I_r(s) = \frac{1}{Z_{\Omega(s)}} \sum_{s_i' \in \Omega(s)} (1 - T(s_i'))I_0(s_i'), \tag{5}$$

where $\Omega(s)$ denotes the 2D neighborhood centered at point s, and Z_Ω indicates the number of points in $\Omega(s)$. Given $I_r(s)$, $\mu(s)$ and $D(s)$, we can obtain $I_0(s)$ which represents the intrinsic intensity of a finger-vein image without scattering corruption.

However, solving $I_0(s)$ from a single observed image $I(p)$ with Eq. (4) is a very ill-posed problem. Not only is the extinct coefficient $\mu(s)$ of human skin tissue inconsistent, but the thickness $D(s)$ also varies with different individuals. The values of $I_r(s)$, $\mu(s)$ and $D(s)$ therefore can not be accurately evaluated in practice. This is due to that the light scattering phenomenon in tissues is very complex. Hence, we have to utilize the observation (or captured) image $I(p)$ to estimate the scattering component for implementing scattering removal.

4. The proposed scattering removal algorithm for restoration

In the observation $I(p)$, veins appear shadows due to light absorbtion, which makes vein information sensitive to illumination modification. Hence, finger-vein images should be transformed into their negative versions. In the negative versions, the venous regions turn brighter than their surroundings, veins thus can be regarded as luminous objects. Moreover, in this situation, the skin tissue can be approximately treated as the only opaque layer that blurs vein objects during imaging. This is beneficial for scattering illumination estimation. Thus, we can rewrite the proposed BOM as

$$\hat{I}(p) = \hat{I}_0(s)T(s) + (1 - T(s))\hat{I}_r(s), \tag{6}$$

where $\hat{I}(p)$, $\hat{I}_0(s)$ and $\hat{I}_r(s)$ represent the negative versions of $I(p)$, $I_0(s)$ and $I_r(s)$, respectively. Referring to the image dehazing technique, we here introduce

$$V(s) = (1 - T(s))\hat{I}_r(s). \tag{7}$$

$V(s)$ can be regarded as the total scattering component. Moreover, we can obtain the transmission map,

$$T(s) = 1 - \frac{V(s)}{\hat{I}_r(s)}. \tag{8}$$

$T(s)$ describes the relative portion of light radiation surviving through a medium. Thus, the optical model can be rewritten as

$$\hat{I}(p) = T(s)\hat{I}_0(s) + V(s). \tag{9}$$

Instead of directly computing $\hat{I}_0(s)$, we first estimate the scattering component $V(s)$, and then estimate the intensity of scattered radiation $\hat{I}_r(s)$. Thus, the restored image $\hat{I}_0(s)$ can be obtained based on Eqs. (8) and (9).

4.1. Scattering component estimation

Generally, the distribution of scattering energy is not uniform in a local block $\Omega(s)$ since the skin medium is inhomogeneous. However, it is affirmable that (1) the directions of scattered light rays are random due to the high density of biological cells, and (2) the nearer s_i' to s is, the higher the probability of the scattered light into column H is [40, 41]. Although the direction of scattered light is highly random due to the heterogeneity of skin tissue, the multiple scattering is dominated by near forward scattering events in biological tissues [16, 42]. Hence, it is reasonable that using the local observation to estimate the scattering component.

Here, unlike the solution of scattering component estimation described in [18], $V(s)$ varies locally and spatially on finger-vein imaging plane due to the heterogeneousness of the human skin tissue. In this sense, three practical constraints should be introduced for $V(s)$ estimation:

- For each point s, the intensity $V(s)$ is positive and cannot be higher than the final observed intensity $\hat{I}(p)$, that is, $0 \leq V(s) \leq \hat{I}(p)$;
- $V(s)$ is smooth except the edges of venous regions since the points in $\Omega(s)$ approximate to be same in depth;
- $\hat{I}_r(s)$ tends to be constant in $\Omega(s)$ and $V(s) \leq \hat{I}_r(s) \leq \hat{I}(p)$.

Based on these constraints, to estimate $V(s)$, a fast algorithm described in [20] is modified as

$$V(s) = \max\left(\min\left(w_1 B(s), \hat{I}(p)\right), 0\right), \tag{10}$$

where $B(s) = A(p) - median_{\Omega(p)}\left(\left|\hat{I}(p) - A(p)\right|\right)$, $A(p) = median_{\Omega(p)}\left(\hat{I}(p)\right)$, $\Omega(p)$ denotes the 2D neighborhood centered at point p, w_1 ($\in [0,1]$) is a factor controlling the strength of the estimated scattering component. Next, for removing the estimated scattering effect, we also have to estimate $T(s)$ based on the observation.

4.2. Scattering radiation estimation

To obtain the transmission map $T(s)$, we should compute $I_r(s)$ in advance according to the Eq. 8. Intuitively, we can obtain $\hat{I}_r(s)$ via Eq. (5) directly. However, it is a difficult task since the intrinsic intensity $\hat{I}_0(s_i')$ is unavailable in practice. Hence, considering the physical meaning that the scattered radiation $\hat{I}_r(s)$ depends on the interaction among neighbor points in $\Omega(s)$, we here simply use a local statistic of $\Omega(p)$ to represent $\hat{I}_r(s)$, that is,

$$\hat{I}_r(s) = \frac{w_2}{Z_{\Omega(p)}} \sum_{i=1}^{Z_{\Omega(p)}} \hat{I}(p_i), \tag{11}$$

where $p_i \in \Omega(p)$, $Z_{\Omega(p)}$ indicates the number of points in $\Omega(p)$, and w_2 ($\in [0,1]$) is a factor for making the constraint $V(s) \leq \hat{I}_r(s) \leq \hat{I}(p)$ satisfying. So, based on Eq. (8), we can estimate $T(s)$ accordingly.

4.3. Finger-vein image restoration

Given the estimations of $V(s)$ and $T(s)$, we can approximately restore an original finger-vein image with scattering removal. That is, by solving Eq. (6) with respect to $\hat{I}_0(s)$, we can obtain

$$\begin{aligned} I_0(s) &= 1 - \hat{I}_0(s) \\ &= 1 - \frac{\hat{I}(p) - V(s)}{T(s)}. \end{aligned} \tag{12}$$

Thus, computing $I_0(s)$ pixelwise using Eq. (12) can generate an image $I_0(x,y)$ automatically and effectively. Here, $I_0(x,y)$ represents the restored finger-vein image which appears free of multiple light scattering.

5. Finger-vein image matching

In this section, the Phase-Only-Correlation (POC) measure proposed in [28] is used for simply handling the finger-vein matching problem based on the restored finger-vein images.

Assume that $I_{0_i}(x,y)$ and $I_{0_j}(x,y)$ are two restored images, and $F_i(u,v)$ and $F_j(u,v)$ represent their 2D DFT, respectively, according to the property of Fourier transform, that is,

$$I_{0_i}(x,y) \circ I_{0_j}(x,y) \Longleftrightarrow F_i(u,v)\overline{F_j(u,v)}, \tag{13}$$

where " $\circ$ " denotes a 2D correlation operator, we can compute the cross phase spectrum as

$$R(u,v) = \frac{F_i(u,v)\overline{F_j(u,v)}}{\|F_i(u,v)\overline{F_j(u,v)}\|} = e^{\hat{j}\theta(u,v)}. \tag{14}$$

Let $r(x,y) = \text{IDFT}(R(u,v))$, thus, $r(x,y)$ is called the POC measure. The POC measure has a sharp peak when two restored finger-vein images are similar, whereas it will be near zero for those from different classes, as shown in Fig. 9. Moreover, the POC function is somewhat insensitive to image shifts and noises. This is helpful for accurately measuring the similarities in finger-vein image matching.

It is worth pointing out that, to robustly handle accurate image matching problem, band-limited phase-only-correlation (BLPOC) function has been also proposed in [28] and widely used for image matching in practice [37–39]. Compared with POC, BLPOC is more reliable in measuring the similarities between two images. However, traditional POC is yet more convincing than BLPOC in investigating the qualities of images. This is because the matching result based on POC is more sensitive to image quality than that of BLPOC. Hence, the POC function still can be used as a simple and effective measure to objectively evaluate the performance of the proposed method in scattering removal and venous region enhancement.

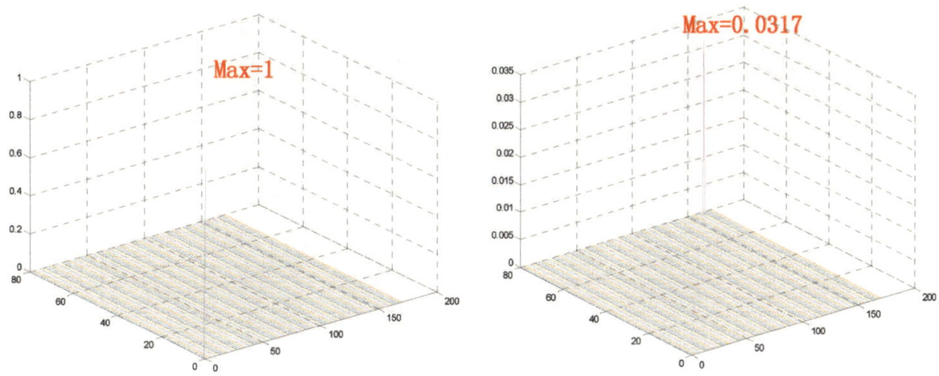

Figure 9. POC measure. Left: $r(x,y)$ of two same finger-vein images. Right: $r(x,y)$ of two finger-vein images from different classes.

6. Experimental results

In this section, the used finger-vein images are captured by a homemade transillumination imaging system with a 760 nm NIR LED array source, and then extracted from raw images by the ROI localization and segmentation method proposed in [5]. The finger-vein image database contains 700 individual finger-vein images from 70 individuals. Each individual contributes 10 forefinger-vein images of the right hand. All cropped finger-vein images are 8-bit gray images with a resolution of 180×100.

6.1. Finger-vein image restoration

Here, some captured finger-vein image samples are collected to demonstrate the validity of the proposed method in finger-vein image restoration. Fig. 10 shows some examples of the estimated $V(x,y)$, $I_r(x,y)$, $T(x,y)$ and restored finger-vein images $I_0(x,y)$. After scattering removal, the contrast of finger-vein images is improved significantly, and the vein networks present in the restored images can be clearly distinguished from the background. This shows that the proposed optical model allowing for the effects of light scattering in skin layer, particularly the multiple scattering, is desirable for describing the mechanism of finger-vein image degradation.

Nevertheless, the proposed method is somewhat sensitive to image noises, as shown in Fig. 10(e). In fact, before lighting the palm-side veins, the NIR rays have been randomly diffused by finger dorsal tissues such as finger-back skin, bone, tendon, fatty tissue and so on. This inevitably gives rise to irregular shadows and noises in the captured finger-vein images, whereas the proposed optical model has not taken account of the effects of finger dorsal tissues except the palm-side skin. As a result, the spatial varied background noises are also strengthened when estimating the scattering components.

In Fig. 11, we compare our method with several common approaches for finger-vein image enhancement. Additionally, we treat the degraded finger-vein images as hazing images, and directly use dehazing method to restore them regardless of the mismatch between the Koschmieder model and the proposed model. Here, a method proposed in [20] is adopted to implement finger-vein image "dehazing", and the results are also shown in Fig. 11.

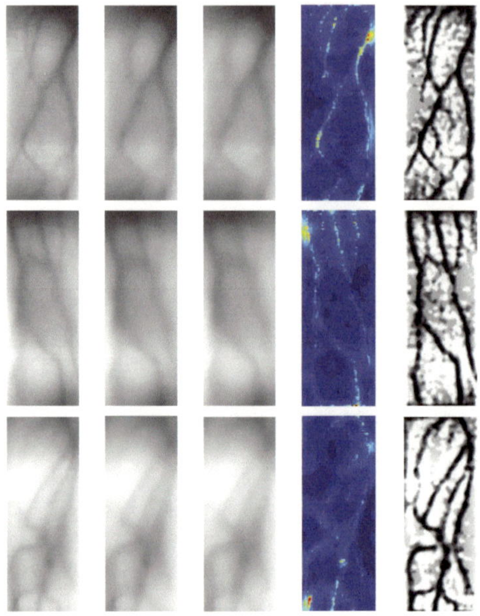

Figure 10. Scattering removal experiments. (a) Some captured finger-vein images $I(x,y)$. (b) The estimated scattering components $V(x,y)$. (c) The estimated scattering radiations $I_r(x,y)$. (d) The estimated transmission maps $T(x,y)$. (e) The restored images $I_0(x,y)$.

In order to evaluate the performance of the proposed method in terms of contrast improvement for finger-vein image, the mean structural similarity index (MSSIM) [13] and the contrast improvement index (CII) [15] are used as two common evaluation criterions. We first randomly choose 50 individual finger-vein images from database as samples, and use these enhancement methods in Fig. 11 to process the finger-vein image samples. Then, we obtain the average MSSIM and the average CII of every enhancement method.

In general, MSSIM is often used to measure the similarity between a processed image and a standard image with perfect quality (*i.e.*, a distortion-free image). The larger the value of MSSIM is, the better an image is improved. This makes a processed image more approximate to its standard quality. However, it is impossible for us to have standard or perfect finger-vein images since the captured images all are degraded due to light scattering. Therefore, we regard the degraded finger-vein images as standard references. Thus, the more the dissimilarity between a processed finger-vein image and its original version is, the better the finger-vein is improved. That is, the lower the value of MSSIM is, the better the quality of a restored image is. CII is often used to measure the improvement of contrast between a processed image and its original version, and the larger the value of CII is, the better the contrast of an improved image is.

Hence, the quality and the visibility of restored finger-vein images can be quantitatively evaluated using MSSIM and CII. In Table 1, we list the two values corresponding to different finger-vein enhancement methods. From Table 1, we can clearly see that the proposed method provides the lowest MSSIM value and the highest CII value. This means the proposed method has better performance in finger-vein image enhancement.

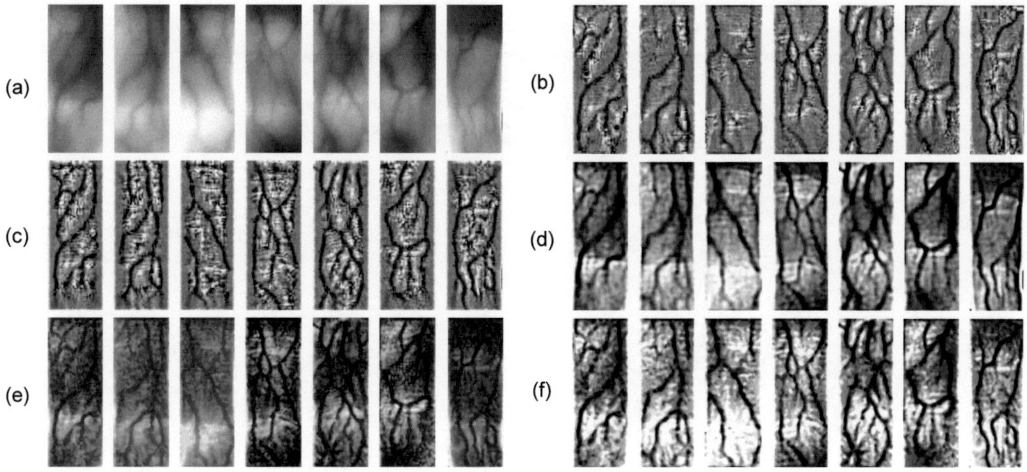

Figure 11. Comparisons with other methods. (a) Some captured finger-vein images. (b) The results from histogram template equalization (HTE) [6]. (c) The results from high frequency emphasis filtering (HFEF) [14]. (d) The results from circular Gabor filtering (CGF) [8]. (e) The results from image dehazing (ImD) [20]. (f) The results from the proposed method.

Methods	Average MSSIM	Average CII
The captured images	1	1
Histogram Template Equalization (HTE)	0.4076	4.4941
High Frequency Emphasis Filtering (HFEF)	0.4239	3.7571
Circular Gabor Filtering (CGF)	0.4141	3.7386
Image Dehazing (ImD)	0.4932	3.3967
The Proposed Method	0.3358	4.6210

Table 1. Quantitative evaluation of different enhancement methods.

6.2. Finger-vein image matching

For finger-vein matching on this database, the number of genuine attempts is 3,150 ($70C_{10}^2$), and the number of impostor attempts is 241,500 ($10 \times 10C_{70}^2$). By respectively using the original images, HTE-based images, HFEF-based images, CGF-based images and the proposed restored images for finger-vein matching under POC (Phase-Only-Correlation) measure, the ROC (receiver operating characteristic) curves are plotted in Fig. 12, where false non-match rates (FNMR) and false match rates (FMR) are shown in the same plot at different thresholds on the POC matching score, and EER (equal error rate) is the error rate where FNMR and FMR are equal.

From Fig. 12, we can clearly see that the proposed method has the best performance of ROC curves and makes the lowest EER. This indicates that the finger-vein images with scattering removal are more discriminative in inter-class. Hence, the proposed method is desirable for improving the accuracy of finger-vein image matching in practice.

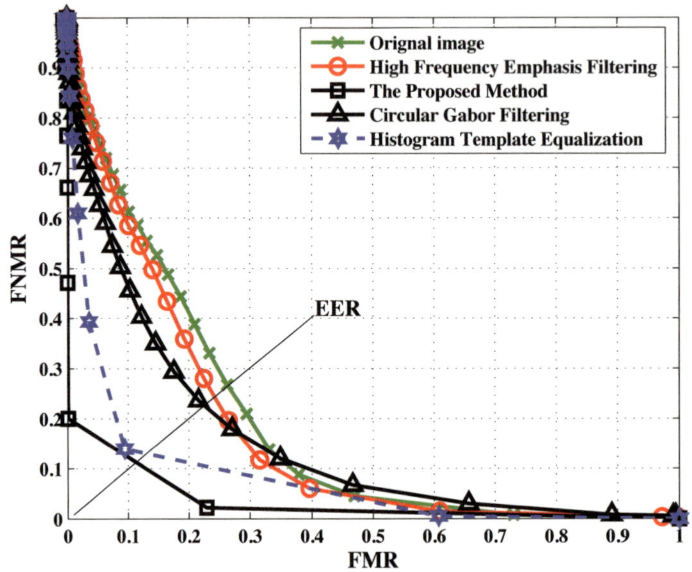

Figure 12. ROC curves of different finger-vein enhancement results.

7. Conclusions

In this chapter, a scattering removal method was introduced for finger-vein image restoration. The proposed method was based on a biological optical model which reasonably described the effects of skin scattering. In this model, the degradation of finger-vein images was viewed as a joint function of the direct light attenuation and multiple light scattering. By properly estimating the scattering components and transmission maps, the proposed method could effectively remove the effects of skin scattering effects from finger-vein images to obtain the restored results. The comparative experiments and quantitative evaluations demonstrated that the proposed method could provide better results compared to the common methods for finger-vein image enhancement and recognition.

Indeed, the proposed method also had its own drawbacks. First, the simplified model in our work did not take into account of the effects of background tissues, which made the proposed method somewhat sensitive to image noises while enhancing the vein patterns. Besides, the rough estimations of the scattering components as well as the scattered radiations could also decrease the performance of the proposed method to some extent. All these shortcomings will be of our further improvement in future work.

Acknowledgements

This work was supported in part by the National Natural Science Foundation of China (Grant No.61073143 and 61063035).

Author details

Jinfeng Yang[1], Yihua Shi[1] and Jucheng Yang[2]

1 Tianjin Key Lab for Advanced Signal Processing, Civil Aviation University of China, China
2 College of Computer Science and Information Engineering, Tianjin University of Science and Technology, China

References

[1] Dhawan, A.P.; Alessandro, B.D.; Fu, X. Optical imaging modalities for biomedical applications, *IEEE Reviews in Biomedical Engineering*, vol.3, pp.69-92, 2010.

[2] Kono, M.; Ueki, H.; Umemura, S. Near-infrared finger vein patterns for personal identification. *Appl. Opt.*, 41, pp.7429-7436, 2002.

[3] Backman, V.; Wax, A. Classical light scattering models. *Biomedical Applications of Light Scattering*; Wax, A., Backman, V.,Eds.; McGraw-Hill: New York, NY, USA, pp.3-29. 2010.

[4] Sprawls, P. Scattered Radiation and Contrast. *The Physical Principles of Medical Imaging*, 2nd ed.; Aspen Publishers, New York, NY, USA, 1993).

[5] Yang, J.F.; Li, X. Efficient Finger vein Localization and Recognition. *Proceedings of the 20th International Conference on Pattern Recognition*, Istanbul, Turkey,23–26 August 2010; pp. 1148-1151.

[6] Wen, X.B.; Zhao, J.W.; Liang, X.Z. Image enhancement of finger-vein patterns based on wavelet denoising and histogram template equalization (in Chinese). *J. Jilin University*, 46, pp.291-292, 2008.

[7] Zhao, J.J.; Xiong, X.; Zhang, L.; Fu, T.; Zhao, Y.X. Study on enhanced algorithm of hand vein image based on CLAHE and Top-hat transform (in Chinese). *Laser Infrared*, 39, pp.220-222, 2009.

[8] Yang, J.F.; Yang, J.L.; Shi, Y.H. Combination of Gabor Wavelets and Circular Gabor Filter for Finger-vein Extraction. *Proceedings of the 5th International Conference on Intelligent Computing*, Ulsan, South Korea, 16-19 September 2009;

[9] Yang, J.F.; Yang, J.L. Multi-Channel Gabor Filter Design for Finger-vein Image Enhancement. In *Proceedings of the 5th International Conference on Image and Graphics*, Xi'an, China, 20-23 September 2009; pp. 87-91.

[10] Yang, J.F.; Yan, M.F. An Improved Method for Finger-vein Image Enhancement. *Proceedings of IEEE 10th International Conference on Signal Processing*, Beijing, China, 24–28 October 2010; pp. 1706-1709.

[11] Wang, K.J.; Ma, H.; Li, X.F.; Guan, F.X.; Liu, J.Y. Finger vein pattern extraction method using oriented filtering technology (in Chinese). *J. Image Graph.*, 16, pp.1206-1212, 2011.

[12] Wang, K.J.; Fu, B.; Xiong, X.Y. A novel adaptive vein image contrast enhancement method based on fuzzy and retinex theory (in Chinese). *Tech. Automation Appl.*, 28, pp.72-75, 2009.

[13] Pi, W.; Shin, J.O; Park, D.S. An Effective Quality Improvement Approach for Low Quality Finger vein Image. *Proceedings of International Conference on Electronics and Information Engineering*, Kyoto, Japan, 1-2 August 2010; pp. V1-424-427.

[14] Gao, X.Y.; Ma, J.S.; Wu, J.J. The research of finger-vein image enhancement algorithm (in Chinese). *Opt. Instrum.*, 32, pp.29-32, 2010.

[15] Oh, J.S.; Hwang, H.S. Feature enhancement of medical images using morphology-based homomorphic filter and differential evolution algorithm. *Int. J. Control Automation Syst.*, 8, pp.857-861, 2010.

[16] Cheong W.F.; Prahl S.A.; Welch A.J. A review of the optical properties of biological tissues. *IEEE J. Quantum Electron.*, 26(12), pp.2166-2185, 1990.

[17] Narasimhan, S.G.; Nayar, S.K. Contrast restoration of weather degraded images. *IEEE Trans. Pattern Anal. Mach. Intell.*, 25, pp.713-724, 2003.

[18] Tan, R.T. Visibility in bad weather from a single image. *Proceedings of IEEE Conference on Computer Vision and Pattern Recognition*, Anchorage, AK, USA, 23–28 June 2008; pp.1-8.

[19] Fattal, R. Single image dehazing. *ACM Trans. Graph.*, 27, pp.1-9, 2008.

[20] Tarel, J.P.; Hautière, N. Fast Visibility Restoration from a Single Color or Gray Level Image. *Proceedings of IEEE 12th International Conference on Computer Vision*, Kyoto, Japan, 29 September–2 October 2009; pp. 2201-2208.

[21] He, K.M.; Sun, J.; Tang, X.O. Single image haze removal using dark channel prior. *IEEE Trans. Pattern Anal. Mach. Intell.*, 33, pp.2341-2353, 2011.

[22] Dumont, E.; Hautière, N.; Gallen, R. A semi-analytic model of fog effects on vision. *Atmospheric Turbulence, Meteorological Modeling and Aerodynamics*; Lang, P.R., Lombargo, F.S., Eds.; Nova Science Publishers: New York, NY, USA, 2011; pp.635-670.

[23] Narasimhan, S.G.; Nayar, S.K. Vision and the atmosphere. *Int. J. Comput. Vis.*,48, pp.233-254, 2002.

[24] Hollis, V. Non-Invasive Monitoring of Brain Tissue Temperature by Near-Infrared Spectroscopy. Ph.D. Dissertation, University of London, London, UK, 2002.

[25] Prasad, P.N. Bioimaging: Principles and Techniques. *Introduction to Biophotonics*; John Wiley & Sons: New York, NY, USA, 2003; pp. 203-209.

[26] Ramachandran, H. Imaging through turbid media. *Current Sci.*, 76, 1pp.334-1340, 1999.

[27] Van Gemert, M.J.C.; Jacques, S.L.; Sterenborg, H.J.C.M.; Star, W.M. Skin optics. *IEEE Trans. Biomed. Eng.*, 36, pp.1146-1154, 1989.

[28] Ito, K.; Nakajima, H.; Kobayashi, K.; Aoki, T.; Higuchi, T. A fingerprint matching algorithm using phase-only correlation. *IEICE Trans. Fundamentals*, E87-A(3), pp.682-691, 2004.

[29] Lee, E.C.; Park, K.R. Restoration method of skin scattering blurred vein image for finger vein recognition, *Electron. Lett.*, vol.45, no.21, pp.1074-1076, 2009.

[30] Lee, E.C.; Park, K.R. Image restoration of skin scattering and optical blurring for finger vein recognition, *Opt. Lasers Eng.*, vol.49, pp.816-828, 2011.

[31] Shimizu, K.; Tochio, K.; Kato, Y. Improvement of transcutaneous fluorescent images with a depth-dependent point-spread function, *Applied Optics*, vol.44, no.11, pp.2154-2161, 2005.

[32] Delpy, D.T.; Cope, M. Quantification in tissue near-infrared spectroscopy, *Phil. Trans. R. Soc. Lond. B.*, vol. 352, pp.649-659, 1997.

[33] Xu, J.; Wei, H.; Li, X.; Wu, G.; Li, D. Optical characteristics of human veins tissue in kubelka-munk model at he-ne laser in vitro, *Journal of Optoelectronics Laser*, vol.13, no.3, pp.401-404, 2002.

[34] Cheng, R.; Huang, B.; Wang, Y.; Zeng, H.; Xie, S. The optical model of human skin. *Acta Laser Biology Sinica*, vol.14, pp.401-404, 2005.

[35] Bashkatov, A.N.; Genina, E.A.; Kochubey, V.I.; Tuchin, V.V. Optical properties of human skin, subcutaneous and mucous tissues in the wavelength rang from 400 to 2000 nm, *J. Phys. D: Appl. Phys.*, vol.38, no.2005, pp.2543-2555, 2005.

[36] Ingle, J.D.J; Crouch, S.R. Spectrochemical analysis. *Prentice Hall*, 1988.

[37] Ito, K.; Aoki, T.; Nakajima, H.; Kobayashi, K.; Higuchi, T. A palmprint recognition algorithm using phase-only correlation, *IEICE Trans. Fundamentals*, vol.E91-A, no.4, pp.1023-1030, Apr. 2008.

[38] Miyazawa, K.; Ito, K.; Aoki, T. Kobayashi, K.; Nakajima, H. An effective approach for iris recognition using phase-based image matching, *IEEE Trans. Pattern Anal. Mach. Intell.*, vol.20, no.10, pp.1741-1756, Oct. 2008.

[39] Zhang, L.; Zhang, L.; Zhang, D.; Zhu, H. Ensemble of local and global information for finger-knuckle-print recognition, *Pattern recognition*, vol.44, no.9, pp.1990-1998, Sep. 2011.

[40] De Boer, J.F., Van Rossum, M.C.W.; Van Albada, M.P.; Nieuwenhuizen, T.M.; Lagendijk, A. Probability distribution of multiple scattered light measured in total transmission, *Phys. Rev. Lett.*, vol.73, no.19, pp.2567-2570, Nov. 1994.

[41] Fruhwirth, R.; Liendl, M. Mixture models of multiple scattering: computation and simulation, *Computer Physics Communications*, vol.141, pp.230-46, Jun. 2001.

[42] Baranoski, G.V.G.; Krishnaswamy, A. An introduction to light interaction with human skin, *RITA*, vol.11, no.1, pp.33-62, 2004.

Chapter 4

Basic Principles and Trends in Hand Geometry and Hand Shape Biometrics

Miroslav Bača, Petra Grd and Tomislav Fotak

Additional information is available at the end of the chapter

http://dx.doi.org/10.5772/51912

1. Introduction

Researchers in the field of biometrics found that human hand, especially human palm, contains some characteristics that can be used for personal identification. These characteristics mainly include thickness of the palm area and width, thickness and length of the fingers. Large numbers of commercial systems use these characteristics in various applications.

Hand geometry biometrics is not a new technique. It is first mentioned in the early 70's of the 20th century and it is older than palm print which is part of dactiloscopy. The first known use was for security checks in Wall Street.

Hand geometry is based on the palm and fingers structure, including width of the fingers in different places, length of the fingers, thickness of the palm area, etc. Although these measurements are not very distinctive among people, hand geometry can be very useful for identity verification, i.e. personal authentication. Special task is to combine some non-descriptive characteristics in order to achieve better identification results. This technique is widely accepted and the verification includes simple data processing. Mentioned features make hand geometry an ideal candidate for research and development of new acquisition, preprocessing and verification techniques.

Anthropologists believe that humans survived and developed to today's state (Homo sapiens) thanks to highly developed brains and separated thumbs. Easily moved and elastic human fist enables us catching and throwing various things, but also making and using various kinds of tools in everyday life. Today, human fist is not used just for that purpose, but also as a personal identifier, i.e. it can be used for personal identification.

Even old Egyptians used personal characteristics to identify people. Since then technology made a great improvement in the process of recognition, and modern scanners based on hand geometry now use infrared light and microprocessors to achieve the best possible comparison of proposed hand geometry patterns.

During the last century some technologies using hand geometry were developed. They ranged from electromechanical devices to electronic scanners. The history of those devices begins in 1971 when US Patent Office patented device for measuring hand characteristics and capturing some features for comparison and identity verification [1-3]. Another important event in the hand geometry history was in the mid 80's when Sidlauskas patented device for hand scanning and founded Recognition Systems Inc. Of Campbell, California [4]. The absolute peek of this biometric characteristic was in 1996 during the Olympic Games in Atlanta when it was used for access control in the Olympic village [5].

Human hand contains enough anatomical characteristics to provide a mechanism for personal identification, but it is not considered unique enough to provide mechanism for complete personal identification. Hand geometry is time sensitive and the shape of the hand can be changed during illness, aging or weight changing. It is actually based on the fact that every person has differently formed hand which will not drastically change in the future.

When placing a hand on the scanner, the device usually takes three-dimensional image of the hand. The shape and length of the fingers are measured, as well as wrists. Devices compare information taken from the hand scanner against already stored patterns in the database. After the identification data are confirmed, one can usually gain access right to secured place. This process has to be quick and effective. It takes less than five seconds for the whole procedure. Today, hand scanners are well accepted in the offices, factories and other business organization environments.

Based on the data used for personal identification, technologies for reading human hand can be divided in three categories:

- Palm technology,
- Hand vein technology,
- Hand geometry and hand shape technology.

The first category is considered the classic approach in the hand biometrics. As mentioned earlier, it is part of dactiloscopy, so methods used here are similar to those used for fingerprints. The size, shape and flow of papillae are measured and minutiae are the main features in the identification process. Image preprocessing and normalization in this category gives us binary image containing papillae and their distances. Because of the different lightning when taking an image, the palm can be divided into five areas [6], although strictly medically speaking, if we consider the muscles, it has only three areas. The areas of the palm are: lower palm, middle palm, upper palm, thenar (thumb part) and hypothenar (little finger part). The location of these areas can be seen in Figure 1.

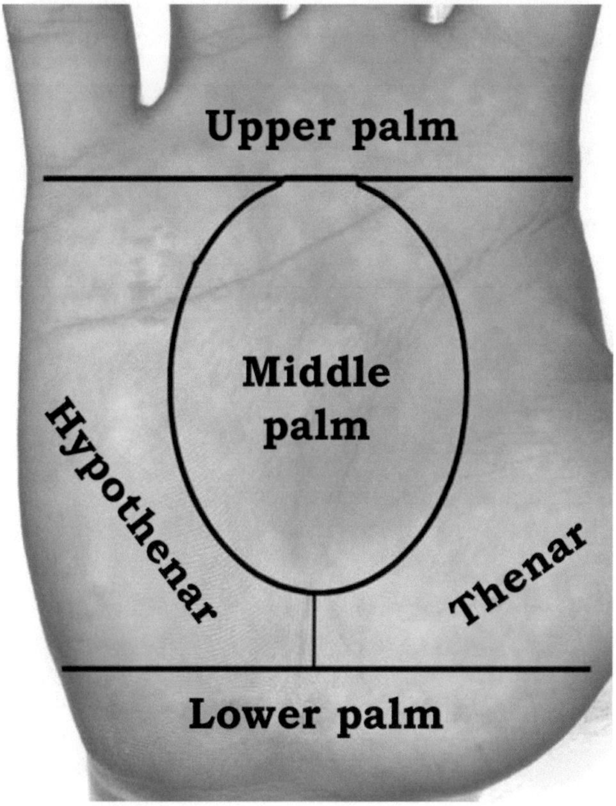

Figure 1. Palm areas according to [6]

Second category uses similar approach for capturing hand image, but instead of using ordinary camera or scanner it rather uses specialized devices containing scanners with infrared light or some other technology that can be used for retrieving image of veins under the human skin. Hand vein biometrics is gaining popularity in the last years and it is likely that this will be one of the main biometric characteristics for the future. Using contactless approach for capturing the structure of human veins gives promising results in this field.

Third category is the primary interest of this chapter. Therefore, it will be explained later in the text.

Hand image taken with digital camera is usually placed on a semitransparent base which is later processed to extract hand shape (usually known as preprocessing of the image to get image data in the form that is suitable for the system it is being used in). It includes extracting small hand curves that can be parts of the one bigger curve which represents hand shape. By using those curves and its characteristics, one can define hand features that will be used in authentication or identification system that is being built.

The first part of the chapter will give an introduction to hand geometry and hand shape, along with description of two different systems for hand geometry. After that, acquiring of characteristics and different extraction techniques will be described. Next chapter will give an overview of new trends in hand geometry. At the end, technology and advantages and disadvantages will be described.

2. Hand geometry and hand shape

Every human hand is unique. In 2002, thirty global features of hand geometry were defined [7]. These features are very exact, but can be represented as global features of contact-less 2D hand geometry. Measures that authors have defined are shown in the Figure 2.

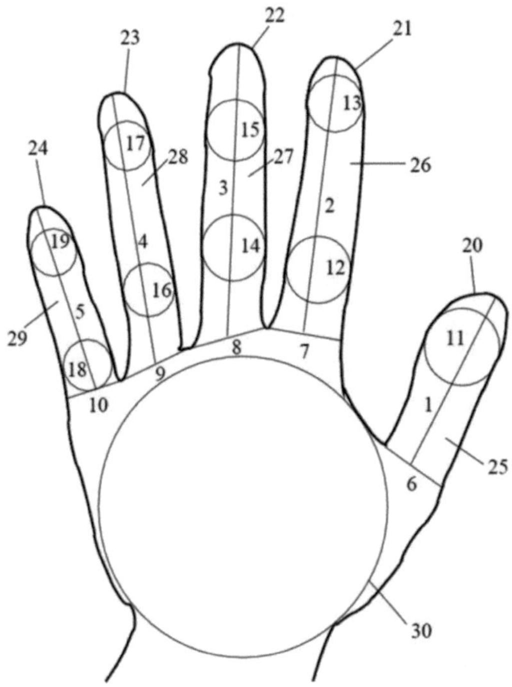

Figure 2. Hand geometry features according to [7]

Features which authors defined in their works and shown in the Figure 2 are following:

1. Thumb length
2. Index finger length
3. Middle finger length
4. Ring finger length
5. Pinkie length
6. Thumb width
7. Index finger width

8. Middle finger width
9. Ring finger width
10. Pinkie width
11. Thumb circle radius
12. Index circle radius lower
13. Index circle radius upper
14. Middle circle radius lower
15. Middle circle radius upper
16. Ring circle radius lower
17. Ring circle radius upper
18. Pinkie circle radius lower
19. Pinkie circle radius upper
20. Thumb perimeter
21. Index finger perimeter
22. Middle finger perimeter
23. Ring finger perimeter
24. Pinkie perimeter
25. Thumb area
26. Index finger area
27. Middle finger area
28. Ring finger area
29. Pinkie area
30. Largest inscribed circle radius

Those features became typical features in the systems that use hand geometry in the identification or authentication process.

Many hand geometry systems have pegs guided hand placement. User has to place his/her hand according to pegs in the device surface. The image of the hand is captured using ordinary digital camera [8]. Length of the fingers, their width, thickness, curvature and relative location of all mentioned features are different among all people. Hand geometry scanners usually use ordinary CCD camera, sometimes with infrared light and reflectors that are being used for image capturing. This type of scanner does not take palm details such as papillae into consideration. It is not interested in fingerprints, palm life lines or other ridges, colors or even some scars on the hand surface. In the combination with reflectors and mirrors, optical device can provide us with two hand images, one from the top and another from the bottom side of the hand.

Other than digital cameras, document scanners are also commonly used for capturing hand image. While systems that use digital camera take images and place it on a semitransparent base to achieve better contrast, document scanners use its technology only and the process is something slower than one with the digital camera.

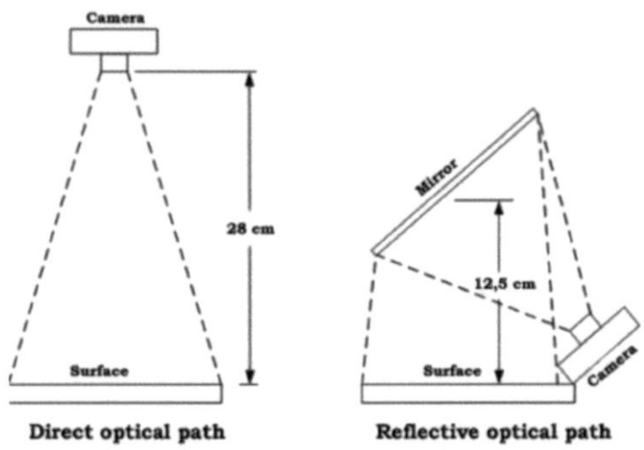

Figure 3. How hand geometry scanners work

Shown in Figure 3, one can see that devices use 28cm optical path length between camera and the surface on which hand is placed on. Reflective optical path minimizes the space needed for building such a device. Device measures a hand couple of times to get a representative sample that will be compared against all others. Using the application defined for given purpose, the processor converts these measurements to biometric pattern. This process is simply called sampling.

2.1. Systems with pegs

Peg based hand geometry systems use pegs on the device board to guide the hand placement on the device. During sampling process scanner prompts a person to put his hand on the board, several times. The board is highly reflective and projects the image of a shaded palm, while the pegs that come out of the surface plate place the fingers in the position necessary for exclusion of a sample. In this way, these systems allow for better measuring compared to systems without pegs, because the hand is fixed to the surface and cannot be shifted. The advantage of this system over the system with no pegs are predefined bases for measurement of characteristics, while the biggest disadvantage is that the system can deform, to a certain extent, the appearance of a hand, so measurements are not very precise, which leads to suboptimal results. It has to be mentioned that various finger positions can effect on variations in measuring features on the fixed axes.

A system that uses pegs was developed by Jain et al. [9]. Their system was able to capture images in 8-bit grayscale, size 640x480 pixels. Authors also developed GUI which helped

http://dx.doi.org/10.5772/51912

users place the hand on the surface. Measuring palm and fingers was made through fourteen intersection points. System provided support through control points and helps in defining the interception points. Two different techniques were used to obtain skin color differences, lightning and noise which are relevant for eigenvector calculation. Researchers found that there are no big differences in system characteristics when using either one of proposed techniques. They acquired 500 images from 50 people. The system was divided in two phases: acquisition and verification. In the first phase the new user was added to database or the existing user was updated. Five images of the same hand were extracted. One had to remove its hand from the device surface before every scanning and place it again according to pegs in the surface. Acquired images were used to obtain eigenvector. This process includes calculating arithmetic mean of eigenvalues. The verification phase represents the process of comparing currently acquired hand image with the one that is already in the database. Two hand images were acquired in this phase and the 'mean' eigenvector was calculated. This vector was compared with the vector in the database which was stored for the user that system was trying to verify.

Let, $F=(f_1, f_2, \ldots, f_d)$ be an n-dimensional eigenvector stored in the database and $Y=(y_1, y_2, \ldots, y_d)$ is an n-dimensional eigenvector of the hand that is being verified. The verification has positive result if the distance between F and Y is smaller than defined threshold. For distance calculating, authors used absolute, weighted absolute, Euclidean and weighted Euclidean distances, with corresponding formulas:

- Absolute distance:

$$\sum_{J=1}^{d} |y_j - f_j| < \alpha \tag{1}$$

- Weighted absolute distance:

$$\sum_{J=1}^{d} \frac{|y_j - f_j|}{\sigma_j} < \omega\alpha \tag{2}$$

- Euclidean distance:

$$\sqrt{\sum_{J=1}^{d} (y_j - f_j)^2} < \tag{3}$$

- Weighted Euclidean distance:

$$\sqrt{\sum_{J=1}^{d} \frac{(y_j - f_j)^2}{\sigma_j}} < \omega \tag{4}$$

Where:

- σ_j^2 is feature variance of jth feature, and

- $_{\alpha}, {}_{\omega\alpha}, {}, {}_{\omega}$ are thresholds for each respective distance metrics

Another research attempt in the field of hand geometry and hand shape has been made in 2000. Sanchez-Reillo and associates developed system which takes 640x640 pixels images in the JPEG format. Surface on which hand had to be placed had 6 guiding pegs. They used 200 images from 20 persons. Not all people had same gender, affiliations or personal habits. Before the features were extracted all images were transformed in the binary form, using the following formula [10]:

$$I_{BW} = \langle\langle I_R + I_G \rangle - I_B \rangle \tag{5}$$

Where:

- I_{BW} is resulting binary image,
- I_R, I_G, I_B are values of red, green and blue channel respectively, and
- $\langle\ \rangle$ is contrast stretching function

Sometimes, digital image does not use its whole contrast range. By stretching lightness values in allowed range the contrast of the image is increasing. This allows better extraction of the hand from the image background. Every 'false' pixel is later (if necessary) removed from the image by using some threshold value. To avoid deviations, image is formatted on the fixed size. Two pegs are used to locate the hand. Afterwards, using *Sobel edge detector*, system can extract hand shape. Final result of this process is image containing hand shape and side view image containing pegs in the predefined positions. First image is used for extracting palm and fingers features. Authors of this paper extracted 31 features to construct eigenvector. They also defined deviation as distance between middle point of the finger and middle point of the line between two fingers and the height on which the finger was measured. Euclidean distance, Hamming distance and Gaussian Mixture Model (GMM) were used for similarities in eigenvectors. This paper is the first that presented hand geometry based identification with satisfying results. Each subject (user) had form 3 to 5 templates stored in the database, each template containing from 9 to 25 features. The GMM gave the best results in all tested cases. With 5 stored templates the system based on GMM achieved 96% identification accuracy, and 97% verification accuracy.

Techniques that are used in hand geometry biometrics are relatively simple and easy to use [11]. Hand geometry systems have tendency to become the most acceptable biometric characteristic, especially comparing to fingerprints or iris [12]. Beside this fact, it has to be mentioned that this biometric technique has some serious disadvantages, and low recognition rate is probably one of the biggest. Most researchers believe that hand geometry itself cannot satisfy needs of modern biometric security devices [8].

2.2. Systems without pegs

As an alternative for systems that used pegs to measure hand geometry features, researchers started to explore hand shape as new biometric characteristic. Researchers in [13] extracted 353 hand shape images from 53 persons. The number of images per person varied from 2 to 15. Pegs were used to place the hand in the right position. They were removed before the comparison and covered with background color. Hand shape was extracted using hand segmentation. During the finger extraction a set of points is produced as shown in Figure 4.

Figure 4. Hand shapes of the same hand extracted, overlaid and aligned [13]

Five fingers were extracted from the hand shape and analyzed separately. To automatize the whole process fingers of the same hand were aligned according to set of all defined points. This alignment is also shown in the Figure 4. The mean distance between two points was defined as Mean Alignment Error (MAE). This error was used to quantify matching results. Positive matching is found if the MAE falls in the predefined set of values. This kind of system achieves False Acceptance Rate (FAR) about 2% and False Rejection Rate (FRR) about 1.5%. This can be comparable to professional and commercial hand geometry systems. The outcome of this approach was larger data storage system because few hundred points needed to be stored for just one hand shape. Authors used randomly created set of 3992 image pairs to create set of interclass distances. By using that set of distances, it is possible to calculate distribution and with very high degree of certainty determine which user is real and which is not.

This was just one way of using hand shape for personal verification. Beside that approach, one can use a palm area size approach. Some researchers like Lay [14], conducted researches based on the palm area size. The hand image was acquired by projecting lattice pattern on the top size of the hand. Image was captured in the lattice frame ant it presented the curvature of the hand. An example of this approach can be seen in Figure 5. Author acquired a hundred images (number of persons is not known), size 512x512 pixels. From those images he extracted templates, size 128x128 pixels.

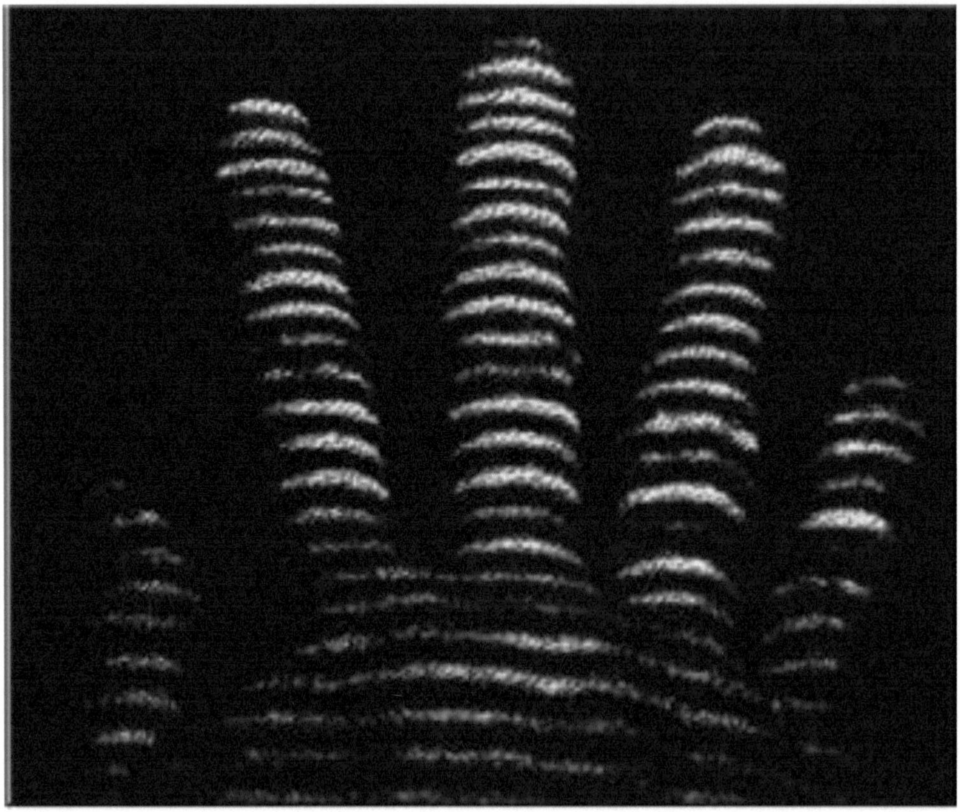

Figure 5. Capturing lattice pattern of the hand

Curvature lattice image was transformed in binary image. This system did not use pegs for hand placement, but one could not move its hand freely. The hand had to be in the right position for the verification process. The system prompted user to place his hand as much as possible the same it was placed during the registration phase. Acquired binary image was coded in quadric tree on seven levels. Those trees were used in the matching process for calculating the similarity of proposed hands. Value less than Root Mean Square (RMS) is proof of better similarity between images. Author claims that he achieved 99.04% verification accuracy, with FAR = FRR = 0.48%.

One can notice that each of the two described systems is capable of competing with the commercial hand geometry systems. The main problem in those systems is relatively small number of users (from 25 to 55 and from 100 to 350 images). This leaves an open question of systems behavior with the larger number of subjects.

An important element (researchers did not consider it) in this field is aging, i.e. the changing of the hand during the time. Hand image is time sensitive, but there is an open question if it is necessary to change the input images of the hand from time to time. This can be done to achieve better recognition rate and event hand features extraction.

http://dx.doi.org/10.5772/51912

Systems without pegs are more tolerant when it comes to placing a hand on the device used for image acquiring.

3. Hand characteristics acquisition

Hand image acquisition is very simple process, especially when it is done in the system without pegs. Hand acquisition system with pegs consists from light source, camera, mirrors and flat surface (with 5 pegs on it). User puts its hand (palm facing down) on the surface. Pegs are used to guide hand placement so the hand would be in the correct position for the system that is being built. Mirror projects side view image of the hand to the camera. In this way, system can obtain hand image and can extract biometric features from the acquired image. The user is being registered to database along with eigenvector of his hand (from now on we call this "eigen-hand"). The acquired image is compared to the already existing images in the database and, if necessary, new eigen-hand is being calculated. A simple way for acquiring image was presented in [9] where the image was taken in 8-bit grayscale, size 640x480 pixels.

The quality of sampling has an effect on the number of false rejected templates, especially in the beginning of the system usage. Sampling depends on large number of factors. For instance, different heights of the biometric device change relative position of the body and hand. This will lead to different hand shape and differently calculated features. Acquiring hand image on the one height and verifying it on another can cause the system to reject a legal user. Besides that, not knowing how the device works can have great impact on the system and make it complicated to work with. If one wants to reduce this complication in verification phase, it can practice putting its hand on the device's surface. Practicing includes correctly placing hand on the surface (no matter whether it uses pegs or not). When a human is born, their hands are almost symmetrical. By getting older there are also some changes in our hands, mainly because of environmental factors. Most people become left- or right-handed leading this hand to become a little bigger that the other one. Young people hands are changing much more that the hands of older people. These processes require that hand geometry and hand shape devices are capable of following those changes and learn how to update every change that is made to person's hand.

Identification systems based on hand geometry are using geometric differences in the human hands. Typical features include length and width of the fingers, palm and fingers position, thickness of the hand, etc. There are no systems that are taking some non-geometric features (e.g. skin color) in consideration. Pegs that some scanners are using are also helpful in determining axes needed for the feature extraction. An example is shown in the Figure 6 where the hand was represented as the vector containing measuring results and 16 characteristic points were extracted:

1. F1 – thumb width on the second phalange (bones that form toes and fingers)
2. F2 – index finger length on the third phalange

3. F3 – index finger length on the second phalange
4. F4 – middle finger length on the third phalange
5. F5 – middle finger length on the second phalange
6. F6 – ring finger width on the third phalange
7. F7 – ring finger width on the second phalange
8. F8 – little finger width on the third phalange
9. F9 – index finger length
10. F10 – middle finger length
11. F11 – ring finger length
12. F12 – little finger length
13. F13 – palm width based on the four fingers
14. F14 – palm width in the thumb area
15. F15 – thickness of the fingers on the first phalange
16. F16 – thickness of the fingers on the second phalange

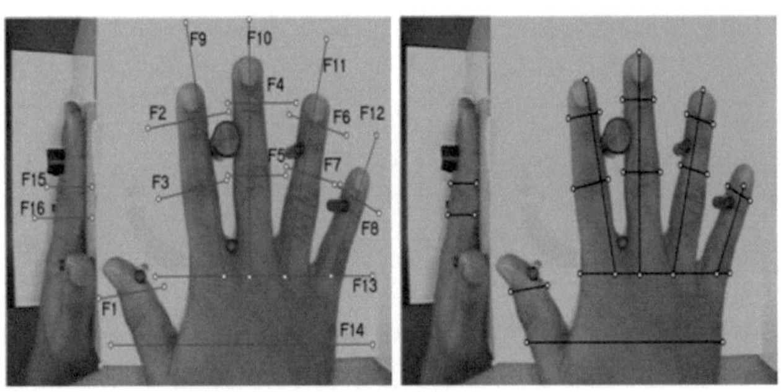

Figure 6. Axes on which hand features are extracted and extracted features [9]

3.1. Extraction techniques

Ross [15] presented two techniques for feature extraction: The Parameter Estimation Technique and The Windowing Technique.

In the Parameter Estimation Technique peg-based acquisition system was used. This approach is called intensity based approach. The other presented technique used fixed windows size and determined points whose intensity was changed along the axes. These techniques will be presented later in the chapter.

http://dx.doi.org/10.5772/51912

Third technique that will be presented here was described in [16]. Since this technique does not have its name we will call it F&K technique which describes hand image through minimum spanning trees.

3.1.1. The parameter estimation technique

In order to offset the effects of background lighting, color of the skin, and noise, the following approach was devised to compute the various feature values. A sequence of pixels along a measurement axis will have an ideal gray scale profile as shown in Figure 7.

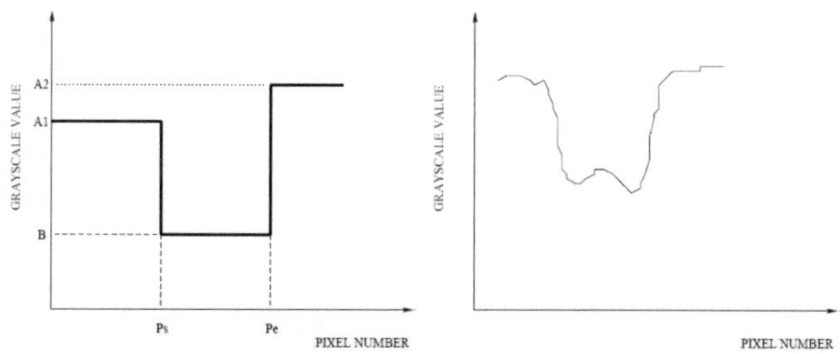

Figure 7. The gray scale profile of pixels along a measurement axis [15]

Total number of pixels considered is referred as *Len*, *Pe* and *Ps* refer to end points within which the object to measured is located and *A1*, *A2* and *B* are the gray scale values.

The actual gray scale profile tends to be spiky as shown in Figure 7 (right image). The first step author presented was to model the profile. Let the pixels along a measurement axis be numbered from 1 to *Len*. Let $X = (x_1, x_2, \ldots, x_{Len})$ be the gray values of the pixels along that axis. The following assumptions about the profile were made:

1. The observed profile (Figure 7 (right)) is obtained from the ideal profile (Figure 7 (left)) by the addition of Gaussian noise to each of the pixels in the latter. Thus, for example, the gray level of a pixel lying between *Ps* and *Pe* were assumed to be drawn from the distribution:

$$G\left(x / B, \sigma_B^2\right) = \frac{1}{\sqrt{2\pi\sigma_B^2}} exp\left\{\frac{-1}{2\sigma_B^2}(x - B)^2\right\} \tag{6}$$

where σ_B^2 is the variance of x in the interval *R*, $Ps < R \leq Pe$.

2. The gray level of an arbitrary pixel along a particular axis is independent of the gray level of other pixels in the line.

Operating under these assumptions, author could write the joint distribution of all the pixel values along a particular axis as:

$$P(X/\theta)=\begin{bmatrix}\prod_{J=1}^{Ps}\frac{1}{\sqrt{2\pi\sigma_{A1}^2}}exp\left\{-\frac{1}{2\sigma_{A1}^2}(x_j-A1)^2\right\}\end{bmatrix}\begin{bmatrix}\prod_{J=Ps+1}^{Pe}\frac{1}{\sqrt{2\pi\sigma_B^2}}exp\left\{-\frac{1}{2\sigma_B^2}(x_j-B)^2\right\}\end{bmatrix}\begin{bmatrix}\prod_{J=Pe+1}^{Len}\frac{1}{\sqrt{2\pi\sigma_{A2}^2}}exp\left\{-\frac{1}{2\sigma_{A2}^2}(x_j-A2)^2\right\}\end{bmatrix} \tag{7}$$

where $\theta=(Ps,\ Pe,\ A1,\ A2,\ B,\ \sigma_{A1}^2,\ \sigma_{A2}^2,\ \sigma_B^2)$ and σ_{A1}^2, σ_{A2}^2 and σ_B^2 are the variances of x in the three intervals [1, *Ps*], [*Ps* + 1, *Pe*] and [*Pe* + 1, *Len*] respectively.

The goal now is to estimate *Ps* and *Pe* using the observed pixel values along the chosen axis (Authors used Maximum Likelihood Estimate-MLE).

By taking algorithm on both sides of (7) one could obtain likelihood function as:

$$L(\theta)=\frac{1}{\sigma_{A1}^2}\sum_{1}^{Ps}(x_j-A1)^2+\frac{1}{\sigma_B^2}\sum_{Ps+1}^{Pe}(x_j-B)^2+\frac{1}{\sigma_{A2}^2}\sum_{Pe+1}^{Len}(x_j-A2)^2+Ps\log\sigma_{A1}^2+(Pe-Ps)\log\sigma_B^2+(Len-Pe)\log\sigma_{A2}^2 \tag{8}$$

The parameters could then be estimated iteratively [15].

The initial estimates of $A1$, σ_{A1}^2, $A2$, σ_{A2}^2, B and σ_B^2 were obtained as follows:

- $A1$ and σ_{A1}^2 were estimated using the gray values of the first N_{A1} pixels along the axis
- $A2$ and σ_{A2}^2 were estimated using the gray values of the pixels from $(Len - N_{A2})$ to *Len*
- B and σ_B^2 were estimated using the gray values of the pixel between $(Len/2 - N_B)$ and $(Len/2 + N_B)$.
- The values of N_{A1}, N_{A2} and N_B were fixed for the system and the values of the *Ps* and *Pe* were set to $Len/2 - 10$ and $Len/2 + 10$ respectively.

3.1.2. The windowing technique

This technique was developed to locate the end points *Ps* and *Pe* from the gray scale profile in Figure 7. A heuristic method was adopted to locate these points. A window of length *wlen* was moved over the profile, one pixel at a time, starting from the left-most pixel.

Let W_i, $0 \le i \le N$, refer to sequence of pixels covered by the window after the *i*th move, with W_N indicating the final position. For each position W_i, author computed four values $Maxval\omega_i$, $Maxindex\omega_i$, $Minval\omega_i$ and $Minindex\omega_i$ as:

$$Maxval\omega_i = \max_{j \in \omega_i} G(j) \tag{9}$$

$$Maxindex\omega_i = arg \max_{j \in \omega_i} G(j) \tag{10}$$

$$Minval\omega_i = \min_{j \in \omega_i} G(j) \tag{11}$$

$$Minindex\omega_i = arg \min_{j \in \omega_i} G(j) \tag{12}$$

Ps and *Pe* could then be obtained by locating the position W_i where $(Maxval\omega_i - Minval\omega_i)$ was the maximum. This indicated a sharp change in the gray scale of the profile.

3.1.3. F&K technique

Fotak and Karlovčec [16] presented a different method of feature extraction. They decided to use mathematical graphs on the two-dimensional hand image. Hand image was normalized by using basic morphological operators and edge detection. They created a binary image from the image captured with an ordinary document scanner. On the binary image the pixel values were analyzed to define the location of characteristic points. They extracted 31 points, shown in the Figure 8.

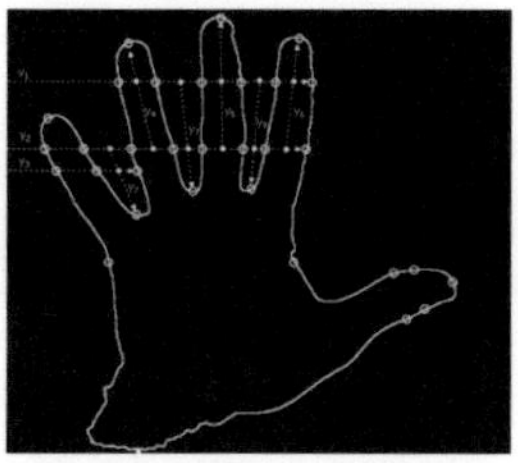

Figure 8. Hand shape and the characteristic hand points defined in [16]

For the hand placement on y-axis a referential point on the top of the middle finger was used. The location of that point was determined by using the horizontal line y1. Using that line, authors defined 6 points that represents the characteristic points of index, middle and ring finger. Using lines y2 and y3 they extracted enough characteristic points for four fingers. Thumb has to be processed in the different manner. To achieve that the right-most point of the thumb had to be identified. Using two vertical lines they found the edges of the thumb. By analyzing points on those lines and their midpoints the top of the thumb could be extracted. Example of the thumb top extracting is shown in the Figure 9.

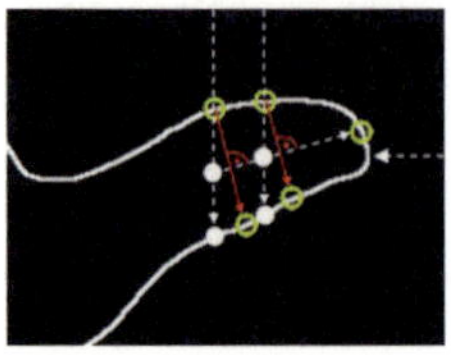

Figure 9. Extracting characteristic points of the thumb

In order to get enough information for their process, each hand had to be scanned four times. For each characteristic point authors constructed the complete graph. The example of characteristic points from four scans and the corresponding complete graph of one point are shown in the Figure 10 and Figure 11 respectively.

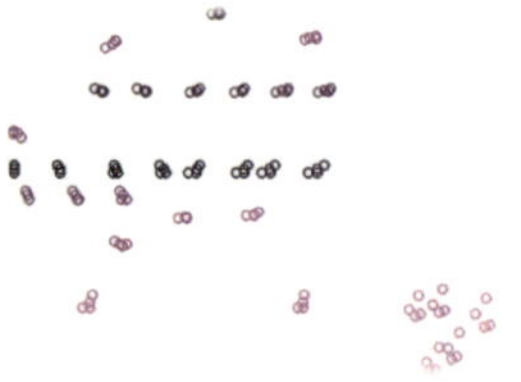

Figure 10. Characteristic points of the four scanning of the hand

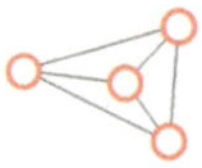

Figure 11. The complete graph of one characteristic point

The number of edges in the complete graph is well known. In order to construct minimum spanning tree this graph needed to be weighted graph. The weights are distances between two graph vertices that are connected with an edge. Distances were measured using Euclidean distance. In the end, Prim algorithm was used to construct minimum spanning tree of one characteristic point. The same procedure was made for each of 31 points. The example of minimum spanning tree of one characteristic point and all minimum spanning trees are shown in the Figure 12 and Figure 13 respectively.

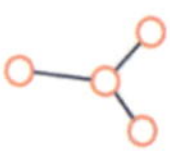

Figure 12. Minimum spanning tree of the graph from the Figure 12

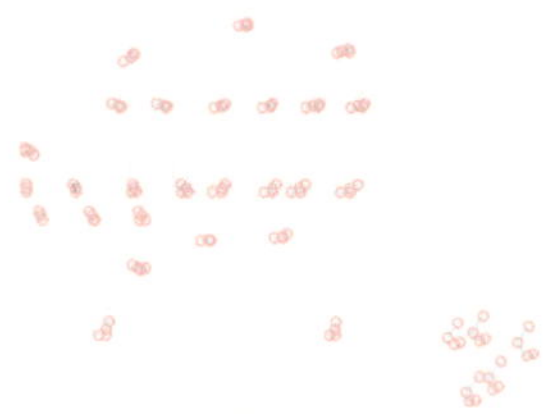

Figure 13. All minimum spanning trees of one user

The verification process is made by comparing every point minimum spanning tree with the location of currently captured corresponding point. The results of the system are very promising for future development, and are FAR = 1.21% and FRR = 7.75%.

4. New trends in hand geometry and hand shape biometrics

So far we described the basics of hand geometry biometrics. In this section we will mention some new trends and new researches in this field. Reading this section requires a great understanding of the hand geometry biometrics and the extraction and verification methods that are mentioned here. We will describe everything in detail, but rather mention some achievements that were produced in last few years.

Hand geometry has been contact-based from its beginnings and still is in almost all commercial systems. Since it has evolved in last 30 years, one can categorize this field as in [17]:

- Constrained and contact-based
- Unconstrained and contact-based

While the first category requires a flat platform and pegs or pins to restrict hand degree of freedom, second one is peg- and pin-free, although still requiring a platform to place a hand (e.g. scanner). Main papers of this category were described earlier in this chapter.

The second category gives users more freedom in the process of image acquisition. This step is considered as the evolution forward from constrained contact-based systems. Some newer works in this field are [18], [19]. In the [18] authors presented a method based on three keys. The system was based on using Natural Reference System (NRS) defined on the hand's layout. Therefore, neither hand-pose nor a pre-fixed position were required in the registration process. Hand features were obtained through the polar representation of the hand's contour. Their system uses both right and left hand which allowed them to consider distance measures for direct and crossed hands. Authors of the second paper [19] used 15 geometric features to analyze the effect of changing the image resolution over biometric system based on hand geometry. The images were diminished from an initial 120dpi up to 24dpi. They used two databases, one acquiring the images of the hand underneath whereas the second database acquires the image over the hand. According to that they used two classifiers: multiclass support vector machine (Multiclass SVM) and neural network with error correction output codes.

There are many different verification approaches in the contact-based hand geometry systems. So far, the GMMs and SVM give the best results but they are far from satisfying for commercial use.

Due to user acceptability, contact-less biometrics is becoming more important. In this approach neither pegs nor platform are required for hand image acquisition. Papers in this field are relatively new according to ones in the contact-based approach. It is for the best to present just new trends in contact-less hand geometry biometrics.

The most used verification methods in this approach are *k – Nearest Neighbor (k-NN)* and SVM. These methods are also the most competitive in the existing literature.

In the last few years, literature on this problem is rapidly increasing. SVM is the most common used verification and identification method. Authors in [20] acquired hand image with static video camera. Using the decision tree they segmented the hand and after that measured the local feature points extracted along fingers and wrists. The identification was based on the geometry measurements of a query image against a database of recorded measurements using SVM. Another use of SVM can be found in the [21]. They also presented biometric identification system based on geometrical features of the human hand. The right hand images were acquired using classic web cam. Depending on illumination, binary images were constructed and the geometrical features (30-40 finger widths) were obtained from them. SVM was used as a verifier. Kumar and Zhang used SVM in their hybrid recognition system which uses feature-level fusion of hand shape and palm texture [22]. They extracted features from the single image acquired from digital camera. Their results proved that only a small subset of hand features are necessary in practice for building an accurate model for identification. The comparison and combination of proposed features was evaluated on the diverse classification schemes: naïve Bayes (normal, estimated, multinomial), decision trees (4 5, LMT), k-NN, SVM, and FFN.

A hybrid system fusing the palmprint and hand geometry of a human hand based on morphology was presented in [23]. Authors utilized the image morphology and concept of Voronoi diagram to cut the image of the front of the whole palm apart into several irregular blocks in accordance with the hand geometry. Statistic characteristics of the gray level in the blocks were employed as characteristic values. In the recognition phase SVM was used.

Beside SVM which is the most competitive method in the contact-less hand geometry verification and identification, the literature contains other very promising methods such as neural networks [24], a new feature called 'SurfaceCode' [25] and template distances matching [17].

Mentioned methods are not the only ones but they have the smallest Equal Error Rate and therefore are the most promising methods for the future development of the contact-less hand geometry biometric systems.

5. The hand recognition technology

Hand features, described earlier in the chapter, are used in the devices for personal verification and identification. One of the leading commercial companies in this field is *Schlage*. In their devices a CCD digital camera is used for acquiring a hand image. This image has size of 32000 pixels. One if their device is shown in Figure 14.

Figure 14. Schlage HandPunch 4000 [26]

The system presented in the Figure X14 consists from light source, camera, mirrors and flat surface with 5 pegs. The user places the hand facing down on a flat plate on which five pins serve as a control mechanism for the proper accommodation of the right hand of the user. The device is connected with the computer through application which enables to see live image of the top side of the hand as well as side view of the hand. The GUI helps in image acquisition while the mirror in the device used to obtain side view of the hand. This gives a partially three-dimensional image of the hand. The device captures two hand images. After the user places its hand on the device, the hand is being captured. The location and the size of the image are determined by segmentation of reflected light from the dark mask. Second image is captured with the same camera but using the mirror for measuring the hand thickness. By using only binary image and the reflected background the system is not capable of capturing scars, pores or tattoos. On the other hand, big rings, bandages or gloves can have great impact on the image so it could lead to false rejection of the hand.

The captured hand silhouette is used to calculate length, width and the thickness of the four fingers (thumb is not included). The system makes 90 measurements which are stored in the 9B size template. For template matching the Euclidean distance is used. The acquisition procedure takes 30 seconds to complete and during that period user has to place its hand on the device four times. Internal processor generates template which is mean template of all readings during this process. Image captured with this device can be seen in the Figure 15.

Figure 15. Hand silhouette captured with Schalge device

6. Conclusion

Hand recognition biometrics is probably the most developed and applicable biometric technique that found its application in many organizations. This is due to its user friendliness. Moreover, hand recognition is a simple technique which is very easy to use and does not require much memory space. Hand geometry is invariant from the environmental impacts and has acceptable privacy violation level. For the image capturing one can use classic CCD cameras which are easy to use (it is easy to obtain hand image) and have a low price.

The biggest disadvantages of hand geometry lie in the following facts. The size of the hand restricts biometric systems on the smaller number of applications. From a hundred randomly chosen persons, at least two will have similar hand geometry. The hand injury can potentially have great impact on the recognition system. Measurements have to be done several times, since in the acquisition process one cannot always obtain all information needed.

It is obvious that this technique is easy to forge by finding the most appropriate hand (one has to find the hand that is "close enough"). The technology based on the hand image is the most common in modern biometric systems.

In this chapter we presented the basics of the hand geometry and hand shape biometrics. Researchers in the field of biometrics found that human hand, especially human palm, contains some characteristics that can be used for personal identification. These characteristics mainly include thickness of the palm area and width, thickness and length of the fingers, etc. Hand recognition biometrics is probably the most developed and applicable biometric technique that found its application in many organizations.

http://dx.doi.org/10.5772/51912

Author details

Miroslav Bača*, Petra Grd and Tomislav Fotak

*Address all correspondence to: miroslav.baca@foi.hr

Centre for biometrics, Faculty of Organization and Informatics, Varaždin, Croatia

References

[1] Ernst R.H. Hand ID System. US Patent. (1971).

[2] Jacoby OH, Giordano AJ, Fioretti WH. Personal Identification Apparatus. US Patent. (1971).

[3] Lay HC. Hand Shape Recognition. US Patent. (1971).

[4] Sidlauskas DP. 3D HHHand Profile Identification Apparatus.US Patent 4736203; (1988).

[5] Van Tilborg, H. C. E., Jajodia, S., & editors, . Encyclopedia of Cryptography and Security 2nd Ed. New York: Springer Science + Business Media, LLC; (2011).

[6] Fotak T. Razvoj biometrijskih tehnika. BSc thesis. University of Zagreb, Faculty of organization and informatics; 2008.

[7] Bulatov, Y., Jambawalikar, S., Kumar, P., & Sethia, S. Hand Recognition System Using Geometric Classifiers. DIMACS Workshop on Computational Geometry, (14-15 November 2002). Piscataway, NJ; 2002., 14-15.

[8] Jain, A., Bolle, R., Pankanti, S., editors, Biometrics., Personal, identification., in, networked., & society, . Norwell: Kluwer Academic Publishers; (1999).

[9] Jain, A., Ross, A., Panakanti, S. A., prototype, hand., geometry-based, verification., & system, A. V. B. P. AVBPA: proceedings of the 2nd International Conference on Audio- and Video-based Biometric Person Authentication, Washington DC; (1999).

[10] Sanchez-Reillo, R., Sanchez-Avila, C., & Gonzales-Marcos, A. (2000). Basic Principles and Trends in Hand Geometry and Hand Shape Biometrics . *IEEE Transactions on Pattern Analysis and Machine Intelligence*, 1168 EOF-1171 EOF.

[11] Jain, A., Hong, L., Prabhakar, S., Biometrics, promising., frontiers, for., the, emerging., & identification, market. Communications of the ACM (2000). , 91-98.

[12] Holmes, J. P., Maxwell, R. L., Righ, L. J. A., performance, evaluation., of, biometric., & identification, devices. Technical Report SANDSandia National Laboratories; (1990). , 91-0276.

[13] Jain, A., & Duta, N. Deformable matching of hand shapes for verification. IEEE International Conference in Image Processing: Proceedings of the IEEE International Conference in Image Processing. Kobe, Japan; (1999).

[14] Lay HC. Hand shape recognition.Optics and Laser Technology (2000).

[15] Ross, A. A., prototype, Hand., Geometry-based, Verification., & System, . MS Project Report; (1999).

[16] Fotak, T., & Karlovčec, M. Personal authentication using minimum spanning trees on twodimensional hand image. Varaždin: FOI; (2009).

[17] De Santos, Sierra. A., Sanchez-Avila, C., Bailador del, Pozo. G., & Guerra-Casanova, J. Unconstrained and Contactless Hand Geometry Biometrics. Sensors (2011). , 11, 10143-10164.

[18] Adan, M., Adan, A., & Vasquez, Torres. R. (2008). Basic Principles and Trends in Hand Geometry and Hand Shape Biometrics . *Image and Vision Computing*, 26(4), 451-465.

[19] Ferrer, Fabregas. J., Faundez, M., Alonso, J. B., & Travieso, C. M. Basic Principles and Trends in Hand Geometry and Hand Shape Biometrics . International Carnahan Conference on Security Technology: Proceedings of the 43rd Annual 2009 International Carnahan Conference on Security Technolog, Zurich; (2009).

[20] Jiang, X., Xu, W., Sweeney, L., Li, Y., Gross, R., & Yurovsky, D. New drections in contact free hand recognition. International Conference in Image Processing : Proceedings of the IEEE International Conference in Image Processing, San Antonio, TX; (2007).

[21] Ferrer, M. A., Alonso, J. B., & Travieso, C. M. Comparing infrared and visible illumination for contactless hand based biometric scheme. International Carnahan Conference on Security Technology: Proceedings of the 42nd Annual IEEE International Carnahan Conference on Security Technology, Prague; (2008).

[22] Kumar, A., & Zhang, D. (2006). Basic Principles and Trends in Hand Geometry and Hand Shape Biometrics . *IEEE Transactions on Image Processing*.

[23] Wang WC, Chen WS, Shih SW.Basic Principles and Trends in Hand Geometry and Hand Shape Biometrics . International Conference on Acoustics: Proceedings of the IEEE International Conference on Acoustics, Speech and Signal Processing, Taipei; (2009).

[24] Rahman, A., Anwar, F., Azad, S. A., Simple, , Effective, Technique., for, Human., Verification, with., & Hand, Geometry. International Conference on Computer and Communication Engineering: Proceedings of the International Conference on Computer and Communication Engineering, Kuala Lumpur; (2008).

[25] Kanhangad, V., Kumar, A., & Zhang, D. Human Hand Identification with 3D Hand Pose Variations. Computer Society Conference on Computer Vision and Pattern Rec-

ognition: Proceedings of the IEEE Computer Society Conference on Computer Vision and Pattern Recognition Workshops, San Francisco, CA; (2010).

[26] Schlage. HandPunch 4000: Biometrics. http://w3.securitytechnologies.com/products/biometrics/time_attendance/HandPunch/Pages/details.aspx?InfoID=18 (accessed 20May (2012).

Chapter 5

Genetic & Evolutionary Biometrics

Aniesha Alford, Joseph Shelton, Joshua Adams, Derrick LeFlore, Michael Payne, Jonathan Turner, Vincent McLean, Robert Benson, Gerry Dozier, Kelvin Bryant and John Kelly

Additional information is available at the end of the chapter

http://dx.doi.org/10.5772/51386

1. Introduction

Genetic & Evolutionary Computation (GEC) is the field of study devoted to the design, development, and analysis of problem solvers based on natural selection [1-4] and has been successfully applied to a wide range of complex, real world optimization problems in the areas of robotics [5], scheduling [6], music generation [7], aircraft design [1], and cyber security [8-11], just to name a few. Genetic and Evolutionary Computations (referred to as GECs) differ from most traditional problems solvers in that they are stochastic methods that evolve a population of candidate solutions (CSs) rather than just operating on a single CS. Due to the evolutionary nature of GECs, they are able to discover a wide variety of novel solutions to a particular problem at hand – solutions that radically differ from those developed by traditional problem solvers [3,12,13].

GECs are general-purpose problem solvers [1,2,4]. Because of this fact and their ability to hybridize well with traditional problem solvers [1], a number of new subfields have emerged. In the field of Evolutionary Robotics [5,14], GECs are used in path planning [15], robot behavior design [16], and robot gait design [17]. In the field of Evolutionary Design [1,18], GECs are being used to evolve lunar habitats [19], emoticons [20], and music [7,21]. GECs have also been used successfully in a wide variety of scheduling applications [22,23] – which in turn has spawn a subfield known as Evolutionary Scheduling [6,24].

Currently we are seeing the emergence of a new and exciting field of study devoted towards the design, development, analysis, and application of GECs to problems within the area of biometrics [25-29]. We refer to this new subfield of study as Genetic and Evolutionary Biometrics (GEB) [25-27,31]. In this chapter, we will provide a brief history of GEB as well as introduce a number of GEB applications (which we refer to as GEBAs). The GEBAs presented in this chapter are actually hybridized forms of traditional methods used within the biometrics research community. These GEBAs typically evolve solutions that are radically different from and, in many instances, more efficient than solutions developed by traditional methods currently used within the biometrics research community.

The remainder of this chapter is as follows. In Section 2, we discussGECs and provide a brief history of the field of GEB. We also present an overview of the Local Binary Patterns (LBP) [32-34] method and in Section 3 we present the GEBAs used in this work. In Section 4, we describe the experiments performed and we present our results. In Section5,we provide an additional discussion of our results, and in Section 6, we provide a summary of our work as well as directions for further research.

2. Background

2.1. Genetic & Evolutionary Computation (GEC)

GECs typically work in the following fashion [1-4,12,13]. Initially, a population of CSs is randomly generated. Each CS is then evaluated and assigned a fitness based on a user-defined evaluation function. Next, parents are selected from the population based on their fitness and are allowed to produce offspring CSs. The offspring are then assigned a fitness and usually replace the worst performing CSs within the current population. This evolutionary process is then repeated until a user-specified stopping condition is satisfied. Figure 1 provides a flowchart of the typical GEC process.

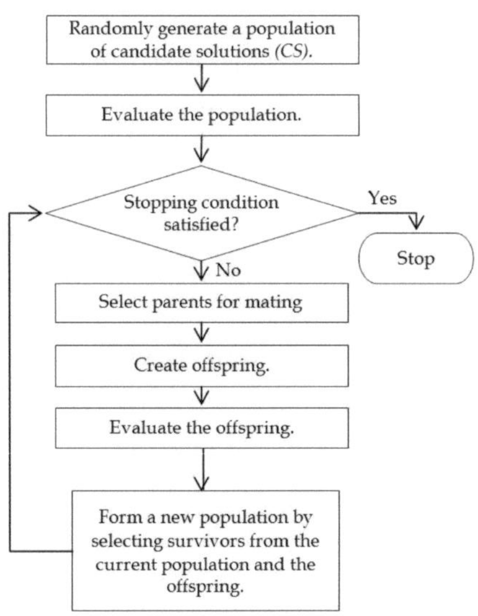

Figure 1. Flowchart of a typical GEC.

2.2. A Brief History of GEB

Within the field of biometrics, GEB applications (GEBAs) have been successfully applied to the areas of feature selection [25,30,31,33,35,36], feature weighting [25,30,31,37,38], feature extraction [26-29], and biometric-based security [9-11,39].

2.2.1. GEBAs for Feature Selection and Weighting

Concerning GEBAs for feature selection, Galbally et al. [35] developed Genetic Algorithms (GAs) [1] for feature selection and applied them in an effort to solve the signature verification problem. The GAs were applied to two training sets which were formed using the signatures of 330 subjects from the MCYT Signature database [40]. The first training set consisted of five signatures of each subject and the second training set consisted of 20 signatures of each subject. A test set was formed using the remaining signatures. Their results showed that the GAs, when compared to the baseline method that used all of the features, were able to reduce the number of features used while improving the recognition accuracy of the system.

Ramadan and Abdel-Kader [36] applied two GECs, Particle Swarm Optimization (PSO) [13] and a GA, for feature selection for a facial recognition problem. Images from the Cambridge ORL database [41] were used to form a training set, which consisted of four images of each of the 40 subjects, and a test set, which consisted of six images of each of the 40 subjects. Two baseline methods, the Discrete Cosine Transform (DCT) [42] and Discrete Wavelet Transform (DWT) [43] methods, were then used to extract the original set of features. Ramadan and Abdel-Kader demonstrated that their GECs could increase the recognition accuracy over the baseline methods while using fewer features. In addition, the PSO used fewer features than the GA.

Kumar et al. [44] also applied two GECs, a Memetic Algorithm (MA) [45] and a GA, for feature selection for a face recognition system. The GECs were tested on two facial databases: the Cambridge ORL database [41] and a subset of 20 subjects from the YaleB database [46]. The following feature extraction techniques were used to create the original feature templates: Principal Component Analysis (PCA) [47], Linear Discriminant Analysis [48], and Kernel PCA [49]. The MA and GA were applied in an effort to reduce the dimensionality of the feature templates as well as to increase the recognition rate. Their results showed the GECs outperformed the baseline methods, which used all of the extracted features, in terms of feature usage and recognition rate. Their results also showed that the MA outperformed the GA.

In [37], Abegaz et al. applied two GEBAs for feature selection and feature weighting for facial recognition. The first GEBA, referred to as Genetic & Evolutionary Feature Selection (GEFeS), evolved subsets of biometric features also in an effort to increase the recognition rate while reducing the number of features used. The second GEBA, referred to as Genetic & Evolutionary Feature Weighting (GEFeW), evolved weights for the features. These GEBAs, which were instances of a Steady-State Genetic Algorithm (SSGA) [1-4] and Estimation of Distribution Algorithms (EDAs) [50], were applied to Eigenface[51] and LBP facial feature templates. Their results showed that GEFeS and GEFeW outperformed the baseline methods, achieving higher recognition rates while using significantly fewer features. Their results also showed that the EDA instance of GEFeW was the best performing GEBA. In addition, the LBP instances outperformed the Eigenface instances.

Alford et al. [38] compared the performances of GEFeS, GEFeW, and a hybrid feature selection and weighting GEBA referred to as Genetic & Evolutionary Feature Weighting/Selection (GEFeWS), for face-only, periocular-only, and face + periocular recognition. The GEBAs were implemented using a SSGA and an EDA, and the original feature sets were formed using the Eigenface and LBP methods. Their results showed that the GEFeS, GEFeW, and GEFeWS instances significantly outperformed the baseline methods in terms of recognition accuracy and feature usage. In addition, the EDA instance of GEFeWS outperformed the other GEBAs. Their results also showed that the performances of the GEBAs using multiple biometric modalities were better than those using only a single modality. In addition, the LBP instances performed better than the Eigenface instances.

Alford et al. [25] extended their work by developing a hybrid GEBA for feature selection and weighting that dramatically reduced the number of features necessary for recognition, increased the recognition rate, and also evolved feature masks (FMs) that generalized well to unseen subjects. The GEBA, known as $GEFeWS_{ML}$ (GEFeWS – Machine Learning), was applied to face-only, periocular-only, and face + periocular LBP templates formed for subjects within the Face Recognition Grand Challenge (FRGC) database [52]. Their results showed that $GEFeWS_{ML}$ achieved higher recognition rates than the baseline methods, while using less than 50% of the extracted features. In addition, FMs evolved via the validation set performed better than those evolved via the training set.

In [31], Alford et al. evaluated the performance of $GEFeWS_{ML}$ on a subset of images extracted from the Craniofacial Longitudinal Morphological Face (MORPH) [53] database. They also tested the cross-generalization ability of the resulting FMs by applying the FMs evolved for the FRGC datasets in [25] to the MORPH test set and applying the FMs evolved for the MORPH to the FRGC test set. Their results showed that the FMs evolved by $GEFeWS_{ML}$ could also generalize well to unseen images from a different database.

2.2.2. GEBAs for Feature Extraction

Concerning GEBAs for feature extraction, Shelton et al. [29] developed a GEBA referred to as Genetic & Evolutionary Feature Extraction (GEFE), which evolved LBP-based feature extractors (FEs) for facial recognition. Unlike the standard LBP method (SLBPM), GEFE evolved FEs that were allowed to overlap and only extracted from a subset of the image. Shelton et al. tested the performance of GEFE using two GECs, a SSGA and an EDA. They also evolved two types of FEs: (a) those that consisted of patches that were of non-uniform size and (b) those that consisted of patches that were of uniform size. Their results showed that the GEFE instances outperformed the SLBPM in terms of accuracy, feature usage, and computational complexity. In addition, the GEFE instances that evolved FEs composed of uniform sized patches outperformed the GEFE instances that evolved non-uniformed sized patches. Their results also showed that the EDA instances of GEFE outperformed the SSGA instances.

Shelton et al. [26] then extended their work, by incorporating the machine learning technique known as cross validation [54], in an effort to evolve FEs that achieve high recognition rates, extract from a small region of the image, and generalize well to unseen subjects. The GEBA, known as $GEFE_{ML}$ (GEFE-Machine Learning), was trained on a subset of images taken from the FRGC database. The evolved FEs were then tested on the images of unseen subjects taken from the FRGC database and Craniofacial Longitudinal Morphological Face (MORPH) database [53]. Their results showed that the $GEFE_{ML}$-evolved FEs, when compared to the SLBPM, used fewer patches, achieved comparable recognition rates on both datasets, and were significantly less expensive in terms of computational complexity. In addition, the resulting FEs generalized well to the unseen subjects from both databases.

In [27], a two-stage process known as Darwinian Feature Extraction (DFE) was developed. This technique used FEs that were evolved by $GEFE_{ML}$ to create Darwinian Feature Extractors (dFEs). The first stage of DFE superimposes a set of FEs to create a hyper FE. This hyper FE is then used to create a probability distribution function (PDF) of the occurrence of extraction per pixel. In the second stage, the PDF is sampled to determine which pixels will be processed via the LBP method. The selected pixels are then grouped using a clustering process. Next, a number of cluster centers are randomly selected within an image, and the selected pixels are then assigned to their closest cluster centers. The SLBPM is then applied to the resulting clusters. Their results showed that dFEs, when compared to the FEs evolved by $GEFE_{ML}$, achieved a higher recognition rate at a reduced computational complexity.

Adams et al. [28] extended the work of [27] by developing three types of Darwinian Feature Extraction – Clustering (DFE_c). Unlike DFE, which uses random cluster centers, DFE_C uses K-Means clustering [55] (DFE_{KM}), Kohonen clustering [56] (DFE_K) and a combination of the two (DFE_{K+KM} and DFE_{KM+K}) to create a user-specified number of clusters. These GEBAs were applied to datasets formed from subjects taken from the FRGC database. Their results showed that DFE_{KM} and DFE_{K+KM} performed as well as DFE in terms of accuracy, while DFE_K and DFE_{KM+K} performed worse than DFE. In addition, their results showed that DFE_{K+KM} outperformed the other DFE_C methods.

2.2.3. *Genetic & Evolutionary Biometric Security*

There has also been an increase in the use of GEBAs for biometric-based security, giving rise to a new field of study known as Genetic & Evolutionary Biometric Security (GEBS). Shelton et al. [9,10] introduced a number biometric-based access control protocols that used disposable FEs and their associated feature vectors (FVs) to mitigate replay attacks on a facial recognition systems. In [9], the researchers showed that the FEs evolved by $GEFE_{ML}$ and their associated FVs were unique from oneanother and achieved high recognition rate. As a result, either the FEs or their associated FVs could be used to mitigate replay attacks by disposing of a particular FE or FV after usage. In [10], Shelton et al. extended their work by demonstrating that permuting the order of feature extraction resulted in the development of FVs with greater distinction from one another. The net effect of this being a further reduction in the possibility of the occurrence of a successful biometric-based replay attack.In [11],

Shelton et al.showed that the dFEscreated by the DFE method could also be used to mitigate replay attacksas well.

Adams et al. [39]developed a method for mitigating image reconstruction attacks from a compromised biometric gallery consisting of biometric templates extracted using the SLBPM. First, they demonstrated how a General Regression Neural Network [57] and a SSGA could be used to reconstruct facial images from the biometric templates. They then developed a neurogenetic method to distort the biometric templates, so that if reconstructed, they would not match with their original biometric templates.

2.3. Local Binary Patterns Method (LBP)

The Local Binary Patterns Method (LBP), which was developed by Ojala et al. [32], is a popular texture descriptor that has been used in a variety of applications [25-28,30, 31, 34, 58-61]. Within the biometrics community, the LBP method has become a very popular feature extraction technique [25-28, 30, 31, 58] due to its computational simplicity and its invariance against monotonic gray level changes [34].

The LBP works as follows. First, an image is segmented into a grid of evenly sized regions, which are referred to as patches. Within each patch, the LBP operator is then used to label each interior pixel by subtracting its intensity value,i_c, from the intensity value of each of its P neighboring pixels at a radius R,i_p, where $p = 0,\ldots, P-1$. A texture, which is essentially a bit pattern, is then formed, as shown in Equation 1, where if the difference between the intensity values is negative, a zero is added to the bit string, otherwise a one.

$$T = \{s(i_0 - i_c),\ s(i_1 - i_c),\ \ldots,\ s(i_{P-1} - i_c)\} \tag{1}$$

$$s\ (i_p - i_c) = \begin{cases} 0, \text{ if } i_p < i_c \\ 1, \text{ if } i_p \geq i_c \end{cases} \tag{2}$$

Each interior pixel can then be represented by a unique LBP code by assigning a binomial weight to the elements in the texture as follows:

$$LBP = \sum_{p=0}^{P-1} s\ (i_p - i_c)\ 2^p \tag{3}$$

Associated with each patch is a histogram where each bin represents the frequency of a particular LBP code. Using a neighborhood size of P, there are 2^P unique LBP codes. However, Ojala et al. [32] showed that only a subset of the possible patterns, known as uniform patterns, are necessary to describe the texture of an image. For our research, uniform patterns are those texture patterns that have at most two one-to-zero or zero-to-one bit transitions when the texture is traversed circularly. These uniform patterns account for a high percentage of the resulting texture patterns and also contain the most texture information

[33]. Therefore, instead of having a histogram consisting of 2^P bins, each histogram would now consist of only $P(P-1)+3$ bins, where $P(P-1)$ bins account for the uniform patterns with exactly two bit transitions, one bin represents the all zero bit pattern, another bin represents the all ones bit pattern, and an additional bin is used to store the frequency of the non-uniform patterns.

The histograms for each patch are then concatenated to form a feature template for the image, which consists of the number of bins, $P(P-1)+3$, times the number of patches used, N, features.

3. The GEBAs

3.1. Genetic & Evolutionary Feature Weighting/Selection—Machine Learning ($GEFeWS_{ML}$)

Genetic & Evolutionary Feature Weighting/Selection—Machine Learning ($GEFeWS_{ML}$) was developed by Alford et al. [25] for hybrid feature weighting and selection for facial and peri-ocular recognition. $GEFeWS_{ML}$ evolves feature masks (FMs) that use a low percentage of features, achieve high recognition rates, and that generalize well to unseen instances. The technique, which is an instance of an Estimation of Distribution Algorithm (EDA) [50], works as follows.

First, the set of available instances is split into a training set, a validation set, and a test set. The EDA then randomly generates an initial population of Q real-valued candidate FMs. Each candidate FM, fm_i, can be represented by a tuple$\langle M_i, fit_i\rangle$where $M_i=\langle \mu_{i,0}, \mu_{i,1}, \ldots, \mu_{i,n-1}\rangle$ represents the set of mask values and where fit_i represents the fitness value. The mask values are initially within the range [0..1]. Any mask value that is lower than 0.5 is set to 0 and the corresponding biometric feature would not be used during comparisons. Otherwise, the mask value is used to weight the corresponding biometric feature.

Next, each candidate FM is applied to the probe and gallery templates within both the training and validation sets. The resulting probe templates are then compared to each gallery template using the Weighted Manhattan Distance (wMD) formula shown in Equation 4, where h_j and h_l are two templates that are being compared, n is the original number of features in the biometric templates, $\mu_{i,k}$ is a FM value, k represents thek^{th} feature, and the function f_{WS} represents the process of feature weighting/selection as performed by $GEFeWS_{ML}$. The subject associated with the template within the gallery set with the smallest weighted Manhattan distance when compared to the probe is considered the match.

$$wMD_{WS}(h_j, h_l, fm_i)=\sum_{k=0}^{n-1} | h_{j,k}-h_{l,k} | f_{WS}(u_{i,k}) \quad (4)$$

$$f_{WS}(u_{i,k}) = \begin{cases} 0 & ,\text{if } u_{i,k} < 0.5 \\ u_{i,k} & ,\text{if } u_{i,k} \geq 0.5 \end{cases} \quad (5)$$

The fitness function shown in Equation 6 is then used to evaluate each candidate FM based on its performance on the training and validation sets, where ε is the number of recognition errors that occurred when the candidate FM was applied to the probe and gallery templates, m is the number of features used by the candidate FM, and where n is the original number of features in the biometric templates.

$$fit_i = 10\varepsilon + \frac{m}{n} \quad (6)$$

The best performing candidate FM on the validation set is then stored and will be referred to as *FM**. Next, the top 50% best performing candidate FMs, based on their performance on the training set, are used to create a probability density function (PDF). The PDF is then sampled to create (1-α)Q offspring, where α is the user-defined percentage (in this case, 25%) of FMs that are allowed to survive into the next generation (known as the elites). The offspring are then evaluated based on their performance on the training and validation sets. Any offspring whose performance on the validation set is better than that of FM* will become the new FM*. A new population is then formed using the (1-α)Q offspring and the αQ elites. This evolutionary process is then continued until a user-specified stopping condition has been satisfied. Once the condition has been met, the best performing FM from the population based on its performance on the training set, which will be referred to as FM^{ts}, as well as FM* are returned. These FMs are then applied to the test set in order to determine how well they generalize to unseen instances.

3.2.Reverse Engineered Feature Extraction (REFE)

Reverse Engineered Feature Extraction (REFE) is a technique that creates feature extractors (FEs) that obtain higher recognition rates than the SLBPM, while using a smaller number of patches, as compared to the SLBPM. This technique works by first analyzing statistically the FMs evolved by $GEFeWS_{ML}$ [25] to determine the percentage of features selected for use within each patch. For each FM, apatch percentage vector (PPV) is calculated by dividing the number of features used in a patch by the number of total features in a patch. For the results presented in this chapter, each image is segmented into 24 patches and each patch consisted of 59 bins. Therefore, the total number of features in a patch is 1416 (24 patches × 59 bins).

Each PPV is then evaluated at each patch position to create a corresponding FM. Because each image is segmented into 24 equally size patches, the PPV is evaluated based on the top 24 patches to the top patch, in terms of their percentage. In addition to the PPVs for the 30 best performing FMs, an average PPV (PPV_{avg}) is also formed. PPV_{avg} is the average percentage of features used at each patch position for the 30 PPVs. Therefore, 31 total PPVs are created. The PPVs were then used to create a set of FEs. Each FE is created by selecting the top user-specified number ofpatches based on the patches PPV value, starting with all 24 patches as a baseline working down to the top performing patch. Ties were broken based on the patch position. A candidate FM is then created from each FE in the following manner. If a patch is selected to be present in the FE, then all of the features extracted by that patch will be used for matching. Otherwise, no features will be extracted from the patch.

3.3.Genetic & Evolutionary Feature Extraction-Machine Learning ($GEFE_{ML}$)

Genetic &Evolutionary Feature Extraction—Machine Learning ($GEFE_{ML}$), which was developed by Shelton et al. [26],evolves LBP-based FEs that result in high recognition accuracies, use a low percentage of features, and generalizes well to unseen images. Unlike the SLBPM, which uses non-overlapping uniform patches that extract from the entire image, $GEFE_{ML}$ evolves FEs with overlapping uniform patches that only extract from a subset of an image. The $GEFE_{ML}$ technique, which is also an instance of an EDA [50], works as follows.

As done with $GEFeWS_{ML,}$ first the set of available instances is split into a training set, a validation set, and a test set. $GEFE_{ML}$ then randomly generates an initial population of Q candidate FEs, where each FE, fe_i, can be represented as a six-tuple,$\langle X_i, Y_i, W_i, H_i, M_i, f_i\rangle$. The first two elements in the tuple represent the x and y coordinates of the centers of the N possible patches, where $X_i=\langle x_{i,0}, x_{i,1}, ..., x_{i,N-1}\rangle$ and $Y_i=\langle y_{i,0}, y_{i,1}, ..., y_{i,N-1}\rangle$. The next two elements represent the widths and heights of the N patches respectively, where $W_i=\langle w_{i,0}, w_{i,1}, ..., w_{i,N-1}\rangle$ and$H_i=\langle h_{i,0}, h_{i,1}, ..., h_{i,N-1}\rangle$. It is important to note that the size of the patches were uniform due to the results presented in [29], therefore, the weights and heights of each patch were equivalent. The final two elements in the six-tuple represent the masking values of each patch, where $M_i=\langle m_{i,0}, m_{i,1}, ..., m_{i,N-1}\rangle$, and wheref_i is the fitness for fe_i. The masking values determine whether a patch is activated or deactivated.

Next, the fitness function shown in Equation 7 is used to evaluate each candidate FE based on its performance on the training and validation sets, where γ represents the percentage of image space (measured in pixels) covered by fe_i.

$$f_i=10\varepsilon+\gamma \tag{7}$$

To evaluate the candidate FEs, eachfe_i is applied to the probe and gallery sets in both the training and validation set to create feature vectors (FVs) for the images. The resulting FVs for the probe and gallery sets are then compared using the Manhattan Distance measure. The subject associated with the template within the gallery set with the smallest Manhattan distance when compared to the probe is considered the match.

The best performing FE on the validation set is then stored and will be referred to as FE^*. As with $GEFeWS_{ML}$, the top 50% best performing candidate FMs, based on their performance on the training set, are used to create a PDF. The PDF is then sampled to create $(1\text{-}\alpha)Q$ offspring, where α = 5%. The offspring are then evaluated based on their performance on the training and validation sets. Any offspring FE that outperforms FE^* becomes the new FE^*. Finally, a new population is formed using the $(1\text{-}\alpha)Q$offspring and the αQ elites. This evolutionary process is then continued until a user-specified stopping condition has been satisfied, after which two FEs are returned: the best performing FE on the training set, FE^{ts}, and FE^*. The returned FEs are then applied to the test set to evaluate how well they generalize to unseen instances in comparison to the SLBPM.

3.4. Darwinian-Based Feature Extraction (DFE) using Random Clustering

Darwinian-based Feature Extraction (DFE) [27] is a two-stage process for developing FEs to be used for facial recognition. In the first stage, a set of FEs evolved by $GEFE_{ML}$ are superimposed onto each other to create a hyper FE. From this hyper FE, a probability distribution function (PDF) is created which is essentially a two-dimensional array that represents the number of times a certain pixel is selected for use by the set of FEs. In the second stage of the process, a Darwinian-based FE (dFE) is created by sampling the PDF via k-tournament selection [62]. This dFE can be represented as a 3-tuple, $\langle c, \mu, \rho \rangle$, where c is the number of clusters in the dFE, μ is the selection pressure of tournament selection, and ρ is the resolution of the clusters. To create a dFE, first a number of pixels,$c \times \beta \times \rho$, where β represents the user-specified number of pixels per cluster, are selected from the PDF for use in the clustering process. Pixels are selected for use via k-tournament selection in which k = μ*σ pixels, where σ represents the total number of positions in the PDF that have been processed at least once, compete for selection. The pixel with the greatest consistency (i.e. the pixel that was used the most by the set of FEs) will be considered the winner of the tournament and will not be allowed to win again. Next, *c* locations within an image are randomly selected to serve as cluster centers. The pixels that were selected for use are then assigned to their closest cluster center. The SLBPM is then applied to the clustered pixels in a manner similar to how the SLBPM is traditionally applied to pixels within a patch. Afterwards, the histograms associated with each cluster are concatenated and are used as the feature vectors for the given images.

3.5. Darwinian-Based Feature Extraction using Kohonen and K-Means Clustering (DFE_{K+KM})

Darwinian Feature Extraction-Clustering [28] usingK-means[55] and Kohonen[56] clustering (DFE_{K+KM}) works as follows. First, Kohonen clustering is applied in the following manner. The algorithm iterates though each of the pixels selected for use, moving the nearest cluster center towards the given pixel. The distance that the center is moved is based on a user specified learning rate. For example, given a learning rate of 0.25, the magnitude that the center is moved would be 25% of the distance between the current pixel and the center. After iterating through all of the pixels, the distance between each center's starting and ending position is calculated. If the locations of the centers have not moved or a user-specified number of iterations have occurred, the Kohonen clustering process is halted. K-Means clustering is then applied to the resulting clusters in the following manner.First, each pixel selected for use via tournament selection is assigned to one of the *K* clusters centers determined by the Kohonen clustering process. Once each pixel has been assigned, the positions of the K centers are recalculated based on the average of the pixels assigned to that center. Once each of the centers has been repositioned, the distance between their old and new position is measured. When the positions of the centers remain constant, the K-Means clustering process is considered complete. The SLBPM is then applied to the clustered pixels and the histograms associated with each cluster are concatenated and are used as the feature vectors for the given images.

4. Experimental Results

4.1. Databases

For our experiments, images were selected from two diverse databases: the Face Recognition Grand Challenge (FRGC) database [52] and the Craniofacial Longitudinal Morphological Face (MORPH) database [53]. The images within the two facial databases were acquired in different manners. The images within the FRGC database were collected in a controlled setting (i.e. controlled lighting, frontal pose, and neutral facial expression) and were acquired in a single sitting. In contrast, the images in the MORPH database were collected in an uncontrolled setting, were acquired over a period of time, and were of diverse ethnicities.

From the FRGC database, 489 subjects were selected. From the MORPH database, 300 subjects were selected. From the subjects selected from each database, three datasets were formed: a training set, a validation set, and a test set. The FRGC datasets were as follows: 163 of the subjects were used to form the training set, which will be referred to as FRGC-163_{trn}; An additional 163 subjects were used to form the validation set, which will be referred to as FRGC-163_{val}; The remaining 163 subjects were used to form the test set, which will be referred to as FRGC-163_{tst}. The MORPH datasets were as follows: 100 subjects were used to form the training set, which will be referred to as MORPH-100_{trn}; 100 subjects were used to form the validation set, which will be referred to as MORPH-100_{val}; the remaining 100 subjects were used to form the test set, which will be referred to as MORPH-100_{tst}.

For each of the facial datasets, three frontal facial images of each subject were selected and used to form the probe and gallery sets. The probe sets consisted of one image per subject, and the gallery sets consisted of the remaining two images per subject. The SLBPM was then used to extract 1416 (24 patches × 59 bins) facial features from each image and served as the baseline for our experiments.

Using these datasets, we performed two experiments. For the first experiment, each GEBA was used to evolve FMs or FEs for the FRGC and MORPH facial templates within the training sets. This will be referred to as '*Opt*' because we are attempting to maximize the recognition accuracy while minimizing the percentage of features used. The resulting FMs/FEs were then applied to the test sets in order to evaluate how well they generalized to unseen subjects within the respective test sets. The application of the FM/FE that performed best on the training set (i.e. FM^{ts} and FE^{ts}) will be referred to as '*Opt-Gen*' because we are evaluating the generalization ability of these FMs/FEs. Similarly, the application of the best performing FM or FE on the validation set (i.e. FM^{ts} and FE^{ts})will be referred to as '*Val-Gen*' because we are evaluating how well these FMs and FEs generalize.

For the second experiment, we evaluated the cross-generalization ability of the resulting FMs/FEs for each GEBA. To do so, the FMs/FEs returned for the FRGC templates were applied to the MORPH test set and the FMs/FEs returned for the MORPH templates were applied to the FRGC test set.

4.2. Results

The results of our experiments were generated as follows. The SLBPM was applied to the training and test sets for the variousdatabases. Its performance served as the baseline for our experiments.

$GEFeWS_{ML}$ was run 30 times on the FRGC, MORPH, and DLFW datasets. The EDA evolved a population of 20 FMs and always retained 5 (α=25%) elites. A maximum of 1000 function evaluations were allowed for each run, and at the end of each run, the best performing FM on the training set, FM^{ts}, and the best performing FM on the validation set, FM^{*}, were returned. These FMs were then applied to their respective test set in order to evaluate their generalization performances.

REFE analyzed the FMs evolved by $GEFeWS_{ML}$for the three datasets. The $GEFeWS_{ML}$ evolved FMs were used to create a number of FEs. For each dataset, 62 PPVs were created (31 corresponding to the FM^{ts}s and 31 corresponding to the FM^{*}s). These PPVs were used to create FMs based on patch position and percentage of features used.The resulting FMs were then applied to their respective test set in order to evaluate their generalization performances.

$GEFE_{ML}$ was also run 30 times on the datasets, evolved a population size of 20 FEs, always retained one elite, and allowed a maximum of 1000 function evaluations per run. At the end of each run, $GEFE_{ML}$ returned the best performing FE on the training set (FE^{ts}), and the best performing FE with respect to the validation set (FE^{*}). The resulting FEs were then applied to the test sets in order to evaluate how well they generalized to the test sets.

To construct a hyper FE, DFE used the 30 FE^{*}s evolved by $GEFE_{ML}$ for the FRGC, MORPH, and DLFW datasets. To test DFE on FRGC, dFEs were created with c values of 16, 12 and 8. These values were chosen based on the average number of patches activated in the 30 FE^{*}s validated on FRGC-163_{val}, which was 16; c values of 12 and 8 came from 75% and 50% of 16 clusters. For each c,a ρ of 100% to 10% was used, using every tenth percentage in between. A selection pressure from 100% to 0% was also used, using every tenth percentage.

To test DFE on MORPH, dFEs were created with c values of 13, 10, and 7. These values were chosen based on the average number of patches activated in the *30* FE^{*}s validated on MORPH-100_{val}, which was 13; c values of 10 and 7 came from 75% and 50% of 16 clusters. For each c,a ρ of 100% to 10% was used, using every tenth percentage in between. A selection pressure from 100% to 0% was also used, using every tenth percentage.

http://dx.doi.org/10.5772/51386

To test the performance of DFE_{K+KM}, the best hyper FEs from both FRGC (using $c = 16$) and MORPH (using $c= 13$) were used in the Kohonen clustering process. The results from Kohonen clustering were then used for K-Means clustering. This process was performed for each of the 30 DFE runs. The resulting feature extractors were then applied to the FRGC and MORPH test sets.

The performances of these methods were separated into equivalence classes using ANOVA and t-tests based on their average recognition accuracy, the percentage of features used, and their computational complexity, which is the number of pixels processed or extracted by each method. Those methods that achieved higher recognition rates, used a lower percentage of features, and had a reduced computational complexity, were considered to be best.

4.2.1. Experiment I

The results of our first experiment are shown in Tables 1 and 2. Table 1 shows the performances of the GEBAs on the FRGC dataset. Table 2 shows the performances of the GEBAs on the MORPH dataset. Within each table, the first column represents the methods, where the asterisk denotes the performance of the GEBAs on the training set. The second column represents the average recognition accuracy for each method. The third column represents the average computational complexity of each method, and the final column represents the average percentage of features used by each method.Note that for the SLBPM, the accuracy was deterministic. In addition, the results for REFE were the performances of the best performing FMs.

With respect to $GEFeWS_{ML}$, the FMs evolved for the training set used an average of 45.02% of the features to achieve a higher recognition rate than the SLBPM. The FRGC Opt-Gen and Val-Gen performances show that the resulting FMs generalized well to the test set. When the generalization performances were compared, the Val-Gen performance was better in terms of accuracy, while the Opt-Gen performance used a lower percentage of features. This may be due to the need for more features for adequate generalization.

REFE performed well on FRGC-163_{tst}. The best performing FM created by analyzing the FM^{ts}s evolved by $GEFeWS_{ML}$ achieved a 93.84% recognition rate while using only 29.16% (7 patches) of the features. The best performing FM created by analyzing the FM^{*}s achieved a higher recognition rate of 94.46% using the same percentage of features. Although REFE did not outperform the SLBPM in terms of recognition accuracy, it's important to note that it significantly reduced the computational complexity of feature extraction by reducing the number of patches from 24 to 7.

In terms of recognition accuracy and feature usage, $GEFE_{ML}$ outperformed the SLBPM on FRGC-163_{trn} and FRGC-163_{tst}. However, the average computational complexity of the FEs evolved by $GEFE_{ML}$ was higher than the computational complexity of the SLBPM. This is due to the fact that the patches within the evolved FEs had a large amount of overlap. This overlap resulted in an increased number of pixels to be processed and, consequently, an increase in computational complexity. Though the computational complexities for FEs evolved by $GEFE_{ML}$ were larger, they were selected due to their superior recognition accuracy when compared to the SLBPM. When the performances of the FE^{ts}s were compared to the FE^{*}s in terms of recognition accuracy, the FE^{*}s (Val-Gen) performed statistically better than the FE^{ts}s (Opt-Gen).

For FRGC-163_{tst}, DFE outperformed the SLBPM in terms of recognition accuracy as well as computational complexity. The recognition accuracy for DFE on FRGC-163_{tst} was 97.24% and the computational complexity was approximately 10% less than the SLBPM.

DFE_{K+KM} also outperformed SLBPM in terms of recognition accuracy and computational complexity. This method achieved a recognition accuracy of 97.20% on FRGC-163_{tst}. Because the hyper FE from DFE was used, it had the same computational complexity as DFE.

When the performances of the GEBAs on the test set were compared in terms of accuracy, DFE and DFE_{K+KM}outperformed the other GEBAs. However, in terms of feature usage and computational complexity, REFE performed best.

Method	Accuracy	Comp. Complexity	% of Features
SLBPM (Training)	92.02%	10379	100.00%
SLBPM (Test)	95.09%	10379	100.00%
$GEFeWS_{ML}$ (Opt)*	97.63%	10379	45.02%
$GEFeWS_{ML}$(Opt-Gen)	94.42%	10379	45.02%
$GEFeWS_{ML}$ (Val-Gen)	94.58%	10379	48.45%
REFE (Opt-Gen)	93.84%	3027	29.16%
REFE (Val-Gen)	94.46%	3027	29.16%
$GEFE_{ML}$ (Opt)*	96.85%	11776	66.67%
$GEFE_{ML}$ (Opt-Gen)	96.64%	11776	66.67%
$GEFE_{ML}$ (Val-Gen)	96.87%	11776	66.67%
DFE (HFE_{val}on Test Set)	97.24%	9011	66.67%
DFE_{K+KM}	97.20%	9011	66.67%

Table 1. FRGC Results.

$GEFeWS_{ML}$ outperformed the SLBPM on MORPH-100_{trn}, using significantly fewer features while significantly increasing the recognition rate over the SLBPM. In addition, the resulting FMs generalized well to the test set. In terms of accuracy, the Val-Gen performances performed better statistically than the Opt-Gen performance. However, the Opt-Gen performances used a lower percentage of features in comparison to the Val-Gen performances.

The REFE created FMs performed well on MORPH-100_{tst}. The best performing FM created with respect to the FM^{ts}s outperformed the SLBPM, achieving a 70.95% recognition rate while using only 41.66% of the features and significantly reducing the computational complexity by using only 10 patches. The best performing FM created with respect to the FM*s also performed well on the test set, achieving a recognition accuracy that was slightly lower than the SLBPM while using only 29.16% (7 patches) of the features.

$GEFE_{ML}$ outperformed the SLBPM on MORPH-100_{trn} and MORPH-100_{tst}. The FE^{ts}s had an average 39.66% recognition accuracy when applied on MORPH-100_{trn}, which was significantly better than the recognition accuracy achieved by the SLBPM. Like the FEs trained on FRGC, the average computational complexities of the FEs were also higher than for the SLBPM. The computational complexity of evolved FEs on the MORPH set were much higher due to the overlap as well as the large dimensions of the patches.However, FEs were still chosen primarily because of the recognition accuracy. In addition, when the performances of the FE^{ts}s were compared to the FE*s in terms of recognition accuracy, the FE*s performed better.

DFE outperformed the SLBPM in terms of recognition accuracy, computational complexity, and feature usage. DFE achieved a recognition rate of 59.73% while having a computational complexity close to 50% less than the SLBPM.

DFE_{K+KM} also outperformed the SLBPM in terms of recognition accuracy, computational complexity, and feature usage. This method achieved a recognition rate of 62.07% while having a computational complexity reduction of nearly 50% with respect to SLBPM.

Comparing the generalization performances of the GEBAs, REFE outperformed the other GEBAs in terms of recognition accuracy, computational complexity, and feature usage.

Method	Accuracy	Comp. Complexity	% of Features
SLBPM (Training)	27.00%	10379	100.00%
SLBPM (Test)	70.00%	10379	100.00%
$GEFeWS_{ML}$ (Opt)*	39.53%	10379	45.99%
$GEFeWS_{ML}$ (Opt-Gen)	61.67%	10379	45.99%
$GEFeWS_{ML}$ (Val-Gen)	64.30%	10379	48.61%
REFE (Opt-Gen)	70.95%	4324	41.66%
REFE (Val-Gen)	67.98%	3027	29.16%
$GEFE_{ML}$ (Opt)*	39.66%	20034	58.33%
$GEFE_{ML}$ (Opt-Gen)	44.37%	20034	58.33%
$GEFE_{ML}$ (Val-Gen)	57.67%	11050	54.17%
DFE (HFE_{val}on Test Set)	59.73%	5525	54.17%
DFE_{K+KM} (HFE_{val}on Test Set)	62.07%	5525	54.17%

Table 2. MORPH Results.

4.2.2. Experiment II

Tables 3 and 4 show the results of our second experiment. Table 3 presents the cross-generalization performances of the MORPH FMs/FEs on the FRGC test set, while Table 4 presents the cross-generalization performances of the FRGC FMs/FEs on the MORPH test set. The first column of each table represents the methods, the second column represents the average recognition accuracy, the third column represents the average computational complexity of each method, and the final column represents the average percentage of features used by each method. As for Experiment I, for the SLBPM, the accuracy was deterministic and the results shown for REFE were the performances of the best performing FMs.

With respect to $GEFeWS_{ML}$, the FM^{ts}s and FM^{*}s evolved for the MORPH dataset generalized well to the FRGC test set. Although the average accuracy waslower than the SLBPM and lower than the results presented in Table 1, it is important to note that the FMs were optimized for the MORPH dataset, while the SLBPM and FMs used for Experiment I were applied directly to and trained on the FRGC test set. In addition, the FMs used less than 50% of the features in contrast to the SLBPM which used 100% of the features. When the Opt-Gen and Val-Gen performances were compared, in terms of accuracy, Val-Gen performed than Opt-Gen. However, Opt-Gen used fewer features.

Method	Accuracy	Comp. Complexity	% of Features
SLBPM (Test)	95.09%	10379	100.00%
$GEFeWS_{ML}$(Opt-Gen)	92.70%	10379	45.99%
$GEFeWS_{ML}$ (Val-Gen)	93.72%	10379	48.61%
REFE (Opt-Gen)	72.97%	4324	41.66%
REFE (Val-Gen)	68.97%	3027	29.16%
$GEFE_{ML}$ (Opt-Gen)	88.41%	20034	58.33%
$GEFE_{ML}$ (Val-Gen)	93.37%	11050	54.17%
DFE (HFE_{val}on Test set)	94.66%	5525	54.17%
DFE_{K+KM}	93.82%	5525	54.17%

Table 3. MORPH to FRGC Cross-Generalization Results.

The best performing FMs created by REFE for the MORPH dataset did not generalize well to $FRGC\text{-}163_{tst}$. Neither FMs outperformed the SLBPM in terms of recognition accuracy. However, the best performing FM with respect to the FM^{ts}s achieved a 72.97% recognition rate while using only 41.66% of the features and while having a more than 50% lower computational complexity. The best performing FM with respect to the FM^{*}s achieved a 68.97% recognition rate while using only 29.16% of the features and also having a 50% lower computational complexity. This reduction in features and processing time (in terms of computational complexity) is important to highlight, especially since the SLBPM was applied directly to the test set.

With respect to $GEFE_{ML}$, the recognition accuracyof the SLBPM was superior to the average accuracy of both the FE^{ts}s as well as the FE^{*}s. However, the percentage of features for $GEFE_{ML}$was 50% less than the SLBPM. The Val-Gen recognition accuracy was also statistically greater than the Opt-Gen accuracy, and the computational complexity was less for Val-Gen than for Opt-Gen.

For DFE, the recognition accuracy was slightly lower than the accuracy of the SLBPM. However, the percentage of features used by DFE, as well the computational complexity of DFE, was far less than for the SLBPM.

DFE_{K+KM} performed well on FRGC-163_{tst}, achieving a recognition rate slightly lower than the SLBPM while having a nearly 50% lower computational complexity and feature usage.

Comparing the cross-generalization performances of the GEBAs, DFE cross-generalized best to the FRGC dataset. The dFEs achieved recognition rates comparable to the SLBPM, while using significantly fewer features and requiring less processing time.

When the FMs evolved by $GEFeWS_{ML}$for FRGC were applied to the MORPH test set, they did not outperform the SLBPM, which was applied directly to the test set. However, the performances of the FM^{ts}s evolved for FRGC were better statistically than the Opt-Gen results presented in Table 2. In addition, the Val-Gen performances for both experiments were statistically equivalent.

The best performing FMs created by REFE for FRGC generalized well to the MORPH test set. The FMs outperformed the SLBPM in terms of accuracy, computational complexity, and feature usage.

With respect to $GEFE_{ML}$, the recognition accuracyof the SLBPM was superior to the average accuracy of both the FE^{ts}sand FE^{*}s. However, there is still a reduction in the percentage of features used by $GEFE_{ML}$. The Val-Gen recognition accuracy was still statistically greater than the Opt-Gen accuracy, though the computational complexity remained the same. The recognition accuracy resulting from cross-generalizing FEs on the MORPH dataset is greater than the accuracy of generalizing FEs in Experiment I.

The recognition accuracy of DFE was less than the recognition accuracy of the SLBPM. However, the percentage of features used by DFE, as well as the computational complexity, was far less than the percentage of feature for the SLBPM.

DFE_{K+KM} outperformed the SLBPM in terms of accuracy, computational complexity, and feature usage. The GEBA achieved a 71.12% recognition rate, while using only 66.67% of the features and processing fewer pixels.

Comparing the performances of the SLBPM and the GEBAs, REFE was the best performing technique, generalizing well to the test set, while processing less than 50% of the available pixels and using less than 30% of the features.

Method	Accuracy	Comp. Complexity	% of Features
SLBPM (Test)	70.00%	10379	100.00%
$GEFeWS_{ML}$ (Opt-Gen)	65.19%	10379	45.02%
$GEFeWS_{ML}$ (Val-Gen)	65.60%	10379	48.45%
REFE (Opt-Gen)	72.98%	3027	29.16%
REFE (Val-Gen)	71.14%	3027	29.16%
$GEFE_{ML}$ (Opt-Gen)	64.76%	11776	66.67%
$GEFE_{ML}$ (Val-Gen)	65.63%	11776	66.67%
DFE (HFE_{val}on Test set)	62.57%	9011	66.67%
DFE_{K+KM}	71.12%	9011	66.67%

Table 4. FRGC to MORPH Cross-Generalization Results.

5. Discussion

In Experiment I, we showed that the GEBAs could evolve FEs and FMs that achieve accuracies comparable to the performance of the SLBPM on the test sets, while using significantly fewer features and a using a lower computational complexity. To further analyze the performances of the GEBAs, the Receiver Operator Characteristic (ROC) curve for the performance of the best FMs/FEs on the test sets were plotted in Figures 2 and 3. The ROC curves for $GEFeWS_{ML}$ were created using the normalized Weighted Manhattan Distance(NwMD) formula shown in Equation 8, and the ROC curves for $GEFE_{ML}$ were created using the normalized Manhattan Distance(NMD) formula shown in Equation 9. For these formulas, h_i and h_j are the feature templates being compared, fm_l is the $GEFeWS_{ML}$ evolved FM, z is the zth featurewithin the templates, n is the total number of extracted features, andthe function f_{WS}, asshown in Equation 5, represents the process of feature weighting/selection as performed by $GEFeWS_{ML}$. The ROC charts plot the true accept rate (y-axis) to the false accept rate (x-axis). For a given threshold from 0.0 to 1.0, all images in the probe dataset were compared to all images in the gallery dataset. If the NMD of the probe image and gallery image was below the threshold, it was considered a match. The true accept rate was increased if the two matching images were of the same subject, while the false accept rate was increased if the images were not of the same subject.

$$NwMD_{WS}(h_i, h_j, fm_l)=\sum_{z=0}^{n-1}\frac{|h_{i,z}-h_{j,z}|f_{WS}(u_{i,z})}{\max(h_{i,z}, h_{j,z})f_{WS}(u_{i,z})} \quad (8)$$

$$NMD(h_i, h_j)=\sum_{z=0}^{n-1}\frac{|h_{i,z}-h_{j,z}|}{\max(h_{i,z}-h_{j,z})} \quad (9)$$

Figures 2 and 3 show the ROC curves of the SLBPM, and the best performing FM^{ts}, FM^{*}, FE^{ts}, and FE^{*} on FRGC-163_{tst} and MORPH-100_{tst} respectively. The evolved FMs and FEs seem to perform comparable to the SLBPM while using significantly fewer features. It also appears that the FEs perform better than the SLBPM and the FMs on both datasets.

In addition, Figure 4 shows the graph of the accuracy of the best performing REFE created FMs on FRGC-163_{tst} and MORPH-100_{tst}. By using only the patches that correspond to the highest feature usages, one can achieve recognition accuracies better than using all 24 patches as done by the SLBPM.

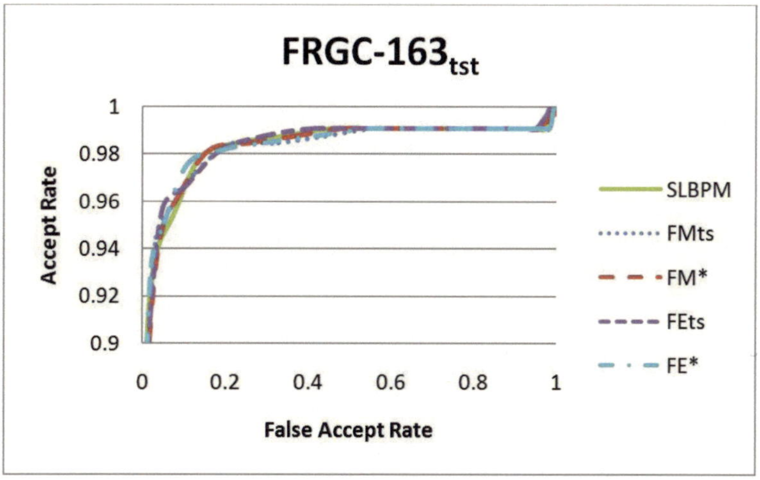

Figure 2. ROC curves for the SLBPM and the best performing FMs and FEs on FRGC-163_{tst}.

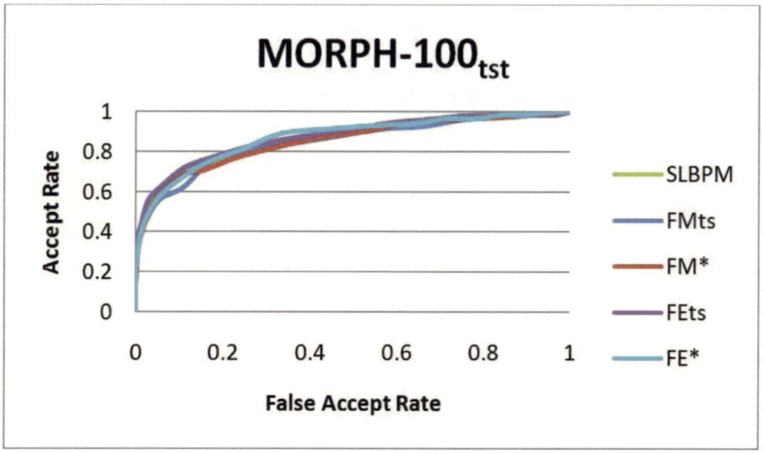

Figure 3. ROC curves for the SLBPM and the best performing FMs and FEs on MORPH-163_{tst}.

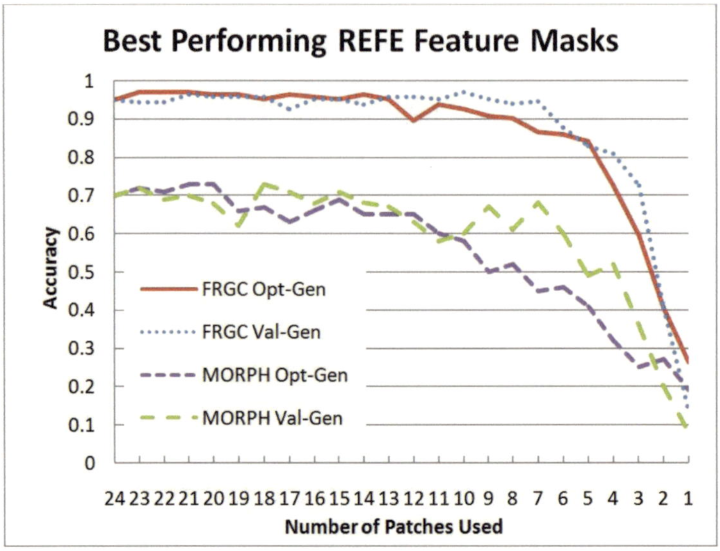

Figure 4. Performance of the best REFE feature masks for FRGC and MORPH test sets.

6. Conclusions and Further Work

In conclusion, we presented several GEBAs for feature selection/weighting and for feature extraction. The GEBAs were applied to images of subjects taken from two facial. The resulting FMs/FEs developed for each database were then applied to instances of each unrelated database to test the notion of cross-generalization. Our results showed that the GEBAs achieved recognition rates comparable to the SLBPM while using significantly fewer features and a considerably lower computational complexity.

Further work will be devoted towards the use of these GEBAs to develop more secure biometric systems.

Acknowledgements

This research was funded by the Office of the Director of National Intelligence (ODNI), Center for Academic Excellence (CAE) for the multi-university Center for Advanced Studies in Identity Sciences (CASIS) and by the National Science Foundation (NSF) Science & Technology Center: Bio/computational Evolution in Action CONsortium (BEACON). The authors would like to thank the ODNI and the NSF for their support of this research.

Author details

Aniesha Alford[1], Joseph Shelton[2*], Joshua Adams[2], Derrick LeFlore[2], Michael Payne[2], Jonathan Turner[2], Vincent McLean[2], Robert Benson[2], Gerry Dozier[2], Kelvin Bryant[2] and John Kelly[1]

*Address all correspondence to: jasheltl@ncat.edu

1 Department of Electrical and Computer Engineering, North Carolina A&T State University, USA

2 Department of Computer Science, North Carolina A&T State University, USA

References

[1] Davis, L. (1991). Handbook of genetic algorithms. Van Nostrand Reinhold, New York.

[2] Dozier, G., Homaifar, A., Tunstel, E., & Battle, D. (2001). An Introduction to Evolutionary Computation (Chapter 17). Intelligent Control Systems Using Soft Computing Methodologies, A. Zilouchian& M. Jamshidi (Eds.), CRC press , 365-380.

[3] Engelbrecht, A. P. (2007). Computational Intelligence: An Introduction,. John Wiley & Sons, Ltd.

[4] Fogel, D. (1995). Evolutionary Computation: Toward a New Philosophy of Machine Intelligence,. IEEE Press.

[5] Nolfi, S., & Floreano, D. (2000). Evolutionary robotics- the biology, intelligence, and technology of self-organizing machines. In: Intelligent Robotics and Automation Agents. MIT Press Cambridge, MA.

[6] Dahal, K. P., Tan, K. C., & Cowling, P. I. (2007). Evolutionary Scheduling. Springer Verlag 978-3-54048-582-7 pages., 628.

[7] Miranda, E. R., & Biles, J. A. (2007). Evolutionary Computer Music. Springer-Verlag, New York, Inc., Secaucus, NJ, USA.

[8] Dasgupta, D. (1999). An overview of artificial immune systems and their applications. In Dasgupta, D., editor, Artificial Immune System and Their Applications Springer-Verlag , 3-23.

[9] Shelton, J., Bryant, K., Abrams, S., Small, L., Adams, J., Leflore, D., Alford, A., Ricanek, K., & Dozier, G. (2012). Genetic & Evolutionary Biometric Security: Disposable Feature Extractors for Mitigating Biometric Replay Attacks. *Proceedings of the 10th Annual Conference on Systems Engineering Research (CSER).*

[10] Shelton, J., Dozier, G., Adams, J., & Alford, A. (2012). Permutation-Based Biometric Authentication Protocols for Mitigating Replay Attacks. Paper presented at Proceedings of the 2012 IEEE World Congress on Computational Intelligence (WCCI).

[11] Shelton, J., Adams, J., Alford, A., Venable, M., Neal, S., Dozier, G., & Bryant, K. (2012). Mitigating Replay Attacks Using Darwinian-Based Feature Extraction. *IEEE Symposium on Computational Intelligence for Security and Defense Applications.*

[12] Goldberg, D. E. (1989). Genetic Algorithms in Search, Optimization & Machine Learning. Addison-Wesley Publishing Company, Inc., Reading, Massachusetts.

[13] Kennedy, J., Eberhart, R. C., & Shi, Y. (2001). *Swarm Intelligence*, Morgan Kaufmann.

[14] Nolfi, S., & Floreano, D. (2000). Evolutionary Robotics:The Biology, Intelligence and Technology of Self-Organizing Machines. MIT Press.

[15] Vadakkepat, P., Chen, Tan. K., & Ming-Liang, W. (2000). Evolutionary artificial potential fields and their application in real time robot path planning. *Proceedings of the 2000 Congress on Evolutionary Computation*, 256-263, 1.

[16] Hoffmann, F., & Pfister, G. (1997, November). Evolutionary design of a fuzzy knowledge base for a mobile robot. *International Journal of Approximate Reasoning*, 17(4), 447-469.

[17] Harvey, I., Husbands, P., Cliff, D.., Thompson, A., & Jakobi, N. (1997, June). Evolutionary robotics: the Sussex approach. *Robotics and Autonomous Systems*, 20(2-4), 205-224.

[18] Bentley, P. J. (1999). Evolutionary design by computers. San Francisco, Morgan Kaufmann.

[19] Gargiulo, A. A., Schnell, A. R., Tinker, M. L., Dozier, G., & Garrett, A. (2000). Use of Evolutionary Computation for Three-Dimensional Structural Design of a Lunar Habitat. http://nxt.ncat.edu/pdf/Use%20of%20EC_for_Prelim_Struct_Design_Lunar_Habitat.pdf.

[20] Dozier, G., Carnahan, B., Seals, C., Kuntz, L. A., & Ser-Geon, Fu. (2005). An interactive distributed evolutionary algorithm (IDEA) for design. 2005 IEEE International Conference on Systems, Man and Cybernetics, 10-12 Oct , 1, 418-422.

[21] Miranda, E. R. (2004). At the Crossroads of Evolutionary Computation and Music: Self-Programming Synthesizers, Swarm Orchestras and the Origins of Melody. *Evolutionary Computation*, 12(2), 137-158.

[22] Murata, T., Ishibuchi, H., & Tanaka, H. (1996, September). Multi-objective genetic algorithm and its applications to flowshop scheduling. *Computers & Industrial Engineering*, 30(4), 957-968.

[23] Hart, E., Ross, P., & Corne, D. (2005). Evolutionary Scheduling: A Review. *Genetic Programming and Evolvable Machines*, 6(2), 191-220.

[24] Dahal, K. P., Tan, K. C., & Cowling, P. I. (2007). Evolutionary Scheduling. *Springer Berlin /Heidelberg*, 317-330.

[25] Alford, A., Steed, C., Jeffrey, M., Sweet, D., Shelton, J., Small, L., Leflore, D., Dozier, G., Bryant, K., Abegaz, T., Kelly, J. C., & Ricanek, K. (2012). Genetic & Evolutionary Biometrics: Hybrid Feature Selection and Weighting for a Multi-Modal Biometric System. *IEEE SoutheastCon 2012.*

[26] Shelton, J., Alford, A., Abegaz, T., Small, L., Leflore, D., Williams, J., Adams, J., Dozier, G., Bryant, K., Ricanek, K., & Woodard, D. L. (2012). Genetic & Evolutionary Biometric Security: Feature Extraction from a Machine Learning Perspective. *IEEE SoutheastCon 2012.*

[27] Shelton, J., Venable, M., Neal, S., Adams, J., Alford, A., & Dozier, G. (2012). *Pixel Consistency, K-Tournament Selection, and Darwinian-Based Feature Extraction, Midwest Artificial Intelligence and Cognitive Science (MAICS) Conference.*

[28] Adams, J., Shelton, J., Small, L., Venable, M., Neal, S., Kim, J., & Dozier, G. (2012). Darwinian-based Feature Extraction using K-means and Kohonen Clustering. Paper presented at Midwest Artificial Intelligence and Cognitive Science (MAICS) Conference.

[29] Shelton, J., Dozier, G., Bryant, K., Smalls, L., Adams, J., Popplewell, K., Abegaz, T., Woodard, D., & Ricanek, K. (2011). Genetic and Evolutionary Feature Extraction via X-TOOLSS. in The 8th Annual International Conference on Genetic and Evolutionary Methods (GEM).

[30] Alford, A., Bryant, K., Abegaz, T., Dozier, G., Kelly, J., Shelton, J., Small, L., Williams, J., & Woodard, D. L. (2011). Genetic & Evolutionary Methods for Biometric Feature Reduction. Special Issue on: "Computational Intelligence in Biometrics: Theory, Methods and Applications", Guest Editor: Qinghan Xiao, International Journal of Biometrics.

[31] Alford, A., Adams, J., Shelton, J., Bryant, K., Kelly, J. C., & Dozier, G. (2012). Analyzing the Cross-Generalization Ability of a Hybrid Genetic & Evolutionary Application for Multibiometric Feature Weighting and Selection. *Genetic and Evolutionary Computation Conference (GECCO-2012).*

[32] Ojala, T., Pietikainen, M., & Harwood, D. (1996). A comparative study of texture measures with classification based on feature distributions. *Pattern Recognition, 29*, 51-59.

[33] Ojala, T., Pietikainen, M., & Mäenpää, T. (2002). MultiresolutionGray-scale and Rotation Invariant Texture Classification with Local Binary Patterns. *Proceedings of IEEE Trans. Pattern Analysis and Machine Intelligence*, 24(7), 971-987.

[34] Marcel, S., Rodriguez, Y., & Heusch, G. (2006). On The Recent Use of Local Binary Patterns for Face Authentication. *International Journal of Image and Video Processing-Special Issue on Facial Image Processing*, 1-9.

[35] Galbally, J., Fierrez, J., Freire, M., & Ortega-Garcia, J. (2007). Feature Selection Based on Genetic Algoirthms for On-Line Signature Verification. Paper presented at IEEE Workshop on Automatic Identification Advanced Technologies Alghero, Italy. 198-203.

[36] Ramadan, R. M., & Abdel-Kader, R. F. (2009, June). Face Recognition Using Particle Swarm Optimization-Based Selected Features. *International Journal of Signal Processing, Image Processing and Pattern Recognition*, 2(2).

[37] Abegaz, T., Dozier, G., Bryant, K., Adams, J., Mclean, V., Shelton, J., Alford, A., Ricanek, K., & Woodard, D. L. (2011). Applying GECs for Feature Selection and Weighting using X-TOOLSS". *The 8th Annual International Conference on Genetic and Evolutionary Methods(GEM).*

[38] Alford., A., Popplewell, K., Dozier, G., Bryant, K., Kelly, J., Adams, J., Abegaz, T., Shelton, J., Woodard, D. L., & Ricanek, K. (2011). Hybrid GEMs for Multi-Biometric Recognition via X-TOOLSS. *The 8th Annual International Conference on Genetic and Evolutionary Methods (GEM).*

[39] Adams, J., Dozier, G., Bryant, K., Shelton, J., Alford, A., Abegaz, T., & Leflore, D. (2012, 15-18 March). Neurogenetic Reconstruction of Biometric Templates: A New Security Threat? Paper presented at IEEE Southeast Con 2012, Orlando, FL.

[40] Garcia- Ortega, J., Fierrez-Aguilar, J., Simon, D., Gonzalez, J., Faundez-Zanuy, M., Espinosa, V., Satue, A., Hernaez, I., Igarza, J. J., Vivaracho, C., Escudero, C., & Moro, Q. I. (2003, December). MCYT baseline corpus: a bimodal biometric database. *IEEE Proc. Vis. Image Signal Process.*, 150(6), 395-401.

[41] AT&T Laboratories Cambridge. (2000). ORL Face Database. http://www.cl.cam.ac.uk/research/dtg/attarchive/facedatabase.html.

[42] Ahmed, N., Natarajan, T., & Rao, K. R. (1974, Jan). Discrete Cosine Transform. *IEEE Transactions on Computers*, C-23(1), 90-93.

[43] Shensa, M. J. (1992, Oc). The Discrete Wavelet Transform: Wedding the À Trous and Mallat Algorithms. *IEEE Transactions on Signal Processing*, 40(10), 2464-2482.

[44] Kumar, D., Kumar, S., & Rai, C. S. (2009). Feature selection for face recognition: a memetic algorithmic approach. *Journal of Zhejanga University Science A*, 10(8), 1140-1152.

[45] Neri, F., Cotta, C., & Moscato, P. (2012). Handbook of Memetic Algorithms. *Studies in Computational Intelligence*, Springer, 379.

[46] PAMI. (2001). The Extended Yale Face Database B. http://vision.ucsd.edu/~leekc/ExtYaleDatabase/ExtYaleB.html.

[47] Jollife, I. T. (1986). *Principal Component Analysis.*, New York, Springer-Verlag.

[48] Mika, S., Ratsch, G., Weston, J., Scholkopf, B., & Mullers, K. R. (1999, Aug). Fisher discriminant analysis with kernels," Neural Networks for Signal Processing IX, 1999.

Paper presented at Proceedings of the 1999 IEEE Signal Processing Society Workshop. 41-48.

[49] Schölkopf, B., Smola, A., & Müller, K. R. (1997). Kernel Principal Component Analysis. *ARTIFICIAL NEURAL NETWORKS- ICANN'97, Lecture Notes in Computer Science*, 1327, 583-588.

[50] Larrañaga, P., & Lozano, J. A. (2002). Estimation of Distribution Algorithms: A new tool for evolutionary computation. Springer.

[51] Turk, M., & Pentland, A. (1991). Eigenfaces for recognition. *Journal of Cognitive Neuroscience*, 13(1), 71-86.

[52] Phillips, P. J., Flynn, P. J., Scruggs, T., Bowyer, K. W., Chang, J., Hoffman, K., Marques, J., Min, J., & Worek, W. (2005). Overview of face recognition grand challenge. Paper presented at Proc. IEEE Conference on Computer Vision and Pattern Recognition.

[53] Ricanek, K., & Tesafaye, T. (2006, April 10-12.) MORPH: A Longitudinal Image Database of Normal Adult Age-Progression". Paper presented at Proceedings of the 7th International Conference on Automatic Face and Gesture Recognition. 341-345.

[54] Mitchell, T. M. (1997). *Machine Learning*, McGraw-Hill Companies, Inc.

[55] Kanungo, T., Mount, D., Netanyahu, N., Piatko, C., Silverman, R., & Wu, A. (2002, July). An Efficient k-Means Clustering Algorithm: Analysis and Implementation. *IEEE Transactions on Pattern Analysis and Machine Intelligence*, 24(7).

[56] Kohonen, T. (1990). The self-organising map. *Proceedings IEEE*, 78(9), 1464-1480.

[57] Specht, D. F. (1991, Nov). A general regression neural network. *IEEE Transactions on Neural Networks*, 2(6), 568-576.

[58] Miller, P. E., Rawls, A. W., Pundlik, S. J., & Woodard, D. L. (2010). Personal identification using periocular skin texture. Proceedings of the 2010 ACM Symposium on Applied Computing (SAC'10). ACM, New York, NY, USA, 1496-1500.

[59] Srensen, L., Shaker, S. B., & de Bruijne, M. (2010, Feb). Quantitative analysis of pulmonary emphysema using local binary patterns. *IEEE Transactions on Medical Imaging*, 29(2), 559-569.

[60] Unay, D., Ekin, A., Cetin, M., Jasinschi, R., & Ercil, A. (2007, August 23-26,). Robustness of Local Binary Patterns in Brain MR Image Analysis. Paper presented at Proceedings of the 29th Annual International Conference of the IEEE Engineering in Medicine and Biology Society (EMBS), Lyon, France,. 2098-2101.

[61] Woodard, D., Pundlik, S., Lyle, J., & Miller, P. (2010). Periocular region appearance cues for biometric identification. CVPR Workshop on Biometrics. San Francisco, CA , 162-169.

[62] Miller, B. L., & Goldberg, D. E. (1996, June). Genetic algorithms, selection schemes, and the varying effects of noise. *Evol. Comput*, 4(2), 113-131.

Section 2

Performance Evaluation

Chapter 6

Performance Evaluation of Automatic Speaker Recognition Techniques for Forensic Applications

Francesco Beritelli and Andrea Spadaccini

Additional information is available at the end of the chapter

http://dx.doi.org/10.5772/52000

1. Introduction

Speaker recognition is a biometric technique employed in many different contexts, with various degrees of success. One of the most controversial usage of automatic speaker recognition systems is their employment in the forensic context [1, 2], in which the goal is to analyze speech data coming from wiretappings or ambient recordings retrieved during criminal investigation, with the purpose of recognizing if a given sentence had been uttered by a given person.

Performance is one of the fundamental aspects of an FASR (Forensic Automatic Speaker Recognition) system. It depends strongly on the variability in the speech signal, noise and distortions in the communications channel. The recognition task faces multiple problems: unconstrained input speech, uncooperative speakers, and uncontrolled environmental parameters. The speech samples will most likely contain noise, may be very short, and may not contain enough relevant speech material for comparative purposes. In automatic or semi-automatic speaker recognition, background noise is one of the main causes of alteration of the acoustic indexes used in the biometric recognition phase [3, 4]. Each of these variables makes reliable discrimination of speakers a complicated and daunting task.

Typically the performance of a biometric system is determined by the errors generated by the recognition. There are two types of errors that can occur during a verification task: (a) false acceptance when the system accepts an imposter speaker; and (b) false rejection when the system rejects a valid speaker. Both types of errors are a function of the decision threshold. Choosing a high threshold of acceptance will result in a secure system that will accept only a few trusted speakers, however, at the expense of high false rejection rate (FRR) or False Non Match Rate (FNMR). Similarly choosing a low threshold would make the system more user friendly by reducing false rejection rate but at the expense of high false acceptance rate (FAR) or False Match Rate (FMR). This trade-off is typically depicted using a decision-error trade-off (DET) curve. The FAR and FRR of a verification system define different operating points on the DET curve.

In general, to understand what are the causes that contribute most to the total error of an FASR system, it is important to evaluate the performance of individual blocks or phases of the system. Knowing the impact on the performance of individual subsystems of a speaker recognition algorithm (manual, semiautomatic or automatic) allows us to understand what aspects should be better cared for if you want to achieve the performance targets required by the FASR system.

As of the writing of this document, semi-automatic speaker recognition techniques are still employed in Italian courts; this means that an expert witness analyzes the speech data with the aid of some *ad hoc* software, that usually gives the freedom to change some parameters that can affect the final outcome of the identification.

It is obvious that human errors can lead to wrong results, with disastrous consequence on the trial.

In this chapter, we will analyze how efficiently and reliably can state-of-the-art speaker recognition techniques be employed in this context, what are their limitations and their strengths and what must be improved in order to migrate from old-school manual or semi-automatic techniques to new, reliable and objective automatic methods.

It is well-known that speech signal quality is of fundamental importance for accurate speaker identification [5]. The reliability of a speech biometry system is known to depend on the amount of available data, in particular on the number of vowels present in the sequence being analysed, and the quality of the signal [6]; the former affects the resolution power of the system, while the latter impacts the correct estimation of biometric indexes.

In this chapter, we will analyze the behaviour of some speaker recognition techniques when the environment is not controlled and the speech sequences are disturbed by background noise, a very frequent condition in real-world forensic data.

This chapter is organized as follows: in Section 2 we will describe the baseline speaker recognition systen and the speech and noise databases used for the experiments; in Section 3 we will analyze the performance of two Signal-to-Noise (SNR) estimation algorithms; in Section 4 we will analyze the performance of a speaker recognition toolkit; in Section 5 we will analyze the impact of Voice Activity Detection (VAD) algorithms on the recognition rates; finally, in Section 6 we will draw our conclusions.

2. Baseline speaker recognition system and speech/noise databases

2.1. Alize/LIA_RAL

The speaker verification system used in all the experiments is based on ALIZE/LIA_RAL , that is described in this section.

The ALIZE/LIA_RAL toolkit is developed jointly by the members of the ELISA consortium [8], and consists of two separate components: Alize, that is the low-level statistical framework, and LIA_RAL, that is the set of high-level utilities that perform each of the tasks of a state-of-the-art speaker recognition system. The latter is also sometimes referred to as Mistral[9].

One of its main advantages is the high level of modularity of the tools: each program does not directly depend on the others and the data between the modules is exchanged via text

http://dx.doi.org/10.5772/52000

files whose format is simple and intuitive. This means that researchers can easily change one of the components of the system with their own program, without having to modify its source code but only adhering to a set of simple file-based interfaces.

In this section, we will briefly describe all the components of a typical experiment that uses the ALIZE/LIA_RAL toolkit.

2.1.1. Feature extraction

LIA_RAL does not contain any module that performs feature extraction; all the experiments in this chapter used the Speech Signal Processing Toolkit (SPro) [10] for feature extraction tasks. SPro allows to extract different types of features, using filter-banks, cepstral analysis and linear prediction.

2.1.2. Frames selection

The second step of the recognition process is to remove the frames that do not carry useful information. When dealing with the speech signal, this task is carried on by VAD algorithms, some of which will be described in Section 5. Each of these VAD algorithms was implemented by a different program, and their output was always converted to a format that is compatible with the LIA_RAL toolkit.

The default VAD algorithm in LIA_RAL, described in Section 5.3, is implemented in the utility *EnergyDetector*.

2.1.3. Feature normalization

The third step is the feature normalization, that changes the parameters vectors so that they fit a zero mean and unit variance distribution. The distribution is computed for each file.

The tool that performs this task is called *NormFeat*.

2.1.4. Models training

To use the UBM/GMM method [11], it is necessary to first create a world model (UBM), that represents all the possible alternatives in the space of the identities enrolled in the system; then, from the UBM, the individual identity templates are derived from the UBM using the Maximum A-Posteriori (MAP) estimation algorithm.

The tool used for the computation of the UBM is *TrainWorld*, while the individual training models are computed using *TrainTarget*.

2.1.5. Scoring

The computation of scores is done via the *ComputeTest* program, that scores each feature set against the claimed identity model and the UBM, and gives as output the log-likelihood ratio.

In order to take a decision, the system has then to compare the score with a threshold, and then accept or reject the identity claim. The decision step is implemented in LIA_RAL utility *Scoring*, but in this chapter we have not used it.

2.2. The TIMIT speech database

All the speaker recognition experiments described in this chapter use as a speech database a subset of the TIMIT (Texas Instrument Massachusetts Institute of Technology) database, that will be briefly described in this section.

The TIMIT database contains speech data acquired from 630 people, that are split in subsets according to the Dialect Region to which each of them belongs. Each DR is further split in training and test set. The number of speakers contained in each DR, and their division in training and test set are reported in Table 1.

Dialect Region	Total	Training	Test
New England (DR1)	49	38	11
Northern (DR2)	102	76	26
North Midland (DR3)	102	76	26
South Midland (DR4)	100	68	32
Southern (DR5)	98	70	28
New York City (DR6)	46	35	11
Western (DR7)	100	77	23
Moved around (DR8)	33	22	11
Totals:	630	462	168

Table 1. Composition of the TIMIT data set

This database was explicitly designed to provide speech researchers with a phonetically rich dataset to use for research in speech recognition, but it is widely adopted also in the speaker recognition research community.

It contains three types of sentences, dialectal (SA), phonetically-compact (SX) and phonetically diverse (SI). The total number of spoken sentences is 6300, 10 for each of the 630 speakers. There is some superposition between speakers, because there are sentences that are spoken by more than one person. Each person, however, has to read 2 SA sentences, 5 SX sentences and 3 SI sentences.

The database also contains annotations about the start and end points of different lexical tokens (phonemes, words and sentences). This was especially useful for the research on SNR and VAD, because we could compare our algorithms with ground truth provided by the database itself.

2.3. The noise database

The noise database comprises a set of recordings of different types of background noise, each lasting 3 minutes, sampled at 8 kHz and linearly quantized using 16 bits per sample. The types of noise contained in the database fall into the following categories:

- **Car**, recordings made inside a car;

- **Office**, recordings made inside an office during working hours;
- **Factory**, recordings made inside a factory;
- **Construction**, recordings of the noise produced by the equipment used in a building site;
- **Train**, recordings made inside a train;

3. Performance evaluation of SNR estimation algorithms

In forensics, one of the most widely adopted methods to assess the quality of the intercepted signal is based on the estimation of the Signal to Noise Ratio (SNR), that should not be lower than a critical threshold, usually chosen between 6 and 10 dB [6]. It is possible to estimate the SNR using manual or semi-automatic methods. Both of them exploit the typical ON-OFF structure of conversations, which means that on average there are times when there is a speech activity (talkspurt) and times when nobody is talking, and the signal is mainly composed by environmental noise recorded by the microphone (background noise). With manual methods, the SNR is estimated choosing manually the segment of talkspurt and the segment of background noise immediately before or after the talkspurt. The estimation is computed by the following formula:

$$SNR_{est} = \frac{P_{talk} - P_{noise}}{P_{noise}} \tag{1}$$

Semi-automatic estimation methods use a Voice Activity Detection (VAD) algorithm that separates the ON segments from the OFF segments in a given conversation, and use those segments to estimate the SNR [12, 13].

Both algorithms do not give an exact value of the SNR, because the noise sampled for the SNR estimation is different from the noise that degraded the vocal segment for which the SNR is being estimated. This happens because the noise level can be measured only when the speakers are not talking, in an OFF segment.

Sometimes the estimation error causes the elimination of good-quality data (under-estimation of the SNR), while sometimes it causes the usage of low-quality biometric data that was probably corrupted by noise in the subsequent identification process (over-estimation of the SNR)

In this section, we will discuss about the accuracy of the SNR estimation methods, comparing their average estimation error to the real SNR.

3.1. Speech and background noise database

In this experiment, we used speech data coming from 100 people, half female and half male, randomly selected from the DR1 subset of the TIMIT database

The 10 sentences spoken by each person, sampled at 8 kHz and linearly quantized using 16 bits per sample, have been used to produce a clean conversation composed by talkspurt segments (ON) normalized to an average power level of $-26dB_{ovl}$ and silence segments (OFF). The ON-OFF statistics were chosen using the model proposed in [14].

We used 4 kinds of background noise: Car, Office, Stadium, Construction.

For each type of noise, the clean sequence was digitally summed to the noise, in order to get sequences with four different real SNRs in the activity segments: 0, 10, 20 and 30 dB.

3.2. SNR estimation methods

Both analyzed SNR estimation methods exploit the manual phonetic marking offered by the TIMIT database. In particular, for the sake of simplicity, we selected a restricted subset of vowel sounds ("ae", "iy", "eh", "ao"), of which only the central 20 ms were considered.

The manual SNR estimation method computes the estimated SNR as the ratio between the power of the signal of the current vowel, (P_{talk}) lasting 20ms, to the power of noise, (P_{noise}), measured at the nearest OFF segment and lasting 20 ms. The classification of the signal in ON and OFF segments is done manually.

The semi-automatic method uses the VAD algorithm to automatically classify ON and OFF segments. The VAD used is the one standardized by the ETSI for the speech codec AMR [15]. In this case, the noise power is measured using the nearest OFF segment classified by the VAD.

The values obtained by the two algorithms have then been compared to the real SNR, computed as the ratio between the power of the vowel measured on the clean signal and the power of the background noise measured in the same temporal position but on the noise sequence.

3.3. Results

The first analysis that we present is the computation of the average estimation errors. In each subplot, two axis represent the SNR and the vowel, while the third one represents the average estimation error.

Figure 1 shows the average estimation error for the manual method, while Figure 2 shows the same error, but for the semi-automatic method.

The performance of both methods are similar for the Car and Noise, with an average error between 3 and 5 dB of difference with the reference SNR.

A comparison of the errors reveals that the usage of the automatic method increases the average error by 1 dB in case of the Car, Construction and Office noises, while the increase is larger (between 2 and 5 dB) for the Stadium noise.

Even though the VAD impact on the SNR estimation depends on the type of noise, it however does not lead to heavily poorer performance because on average the error grows by only 1-2 dB.

In both cases, when the reference SNR is 0 dB it can be seen that the "iy" vowel is subject to a high sensitivity for each kind of noise. The average estimation error generally is larger by 20-30% with respect to the other vowels.

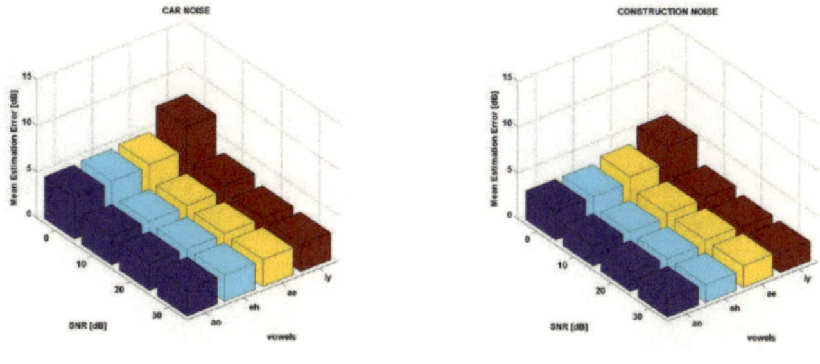

(a) Car, Construction

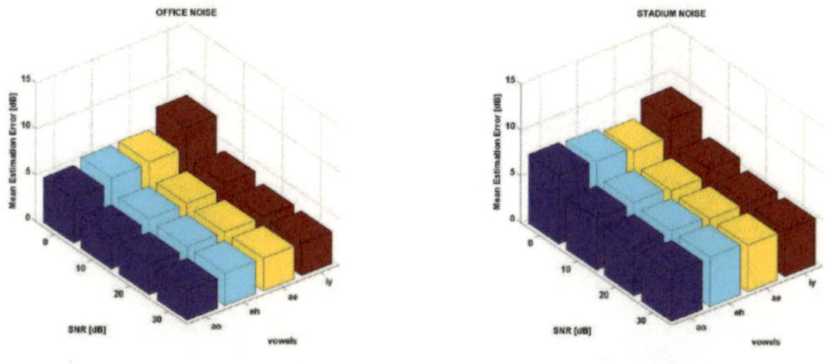

(b) Office, Stadium

Figure 1. Average SNR estimation errors for the manual method

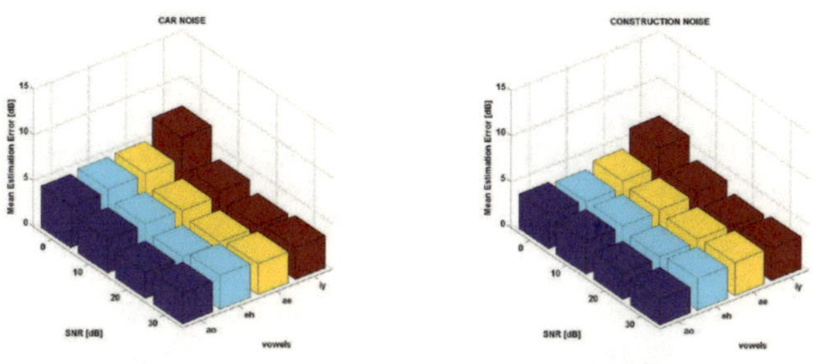

(a) Car, Construction

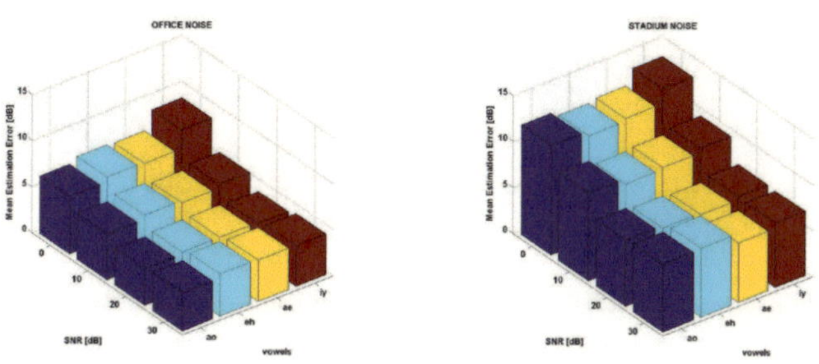

(b) Office, Stadium

Figure 2. Average SNR estimation errors for the semi-automatic method

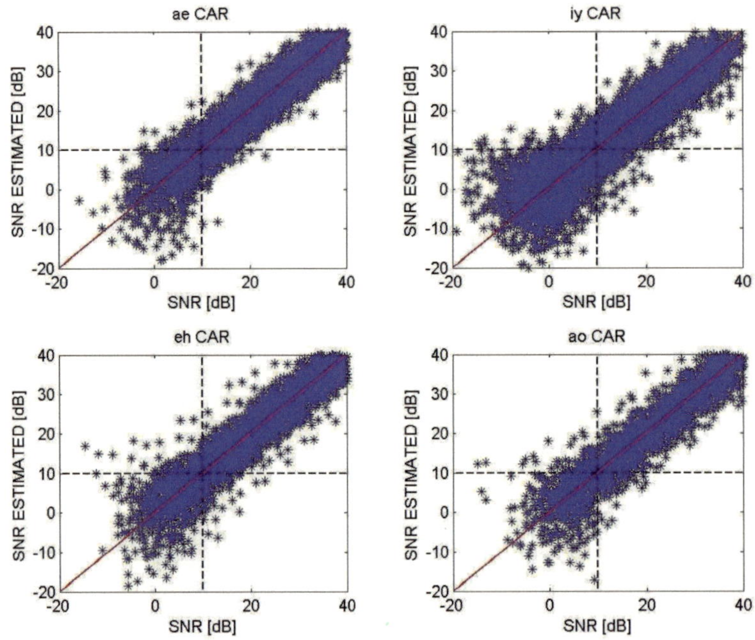

(a) Car

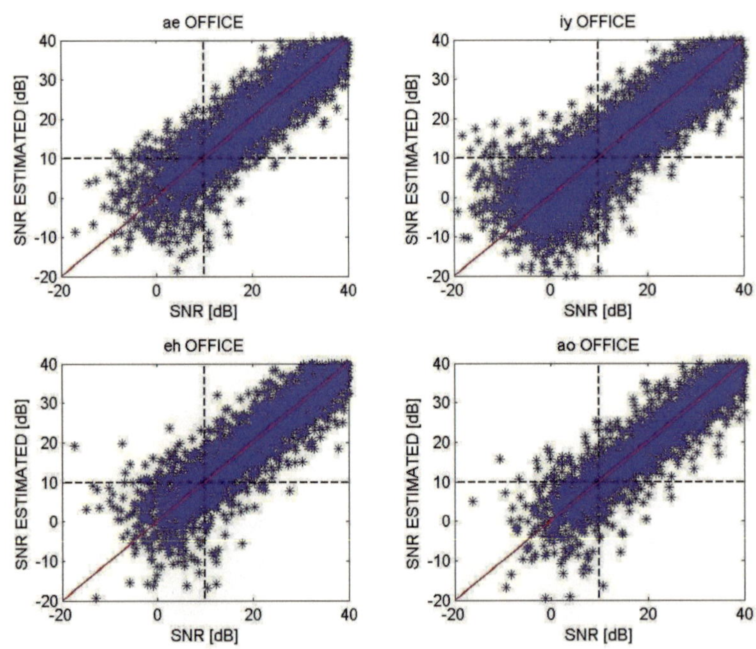

(b) Office

Figure 3. Real vs. estimated SNR, manual method

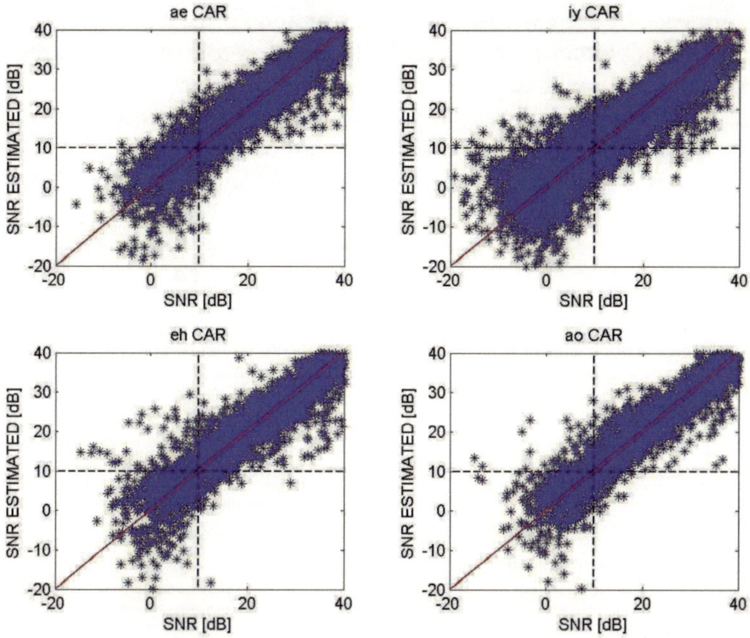

(a) Car

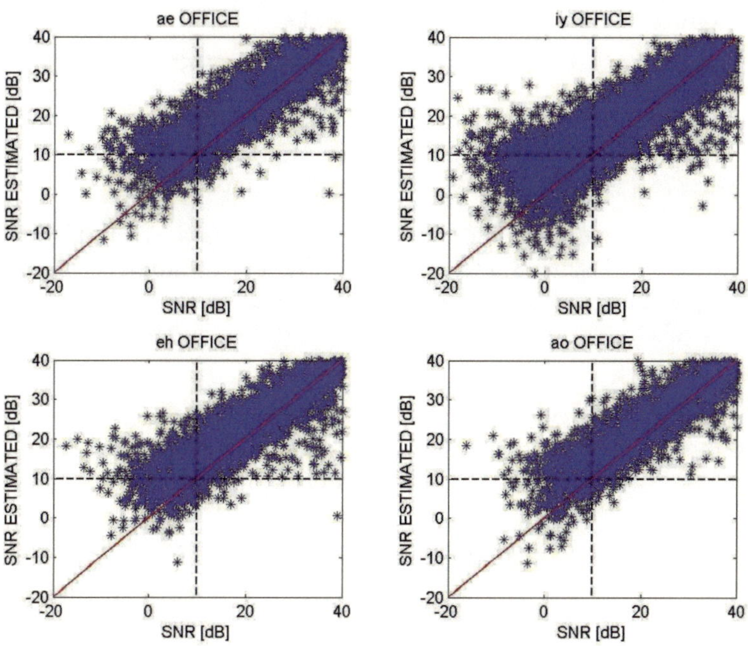

(b) Office

Figure 4. Real vs. estimated SNR, semi-automatic method

The plots in Figure 3 and Figure 4 show the correlation between the real SNR and the estimated SNR for each of the 4 vowels in case of Car and Office noise. If we assume a critical threshold for rejecting a biometric sample of 10 dB, it is possible to outline 4 regions in each of these plots: the upper-left one, that encompasses data erroneously used because the SNR was over-estimated; the lower-right region, that comprises data erroneously discarded because the SNR was under-estimated, and the remaining regions (upper-right and lower-left), that contain data that were correctly discarded or used for the subsequent identity verification phases.

Car noise	**ae**	**iy**	**eh**	**ao**
Bad data used	15.39%	11.63%	15.34%	16.82%
Good data discarded	5.49%	6.75%	4.49%	4.91%
Office noise	**ae**	**iy**	**eh**	**ao**
Bad data used	22.14%	14.95%	21.76%	17.70%
Good data discarded	5.97%	7.97%	6.41%	6.00%

Table 2. Percentage errors for the manual method

Car noise	**ae**	**iy**	**eh**	**ao**
Bad data used	18.56%	15.42%	18.11%	18.77%
Good data discarded	4.94%	6.86%	4.61%	4.33%
Office noise	**ae**	**iy**	**eh**	**ao**
Bad data used	60.45%	42.70%	58.55%	56.46%
Good data discarded	2.35%	3.28%	1.53%	1.59%

Table 3. Percentage errors for the semi-automatic method

Tables 2 and 3, respectively, for manual and semi-automatic methods, show the error percentages depicted in Figure 3 and Figure 4. The semi-automatic method induces an increment of the percentage of low-quality data that is used for subsequent elaboration for the Office noise, while the percentages for the Car noise are similar to the ones of the manual method.

In the end, comparing the percentage of low-quality data erroneously used, it can be deduced that each vowel reacts in different ways: for instance, the “iy” vowel is one of the most robust. A similar comparison can be carried out in terms of high-quality data erroneously discarded.

4. Performance evaluation of Alize-LIA_RAL

In this section we present a study on how a speaker recognition system based on the Alize/LIA_RAL toolkit behaves when the data is affected by background noise. In particular, the section shows both the performance using a "clean" database and the robustness to the degradation of various natural noises, and their impact on the system. Finally, the impact of the duration of both training and test sequences is studied.

http://dx.doi.org/10.5772/52000

4.1. Speech and background noise database

For this experiment, we used the training portion of the DR1 TIMIT subset, that contains 38 people.

We generated the clean and noisy databases using the same protocol described in Section 3.1.

4.2. Performance evaluation and results

In order to verify the performance of our system, we computed the genuine match scores and the impostor match scores for different types of noises and signal-to-noise ratio (SNR). The Detection Error Trade-off of each test case is shown in the following figures.

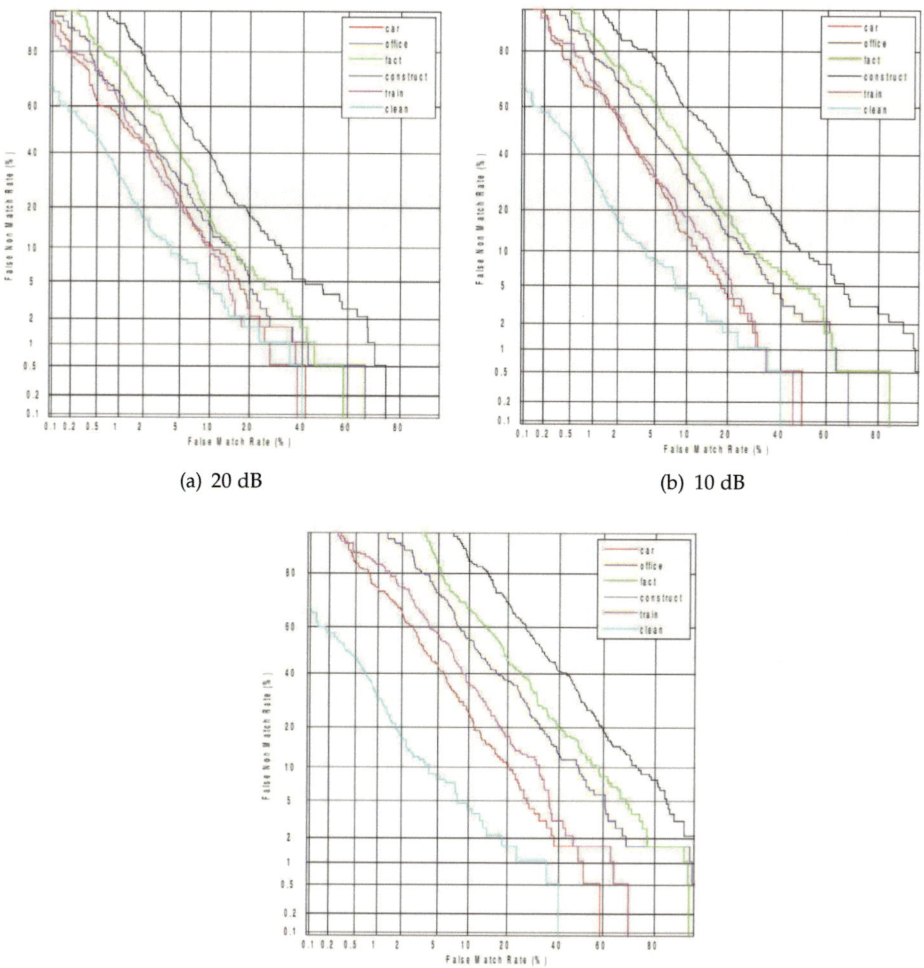

(a) 20 dB

(b) 10 dB

(c) 0 dB

Figure 5. DET vs. Noise type

Figures 5 compare the performance on the basis of noise type for: (a) SNR=20 dB, (b) SNR=10 dB, (c) SNR=0 dB. In all cases we can notice major performance degradation after raising the noise level volume and a different impact on the system performance made by various noise types. In particular, car noise has less impact (EER=13 %) while construction noise is the most degrading noise type (EER=24 %). Algorithm performance in clean sequences points out an EER value of about 8 %, so the impact of the noise compromises the performance for EER percentage basis ranging from 5 to 15 %.

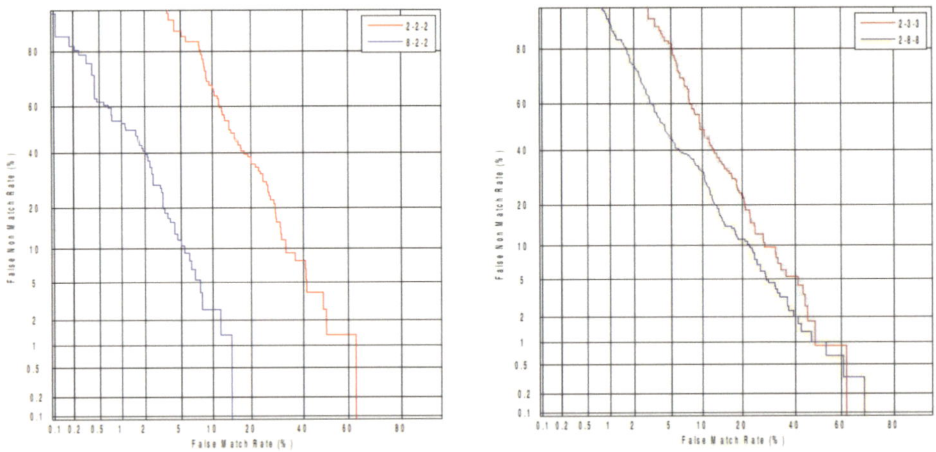

(a) 2-2-2 vs. 8-2-2

(b) 2-3-3 vs. 2-8-8

Figure 6. Training length vs. test length

Another important result is the discovered relation about the recognition performance and the duration of the training and testing sequences. Figure 6(a) compares the DET achieved using clean sequences spanning the following durations:

- 2 training sequences (duration 6,24 sec), 2 true test sequences (duration 6,24 sec) and 2 false test sequences (6,24 sec);
- 8 training sequences (duration 25 sec), 2 true test sequences (6,24 sec) and 2 false test sequences (6,24 sec);

In this case the real impact of the training duration on the total system performance is evident.

Figure 6(b) shows the opposite case where a different duration of the test sequences is applied, in particular:

- 2 training sequences (duration 6,24 sec), 3 true test sequences (duration 9,36 sec) and 3 false test sequences (9,36sec);
- 2 training sequences (6,24 sec), 8 true test sequences (25 sec) and 8 false test sequences (25 sec).

http://dx.doi.org/10.5772/52000

In this case the different durations of the test sequences does not have much impact and the performance are very similar. Therefore, from this result it emerges that, for automatic speaker recognition, it is better to use longer duration sequences for training and shorter duration sequences for testing.

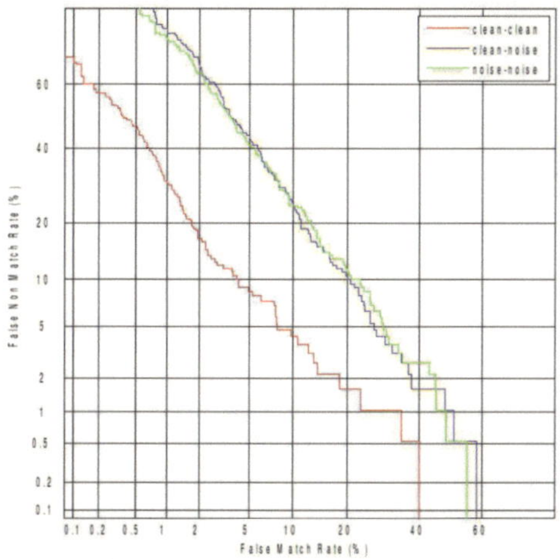

Figure 7. Clean-clean, Clean-Noisy, Noisy-Noisy

Finally, Figure 7 compares system performance in three different modalities: comparison of clean type training and testing sequences, comparison of clean training sequence and degraded testing sequence by car noise with SNR 0dB, and comparison of training and testing sequences both degraded by car noise with SNR 0dB. Analysing the three DET curves it is possible to see that employing one noisy sequence in the training phase does not contribute to the improvement of the performance, which remains similar to the clean-noisy case. Generally, we can therefore conclude that speaker identification performance is sensitive to the degradation of one of the compared sequences (phonic test and testing).

5. Performance evaluation of voice activity detection algorithms

The performance of biometric speaker verification systems is largely dependent on the quality level of the input signal [11]. One of the most important components of such a system is the Voice Activity Detection (VAD) algorithm, as it has the duty of separating speech frames and noise frames, discarding the latter and feeding the speech frames to the rest of the system. This task becomes quite challenging as the Signal-to-Noise Ratio (SNR) of the input signal goes down [12] [13].

A VAD algorithm can use many techniques to classify speech and noise, such as an energy threshold or the analysis of the spectral characteristics of the audio signal. Due to these differences, different algorithms can behave differently in a given noise condition, and this is the reason for the study presented by this section.

The context in which we operate is the analysis of phone tappings in forensic investigations, and our task is to determine whether the conversation was carried on by a suspect or not. Those tappings are often noisy, so we generated from a speech database some audio files with the typical ON-OFF statistics of phone conversations and artificially added to them background noise in order to evaluate the performance of VAD algorithms and speaker identification at different SNR levels[3].

Our objective is to demonstrate that the usage of a single VAD is not the optimal solution, however, biometric identification performance can be improved by introducing a noise estimation component that can dynamically choose the best VAD algorithm for the estimated noise condition.

5.1. The speech database

For our task we selected a TIMIT subset composed by 253 speakers, namely the union of DR sets 1, 2 and 3. Of those speakers, 63 were destined to train the UBM and 190 were used to train the identity models and to compute the match scores. With those speakers, we obtained 190 genuine match scores and 35910 ($190 \cdot 189$) impostor match scores for each simulation.

The speech files were used to generate two one-way conversation audio files, each containing speech material from 5 speech files and with an activity factor of 0.4, using the algorithm described in Section 5.2. In the case of the UBM speakers, both sequences were processed for the training phase, while in the case of identity models one sequence was used for the model training and the other was used for the computation of match scores.

The whole database was downsampled to 8kHz, to better match the forensic scenario, and normalized to an average power level of -26dB_{ovl}.

5.2. Generation of one-way conversations

In order to simulate the forensic scenario, and to give realistic input data to the VAD algorithms, we generated for each speaker two audio files that mimic one side of a two-people conversation, inserting speech and pauses according to the model described in [16], that will now be briefly described.

According to this model, a conversation can be modelled as a Markov chain, whose state can be one of the following: A is talking, B is talking, Mutual silence, Double talk. A and B are the two simulated speakers.

The chain is depicted in Figure 8, along with the transition probabilities between the states.

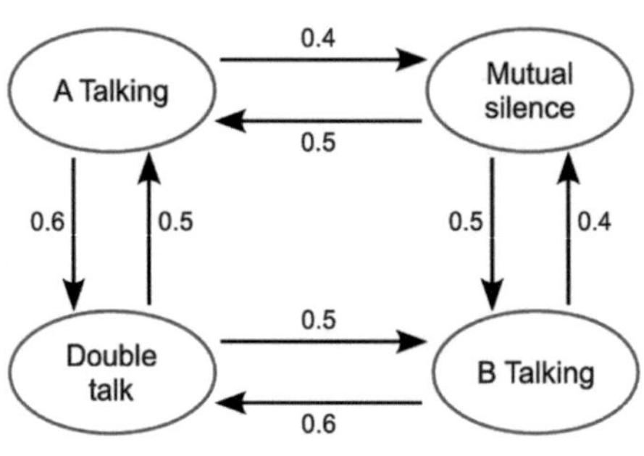

Figure 8. Markov chain used to generate the conversations

The permanence in each of these states is given by the following equations:

$$T_{st} = 0.854\ \ln(1 - x_1)$$
$$T_{dt} = 0.226\ \ln(1 - x_2)$$
$$T_{ms} = 0.456\ \ln(1 - x_3)$$

where $0 < x_1, x_2, x_3 < 1$ are random variables with uniform distribution. T_{st} is the permanence time in the states in which a single speaker is talking, T_{dt} is associated to the double talk state and T_{ms} is used for the mutual silence state.

This model represents a two-way conversation, but we are interested in generating speech for one of the two sides of the conversation. So when the model is in the state "A is speaking" or "Mutual talk", the generator adds speech material to the output sequence, while in the other two states the generator adds silence.

For this experiment, we used the Car, Office and Factory noises.

5.3. The LIA_RAL VAD

The LIA_RAL VAD is an energy-based off-line algorithm that works by training a GMM on the energy component of the input features. It then finds the Gaussian distribution with the highest weight w_i and uses its parameters to compute an energy threshold according to the following formula:

$$\tau = \mu_i - \alpha\sigma_i$$

where α is a user-defined parameter, and μ_i and σ_i are the parameters of the selected gaussian mixture Λ_i.

The energy threshold is then used to discard the frames with lower energy, keeping only the ones with a higher energy value.

5.4. The AMR VAD

The Adaptive Multi-Rate (AMR) Option 1 VAD [15] is a feature-based on-line algorithm that works by computing the SNR ratio in nine frequency bands, and decides which frames must be kept by comparing the SNRs to band-specific thresholds.

Note that this VAD is not optimized for speaker verification tasks, as it has the objective of minimizing the decision time, and it is designed to be used in real-time speech coding applications, while in a forensic biometric system the delay is not a significant parameter to minimize, and thus the VAD could use information from all the input signal to make its decision, as the LIA_RAL VAD does.

5.5. Evaluating VAD performance

In order to evaluate the VAD performance, we need to compare the results of the classification on a given input signal with a reference ideal classification that we know for sure to be correct.

In our experimental set-up, this ideal classification is derived by labelling the start and the end of speech segments generated by the model described in Section 5.2. This classification does not take into account pauses that can occur during the TIMIT spoken sentences, but it is a good approximation of an ideal classification.

The VAD classifier can misinterpret a given input frame in two ways: detecting a noise frame as speech (Noise Detected as Speech, NDS) or classifying a speech frame as noise (Speech Detected as Noise, SDN).

Those two errors are then further classified according to the position of the error with respect to the nearest word; see [17] for a discussion of those parameters.

For our analysis, we are not interested in the time when the misclassification occurs, as it is mainly useful when evaluating the perception effects of VAD errors [18], so we use the two NDS and SDN parameters, defined as follows for a single conversation:

$$
\begin{aligned}
NDS_{\%} &= \frac{N_{NDS} \cdot f}{C} \\
SDN_{\%} &= \frac{N_{SDN} \cdot f}{C}
\end{aligned}
$$

where N_{NDS} and N_{SDN} are, respectively, the number of NDS and SDN frames, f is the frame length expressed in seconds and C is the duration of the conversation expressed in seconds.

We then define a Total Error Rate (TER), as:

$$TER_{\%} = NDS_{\%} + SDN_{\%} \tag{2}$$

The TER is the percentage of audio frames that are misclassified by the VAD.

5.6. Experimental results

The starting point of our experiments is the creation of 9 noisy speech databases, obtained by summing to the one-way conversation speech database described in Section 5.2 the Car, Office and Factory noises, artificially setting the SNR to 20 dB, 10 dB and 0 dB.

Next the Equal Error Rate (EER) was computed over each database, first with the ideal segmentation and then by swapping this segmentation with the ones generated by the LIA_RAL VAD and by the AMR VAD, for a total of 27 simulations.

Finally, the VAD errors were computed using the metrics defined in Section 5.5.

http://dx.doi.org/10.5772/52000

In the clean case (Table 4), we reported the average $\overline{NDS_{\%}}$, $\overline{SDN_{\%}}$ and $\overline{TER_{\%}}$, computed over all the speech samples used to run the speech verification simulations, one time for each VAD algorithm (including the ideal VAD).

In the noisy cases (Tables 5, 6, 7), since for each VAD the simulation was run once for each SNR level, the reported VAD error metrics are the average of the average of the value of each metric (denoted with μ) computed over all the speech samples, and their standard deviations σ are reported in order to better understand the nature of the data presented. Obviously, the VAD errors of the ideal VAD are always zero, so the standard deviation is omitted from the tables.

5.7. Analysis of the results

VAD algorithm	EER (%)	$\overline{NDS_{\%}}$	$\overline{SDN_{\%}}$	$\overline{TER_{\%}}$
ideal	**3.76**	0	0	0
AMR	4.36	1.08	4.81	5.89
LIA_RAL	3.77	4.33	31.74	36.07

Table 4. Results for clean speech

	EER (%)			VAD Errors ($\mu \pm \sigma$, %)		
VAD	0dB	10dB	20dB	$\overline{NDS_{\%}}$	$\overline{SDN_{\%}}$	$\overline{TER_{\%}}$
ideal	5.77	3.60	3.55	0	0	0
AMR	**4.95**	**4.77**	**3.38**	7.30 ± 1.55	4.88 ± 0.34	12.18 ± 1.89
LIA_RAL	6.49	5.43	4.87	3.95 ± 0.12	34.38 ± 0.24	38.33 ± 0.36

Table 5. Results table for CAR noise

	EER (%)			VAD Errors ($\mu \pm \sigma$, %)		
VAD	0dB	10dB	20dB	$\overline{NDS_{\%}}$	$\overline{SDN_{\%}}$	$\overline{TER_{\%}}$
ideal	8.52	5.69	4.10	0	0	0
AMR	9.77	5.39	**3.75**	41.23 ± 5.24	5.08 ± 0.30	46.31 ± 5.53
LIA_RAL	**6.97**	**5.21**	4.00	0.83 ± 0.85	19.39 ± 3.52	20.22 ± 4.37

Table 6. Results table for OFFICE noise

Looking at Table 4, the first question is why the ideal segmentation yields an EER that is very close to the one that the LIA_RAL VAD obtained, in spite of a greater $\overline{TER_{\%}}$.

This is because the ideal segmentation does not focus only on vocalized sounds, that are known to carry the information that is needed to determine the identity of the speaker, but rather is an indicator of when the generator described in Section 5.2 introduced speech in the audio sequence. This therefore includes some sounds, like fricatives, that should be left out when doing biometric identity comparisons. This also explains the worse performance

	EER (%)			VAD Errors ($\mu \pm \sigma$, %)		
VAD	0dB	10dB	20dB	$\overline{NDS_{\%}}$	$\overline{SDN_{\%}}$	$\overline{TER_{\%}}$
ideal	7.84	5.01	4.70	0	0	0
AMR	7.27	**5.02**	**3.42**	13.64 ± 1.04	6.12 ± 1.33	19.76 ± 2.49
LIA_RAL	**6.58**	5.93	4.37	3.13 ± 1.44	16.87 ± 3.40	20.00 ± 4.84

Table 7. Results table for FACTORY noise

of the ideal VAD in other cases like OFFICE, FACTORY 0 dB, etc. Analyzing the average errors made by the VAD algorithms, it is clear that the AMR VAD usually tends to be more conservative in the decision of rejection of speech, because its $\overline{NDS_{\%}}$ is always greater than LIA_RAL's; on the other hand, LIA_RAL always has a greater $\overline{SDN_{\%}}$ than AMR, and this means that it tends to be more selective in the decision of classifying a frame as noise.

The results for the CAR noise show that the AMR VAD always performs better than the LIA_RAL VAD in terms of EER, and it is supported by a significantly lower TER.

The OFFICE noise results do not show a clear winner between the two algorithms, as for high SNR the AMR VAD performs better, but as the SNR decreases, the LIA_RAL algorithm outperforms the AMR VAD. A similar pattern can be seen in the FACTORY results.

6. Conclusions and future work

In this chapter, we analyzed many of the problems that currently affect forensic speaker recognition. It is clear from the results of the previous sections that there is still no universal approach for speaker recognition in forensic context, and also that this applies to some of the smaller sub-problems.

More specifically, some ideas for future work in the SNR estimation area are:

- develop more effective SNR estimation algorithms, that can guarantee a lower average error and, most importantly, lower variance;
- estimate SNR in the sub-bands of interest of the main biometric indices adopted [3], typically in the fundamental frequency and in the first three formants;
- identify the critical SNR thresholds for each vowel and for each kind of noise by evaluating the impact of the noise on the whole identification process;
- use automatic environmental noise classifiers that allow to choose an SNR estimation model and critical thresholds tailored to the kind of noise [13] [19]

Regarding the selection of VAD algorithms, in the forensic context, where accuracy is truly important and results can be collected off-line, multiple VAD algorithms with different characteristics could be used, and all the identification decisions computed using them could then be fused using a majority rule or other fusion rules. In those critical kinds of analysis, it would be important that most of the decisions agreed between them, or else the disagreement could be an indicator that the choice of the VAD algorithm has a greater weight than desired.

More broadly, based on the results of the research work described in this chapter, it is clear that both the SNR estimation and VAD algorithm selection problems could benefit from an adaptive approach that first estimates the characteristics of background noise and then select the algorithm that performs better in that context [20].

Author details

Francesco Beritelli* and Andrea Spadaccini

* Address all correspondence to: francesco.beritelli@dieei.unict.it

DIEEI Dipartimento di Ingegneria Elettrica Elettronica e Informatica, University of Catania, Italy

7. References

[1] Philip Rose. *Forensic Speaker Recognition.* Taylor and Francis, 2002.

[2] J.P. Campbell, W. Shen, W.M. Campbell, R. Schwartz, J.-F. Bonastre, and D. Matrouf. Forensic speaker recognition. *Signal Processing Magazine, IEEE*, 26(2):95 –103, march 2009.

[3] F. Beritelli. Effect of background noise on the snr estimation of biometric parameters in forensic speaker recognition. In *Proceedings of the International Conference on Signal Processing and Communication Systems (ICSPCS)*, 2008.

[4] Kichul Kim and Moo Young Kim. Robust speaker recognition against background noise in an enhanced multi-condition domain. *Consumer Electronics, IEEE Transactions on*, 56(3):1684 –1688, aug. 2010.

[5] J. Richiardi and A. Drygajlo. Evaluation of speech quality measures for the purpose of speaker verification. In *Proceedings of Odyssey, The Speaker and Language Recognition Workshop*, 2008.

[6] M. Falcone, A. Paoloni, and N. De Sario. Idem: A software tool to study vowel formant in speaker identification. In *Proceedings of the ICPhS*, pages 145–150, 1995.

[7] T. May, S. van de Par, and A. Kohlrausch. Noise-robust speaker recognition combining missing data techniques and universal background modeling. *Audio, Speech, and Language Processing, IEEE Transactions on*, 20(1):108 –121, jan. 2012.

[8] The ELISA consortium. The elisa consortium, the elisa systems for the nist'99 evaluation in speaker detection and tracking. *Digital Signal Processing*, 10, 2000.

[9] Eric Charton, Anthony Larcher, Christophe Levy., and Jean-Francois Bonastre. Mistral: Open source biometric platform, 2010.

[10] G. Gravier. SPro: speech signal processing toolkit, 2003.

[11] Douglas A. Reynolds and Richard C. Rose. Robust text-independent speaker identification using gaussian mixture speaker models. *IEEE Transactions on Speech and Audio Processing*, 3:72–83, 1995.

[12] F. Beritelli, S. Casale, and S. Serrano. A low-complexity speech-pause detection algorithm for communication in noisy environments. *European Transactions on Telecommunications*, 15:33–38, January/February 2004.

[13] F. Beritelli, S. Casale, and S. Serrano. Adaptive v/uv speech detection based on acoustic noise estimation and classification. *Electronic Letters*, 43:249–251, February 2007.

[14] P. T. Brady. A model for generating on-off speech patterns in two-way conversation. *Bell Syst. Tech. J.*, pages 2445–2472, September 1969.

[15] ETSI. Gsm 06.94, digital cellular telecommunication system (phase 2+); voice activity detector (vad) for adaptive multi rate (amr) speech traffic channels; general description. *Tech. Rep. V. 7.0.0*, February 1999.

[16] ITU-T Recommendation P. 59: Artificial conversational speech, March 1993.

[17] F. Beritelli, S. Casale, and A. Cavallaro. A robust voice activity detector for wireless communications using soft computing. *IEEE J. Select. Areas Commun*, 16:1818–1829, December 1998.

[18] F. Beritelli, S. Casale, G. Ruggeri, and S. Serrano. Performance evaluation and comparison of g.729/amr/fuzzy voice activity detectors. *IEEE Signal Processing Letters*, 9:85–88, March 2002.

[19] L. Couvreur and M. Laniray. Automatic noise recognition in urban environments based on artificial neural networks and hidden markov models. In *Proceedings of INTERNOISE*, 2004.

[20] F. Beritelli, S. Casale, A. Russo, and S. Serrano. A speech recognition system based on dynamic characterization of background noise. In *Proceedings of the 2006 IEEE International Symposium on Signal Processing and Information Technology*, pages 914–919, 2006.

Chapter 7

Evaluation of Biometric Systems

Mohamad El-Abed and Christophe Charrier

Additional information is available at the end of the chapter

http://dx.doi.org/10.5772/52084

1. Introduction

Biometrics is considered as a promising solution among traditional methods based on "what we own" (such as a key) or "what we know" (such as a password). It is based on "what we are" and "how we behave". Few people know that biometrics have been used for ages for identification or signature purposes. In 1928 for example, fingerprints were used for women clerical employees of Los Angeles police department as depicted in Figure 1. Fingerprints were also already used as a signature for commercial exchanges in Babylon (-3000 before JC). Alphonse Bertillon proposed in 1879 to use anthropometric information for police investigation. Nowadays, all police forces in the world use this kind of information to resolve crimes. The first prototypes of terminals providing an automatic processing of the voice and digital fingerprints have been defined in the middle of the years 1970. Nowadays, biometric authentication systems have many applications [1]: border control, e-commerce, *etc.* The main benefits of this technology are to provide a better security, and to facilitate the authentication process for a user. Also, it is usually difficult to copy the biometric characteristics of an individual than most of other authentication methods such as passwords.

Despite the obvious advantages of biometric systems, their proliferation was not as much as attended. The main drawback is the uncertainty of the verification result. By contrast to password checking, the verification of biometric raw data is subject to errors and represented by a similarity percentage (100% is never reached). Others drawbacks related to vulnerabilities and usability issues exist. In addition, in order to be used in an industrial context, the quality of a biometric system must be precisely quantified. We need a reliable evaluation methodology in order to put into obviousness the benefit of a new biometric system. Moreover, many questions remain: Shall we be confident in this technology? What kind of biometric modalities can be used? What are the trends in this domain? The objective of this chapter is to answer these questions, by presenting an evaluation methodology of biometric systems.

Figure 1. Women clerical employees of Los Angeles Police Department getting fingerprinted and photographed in 1928 (source [2]).

The outline of the chapter is defined as follows: In Section 2, we present the general concepts of biometric systems as well as their limitations. We then present in Section 3 the evaluation aspects of biometric systems related to 1) data quality, 2) usability and 3) security. In Section 4, we focus on emerging trends in this research field. They mainly have for objective to define efficient biometric systems that respect the privacy of an individual and permit a good usability. A conclusion of the chapter is then given in Section 5.

2. Concepts and definitions

2.1. Biometrics

The term biometrics is originally Greek, "bios" and "metron", literally meaning "measurement of life". In its first meaning, it was defined as a *Part of biological science which applies statistical methods and probabilistic formulas to living beings*. In computer security, biometrics refers to authentication techniques that rely on measurable physical characteristics that can be automatically checked.

2.2. Biometric modalities

Each biometric information that can discriminate individuals is considered as a biometric modality. An example of biometric modalities is presented in Figure 2. An ideal biometric information should respect the following properties:

- Universality: all individuals must be characterized by this information.
- Uniqueness: this information must be as dissimilar as possible for two different individuals.
- Permanency: it should be present during the whole life of an individual.
- Collectability: it can be measured in an easy manner.
- Acceptability: it concerns the possibility of a real use by users.

http://dx.doi.org/10.5772/52084

Table 1 presents a comparison study of biometric modalities in terms of universality, uniqueness, permanency, collectability and acceptability. From this table, we can deduce that none biometric information satisfies simultaneously all these properties. As for example, DNA analysis is one of the most efficient techniques to verify the identity of an individual or to identify him/her. Nevertheless, it cannot be used for logical or physical access control not only for time computation reasons, but also because nobody would be ready to give some blood to make the verification. Hence, important attention should be done when choosing a specific modality for a specific application and a target population.

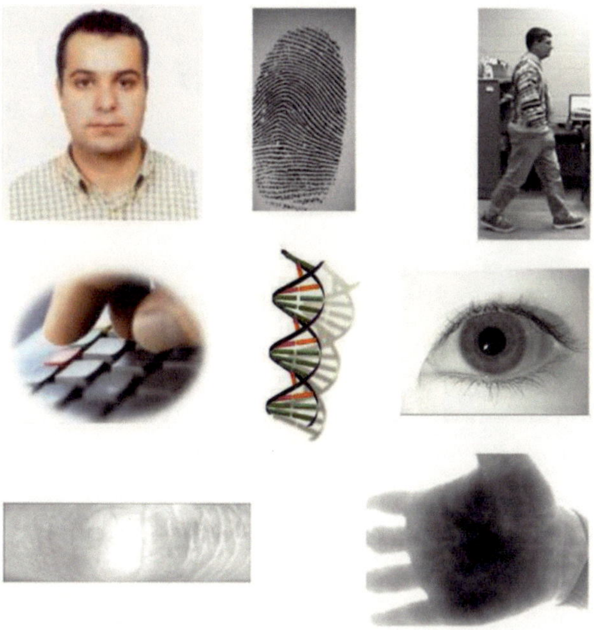

Figure 2. An example of biometric modalities. From left to right, top to bottom, face, fingerprint, gait, keystroke dynamics, DNA, iris, finger knuckle and hand veins information.

Information	U	N	P	C	A	E
DNA	Yes	Yes	Yes	Poor	Poor	*****
Gait	Yes	No	Poor	Yes	Yes	***
Keystroke dynamics	Yes	Yes	Poor	Yes	Yes	****
Voice	Yes	Yes	Poor	Yes	Yes	****
Iris	Yes	Yes	Yes	Yes	Poor	*****
Face	Yes	No	Poor	Yes	Yes	****
Hand geometry	Yes	No	Yes	Yes	Yes	****
Fingerprint	Yes	Yes	Yes	Yes	Fair	****

Table 1. Comparison study of biometric modalities in terms of universality (U), uniqueness (N), permanency (P), collectability (C), acceptability (A) and performance (E). For the performance, the number of stars is related to the modality's performance (i.e., EER) in the literature [3].

2.3. The general scheme of a biometric system

The biometric authentication process is divided into three main functionalities:

- **Enrolment**
  It constitutes the initial process of collecting biometric data samples from a person and subsequently creates a reference template representing a user's identity to be used for later comparison. An example of users' templates of different modalities is given in Figure 3.

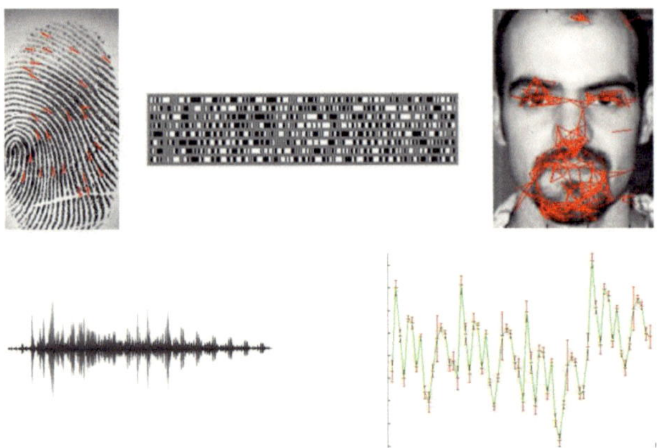

Figure 3. An example of biometric templates. From left to right, top to bottom, extracted minutia from a fingerprint, iris code, facial-based graph using keypoints, vocal and keystroke dynamics signals.

- **Verification**
  It provides a matching score between the biometric sample provided by the user and his/her template. The matching score is defined between 0% and 100% (100% is quite impossible to be reached).
- **Identification**
  It consists of determining the identity of an unknown individual from a database of individuals. In this case, the system can then either attribute the identity corresponding to the most similar profile found in the database to the unknown individual (or a list of the most similar profiles), or reject the individual.

2.4. Architecture of a biometric system

The generic architecture of a biometric system consists of five main modules as depicted in Figure 4:

- Capture module: It consists of capturing the biometric raw data in order to extract a numerical representation. This representation is then used for enrollment, verification or identification.
- Signal processing module: It allows the reduction of the extracted numerical representation in order to optimize the quantity of data to store during the enrollment phase, or to facilitate the processing time during the verification and identification phases. This module can have a quality test to control the captured biometric data.

- Storage module: It is used to store biometric individuals' templates.
- Matching module: It is used to compare the extracted biometric raw data to one or more previously stored biometric templates. The module therefore determines the degree of similarity (or of divergence) between two biometric vectors.
- Decision module: It is used to determine if the returned index of similarity is sufficient to determine the identity of an individual.

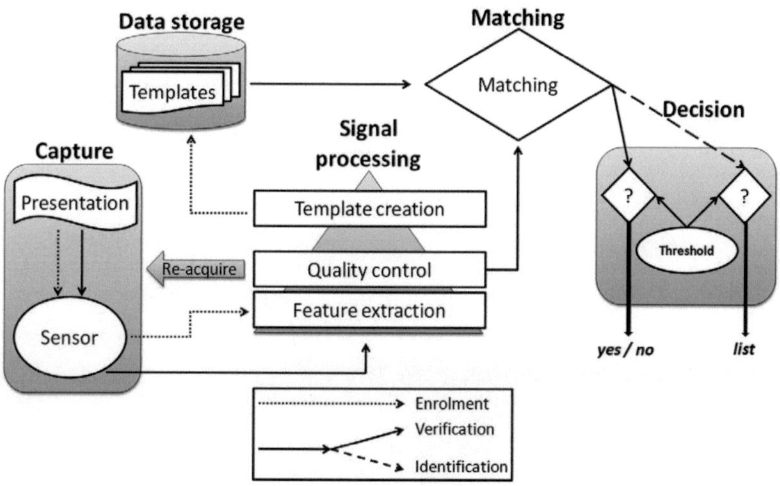

Figure 4. Generic architecture of a biometric system (source [4]).

2.5. Biometric systems limitations

Despite the advantages of biometric systems in terms of easy to use and to provide a better security comparing to traditional solutions, their use is limited to specific kind of applications (such as e-passport). These systems suffer from several limitations which may significantly decrease their widespread of use such as:

- Performance limitation: By contrast to password checking, the verification of biometric raw data is subject to errors and represented by a similarity percentage (100% is never reached). Verification errors are due to many reasons such as the variations of human characteristics (*e.g.*, occlusions [5]), environmental factors (*e.g.*, illuminations [6]) and cross-device matching [7]. This kind of acquisition artifacts may deeply affect the performance of biometric systems and hence, decrease their use in real life applications.
- Acceptability limitations: The use of biometric systems is related its perceived acceptability and satisfaction. Table 1 shows that not all the biometric modalities are accepted. However, the acceptability is also related to its context of use and the target population. Jain et al. (2004) [1] categorize the fundamental barriers in biometrics into three main categories: 1) accuracy in terms of errors, 2) scale or size of the database and 3) usability in terms of easiness to use, acceptability, *etc.* One government can decide that an individual would be identified through a biometric data embedded in the passport. For logical or physical access control in a company, it is more difficult to impose a system that would be not accepted by users.

- Architecture limitations: Several existing works [8–11] show the vulnerability of biometric systems. Ratha *et al.* have identified eight locations of possible attacks in a generic biometric system as depicted in Figure 5. Maltoni *et al.* present several drawbacks of biometric systems related to circumvention, repudiation, contamination, collusion and coercion threats. In addition to these presented threats, several works (such as [11]) present attacks on biometric systems related to the identified points presented in Figure 5. An example of type-1 attacks (*i.e.*, sensor) is given in Figure 6.

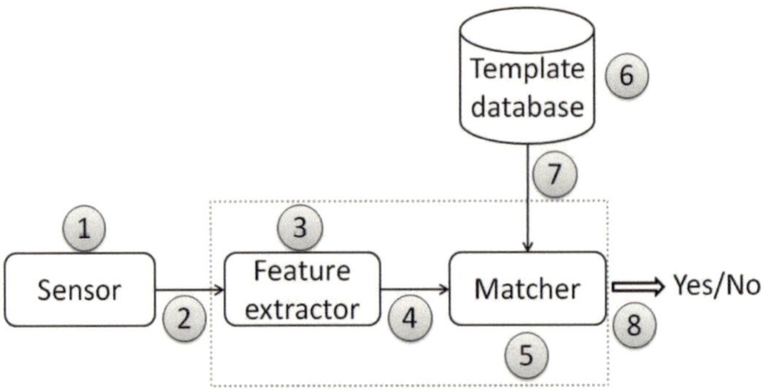

Figure 5. Possible attack points in a generic biometric system: Ratha *et al.* model.

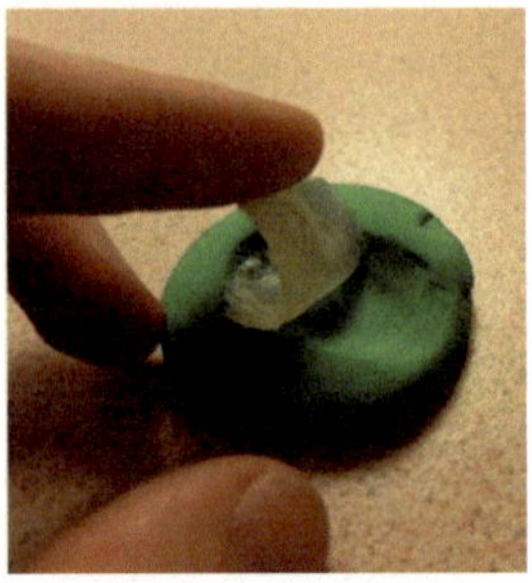

Figure 6. A prosthetic finger created out of latex at the GREYC research laboratory.

3. Evaluation of biometric systems

As shown in the previous section, biometric systems have several limitations which may significantly decrease their use in real life applications. Therefore, the evaluation of biometric systems is carefully considered in the literature. Such kind of evaluation can be categorized into three main categories as depicted in Figure 7: 1) data quality, 2) usability and 3) security. In this section, we present these evaluation aspects followed by a discussion.

3.1. Data quality

The quality assessment of biometric raw data is receiving more and more attention since it is considered as one of the main factors affecting the overall performance of biometric systems. This is mainly due to the acquisition artefacts such as illumination. Therefore, controlling the quality of the biometric raw data is absolutely necessary. Using the quality information, poor quality samples can be removed during the enrollment phase or rejected during the

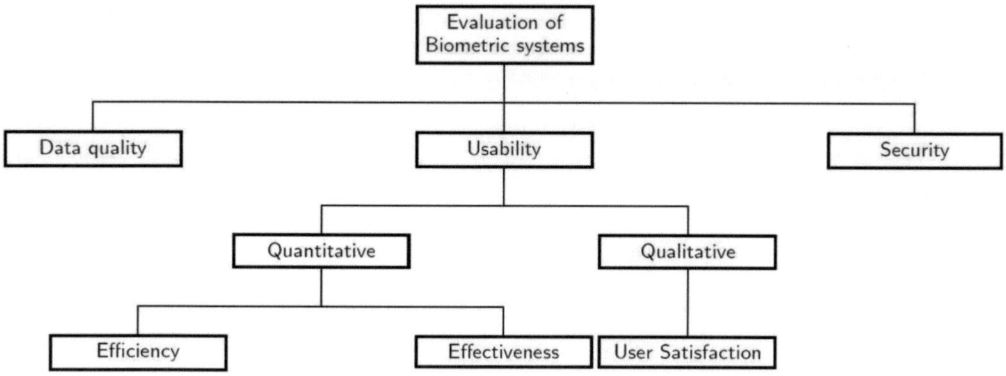

Figure 7. Evaluation aspects of biometric systems: data quality, usability and security.

verification. Such information could be also used for soft biometrics and multimodal approaches [12, 13].

According to the International Organization for Standardization [14], the quality assessment of biometric raw data is divided into three points of view as illustrated in Figure 8:

- Character: refers to the quality of the physical features of the individual.
- Fidelity: refers to the degree of similarity between a biometric sample and its source.
- Utility: refers to the impact of the individual biometric sample on the overall performance of a biometric system.

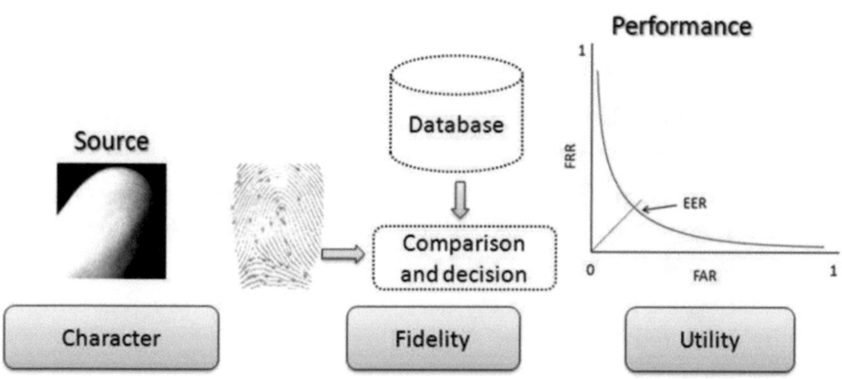

Figure 8. Quality assessment of biometric raw data: character, fidelity and utility.

In biometrics, there is an international consensus on the fact that the quality of a biometric sample should be related to its recognition performance [15]. Therefore, we present in this section an overview of the existing morphological-based quality metrics related to the *utility* point of view.

Alonso-Fernandez et al. (2007) [16] present an overview of existing fingerprint quality metrics. The authors show the impact of bad quality samples on the performance of biometric systems. Many other fingerprint quality algorithms exist [17–19]. The presented methods have shown their efficiency in predicting the quality of fingerprints images. An example of these metrics is the NIST Fingerprint Image Quality metric (NFIQ) [20] proposed by the NIST. NFIQ metric is dedicated to fingerprint quality evaluation.

Krichen et al. (2007) [5] present a probabilistic iris quality measure based on a Gaussian Mixture Model (GMM). The authors compared the efficiency of their metric with existing ones according two types of alterations (occlusions and blurring) which may significantly decrease the performance of iris recognition systems. Other iris quality metrics are presented in [21, 22].

He et al. (2008) [23] present a hierarchical model to compute the biometric sample quality at three levels: database, class and image quality levels. The method is based on the quantiles of genuine and impostor matching score distributions.

Zhang & Wang (2009) [6] present an asymmetry-based quality assessment method of face images. The method uses SIFT descriptor for quality assessment. The presented method has shown its robustness against illumination and pose variations. Another asymmetry-based method is presented in [24, 25].

Abed, Giot, Hemery, Charrier & Rosenberger (2011) [26] present a quality assessment method based on the use of two types of information: 1) image quality and 2) pattern-based quality using the SIFT descriptor. The presented metric has the advantages of being multimodal (face, fingerprint and hand veins), and independent from the used authentication system.

3.2. Usability

According to ISO 13407:1999 (1999), usability is defined as "*The extent to which a product can be used by specified users to achieve specified goals with effectiveness, efficiency, and satisfaction in a specified context of use*".

- Efficiency which means that users must be able to accomplish the tasks easily and in a timely manner. It is generally measured as a task time.
- Effectiveness which means that users are able to complete the desired tasks without too much effort. It is generally measured by common metrics including completion rate and number of errors such failure-to-enroll rate (FTE).
- User satisfaction which measures users' acceptance and satisfaction regarding the system. It is generally measured by studying several properties such as easiness to use, trust, *etc.*

We present in Section 3.2.1 the existing works related to performance (Efficiency and Effectiveness), whereas in Section 3.2.2 the acceptance and users' satisfaction aspect.

3.2.1. Performance

As shown in Section 2.5, biometric systems are subject to several kinds of errors. We present in this section an overview of the most used performance metrics [4, 28] in the literature, followed by a presentation of the existing evaluation competitions and platforms.

3.2.1.1 Metrics

1. Fundamental performance metrics
   - Failure-to-enroll rate (FTE): proportion of the user population for whom the biometric system fails to capture or extract usable information from the biometric sample.
   - Failure-to-acquire rate (FTA): proportion of verification or identification attempts for which a biometric system is unable to capture a sample or locate an image or signal of sufficient quality.
   - False-match-rate (FMR): the rate for incorrect positive matches by the matching algorithm for single template comparison attempts.
   - False-non-match rate (FNMR): the rate for incorrect negative matches by the matching algorithm for single template comparison attempts.

   In addition to these error metrics, other performance metrics are used in order to ensure the operational use of biometric systems such as: 1) average enrollment time, 2) average verification time, 3) average and maximum template size and 4) maximum amount of memory allocated.
2. Verification system performance metrics
   - False rejection rate (FRR): proportion of authentic users that are incorrectly denied. If a verification transaction consists of a single attempt, the false reject rate would be given by:

   $$FRR(\tau) = FTA + FNMR(\tau) * (1 - FTA) \quad (1)$$

   - False acceptation rate (FAR): proportion of impostors that are accepted by the biometric system. If a verification transaction consists of a single attempt, the false accept rate would be given by:

   $$FAR(\tau) = FMR(\tau) * (1 - FTA) \quad (2)$$

   - Receiver operating characteristic curve (ROC): plot of the rate of FMR as well as FAR (*i.e.*, accepted impostor attempts) on the x-axis against the corresponding rate of FNMR as well as FRR (*i.e.*, rejected genuine attempts) on the y-axis plotted parametrically as a function of the decision threshold. An illustration of a ROC curve is presented in Figure 9.
   - Equal Error Rate (EER): this error rate corresponds to the point at which the FAR and FRR cross (compromise between FAR and FRR). It is widely used to evaluate and to compare biometric authentication systems. More the EER is near to 0%, better is the performance of the target system.
3. Identification system performance metrics
   - Identification rate (IR): the identification rate at rate r is defined as the proportion of identification transactions by users enrolled in the system in which the user's correct identifier is among those returned.

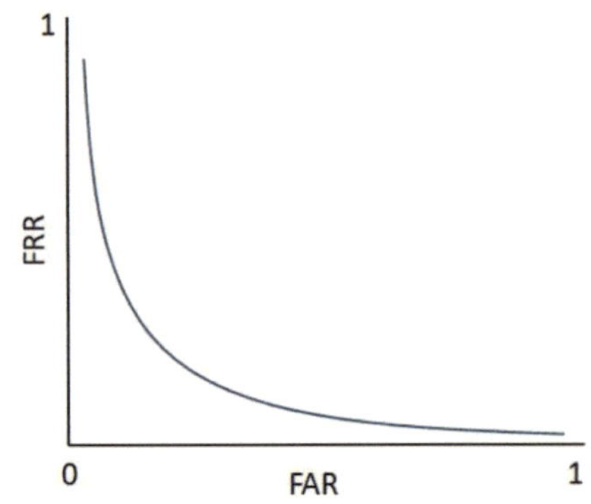

Figure 9. Example of a ROC curve: FAR against FRR.

- False-negative identification-error rate (FNIR): proportion of identification transactions by users enrolled in the system in which the user's correct identifier is not among those returned. For an identification transaction consisting of one attempt against a database of size N, it is defined as:

$$FNIR(\tau) = FTA + (1 - FTA) * FNMR(\tau) \tag{3}$$

- False-positive identification-error rate (FPIR): proportion of identification transactions by users not enrolled in the system, where an identifier is returned. For an identification transaction consisting of one attempt against a database of size N, it is defined as:

$$FPIR = (1 - FTA) * (1 - (1 - FMR)^N) \tag{4}$$

- Cumulative match characteristic curve (CMC): graphical presentation of results of an identification task test, plotting rank values on the x-axis and the probability of correct identification at or below that rank on the y-axis. Examples of CMC curves are given in Figure 10.

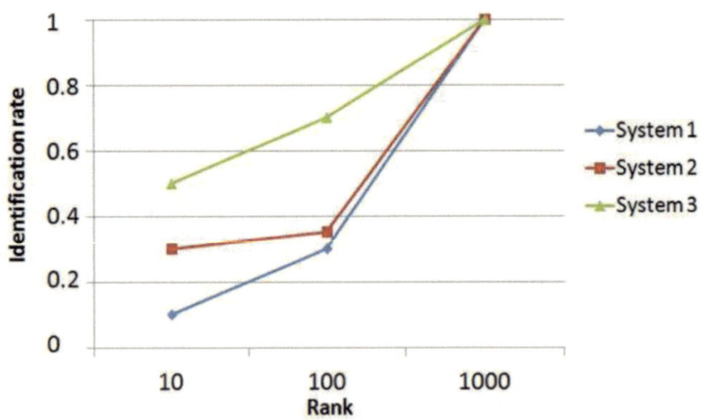

Figure 10. Examples of CMC curves of three biometric systems.

3.2.1.2 Competitions

Several biometric competitions are done in order to compare the performance of biometric systems and are divided into two categories: 1) monomodal and 2) multimodal competitions.

1. Monomodal competitions
   - Signature Verification Competition (SVC) [29]: It is a dynamic signature-based competition organized with the International Conference on Biometric Authentication (ICBA) in 2004. The EER is used as a performance metric.
   - Fingerpint Verification Competition (FVC): It consists of a series of fingerprint-based competitions (http://bias.csr.unibo.it/fvc2006/) organized in 2000, 2002, 2004 and 2006. The participants have tested their algorithms by providing both executables corresponding to the *enrollment* and *verification* phases. Four databases, three real and one synthetic using *SFinGe* software, are used during FVC2006 competition. Different performance metrics are used such as: the distribution of genuine and impostor scores, average and maximum template size, average enrollment and verification time, FTE and ROC curves.
   - Face Recognition Vendor Test (FRVT) and Iris Challenge Evaluation (ICE): both competitions were organized by the National Institute of Standards and Technology (NIST). The ROC curves are used as a performance metric.
   - Speaker Recognition Evaluation (SRE): It consists of a series of voice-based competitions organized by the NIST (http://www.itl.nist.gov/iad/mig/tests/sre/).
2. Multimodal competitions
   - BioSecure Multimodal Evaluation Campaign (BMEC): It is a competition organized by BioSecure (http://biosecure.it-sudparis.eu) in 2007. The BioSecure multimodal database [30] is used within the competition. The used experimental protocol and the results are detailed by by Mayoue et al. (2009) [31].
   - Multiple Biometric Grand Challenge (MBGC) [32]: It is a multimodal competition organized by the NIST in 2009. The main goal of this competition is to enhance the performance of face and iris-based systems over several acquisition conditions. It also consists of evaluating multimodal algorithms (image and score levels) of both modalities.

3.2.1.3 Platforms

- BioSecure Reference and Evaluation framework: BioSecure presents in [33] an evaluation framework based on open-source reference systems, publicly available databases, evaluation protocols and benchmarking results. The framework is available at http://svnext.it-sudparis.eu/svnview2-eph/ref_syst/ and has been used for the first time during the BioSecure Multimodal Evaluation Campaign (BMEC) in 2007. ROC curves and their corresponding EERs are used as a performance indicator.
- GREYC-Keystroke: It is a keystroke-based evaluation platform [34] developed at the GREYC research laboratory. GREYC-Keystroke software is also used to create keystroke databases in order to compare keystroke dynamics algorithms in the literature. Several performance metrics are used such as: the distribution of genuine and impostor scores, ROC curves and the FTA rate.

- Fingerprint Verification Competition-onGoing (FVC-onGoing): FVC-onGoing is an online fingerprint-based evaluation tool accessible at https://biolab.csr.unibo.it/FVCOnGoing. It is the evolution of the series of FVC competitions presented in the previous section. The used performance metrics are: acquisition errors (FTE and FTA), FNMR for a fixed FMR and vice-versa, average enrollment and verification time, maximum template size, genuine and impostor scores distribution, ROC curves and their corresponding EERs.

3.2.2. Users' acceptance and satisfaction

Traditional evaluation methods have worked well to evaluate emerging technologies, new biometric modalities, and algorithm revisions. Many databases have been collected (such as ENSIB face database [35]), many competitions and platforms have been proposed whose objective is mainly to compare enrollment and verification/identification algorithms in the literature. Many metrics have been defined by the International Organization for Standardization ISO/IEC 19795-1 (2006) [4] in terms of error computations, time computation, memory allocations, *etc.* These statistical measures allow in general a precise performance characterization of a biometric system. Nevertheless, these works are dedicated to quantify the system performance (algorithms, processing time, *etc.*) without taking into account user' view within the evaluation process. However, the biometric process is considered as a two-way interaction, between the user and the system. Therefore, taking into account user's view when designing biometric systems is considered as a crucial requirement to the widespread of use of this technology.

According to Smith (2003) [36], some members of the human-computer interaction (HCI) community believe that interfaces of security systems do not reflect good thinking in terms of creating a system that is easy to use, while maintaining an acceptable level of security. Nowadays, several studies have been done to quantify users' acceptability and satisfaction of biometric systems such as:

- The Opinion Research Corporation International ORC (2002) [37] presents the results of a phone survey conducted on 2001 and 2002. The survey has been conducted among national probability samples of 1017 and 1046 adults, respectively, living in United States. The 2001 study showed that 77% of individuals feel that finger-imaging protects individuals against fraud. For privacy issues, 87% in 2001 and 88% in 2002 are worried for the misuse of personal information. The study indicates a good percentage of acceptance, more than 75%, for U.S. law enforcement authorities requiring fingerprint scans to verify identity for passports, at airport check-ins and to obtain a driver license (see [37] for more details).
- The National Institute of Standards and Technology (NIST) has performed a usability test on fingerprints [38]. The survey was conducted on 300 adults recruited from a pool of 10,000 people. There were 151 women and 149 men ranging in ages from 18 to over 65 years. 77% of participants were in favor to provide fingerprint images as a mean of establishing identity for passport purposes. 2% of participants have expressed concerns about the cleanliness of the devices with which they would have physical contact. Another study has been done by NIST to examine the impact on fingerprint capture performance of angling the fingerprint scanners (flat, 10, 20 and 30 degrees) on the existing counter heights (99, 114.3 and 124.5 cm) is presented in in Theofanos et al. (2008) [39].

- Abed *et al.* [40] present a modality-independent evaluation methodology to study users' acceptance and satisfaction of biometric systems. It uses a survey questionnaire for data collection, and some data mining tools for their analysis. Three factors are identified as possible factors influencing respondents' acceptance and satisfaction: 1) the robustness of a systems against attacks, 2) its easiness to use and 3) the computation time during the verification phase. The authors then argue that even if the performance of a biometric system outperformed another one, it will not necessarily mean that it will be more operational or acceptable.
- Other studies presented in [41–48] have highlighted several points about biometric systems such as:
    - Acceptance is linked to the number of uses of the biometrics in general, and information provided by the biometric device can also improve user acceptance.
    - There is a potential concern about the misuse of personal data (*i.e.*, templates) which is seen as violating users' privacy and civil liberties. Another important concern is the probability that criminals may perpetrate heinous acts to gain access. This could include stalking or assaulting individuals to steal their biometric information.
    - Individuals complain that once the biometric template is stolen, it is compromised forever. There are also concerns about hygiene with touching such devices and health risks for more advanced technologies such as iris or retina.

3.3. Security

As shown in Section 2.5, biometric systems present several drawbacks which may significantly decrease their use in a an accurate way. Therefore, it is important that biometric systems be designed to withstand the presented threats when employed in security-critical applications and to achieve an end to end security. Despite the vulnerabilities of biometric systems, few are the works exist in comparison to the performance and quality aspects. Here is an overview of the works related to the security issue of biometric systems.

The International Organization for Standardization ISO/IEC FCD 19792 [49] presents a list of several threats and vulnerabilities of biometric systems. The standard also addresses privacy concerns when dealing with biometric systems. The standard does not present a security evaluation of biometric systems. It aims to guide the evaluators by giving suggestions and recommendations that should be taken into account during the evaluation process.

The Common Criteria Biometric Evaluation Working Group [50] presents a list of threats that may need to be considered when evaluating biometric systems.

Dimitriadis & Polemi (2004) [51] present a security comparison study of several biometric technologies in order to be used as an access control system for stadiums. The presented method can be used easily in comparing biometric systems since it is a quantitative-based method.

Attack tree technique introduced by [52], provides a structure tree to conduct security analysis of protocols, applications and networks. However, attack trees are dependent from the intended system and its context of use. Therefore, it is infeasible to be used for a generic evaluation purpose. An example of its use for the security evaluation of fingerprint recognition systems is presented by [53].

Matyás & Ríha (2002) [54] propose a security classification of biometric systems. Their proposal classifies biometric systems into four categories according to their security level. However, their model could not be considered as discriminative to compare the security level of biometric systems.

Abed et al. (2012) [55] present an on-line platform (*Security EvaBio*) to the security evaluation of biometric systems available at: http://www.epaymentbiometrics.ensicaen.fr/securityEvaBio/. A snapshot of the on-line platform is given in Figure 11. The platform implements a quantitative-based security assessment method based on the notion of risk factors, to allow easily the evaluation and comparison of biometric systems. It also contains a database of common threats and vulnerabilities of biometric systems which may be used by other researchers to quantify their developed systems in a quantitative or qualitative way.

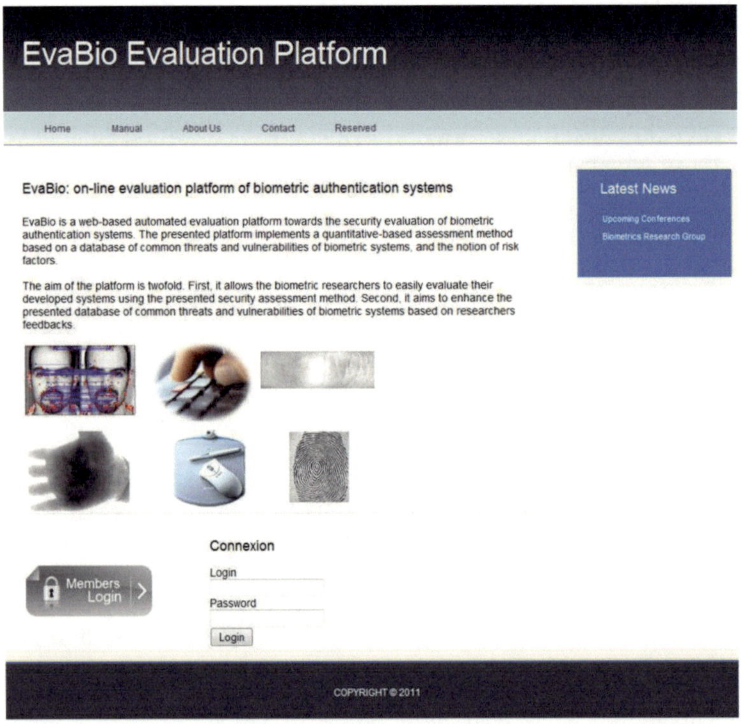

Figure 11. A snapshot of the Security EvaBio platform [55] developed at the GREYC research laboratory.

3.4. Discussion

Biometric systems are shown as a promising solution to authenticate individuals. However, their proliferation is not as much as attended. In this chapter, we see that biometric technology presents several drawbacks which may decrease their widespread of use in real life applications. Therefore, the evaluation of such systems is considered as a key challenge in this research field. Despite this, few are the works that address the evaluation aspects in comparison to recognition algorithms. More generally speaking, most of the existing works aim to present a better recognition algorithm in terms of performance (*e.g.*, using the EER) without taking into account the other evaluation aspects in terms of data quality, users' acceptance and security. From the presented evaluation works, we can put into obvious these points:

- For the quality aspect, we see that most of the existing quality metrics are modality-dependent (such as NFIQ metric). A step forward is presented by Abed *et al.* which present a multimodal quality metric to evaluate the quality of biometric raw data. However, the presented quality metric do not detect luminance alteration which is considered as an important alteration especially in a facial-based modality. In addition, we believe that more works are required to be done in this evaluation aspect to ensure the accuracy of applications using **only one** biometric information as a reference (*e.g.*, one facial image in e-passport).
- For the security aspect, we see also that most of the existing works aim to present scenarios of attacks (such as hill-climbing attacks) on biometric systems. Few are the works dedicated to the security evaluation of such systems. We believe that more works should be done in this research area in order to ensure the accuracy of biometric systems.

Finally, we believe that taking into account simultaneously the presented evaluation aspects is important when evaluating and comparing biometric systems. In other words, a biometric systems providing 0% errors but not easy to use is not really important (such as DNA-based authentication systems).

4. Future trends

In this section, we present some future trends in biometrics research field. We focus only on those related to the evaluation of biometric systems.

4.1. Evaluation of multimodal-based biometric systems

In order to increase the performance of biometric systems, it is possible to combine different information for the decision making [56]. Different alternatives are available such as combining two different biometric systems (*e.g.*, face and fingerprint), using two sensors of the same modality (optical and sweeping fingerprint sensors), using two different algorithms given a single capture, exploiting different representations of a single biometric modality (2D and 3D face information) ... Of course, the combination of the decision results given by these multiple biometric sensors can be realized by different techniques from the easiest way based on a logical combination (conjunction) to more complicated methods such as those based on fuzzy logic [57].

Even if the global performance of multi-modal biometric systems is improved, two main drawbacks make this solution rarely used in our daily life. The first one is due to the cost that is, of course, increased as many sensors are necessary. The second one concerns the usability for users that have to make many operations to be authenticated.

4.2. Evaluation of privacy by design biometric systems

One of the main drawbacks of biometrics is the impossibility to revoke the biometric data of a user if they are compromised [58]. Another problem, which is related to the acceptance by the users, is the respect of privacy: how can people be sure that their personal data collected during the enrollment will not be stolen or diverted and used for other purposes?

Over the last decade, a new innovative research field has emerged, trying to protect biometric templates. Nowadays, several protection schemes exist, but unfortunately not yet mature for large scale deployment. Examples of such schemes are fuzzy commitment [59], fuzzy vault scheme [60], and the BioHashing principle presented in several works by [61] and [62].

4.3. Quality assessment of 3D-based face data

In comparison to the 2D-based face recognition, 3D technology is considered as a promising solution to enhance the performance of biometric systems [63]. We believe also that this technology is an efficient solution to detect type-1 fakes (*e.g.*, presentation of a face image of good quality to the sensor). Moreover, quality assessment is required nowadays especially after the growing of this technology (such as 3D films like Avatar, *etc.*).

Despite the advantages of 3D technology in comparison to the 2D, none of the works exist to assess the quality of 3D biometric raw data. In addition, very few are the works addressing the quality assessment of 3D images/videos content. We can cite paired comparison is one of the standardized test methodologies toward the quality assessment of 3D images/videos. We can cite also a recent method toward the 3D quality assessment presented by [64].

5. Conclusion

Biometric systems are increasingly used in our daily life to manage the access of several resources. Several biometric technologies exist toward this goal, going from physiological-based features (such as face) to behavioral-based features (such as keystroke dynamics). However, a key issue to be considered is the evaluation of such systems. This is mainly important to ensure efficient biometric systems that respect the privacy of an individual, and to permit a good usability. In this chapter, we have presented an overview of the existing evaluation aspects of biometric systems based on: 1) **Data quality** which ensures that the quality of the acquired biometric raw data is of sufficient quality. This is mainly important for applications using only one biometric information as a reference (*e.g.*, e-passport); 2) **Usability** which ensures the operational use of the biometric system in terms of users' acceptability and satisfaction; and 3) **Security** which ensures the use of the system in an accurate way by avoiding well known attacks (such as a dummy finger). We have seen in this chapter the limitations of biometric systems, which constitute a main drawback to its proliferation. We have seen also that the existing evaluation works related to the data quality and security aspects are very few in comparison to the performance ones. Therefore, it is important to take more attention to these both evaluation aspects (data quality and security). Finally, we believe that the three evaluation aspects should be take into account simultaneously when evaluating and comparing biometric systems.

Acknowledgment

The authors would like to thank the French Research Ministry for their financial support of this work.

Author details

Mohamad El-Abed[1],
Christophe Charrier[2] and Christophe Rosenberger[2]

1 College of Science & Information Systems, Rafic Hariri University, Meshref Lebanon
2 Université de Caen Basse-Normandie, Caen, France

References

[1] A. K. Jain, S. Pankanti, S. Prabhakar, L. Hong, and A. Ross. Biometrics: A grand challenge. *International Conference on Pattern Recognition (ICPR)*, 2:935–942, 2004.

[2] Women clerks –california–los angeles county. digital2.library.ucla.edu, 1928.

[3] J. Mahier, M. Pasquet, C. Rosenberger, and F. Cuozzo. Biometric authentication. *Encyclopedia of Information Science and Technology*, pages 346–354, 2008.

[4] ISO/IEC 19795-1. Information technology – biometric performance testing and reporting – part 1: Principles and framework, 2006.

[5] E. Krichen, S. Garcia Salicetti, and B. Dorizzi. A new probabilistic iris quality measure for comprehensive noise detection. In *IEEE Third International Conference on Biometrics : Theory, Applications and Systems (BTAS)*, pages 1–6, 2007.

[6] G. Zhang and Y. Wang. Asymmetry-based quality assessment of face images. In *Proceedings of the 5th International Symposium on Advances in Visual Computing (ISVC)*, volume 5876, pages 499–508, 2009.

[7] N. Poh, J.V. Kittler, and T. Bourlai. Quality-based score normalization with device qualitative information for multimodal biometric fusion. *IEEE Transactions on Systems, Man, and Cybernetics*, 40:539–554, 2010.

[8] N. K. Ratha, J. H. Connell, and R. M. Bolle. An analysis of minutiae matching strength. In *Audio- and Video-Based Biometric Person Authentication*, pages 223–228, 2001.

[9] T. V. der Putte and J. Keuning. Biometrical fingerprint recognition: Don't get your fingers burned. In *Proceedings of the Fourth Working Conference on Smart Card Research and Advanced Applications*, volume 31, pages 289–306, 2000.

[10] D. Maltoni, D. Maio, A. K. Jain, and S. Prabhakar. *Handbook of Fingerprint Recognition.* Springer-Verlag, 2003.

[11] U. Uludag and A. K. Jain. Attacks on biometric systems: A case study in fingerprints. In *Proc. SPIE-EI 2004, Security, Seganography and Watermarking of Multimedia Contents VI*, volume 5306, pages 622–633, 2004.

[12] N. Poh, T. Bourlai, and J. Kittler. A multimodal biometric test bed for quality-dependent, cost-sensitive and client-specific score-level fusion algorithms. *Pattern Recognition*, pages 1094–1105, 2010.

[13] N. Poh, T. Bourlai, J. Kittler, L. Allano, F. Alonso-Fernandez, O. Ambekar, J. Baker, B. Dorizzi, O. Fatukasi, J. Fierrez, H. Ganster, J. Ortega-Garcia, D. Maurer, A. A. Salah, T. Scheidat, and C. Vielhauer. Benchmarking quality-dependent and cost-sensitive score-level multimodal biometric fusion algorithms. *Transactions on Information Forensics and Security*, 4(4):849–866, 2009.

[14] ISO/IEC 29794-1. Biometric quality framework standard, first ed. jtc1/sc37/working group 3, 2006.

[15] P. Grother and E. Tabassi. Performance of biometric quality measures. *IEEE Transactions on Pattern Analysis and Machine Intelligence*, 29:531–543, 2007.

[16] F. Alonso-Fernandez, J. Fierrez, J. Ortega-Garcia, J. Gonzalez-Rodriguez, H. Fronthaler, K. Kollreider, and J. Bigun. A comparative study of fingerprint image-quality estimation methods. *IEEE Transactions on Information Forensics and Security*, 2:734–743, 2007.

[17] L. Shen, A. C. Kot, and W. M. Koo. Quality measures of fingerprint images. In *Proceedings of the 3rd International Conference on Audio- and Video-Based Biometric Person Authentication (AVBPA)*, pages 266–271, 2001.

[18] Y. Chen, S. C. Dass, and A. K. Jain. Fingerprint quality indices for predicting authentication performance. In *5th International Conference Audio- and Video-Based Biometric Person Authentication (AVBPA)*, volume 3546, pages 160–170, 2005.

[19] S. Lee, C. Lee, and J. Kim. Model-based quality estimation of fingerprint images. In *IAPR/IEEE International Conference on Biometrics (ICB'06)*, pages 229–235, 2006.

[20] E. Tabassi and C.L. Wilson. A novel approach to fingerprint image quality. In *International Conference on Image Processing (ICIP)*, pages 37–40, 2005.

[21] Y. Chen, S.C. Dass, and A.K. Jain. Localized iris image quality using 2-d wavelets. In *International Conference on Biometrics (ICB)*, 2006.

[22] N. D. Kalka, J. Zuo, N. A. Schmid, and B. Cukic. Image quality assessment for iris biometric. In *Proc. SPIE 6202*, 2006.

[23] Q. He, Z.A. Sun, T.N. Tan, and Y. Zou. A hierarchical model for the evaluation of biometric sample quality. In *International Conference on Pattern Recognition (ICPR)*, pages 1–4, 2008.

[24] X.F. Gao, S.Z. Li, R. Liu, and P.R. Zhang. Standardization of face image sample quality. In *International Conference on Biometrics (ICB'07)*, pages 242–251, 2007.

[25] J. Sang, Z. Lei, and S. Z. Li. Face image quality evaluation for ISO/IEC standards 19794-5 and 29794-5. In *Proceedings of the Third International Conference on Advances in Biometrics (ICB)*, pages 229–238, 2009.

[26] M. El Abed, R. Giot, B. Hemery, C. Charrier, and C. Rosenberger. A SVM-based model for the evaluation of biometric sample quality. In *IEEE International Workshop on Computational Intelligence in Biometrics and Identity Management*, pages 115–122, 2011.

[27] ISO 13407:1999. Human centred design process for interactive systems, 1999.

[28] James P. Egan. Signal detection theory and ROC-analysis. by Academic Press, New York, 1975.

[29] D.Y. Yeung, H. Chang, Y.M. Xiong, S. George, R. Kashi, T. Matsumoto, and G. Rigoll. SVC2004: First International Signature Verification Competition. In *International Conference on Biometric Authentication (ICBA'04)*, pages 16 – 22, 2004.

[30] BIOSECURE. Biosecure Multimodal Biometric Database. http://www.biosecure.info/, 2008.

[31] A. Mayoue, B. Dorizzi, L. Allano, G. Chollet, J. Hennebert, D. Petrovska-Delacrétaz, and F. Verdet. *Guide to biometric reference systems and performance evaluation*, chapter The BioSecure multimodal evaluation campaign 2007 (BMEC'2007), pages 327–372. 2009.

[32] P. J. Phillips, P. J. Flynn, J. R. Beveridge, W. T. Scruggs, A. J. O'Toole, D. S. Bolme, K. W. Bowyer, B. A. Draper, G. H. Givens, Y. M. Lui, H. Sahibzada, J. A. Scallan, and S. Weimer. Overview of the multiple biometrics grand challenge. In *International Conference on Biometrics (ICB'09)*, pages 705 – 714, 2009.

[33] D. Petrovska and A. Mayoue. Description and documentation of the biosecure software library. Technical report, BioSecure, 2007.

[34] R. Giot, M. El Abed, and C. Rosenberger. Greyc keystroke : a benchmark for keystroke dynamics biometric systems. In *IEEE Third International Conference on Biometrics : Theory, Applications and Systems (BTAS)*, pages 1–6, 2009.

[35] B. Hemery, C. Rosenberger, and H. Laurent. The ENSIB database : a benchmark for face recognition. In *International Symposium on Signal Processing and its Applications (ISSPA), special session "Performance Evaluation and Benchmarking of Image and Video Processing"*, 2007.

[36] S. Smith. Humans in the loop: Human computer interaction and security. *IEEE Security & Privacy*, 3:75–79, 2003.

[37] ORC. Public Attitudes Toward the Uses of Biometric Identification Technologiesby Government and the Private Sector. Technical report, Opinion Research Corporation International (ORC), 2002.

[38] M. Theofanos, B. Stanton, S. Orandi, R. Micheals, and N.F. Zhang. Usability testing of ten-print fingerprint capture. Technical report, National Institute of Standards and Technology (NIST), 2007.

[39] M. Theofanos, B. Stanton, C. Sheppard, R. Micheals, N. Zhang, J. Wydler, L. Nadel, and W. Rubin. Usability testing of height and angles of ten-print fingerprint capture. Technical report, National Institute of Standards and Technology (NIST), 2008.

[40] M. El Abed, R. Giot, B. Hemery, and C. Rosenberger. Evaluation of biometric systems: A study of users' acceptance and satisfaction. *Inderscience International Journal of Biometrics*, pages 1–26, 2011.

[41] F. Deane, K. Barrelle, R. Henderson, and D. Mahar. Perceived acceptability of biometric security systems. *Computers & Security*, 14:225–231, 1995.

[42] L. Coventry, A. De Angeli, and G. Johnson. Honest it's me! self service verification. In *The ACM Conference on Human Factors in Computing Systems (CHI)*, pages 1–4, 2003.

[43] J. Moody. Public perceptions of biometric devices: The effect of misinformation on acceptance and use. In *the Informing Science and Information Technology Education*, volume 1, pages 753–761, 2004.

[44] L. A. Jones, A. I. Antón, and J. B. Earp. Towards understanding user perceptions of authentication technologies. In *ACM Workshop on Privacy in the Electronic Society*, pages 91–98, 2007.

[45] S. J. Elliott, S. A. Massie, and M. J. Sutton. The perception of biometric technology: A survey. *Automatic Identification Advanced Technologies*, pages 259–264, 2007.

[46] A. P. Pons and P. Polak. Understanding user perspectives on biometric technology. *Communications of the Association for Computing Machinery (ACM)*, 51(9):115–118, 2008.

[47] R. Giot, M. El Abed, and C. Rosenberger. Keystroke dynamics authentication for collaborative systems. *Collaborative Technologies and Systems, International Symposium*, pages 172–179, 2009.

[48] M. El Abed, R. Giot, B. Hemery, and C. Rosenberger. A study of users' acceptance and satisfaction of biometric systems. In *International Carnahan Conference on Security Technology (ICCST)*, pages 170–178, 2010.

[49] ISO/IEC FCD 19792. Information technology – security techniques – security evaluation of biometrics, 2008.

[50] Common criteria for information technology security evaluation. Technical report, 1999.

[51] C. Dimitriadis and D. Polemi. Application of multi-criteria analysis for the creation of a risk assessment knowledgebase for biometric systems. In *international conference on biometric authentication (ICB)*, volume 3072, pages 724–730, 2004.

[52] B. Schneier. Attack trees. *Dr. Dobb's Journ. of Softw. Tools*, 1999.

[53] O. Henniger, D. Scheuermann, and T. Kniess. On security evaluation of fingerprint recognition systems. In *Internation Biometric Performance Testing Conference (IBPC)*, pages 1–10, 2010.

[54] V. Matyás and Z. Ríha. Biometric authentication - security and usability. In *Proceedings of the IFIP TC6/TC11 Sixth Joint Working Conference on Communications and Multimedia Security*, pages 227–239, 2002.

[55] M. El Abed, P. Lacharme, and C. Rosenberger. Security evabio: An analysis tool for the security evaluation of biometric authentication systems. In *the 5th IAPR/IEEE International Conference on Biometrics (ICB)*, pages 1–6, 2012.

[56] A. Ross, K. Nandakumar, , and A.K. Jain. *Handbook of Multibiometrics*. Springer, 2006.

[57] A. Azzini, S. Marrara, R. Sassi, and F. Scotti. A fuzzy approach to multimodal biometric authentication. In *Knowledge-Based Intelligent Information and Engineering Systems*, number 8, pages 801–808, 2007.

[58] A. K. Jain, K. Nandakumar, and A. Nagar. Biometric template security. *EURASIP Journal on Advances in Signal Processing*, 2008:1–17, 2007.

[59] A. Juels and M. Wattenberg. A fuzzy commitment scheme. In *ACM Conference on Computer and Communication Security*, pages 28–36, 1999.

[60] A. Juels and M. Sudan. A fuzzy vault scheme. In *IEEE International Symposium on Information Theory*, pages 237–257, 2001.

[61] A. Goh and C. Ngo. *Computation of Cryptographic Keys from Face Biometrics*. Lecture Notes in Computer Science. Springer, Berlin, 2003.

[62] R. Belguechi, C. Rosenberger, and S.A. Aoudia. Biohashing for securing minutia template. In *Proceedings of the 20th International Conference on Pattern Recognition (ICPR'10)*, pages 1168–1171, 2010.

[63] S. Berretti, A. D. Bimbo, P. Pala, B. B. Amor, and M. Daoudi. A set of selected sift features for 3D facial expression recognition. In *Proceedings of the 20th International Conference on Pattern Recognition (ICPR)*, pages 4125–4128, 2010.

[64] J. Lee, L. Goldman, and T. Ebrahimi. A new analysis method for paired comparison and its application to 3d quality assessment. In *Proceedings of the 19th ACM International Conference on Multimedia*, pages 1281–1284, 2011.

Section 3

Security and Template Protection

Chapter 8

Multi-Biometric Template Protection: Issues and Challenges

Christian Rathgeb and Christoph Busch

Additional information is available at the end of the chapter

http://dx.doi.org/10.5772/52152

1. Introduction

The term biometrics refers to "automated recognition of individuals based on their behavioral and biological characteristics" (ISO/IEC JTC1 SC37). Several physiological (static) as well as behavioral (non-static) biometric characteristics have been exploited [1] such as fingerprints, iris, face, hand, voice, gait, keystroke dynamics, etc., depending on distinct types of applications (see Figure 1). Biometric traits are acquired applying adequate sensors and distinctive feature extractors are utilized in order to generate a biometric template (reference data) in the enrollment process. During verification (authentication process) or identification (identification can be handled as a sequence of biometric comparisons against the enrollment records in a reference databse) the system processes another biometric measurement from which an according template is extracted and compared against the stored template(s) yielding acceptance/ rejection or hit/ no-hit, respectively.

The presented work is motivated by very recent advances in the fields of *multi-biometric recognition* [2] and *biometric template protection* [3]. Automatic recognition systems based on a single biometric indicator often have to contend with unacceptable error rates [4]. Multi-biometric systems have improved the accuracy and reliability of biometric systems [2]. Biometric vendors are already deploying multi-biometric systems (e.g. fingerprint and finger vein by SAFRAN Morpho[1]) and multi-biometric recognition is performed on large-scale datasets (e.g. within the Aadhaar project [5] by the Unique Identification Authority of India (UIDAI)). However, security of multi-biometric templates is especially crucial as they contain information regarding multiple traits of the same subject [6]. The leakage of any kind of template information to unauthorized individuals constitutes serious security and privacy risks, e.g. permanent tracking of subjects without consent [7] or reconstruction of original biometric traits (e.g. fingerprints [8] or iris textures [9]) might become a realistic threat. Therefore, biometric template protection technologies have been developed in order to protect privacy and integrity of stored biometric data. However, so far, template protection schemes which provide provable security/ privacy, and achieve practical recognition rates

[1] SAFRAN Morpho, France, http://www.morpho.com/

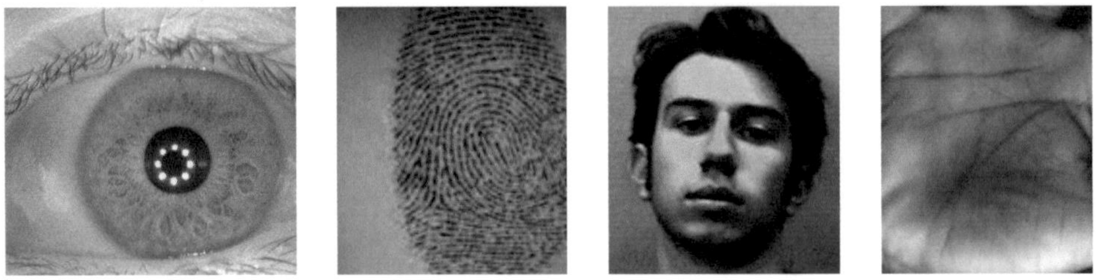

(a) Iris (b) Fingerprint (c) Face (d) Palmprint

Figure 1. Examples of physiological (static) biometric characteristics.

have remained elusive, even on small datasets. This bookchapter provides a comprehensive overview of biometric fusion, biometric template protection, and, in particular, possible ways of how to combine these technologies.

The remainder of this bookchapter is organized as follows: Section 2 briefly summarizes advantages and issues of multi-biometric recognition. Template protection technologies are reviewed in Section 3. In Section 4 multi-biometrics and template protection are combined and related works are summarized. Subsequently, a theoretical framework for multi-biometric template protection is introduced and major issues and challenges evolving from incorporating biometric fusion to template protection technologies are discussed in detail in Section 5. Finally, a summary is given in Section 6.

2. Multi-biometric recognition

Whenever biometric verification systems based on single biometric indicators have to deal with noisy sensor acquisition, restricted degrees-of-freedom, or non-universality unpractical performance rates are yielded [4]. Such drawbacks, which represent common scenarios when operating biometric recognition systems, raise the need for multi-biometric recognition [2] or other approaches that can increase the recognition accuracy. As previously mentioned, a fusion of multiple biometric indicators have been shown to improved the accuracy and reliability of biometric systems.

2.1. Categorization

Fusion in biometric systems is commonly categorized according to the level within which the fusion is performed. ISO/IEC TR 24722:2007 coarsely distinguishes three possible levels of fusion: (1) fusion at feature level, (2) fusion at score level, and (3) fusion at decision level. Figure 2 illustrates these different types of biometric fusion.

1. *Feature Level Fusion*: biometric fusion on feature level comprises the construction of a new feature vector of higher dimensionality composed of (a selection of) feature elements of various feature vectors generated a priori. The new feature vector should turn out to be more discriminative than each single one [4].
2. *Score Level Fusion*: on this level of fusion matching scores are returned by each individual subsystem and obtained scores are combined. Once scores are properly normalized they can be combined in different ways (e.g. by weighted sum-rule) such that the fusion of normalized scores leads to a more accurate overall system.

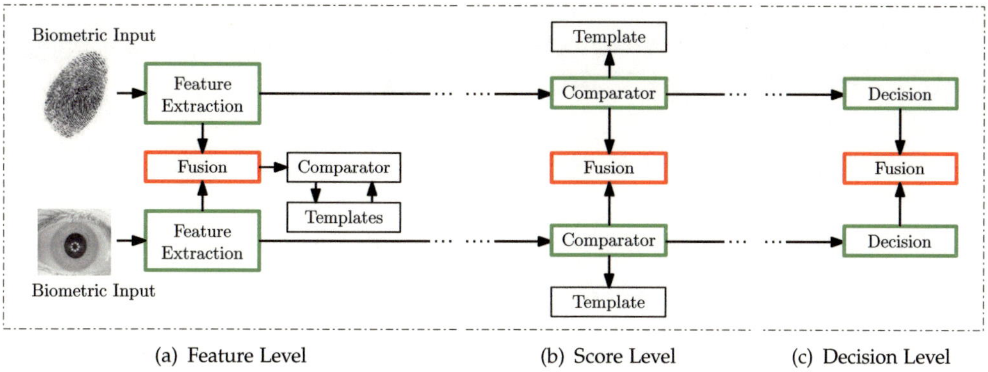

Figure 2. Biometric fusion: different levels of fusion within a biometric recognition system.

3. *Decision Level Fusion*: a fusion of final decisions (in general accept/ reject) is referred to as decision level fusion. Various final decisions of independent subsystems can be fused (e.g. by applying a majority voting) in order to increase the accuracy (security) or universality (convenience) of the entire system [2].

2.2. Advantages

Multi-biometric recognition systems offer several advantages compared to conventional biometric systems. There is a common and intuitive assumption that the combination of multiple biometrics improves performance as multiple multiple sources of information are involved. By combining multiple sources of information, it is possible to improve systems biometric performance, increase population coverage, deter spoofing, and facilitate indexing [10]. While several fusion levels are possible in multi-biometric systems (see Chapter 2.1), biometric fusion on the score level represents the most popular one due to the ease in accessing and consolidating comparison scores. Performance gain is achieved in case uncorrelated traits are applied in a multi-biometric recognition systems. Incorporating subject-specific parameters may further increase accuracy of these systems.

However, in case a strong (highly discriminative) biometric characteristic is combined with a weak one, the resulting decision environment is in a sense averaged, and the combined performance will lie somewhere between that of the two tests conducted individually. Hence, biometric fusion is not straight forward, but highly depends on the choice of characteristics, features, fusion type, etc.

2.3. Issues

Besides common issues like requirements for stronger user incorporation of feature level fusion of different feature representations, one major issue regarding multi-biometric recognition we want to emphasize on is the central storage of multiple biometric templates of a single subject. Compared to conventional biometric systems based on a single biometric indicator, multiple sources of information, i.e. more biometric reference data, has to be stored for each subject registered with a multi-biometric system. In a multi-biometric system the overall complexity increases as multiple SDK need to be maintained and the use of multiple

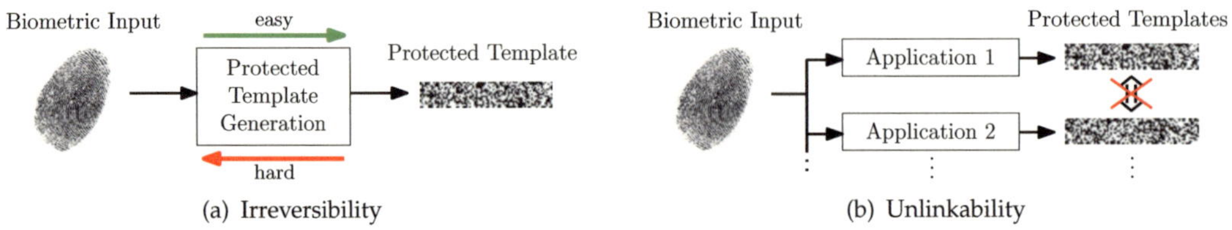

Figure 3. Biometric template protection: properties of (a) irreversibility and (b) unlinkability.

sensors results in a stronger dependency on fully operational hardware. Biometric system can be compromised in a number of ways [7], and leakage of biometric template information to unauthorized individuals constitutes serious security and privacy threats [6]. For instance, in case n different comparison scores are combined performing score level fusion, n different biometric templates have to be stored for each subject registered with the system.

This major drawback of biometric fusion raises the need for multi-biometric template protection. More precisely, the storage of multiple biometric records of a fused template of biometric features extracted from different biometric traits has to be protected.

3. Template protection

The industry has long claimed that one of the primary benefits of biometric templates is that original biometric signals acquired to enroll a data subject cannot be reconstructed from stored templates. Several techniques (e.g. [8, 11]) have proven this claim wrong. Since most biometric characteristics are largely immutable, a compromise of raw biometric data or biometric templates might result in a situation that a subject's biometric characteristics are essentially *burned* and not usable any longer from the security perspective. Biometric template protection technologies offer significant advantages to enhance the privacy and security of biometric systems, providing reliable biometric authentication at a high security level.

3.1. Categorization

Biometric template protection schemes are commonly categorized as (1) biometric cryptosystems (also referred to as helper data-based schemes) and (2) cancelable biometrics (also referred to as feature transformation). Biometric cryptosystems are designed to securely bind a digital key to a biometric or generate a digital key from a biometric [12], offering solutions to biometric-dependent key-release and biometric template protection [13, 14]. Cancelable biometrics consist of intentional, repeatable distortions of biometric signals based on transforms which provide a comparison of biometric templates in the transformed domain [7]. Both technologies are designed to meet two major requirements of biometric information protection (ISO/IEC 24745): (1) *irreversibility*, i.e. it should be computationally hard to reconstruct the original biometric template from the stored reference data (protected template), while it should be easy to generate the protected biometric template; (2) *unlinkability*, i.e. different versions of protected biometric templates can be generated based on the same biometric data (renewability), while protected templates should not allow cross-matching (diversity). Schematic illustrations of both properties are shown in Figure 3(a) and Figure 3(b).

Advantage	Description
Privacy protection	Within biometric cryptosystems and cancelable biometrics the original biometric template is obscured such that a reconstruction is hardly feasible.
Secure key release	Biometric cryptosystems provide key release mechanisms based on biometrics.
Pseudonymous authentication	Authentication is performed in the encrypted domain and, thus, the biometric reference is a pseudonymous identifier.
Revocability and renewability of templates	Several instances of secured templates can be generated.
Increased security	Biometric cryptosystems and cancelable biometrics prevent from several traditional attacks against biometric systems.
More social acceptance	Biometric cryptosystems and cancelable biometrics are expected to increase the social acceptance of biometric applications.

Table 1. Major advantages of technologies of biometric template protection.

3.2. Advantages

Biometric cryptosystems and cancelable biometrics offer several advantages over generic biometric systems. Most important advantages are summarized in Table 1. These major advantages over conventional biometric systems call for several applications. In order to underline the potential of both technologies two essential use cases are discussed in detail. With respect to the design goals, biometric cryptosystems and cancelable biometrics offer significant advantages to enhance the privacy and security of biometric systems, providing reliable biometric authentication at an high security level. Several new issues and challenges arise deploying these technologies [13].

3.3. Issues

One fundamental challenge, regarding template protection, represents the issue of alignment, which significantly effects recognition performance. Biometric templates are obscured within both technologies, i.e. alignment of obscured templates without leakage is highly non-trivial. For instance, if iris biometric textures or templates (iris-codes) are transformed in a non-row-wise manner, e.g. block permutation of preprocessed textures or a permutation of iris-code bits. Consequentially, additional information, which must not lead to template reconstruction, has to be stored [3].

Focusing on biometric template protection technologies it is not actually clear which biometric characteristics to apply in which type of application. In fact it has been shown that even the iris may not exhibit enough reliable information to bind or extract sufficiently long keys providing acceptable trade-offs between accuracy and security. Stability of biometric features is required to limit information leakage of stored helper data. In addition, feature adaptation schemes that preserve accuracy have to be utilized in order to obtain common representations of arbitrary biometric characteristics (several approaches to extract fixed-length binary fingerprint templates have been proposed, e.g. [15, 16]).

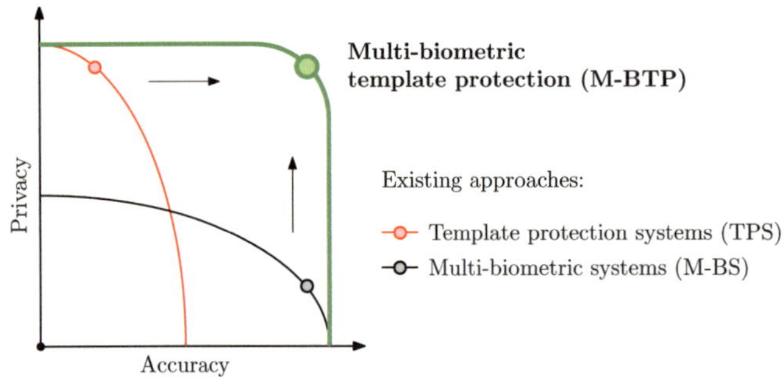

System	Privacy	Accuracy
TPS	high	low
M-BS	low	high
M-BTP	high	high

Figure 4. Privacy/ accuracy relation: multi-biometrics and template protection systems.

As plenty different approaches to biometric cryptosystems and cancelable biometrics have been proposed a large number of pseudonyms and acronyms have been dispersed across literature such that attempts to represented biometric template protection schemes in unified architectures have been made [17]. Standardization on biometric template protection has been achieved in the ISO/IEC 24745 standard providing guidance on the protection of an individual's privacy during the processing of biometric information.

4. Multi-biometric template protection

As previously mentioned, a lack of security represents a major drawback of multi-biometric recognition systems [6]. On the other hand, biometric template protection technologies generally reveal unpractical accuracy compared to underlying recognition algorithms [3]. These facts motivate the incorporation of template protection technologies to multi-biometric recognition systems, and vice versa.

4.1. Combining the best of two worlds

With respect to the described design goals, i.e. *breaking the trade-off* between accuracy and security, multi-biometric template protection systems offer significant advantages, improving public confidence and acceptance of biometrics. In addition, multi-biometrics provide low error rates compared to uni-biometric systems even under unconstrained circumstances paving the way for practical deployment of template protection systems. The relation between approaches to multi-biometric recognition and biometric template protection is schematically illustrated in Figure 4, highlighting the potential of multi-biometric template protection.

4.2. Related work

Focusing on the current state-of-the-art in biometric template protection key approaches to biometric cryptosystems and cancelable biometrics are summarized in Table 2. Representing one of the simplest key binding approaches the fuzzy commitment scheme [18] has been successfully applied to iris [19] (and other biometrics). The fuzzy vault scheme [20] which represents one of the most popular biometric cryptosystem has frequently been applied to fingerprints. Early approaches (e.g. [21]), which required a pre-alignment of biometric templates, have demonstrated the potential of this concept. Several techniques (e.g. [22, 23]) to overcome the shortcoming of pre-alignment have been proposed. Quantization schemes

http://dx.doi.org/10.5772/52152

Author(s)	Applied Technique	Modality	FRR / FAR (%)	Remarks
[19]	Fuzzy Commitment	Iris	0.42 / 0.0	small test set
[34]			5.62 / 0.0	short key
[21]	Fuzzy Vault	Fingerprints	20-30 / 0.0	pre-alignment, >1 enroll sam.
[23]			4.0 / 0.004	>1 enroll sam.
[35]		Iris	5.5 / 0.0	–
[36]	Quantization	Online Sig.	28.0 / 1.2	>1 enroll sam.
[24]			7.05 / 0.0	short key
[26]	Password-Hardening	Voice	>2.0 / 2.0	short key
[37]	BioHashing	Face	0.0 / 0.0	non-stolen token
[38]	Block Permutation, Surface Folding	Fingerprints	$\sim$35 / 10^{-4} $\sim$15 / 10^{-4}	–
[39]	BioConvolving	Online Sig.	10.81 EER	–
[33]	BioHashing	Face	0.0002 EER	non-stolen token

Table 2. Experimental results of key approaches to biometric template protection schemes.

(e.g. [24, 25]) have been applied to several physiological and behavioral biometrics, while focusing on reported performance rates, these schemes require further studies in order to improve accuracy. Besides, approaches which aim at "salting" existing passwords with biometric features have been proposed [26]. Within the BioHashing approach [27] biometric features are projected onto secret domains applying user-specific tokens prior to a key-binding process. Variants of this approach have been exposed to reveal unpractical performance rates under the stolen-token scenario [28]. With respect to recognition rates, the vast majority of biometric template protection schemes are by no means comparable to conventional biometric systems. While numerous approaches to biometric cryptosystems generate rather short keys at unacceptable performance rates, several enrollment samples may be required as well, (e.g. four samples in [21]). Approaches which report practical recognition rates are tested on rather small datasets (e.g. 70 persons in [19]) which must not be interpreted as significant. In addition, the introduction of additional tokens, be it random numbers or secret PINs, often clouds the picture of reported results.

First approaches to non-invertible transforms [7] (representing an instance of cancelable biometrics), which have been applied to face and fingerprints, include block-permutation and surface-folding. Diverse proposals (e.g. [29, 30]) have shown that recognition performance decreases noticeably compared to original biometric systems. Additionally, it is doubtable if sample images of transformed biometric images are non-invertible. BioHashing [27] (without key-binding) represents the most popular instance of biometric salting yielding a two-factor authentication scheme. Since additional tokens have to be kept secret (e.g. [31, 32]) result reporting turns out to be problematic. Perfect recognition rates have been reported (e.g. in [33]) while the opposite was found to be true [28] within the stolen-token scenario.

Focusing on the incorporation of multiple biometrics in template protection schemes several approaches have been proposed. Most notable approaches are summarized in Table 3. One of the first approach to a multi-biometric cryptosystem based on the fuzzy commitment scheme was proposed by [40], in which binary fingerprint and face features are combined. In [41] two different feature extraction algorithms are applied to 3D face data yielding a single

Author(s)	Applied Technique	Modality	FRR / FAR (%)	Remarks
[40]	Multi-biometric Fuzzy Commitment	Fingerprint and Face	0.92 / >0.001	–
[41]		3D Face and 3D Face	$\sim$ 2.5 EER	single sensor scenario
[42]		Iris and Iris	5.56 / 0.01	single sensor scenario
[43]	Multi-biometric Fuzzy Vault	Fingerprint and Iris	1.8 / 0.01	–
[6]		Fingerprint, Face and Iris	1.0 / 0.0	–
[44]	Token-based Scrambling	Face and Face	$\sim$ 15.0 EER	single sensor scenario

Table 3. Experimental results of approaches to multi-biometric template protection schemes.

sensor scenario[2]. The authors provide results for feature level, score level and decision level fusion. In order to obtain a comparison score the number of errors corrected by the error correction code are estimated, i.e. scores are only available in case of successful decoding. Best results are obtained for the multi-algorithm fusion at feature level. [42] propose a sensible rearrangement of bits in iris codes in order to provide a uniform distribution of error probabilities. The rearrangement allows a more efficient execution of error correction codes combining the most reliable bits generated by different feature extraction algorithms. [43] proposed a multi-biometric cryptosystem fuzzy vault based on fingerprint and iris. The authors demonstrate that a combination of biometric modalities leads to increased accuracy and, thus, higher security. A FRR of 1.8% at a FAR of $\sim$0.01% is obtained, while the corresponding FRR values of the iris and fingerprint fuzzy vaults are 12% and 21.2%, respectively. [44] combine two different feature extraction methods to achieve cancelable face biometrics. PCA and ICA (independent component analysis) coefficients are extracted and both feature vectors are randomly scrambled and added in order to create a transformed template. In rather recent work [6] report results on multi-biometric fuzzy commitment schemes and fuzzy vault schemes based on fingerprint, face and iris. In order to obtain a common feature representation for each type of template protection scheme the authors propose different embedding algorithms, e.g. for mapping a binary string to a point set. best results are obtained for a multi-biometric fuzzy vault scheme. Compared to feature level fusion and score level fusion, recently [45] proposed a multi-biometric template protection system employing decision level fusion of multiple protected fingerprint templates.

Several other ideas of using a set of multiple biometric characteristics within biometric template protections schemes have been proposed [46–51].

[2] Note that in general single sensor scenarios are more challenging than those based on multiple sensors, since, in case of noise occurrence, each feature extractor has to deal with signal degradation.

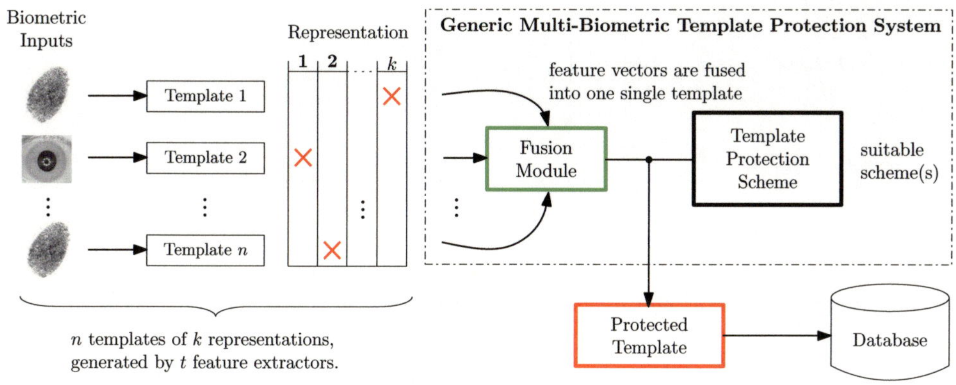

Figure 5. A framework of a generic multi-biometric template protection at feature level.

That is, a rearrangement of biometric feature vectors in order to provide a uniform distribution of errors improves the overall accuracy of the system.

5. Issues and challenges

Besides already mentioned issues of multi-biometric recognition (see Chapter 2.3) and template protection technologies (see Chapter 3.3), which may be solved through multi-biometric template protection, several further issues might occur which have to be dealt with. From designing a generic framework for multi-biometric template protection at a coarse level different evolving issues will be discussed in detail.

5.1. Generic framework for multi-biometric template protection

The major goal of research in the area of multi-biometric template protection is to generate a *generic framework* of constructing multi-biometric template protection schemes, i.e. a code of practice according to various aspects for incorporating different biometric templates in one or more template protection system(s), yielding multi-biometric template protection. From existing research it appears that biometric fusion on feature level is most suitable for template protection schemes [6, 40–42]. While preliminary scores are not available within the vast majority of biometric cryptosystems, cancelable biometric systems based on score level fusion can be constructed analogue to conventional biometric systems. For both technologies biometric fusion based on decision level can easily be implemented combining final decisions. Figure 5 shows a schematic impression of how such a framework (based on feature level fusion) could look like.

In order to provide generic multi-biometric template protection the system should be capable of incorporating n different biometric templates, which need not exhibit a common feature representation, i.e. k different representation may be involved. In a fusion module a common representation of feature vectors is established and feature vectors are combined in a sensible manner. Subsequently, an adequate template protection scheme is applied to protect the multi-biometric template. Focusing on a generic fusion of multiple biometric templates in a template protection system several issues evolve.

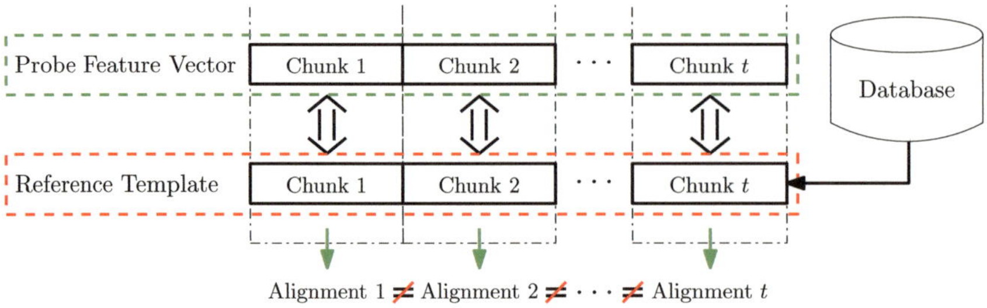

Figure 6. Template alignment within a multi-biometric template protection scheme.

5.2. Template alignment

Focusing on distinct biometric characteristics, e.g. iris, alignment within a template protection scheme can still be feasible. For instance, within an iris biometric fuzzy commitment scheme template alignment can be achieved by applying decommitments at various shifting positions. Within conventional biometric systems align-invariant approaches have been proposed for several biometric characteristics. So far, hardly any suggestions have been made to construct align-invariant biometric cryptosystems or cancelable biometrics. Still, focusing on technologies of biometric template protection, feature alignment significantly effects recognition performance. Biometric templates are obscured within template protection systems, i.e. alignment of protected templates is highly non-trivial [52]. Feature level fusion of biometric templates potentially aggravates a proper alignment of protected templates (optimal alignments vary for incorporated templates), while auxiliary data for the use of alignment may leak information on stored templates. More precisely, a combined feature vector may consist of t chunks of feature elements generated by t diverse feature extractors. In order to establish a proper alignment of the entire feature vector, chunks of feature elements need to be aligned individually. In general a common optimal alignment which is valid for all chunks of feature elements is rather unlikely. Hence, additional helper data is required which at least has to mark start and end points of such chunks. Figure 6 provides an schematic illustration of this issue.

As previously mentioned an adaption of biometric feature vectors to template protection schemes is considered inevitable in order to achieve practical recognition rates. However, generally a rearrangement of features within biometric templates makes conventional template alignment infeasible. Again, in order to align protected templates properly, additional helper data (e.g. reverse permutations) need to be stored (cf. [22, 23]), in a global or subject-specific manner. The additional storage of helper data is essential but will cause information leakage, i.e. potential impostors may utilize the additional helper data in order to compromise or cross-match protected templates, in case of subject-specific helper data.

5.3. Combination of modalities

In fact it has been shown that distinct biometric modalities (e.g. fingerprint or iris) exhibit enough reliable information to bind or extract sufficiently long keys providing acceptable trade-offs between accuracy and security, where the best performing schemes are based on fuzzy commitment and fuzzy vault. However, practical error correction codes are designed for communication and data storage purposes such that a perfect error correction code for a desired code length has remained evasive (optimal codes exist only theoretically under certain assumptions [53]). The fact that false rejection rates are lower bounded by error correction capacities [54] emerges a great challenge since unbounded use of error correction (if applicable) makes the system even more vulnerable [55]. Other characteristics such as voice or keystroke dynamics (especially behavioral characteristics) were found to reveal only a small amount of stable information [26], but can still be applied to improve the security of an existing secret. While for some characteristics extracting of a sufficient amount of reliable features seems to be feasible it still remains questionable if these features exhibit enough entropy. In case extracted features do not meet requirements of discriminativity, systems become vulnerable to several attacks (e.g. false acceptance attacks). In addition, stability of biometric features is required to limit information leakage of stored helper data as well as a sufficient secret length. Focusing on multi-biometric template protection schemes which perform biometric fusion at feature level a single sensor fusion scenario could be applied in order to overcome the issue of alignment. Any combination of biometric feature vectors extracted from a single biometric signal alleviates the construction of a multi-biometric template protection scheme, in case these feature extractors apply the same mode of operation when analyzing biometric data. For instance, if two different iris biometric feature extractors extract binary iris-codes from pre-processed textures and operate on same block sizes extracting the same number of bits per block, a single optimal alignment for both extracted feature vectors exists.

Due to the sensitivity of template protection schemes multiple enrollment samples are required and thus, compared to conventional biometric systems, more user-cooperation (compared to conventional biometric systems) is demanded in order to decrease intra-class variation, while sensoring and preprocessing require improvement as well. Furthermore, from the usability side of view it has to be analyzed which combinations of biometric modalities are applicable (e.g. iris and face or fingerprint and hand geometry) [2]. In order to keep the multi-biometric system usable only those modalities should be combined that allow acquisition of multiple samples with "one" single capture device (e.g. capturing two iris images and one face image with multiple cameras that are integrated in one capture device). Only then the capture time and consequently the transaction time will remain constant.

5.4. Feature representation

While different template protection systems incorporating multiple biometric traits have been proposed, these turn out to be custom-built according to applied biometric feature representations and applied template protection schemes. Multi-biometric template protection schemes in literature have been proposed for numerous types of template protection requiring different feature representations (a detailed overview can be found in [3]). While some techniques have been applied to distinct template protection systems (e.g. fuzzy commitment scheme or fuzzy vault scheme) a detailed analysis of pros and cons of these schemes regarding the application of multi-biometrics has remained elusive. Such investigation involves factors such as scalability, i.e. the vast majority of template protection schemes require fixed-length feature vectors and are only scalable in discrete iterations (e.g. by adding a distinct number of chunks of error correction codewords). Biometric template protection schemes are designed for a distinct representation of feature vectors, e.g. fuzzy commitment schemes require binary biometric templates as input while fuzzy vault schemes require real-valued biometric templates. A fusion of binary iris-codes and minutiae triples can still be performed without a successive application of different types of template protection schemes (e.g. in [43]). However, as this is not the case in general, embedding functions are required in order to perform mappings between different feature representations; such mappings must not cause a drastic loss of information.

Since different template protection schemes require distinct feature representations a generic framework for multi-biometric template protection should be able to handle diverse inputs of feature vectors. This issue can be solve in two ways:

1. *Unified representation*: by establishing a common representation of biometric features (e.g. by quantizing feature vectors [24]) or
2. *Different template protection schemes*: by combining different types of template protection schemes according to the provided feature vectors (e.g. fuzzy commitment scheme and fuzzy vault scheme [43]).

It is expected that the first opportunity degrades discriminativity of feature vectors while the second is expected to cause security vulnerabilities of protected templates. In order to prevent impostors from attacking separately stored protected templates biometric fusion can be performed at "secret level", i.e. each applied template protection scheme contributed a chunk of bits while the final secret is constructed from calculating a hash of the concatenation of all bit chunks. Still, representation of feature vectors represents one of the most critical issues.

5.5. System security

Focusing on the possible levels of fusion existing approaches to feature-level fusion in template protection systems merely involve a trivial concatenation of biometric templates (e.g. [40, 41]). It has been demonstrated, to some extent, that a more-sophisticated feature-level fusion leads to improved accuracy as well as template security [42]. However, more detailed analysis of adapting multiple biometric templates (based on different feature representations) to according template protection schemes on feature level is demanded. While approaches to cancelable biometrics provide a comparison score for each authentication attempt (offering trivial score-level fusion), within biometric cryptosystems subjects are authenticated indirectly via key validities, i.e. comparison scores are not explicitly available. For instance, in [41] comparison scores are equalized with required error correction capacities, however, more sophisticated approaches to multi-biometric cryptosystems based on score level fusion are non-existent. Biometric fusion at decision level implies the incorporation of a significant amount of biometric templates (e.g. to enable majority voting) in a template protection system. For both technologies, biometric cryptosystems and cancelable biometrics, biometric fusion on decision level can be implemented straight-forward. With respect to biometric cryptosystems a way of performing biometric fusion on secret level could be implemented by a (bit-wise) majority vote of released keys. Even tough approaches to cancelable biometric may easily be fused at decision level, recognition performance does not necessarily correlate with results reported for traditional multi-biometric systems. However, by definition, this level of fusion is restricting the system to a separate protection of multiple templates, which need to be secured individually, and can cause further security risks [6].

http://dx.doi.org/10.5772/52152

In the vast majority of approaches to biometric template protection schemes provided security is put on a level with obtained recognition performance, i.e. obtained FAR at a targeted FRR. While analysis with respect to irreversibility and unlinkability is rarely done, some quantities to measure the security of template protection systems have been suggested, e.g. key entropy [56], maximum key size [57], or information leakage of stored helper data [58, 59]. These analysis need to be adapted and extended in order to establish a generic methodology of measuring the security of multi-biometric template protection systems.

Focusing on security/ privacy of template protection schemes several magnitudes have been proposed for uni-biometric template protection schemes (e.g. [56, 58]). With respect to multi-biometric template protection schemes security measures need to be reformulated and extended since additional factors, such as a separate storage of protected templates, take influence on the security provided by the system [6]. We plan to establish a generic modus operandi of estimating the security of any multi-biometric template protection scheme in an information theoretic way. Emphasis will also be put on irreversibility and unlinkability analysis, which is rarely done in existing literature (e.g. in [39]).

6. Summary

The presented bookchapter provides an overview of multi-biometric template protection. While both technologies, multi-biometric recognition [2] and biometric template protection [3], suffer from serious drawbacks a sensible combination of these could eliminate individual disadvantages. Different template protection systems incorporating multiple biometric traits, which have been proposed in literature, are summarized. While, at first glance, multi-biometric template protection seems to solve several drawbacks, diverse issues arise. Based on a theoretical framework for multi-biometric template protection several issues, e.g. template alignment at feature level, are elaborated and discussed in detail. While generic approaches to the construction of multi-biometric template protection schemes have remained elusive we provide several suggestions for designing multi-biometric template protection systems.

Acknowledgement

This work has been supported by the Center for Advanced Security Research Darmstadt (CASED).

Author details

Christian Rathgeb* and Christoph Busch

* Address all correspondence to: christian.rathgeb@cased.de

da/sec – Biometrics and Internet Security Research Group, Hochschule Darmstadt, Darmstadt, Germany

7. References

[1] A. K. Jain, P. J. Flynn, and A. A. Ross. *Handbook of Biometrics*. Springer-Verlag, 2008.

[2] A. Ross, K. Nandakumar, and A. K. Jain. *Handbook of Multibiometrics (International Series on Biometrics)*. Springer-Verlag New York, Inc., Secaucus, NJ, USA, 2006.

[3] C. Rathgeb and A. Uhl. A survey on biometric cryptosystems and cancelable biometrics. *EURASIP Journal on Information Security*, 2011(3), 2011.

[4] A. Ross and A. K. Jain. Information fusion in biometrics. *Pattern Recognition Letters*, 24:2115–2125, 2003.

[5] Unique Identification Authority of India. Aadhaar, 2012. retrieved May, 2012.

[6] A. Nagar, K. Nandakumar, and A. K. Jain. Multibiometric cryptosystems based on feature level fusion. *IEEE Transactions on Information Forensics and Security*, 7(1):255–268, 2012.

[7] N. K. Ratha, J. H. Connell, and R. M. Bolle. Enhancing security and privacy in biometrics-based authentication systems. *IBM Systems Journal*, 40:614–634, 2001.

[8] R. Cappelli, A. Lumini, D. Maio, and D. Maltoni. Fingerprint image reconstruction from standard templates. *IEEE Transactions on Pattern Analysis and Machine Intelligence*, 29(9):1489–1503, 2007.

[9] S. Venugopalan and M. Savvides. How to generate spoofed irises from an iris code template. *Trans. Information Forensics and Security*, 6:385–395, 2011.

[10] A. Ross and A. K. Jain. Multimodal biometrics: An overview. In *Proc. of 12th European Signal Processing Conf. (EUSIPCO'04)*, pages 1221–1224, 2004.

[11] Arun Ross, Jidnya Shah, and Anil K. Jain. From template to image: Reconstructing fingerprints from minutiae points. *IEEE Transactions on Pattern Analysis and Machine Intelligence*, 29(4):544–560, 2007.

[12] A. Cavoukian and A. Stoianov. Biometric encryption. In *Encyclopedia of Biometrics*. Springer Verlag, 2009.

[13] A. Cavoukian and A. Stoianov. Biometric encryption: The new breed of untraceable biometrics. In *Biometrics: fundamentals, theory, and systems*. Wiley, 2009.

[14] A. K. Jain, A. Ross, and U. Uludag. Biometric template security: Challenges and solutions. *in Proc. of European Signal Processing Conf. (EUSIPCO)*, 2005.

[15] J. Bringer and V. Despiegel. Binary feature vector fingerprint representation from minutiae vicinities. In *Proc. of the 4th IEEE Int. Conf. on Biometrics: Theory, applications and systems (BTAS'10)*, pages 1–6, 2010.

[16] H. Xu and R. N.J. Veldhuis. Binary representations of fingerprint spectral minutiae features. In *Proc. of the 20th Int. Conf. on Pattern Recognition (ICPR'10)*, pages 1212–1216, 2010.

[17] J. Breebaart, C. Busch, J. Grave, and E. Kindt. A reference architecture for biometric template protection based on pseudo identities. In *Proc. of the BIOSIG 2008: Biometrics and Electronic Signatures*, pages 25–38, 2008.

[18] A. Juels and M. Wattenberg. A fuzzy commitment scheme. *6th ACM Conf. on Computer and Communications Security*, pages 28–36, 1999.

[19] F. Hao, R. Anderson, and J. Daugman. Combining Cryptography with Biometrics Effectively. *IEEE Transactions on Computers*, 55(9):1081–1088, 2006.

[20] A. Juels and M. Sudan. A fuzzy vault scheme. *Proc. 2002 IEEE Int. Symp. on Information Theory*, page 408, 2002.

[21] T. C. Clancy, N. Kiyavash, and D. J. Lin. Secure smartcard-based fingerprint authentication. *Proc. ACM SIGMM 2003 Multimedia, Biometrics Methods and Applications Workshop*, pages 45–52, 2003.

[22] U. Uludag and A. K. Jain. Fuzzy fingerprint vault. *Proc. Workshop: Biometrics: Challenges Arising from Theory to Practice*, pages 13–16, 2004.

[23] K. Nandakumar, A. K. Jain, and S. Pankanti. Fingerprint-based Fuzzy Vault: Implementation and Performance. *in IEEE Transactions on Information Forensics And Security*, 2:744–757, 2007.

[24] C. Vielhauer, R. Steinmetz, and A. Mayerhöfer. Biometric hash based on statistical features of online signatures. In *ICPR '02: Proc. of the 16 th Int. Conf. on Pattern Recognition (ICPR'02) Volume 1*, page 10123, 2002.

[25] Y. Sutcu, H. T. Sencar, and N. Memon. A secure biometric authentication scheme based on robust hashing. *MMSec '05: Proc. of the 7th Workshop on Multimedia and Security*, pages 111–116, 2005.

[26] F. Monrose, M. K. Reiter, Q. Li, and S. Wetzel. Using Voice to Generate Cryptographic Keys. *Proc. 2001: A Speaker Odyssey, The Speech Recognition Workshop*, 2001. 6 pages.

[27] A. Goh and D. C. L. Ngo. Computation of cryptographic keys from face biometrics. In *Communications and Multimedia Security (LNCS: 2828)*, pages 1–13, 2003.

[28] A. Kong, K.-H. Cheunga, D. Zhanga, M. Kamelb, and J. Youa. An analysis of BioHashing and its variants. *Pattern Recognition*, 39:1359–1368, 2006.

[29] J. Zuo, N. K. Ratha, and J. H. Connel. Cancelable iris biometric. *In Proc. of the 19th Int. Conf. on Pattern Recognition 2008 (ICPR'08)*, pages 1–4, 2008.

[30] J. Hämmerle-Uhl, E. Pschernig, , and A.Uhl. Cancelable iris biometrics using block re-mapping and image warping. *In Proc. of the Information Security Conf. 2009 (ISC'09) LNCS: 5735*, pages 135–142, 2009.

[31] M. Savvides, B.V.K.V. Kumar, and P.K. Khosla. Cancelable biometric filters for face recognition. *ICPR '04: Proc. of the Pattern Recognition, 17th Int. Conf. on (ICPR'04)*, 3:922–925, 2004.

[32] Y. Wang and K.N. Plataniotis. Face based biometric authentication with changeable and privacy preservable templates. In *Proc. of the IEEE Biometrics Symposium 2007*, pages 11–13, 2007.

[33] A. Goh, A. B. J. Teoh, and D. C. L. Ngo. Random multispace quantization as an analytic mechanism for biohashing of biometric and random identity inputs. *IEEE Trans. Pattern Anal. Mach. Intell.*, 28(12):1892–1901, 2006.

[34] J. Bringer, H. Chabanne, G. Cohen, B. Kindarji, and G. Zémor. Optimal iris fuzzy sketches. *in Proc. 1st IEEE Int. Conf. on Biometrics: Theory, Applications, and Systems.*, pages 1–6, 2007.

[35] X. Wu, N. Qi, K. Wang, and D. Zhang. A Novel Cryptosystem based on Iris Key Generation. *Fourth Int. Conf. on Natural Computation (ICNC'08)*, pages 53–56, 2008.

[36] H. Feng and C. C. Wah. Private key generation from on-line handwritten signatures. *Information Management and Computer Security*, 10(18):159–164, 2002.

[37] A. B. J. Teoh, D. C. L. Ngo, and A. Goh. Personalised cryptographic key generation based on FaceHashing. *Computers And Security*, 2004(23):606–614, 2004.

[38] N. K. Ratha, J. H. Connell, and S. Chikkerur. Generating cancelable fingerprint templates. *IEEE Transactions on Pattern Analysis and Machine Intelligence*, 29(4):561–572, 2007.

[39] E. Maiorana, P. Campisi, J. Fierrez, J. Ortega-Garcia, and A. Neri. Cancelable templates for sequence-based biometrics with application to on-line signature recognition. *Trans. on System, Man, and Cybernetics-Part A: Systems and Humans*, 40(3):525–538, 2010.

[40] Y. Sutcu, Q. Li, and N. Memon. Secure biometric templates from fingerprint-face features. In *IEEE Conf. on Computer Vision and Pattern Recognition, CVPR '07*, pages 1–6, 2007.

[41] E. J. C. Kelkboom, X. Zhou, J. Breebaart, R. N. S. Veldhuis, and C. Busch. Multi-algorithm fusion with template protection. In *Proc. of the 3rd IEEE Int. Conf. on Biometrics: Theory, applications and systems (BTAS'09)*, pages 1–7, 2009.

[42] C. Rathgeb, A. Uhl, and P. Wild. Reliability-balanced feature level fusion for fuzzy commitment scheme. In *Proc. of the Int. Joint Conf. on Biometrics (IJCB'11)*, 2011. 1–7.

[43] K. Nandakumar and A. K. Jain. Multibiometric template security using fuzzy vault. In *IEEE 2nd Int. Conf. on Biometrics: Theory, Applications, and Systems, BTAS '08*, pages 1–6, 2008.

[44] M. Y. Jeong, C. Lee, J. Kim, J. Y. Choi, K. A. Toh, and J. Kim. Changeable biometrics for appearance based face recognition. In *Proc. of Biometric Consortium Conf., 2006 Biometrics Symposium*, pages 1–5, 2006.

[45] B. Yang, C. Busch, K. de Groot, H. Xu, and R. N. J. Veldhuis. Performance evaluation of fusing protected fingerprint minutiae templates on the decision level. *Sensor-Journal, Special Issue: Hand-Based Biometrics Sensors and Systems*, 2012(12):5246–5272, 2012.

[46] K. Voderhobli, C. Pattinson, and H. Donelan. A schema for cryptographic key generation using hybrid biometrics. *7th annual postgraduate symp.: The convergence of telecommunications, networking and broadcasting, Liverpool*, 2006.

[47] S. Cimato, M. Gamassi, V. Piuri, R. Sassi, and F. Scotti. A multi-biometric verification system for the privacy protection of iris templates. *Proc. of the Int. Workshop on Computational Intelligence in Security for Information Systems CISIS'08*, pages 227–234, 2008.

[48] S. Kanade, D. Petrovska-Delacretaz, and B. Dorizzi. Multi-biometrics based cryptographic key regeneration scheme. In *IEEE 3rd Int. Conf. on Biometrics: Theory, Applications, and Systems, BTAS '09*, pages 1–7, 2009.

[49] V. S. Meenakshi and G. Padmavathi. Security analysis of password hardened multimodal biometric fuzzy vault. *World Academy of Science, Engineering and Technology*, 56, 2009.

[50] A. Jagadeesan, T.Thillaikkarasi, and K.Duraiswamy. Cryptographic key generation from multiple biometric modalities: Fusing minutiae with iris feature. *Int. Journal of Computer Applications*, 2(6):16–26, 2010.

[51] M. Zhang, B. Yang, W. Zhang, and T. Takagi. Multibiometric based secure encryption and authentication scheme with fuzzy extractor. *Int. Journal of Network Security*, 12(1):50–57, 2011.

[52] Anil K. Jain, Karthik Nandakumar, and Abhishek Nagar. Biometric template security. *EURASIP J. Adv. Signal Process*, 2008:1–17, 2008.

[53] F. Willems and T. Ignatenko. Identification and secret-key binding in binary-symmetric template-protected biometric systems. In *Proc. of IEEE Workshop on Information Forensics and Security (WIFS)*, 2010.

[54] E. J. C. Kelkboom, G. G. Molina, J. Breebaart, R. N. J. Veldhuis, T. A. M. Kevenaar, and W. Jonker. Binary biometrics: An analytic framework to estimate the performance curves under gaussian assumption. *Trans. on System, Man, and Cybernetics-Part A: Systems and Humans*, 40(3):555–571, 2010.

[55] A. Stoianov, T. Kevenaar, and M. van der Veen. Security issues of biometric encryption. In *Proc. of the Toronto Int. Conf. Science and Technology for Humanity (TIC-STH)*, pages 34–39, 2009.

[56] I. R. Buhan, J. M. Doumen, P. H. Hartel, and R. N. J. Veldhuis. Fuzzy extractors for continuous distributions. Technical report, University of Twente, 2006.

[57] E. J. C. Kelkboom, J. Breebaart, I. Buhan, and R. N. J. Veldhuis. Analytical template protection performance and maximum key size given a gaussian modeled biometric source. In *Proc. of SPIE defense, security and sensing*, 2010.

[58] T. Ignatenko and F. M. J. Willems. Information leakage in fuzzy commitment schemes. *Trans. on Information Forensics and Security*, 5(2):337–348, 2010.

[59] X. Zhou, A. Kuijper, R. N. J. Veldhuis, and C. Busch. Quantifying privacy and security of biometric fuzzy commitment. In *Int'l Joint Conf. on Biometrics - IJCB2011*, pages 1–8, 2011.

Chapter 9

Generation of Cryptographic Keys from Personal Biometrics: An Illustration Based on Fingerprints

Bon K. Sy and Arun P. Kumara Krishnan

Additional information is available at the end of the chapter

http://dx.doi.org/10.5772/51372

1. Introduction

Biometric approach for authentication is appealing because of its convenience and possibility to offer security with non-repudiation. However, additional hardware such as biometric scanners and complex software for feature extraction and biometric template matching are required if biometric approach is to provide security for protecting sensitive data such as personal health information.

Cryptographic approach, on the other hand, ties data protection mathematically to the *Key* that is utilized to protect it. This allows a data owner to have complete control over one's personal information without relying on, or relinquishing control to, a third party authority. The protection of personal sensitive information is also not tied to complex software and hardware systems that may need constant patches.

Biometric authentication and authorization for data protection could be thought of as enabling security based on "what one is." The lynchpin of biometric security is the use of sufficiently unique, but often imprecise, physiological or behavioral traits to characterize an individual for authentication and identification purposes. The characterization is expressed in form of some biometric signature, which often can be reduced to some feature vector or matrix representation. For example, a biometric face could be expressed in terms of a linearized vector of color distribution [1], EigenMap [2], or Eigen Face components [3]. In our research a fingerprint is expressed in terms of a 320x1 vector of integers containing minutia point information, and a voice signature is expressed in terms of a 20x1 mean vector and a 20x20 covariance matrix of Mel cepstrum characterizing the multi-variant Gaussian distribution of an individual's voiceprint [4]. The security parameter for assessing the strength of a biometrically based approach is typically related to the size of the underlying feature vector (or matrix) and the number of bits for representing a value, as well as the biometric data distribution leading to inter and intra variability --- a main source of false negative or false positive alarms when applying biometric approach for security.

On the other hand, cryptographically based security could be thought of as a security approach based on "what one knows." The lynchpin of cryptographic security is the secret key for decrypting a cipher text that is the encrypted from sensitive data. The security parameter for assessing the strength of a cryptographic approach is typically the key size in terms of the number of bits, and information leakage which can be measured by the information gain on the sensitive data given its corresponding cipher text and the mathematical structure of the cryptographic mechanism for encryption/decryption. In order to mitigate the risk of information leakage, semantic security is desirable. In brief, we say it is semantically secure with IND-CPA property (INDistinguishability under Chosen Plaintext Attack) [5] if one is given the cipher texts of some encryption, one could not tell whether the cipher texts correspond to the encryption of the same text; i.e., the given cipher texts are indistinguishable, thus thwarting a Chosen Plaintext Attack.

In theory, the size of a biometric signature or the size of a secret key in cryptography could be increased indefinitely to increase the security strength. However, in practice, the limitation in the resolution of biometric sensors, among other factors, does not allow the security strength to be scaled proportionally. On the other hand, cryptographic approach has its own drawback too. Since the confidentiality of sensitive data is protected through encryption, one must keep the decryption key as a secret. Generally the secret key is generated and withheld by the party that handles the decryption of the sensitive data. If the secret key is compromised, the confidentiality of the sensitive data is compromised.

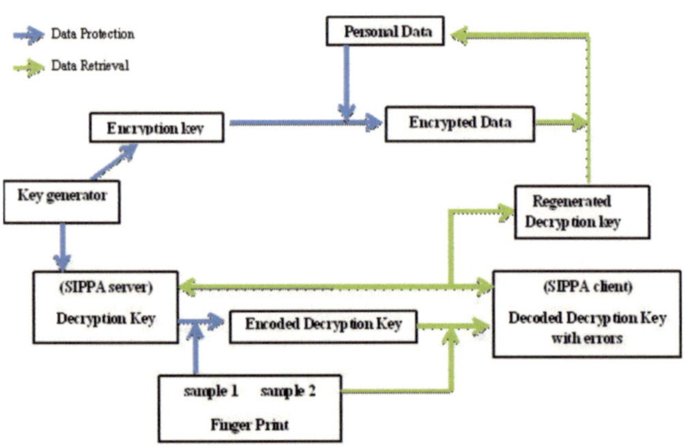

Figure 1. Cryptographic key (re)generation protocol.

The objective of this research is to investigate a secure computation protocol for (re)generating cryptographic key based on biometric signatures. More specifically, we want to protect sensitive personal data based on strong cryptographic approach (e.g., AES256) [6]. But we do not store the secret key anywhere. Instead, we (re)generate the secret key based on an individual's biometric signatures; e.g., fingerprints or voiceprints. In this research we focus on fingerprints. In other words, we use a (cryptographic) key generator to generate the encryption/decryption key pair, and use the key to encrypt the sensitive personal information. Afterward, we discard the key generator and the encryption key. Then, we encode the decryption key using an individual's biometric signatures. The encrypted personal data and the encoded decryption key are given to the individual while the original decryption key will be kept in a separated server without the sensitive personal data. During the retrieval process, the data owner will use his/her biometric signature to *subtract* from the encoded decryption key, and then use it to reconstruct the exact decryption key through SIPPA-2.0 for decrypting the personal information.

The contribution of this research is a cryptographic key (re)generation scheme based on biometrics. The scheme is comprised of the following components:

1. A client/server model is developed for privacy preserving cryptographic key regeneration; where the decryption key --- no (encrypted) personal data --- is stored in the server. In this case, the security and the privacy of the data are still preserved even if the server is compromised. The client party, on the other hand, holds a storage device containing the encrypted sensitive data and the decryption key encoded with personal biometrics. Without the individual's biometrics, decryption key cannot be decoded, thus the confidentiality of the encrypted sensitive data is still preserved even if the storage device is compromised or stolen.

2. A 2-party secure computation protocol, referred to as *SLSSP*(Secure Linear System Solution Protocol), is developed for privacy preserving data comparison based on solving linear equations that yields a solution; and this solution can be used to estimate the similarity or the closeness between the source (server side) data and the target (client side) data.

3. A secure information processing protocol, referred to as SIPPA-2.0 (Secure Information Processing with Privacy Assurance Version 2.0), is developed to realize a 2-party message exchange protocol through which the client and the server could determine how similar their data are to each other by using SLSSP --- without ever revealing their own private data. Furthermore, the client can perfectly reconstruct the server side data if the server provides helper data after the server side determines that the client data is sufficiently similar; whereas the perfect reconstruction is based on a geometrical relationship in the vector space among the helper data and the Eigen components of the client and source data.

4. For proof-of-concept, we implement the cryptographic key regeneration scheme as an Android application for privacy preserving health data management. More specifically, the Android application stores in the memory of a smart phone the encrypted health data and the decryption key encoded by personal fingerprints. During the health data retrieval process, the Android application receives a fingerprint sample (from a fingerprint scanner via a Bluetooth channel) and uses it as an offset to the encoded decryption key to arrive at an estimated decryption key; and then acts as a client to invoke SLSSP and SIPPA for reconstructing a perfect decryption key based on the helper data of the server when the estimated decryption key is sufficiently similar to the actual decryption key.

2. Problem formulation and Related Work

2.1. SLSSP and SIPPA formulation

The concept of SLSSP (formerly referred to as PPCSC) and SIPPA was first introduced in the book chapter of *Biometrics* [7] (INTECH 2011). SLSSP aims at solving the following problem:

Let P1 and P2 be two parties and each has private data (Ai, bi) for i=1,2; whereas Ai is a matrix and bi is a vector. Both parties wish to compute x in (A1+ A2)x = (b1 + b2) without revealing its own private data (Ai, bi) to each other.

In section 6 we will present the protocol design of SLSSP --- which is an improved version of PPCSC. The security and privacy analysis of SLSSP under realistic and reasonable model assumptions will be presented in the appendix. Specifically, the security and privacy of SLSSP will be analyzed under these model assumptions; authenticated communication channels with computational security, the behavior of the participants being rational, and the computational power of the adversary is polynomial bounded[1]. Our SLSSP possess the following two desirable security properties:

(a) The malicious behavior of a party deviating from semi-honest behavior is detectable through verifiable correctness of the private message exchange.

(b) The practical implementation of the homomorphic encryption for SLSSP realizes semantic security with IND-CPA property.

SIPPA-2.0 is the second generation of our secure computation protocol for the following 2-party scenario; where a client party can reconstruct source data of a server party under the following conditions:

(a) The client party must possess some client data that is a "sufficiently good approximation" of the source data, in order to initiate the SIPPA process.

(b) Rather than revealing the source data of the server party to the client party, only some helper data related to the Eigen components of the source data is provided (by the server party) to the client party for reconstructing the source data.

2-party SIPPA-2.0 is a secure process for private data reconstruction with the following desirable security and privacy properties:

(a) The server party retains complete control over the sharing of helper data – thus keeping private the source data - based on the "closeness" between the client and server data.

(b) The server party can determine the "closeness" between the client and server data without the client party ever disclosing it's data to the server party – thus the privacy of both client and server data is respected.

---

1 The analysis presented in the appendix is part of our other paper entitled "SIPPA-2.0 – Secure Information Processing with Privacy Assurance (version 2.0)" appeared in the proceeding of the PST 2012, Paris, France. It is included to make this chapter self-sufficient.

(c) Only if the client and server data are sufficiently close and the server sends the client the helper data, the client can perfectly reconstruct the source data.

The major improvement of SIPPA-2.0 over the previous one is the use of a newly discovered computational geometry that allows perfect data reconstruction from the solution x securely computed in SLSSP. Before we discuss the details of SIPPA-2.0, we first present a survey on related work.

2.2. Related Work

Our research draws from various other works in the literature of biometrics and secure computation. We first discuss the major works in biometrics on which we draw upon, and then the advances in secure computation to which SIPPA-2.0 is related.

Hao et al. [8] [9] were among the pioneers in successfully melding biometrics with cryptography. Iris codes typically contain 10-20% error between samples of the same eye. By utilizing a two tier approach of Hadamard and Reed Solomon Codes to correct both random and burst errors; they achieved a successful *Key* retrieval rate of over 99%. Our research draws from their overall approach of appending a random *Key* with biometrics and then negating this appended biometrics with another biometric sample to retrieve the original cryptographic *Key*. However, SIPPA-2.0 allows us to achieve perfect key reconstruction without using any error correction codes such as Hadamard or Reed Solomon.

Barni et al. [10] utilize a finger-code approach to represent a fingerprint partitioned into sectors from a reference point. Their approach is to utilize these finger-codes to perform fingerprint matching over homomorphic encryption; essentially computing a Euclidean distance between two sets of finger-codes over homomorphic encryption. In contrast to traditional matching methods, such an approach is more privacy aware because the matching process does not expose the biometric sample being matched to the matching agent. Our research draws a few ideas from them including the use of a reference point and sector segmentation to represent fingerprints. However, we notice that any approach applying homomorphic encryption for matching comparison is restricted by using only the matching functions that can be privately computed via the multiplicative or additive properties of the specific homomorphic encryption. In our research, homomorphic encryption is applied in the (SIPPA-2.0) protocol layer which allows not only private data comparison, but source data reconstruction; thus providing additional flexibility on the choice of matching criteria and functions.

Clancy et al. [11] pioneered the use of fingerprints to generate cryptographic Keys. Their essential approach is to use Minutia points as the feature set and Reed-Solomon error correction to handle noise inherent in biometric samples. To describe their approach in their own words:

"Fingerprint minutiae coordinates m_i are encoded as elements in a Finite Field F and the secret Key is encoded in a polynomial f(x) over F[x]. The polynomial is evaluated at the minutiae locations, and the pairs (m_i; $f(m_i)$) are stored along with random (c_i; d_i) chaff points such that $d_i != f(c_i)$. Given a matching Fingerprint, a valid user can separate out enough true points from the chaff points to reconstruct f(x), and hence the original secret Key."

Clancy et al. in their pioneering work achieved a *Key* size of 69 bits, with an EER (Equal Error Rate) at about 30%. Our research also draws inspiration from Clancy et al. in their overall approach of melding a proven biometric modality such as fingerprints with the field of cryptography; bringing forth desirable properties such as non-repudiation into the field of cryptography. In our research we are able to show a much improved result for a similar approach that can accommodate an arbitrary large key size and a much better EER. We will show one such result in the experimental study section of this book chapter.

Recently, non-minutiae methods as features for fingerprint are proposed in addition to the minutiae methods [39, 40], these methods are viable alternatives to consider in trying to improve the performance of many cryptographic key generation protocols.In this research we have primarily focused on minutiae features as data points for our cryptographic key generation protocol. On the other hand, Lalithamani et al. [12] proposed a method utilizing cancellable biometrics to transform a fingerprint into a revocable form; this revocable form is then transformed into an irrevocable viable cryptographic *Key*. The essence of this approach relies on image processing to transform noisy biometric samples into standard representations, from which a cryptographic *Key* is derived. Unfortunately, no practical experimental data was presented utilizing this approach. Nonetheless, this is another indication on the potential interest in combining biometrics with cryptography.

Various secure computation protocols based on cryptographic approach have been developed in the past for privacy preserving data comparison [13] [14]. One main thrust is to rely on Oblivious Transfer (OT) protocols [15] for private joint table lookup. Privacy protection is achieved by transmitting encrypted versions of the entire table using pre-computed public keys. However, even with significant progress in reducing the computational complexity of OT protocols, the relative enormity of the table size coupled with the complexity of encrypting large amounts of data with public key cryptography makes OT based Secure Computation protocols impractical for certain viable privacy preserving applications such as biometrics.

Recent advances in cryptography has led to various cryptosystems that preserve certain operations such as addition [16], multiplication [17], and XOR [18], in the encrypted domain. Such cryptosystems are classified into either Partially Homomorphic (PH) [19] [20] or Fully Homomorphic (FH) [21]. A PH cryptosystem does not allow the evaluation of both addition and multiplication in encrypted domain; and a FH allows the evaluation of unlimited addition and multiplication operations in encrypted domain. A FH cryptosystem would allow [13] the secure evaluation of any function in the encrypted domain where the privacy of the original data is guaranteed if knowing only the function output is not a privacy concern. However the only known semantically secure FH cryptosystems are extremely inefficient for practical use. To put it in context, recently, one of the leading inventors of such a FH cryptosystem Craig Gentry, states that performing a single search query utilizing the best available FH cryptosystem would increase computational complexity by about a trillion [22].

To balance the practical usability and the complexity inherited in a fully homomorphic cryptosytem, we develop SIPPA-2.0 that allows parallelization while relying only on cryptosystems that are Partially Homomorphic for cryptographic key generation from biometric data such as fingerprints. Over the past few years, privacy preserving protocols based on homomorphic cryptosystems have also been developed; e.g., protocol for secure scalar/dot product between vectors [23], protocol for secure Euclidean distance derivation between vectors [24], secure Hamming distance protocol [25], secure evaluation of linear systems [26], and k-mean clustering [27]. These protocols are practically usable in biometric applications and utilize semantically secure Partially Homomorphic (PH) cryptosystems to achieve metric specific privacy preserving biometric authentication. SIPPA-2.0 takes the current state-of-the-art one step further by facilitating not just private data comparison which can be used for privacy preserving biometric authentication, but also private data reconstruction for biometric information retrieval.

3. Theoretical Foundation of SIPPA-2.0

The theoretical foundation of SIPPA-2.0 is built upon two main theorems. We first summarize the important findings of the theorems, and then present the rigorous formulation and proof, followed by the use of the theorems to realize the SIPPA-2.0 protocol for private reconstruction of the server source data by the client.

Let P1 and P2 be the SIPPA-2.0 server and client respectively. Let **de** and **dv** be the column vector representing private data of P1 and P2 respectively. Let (λ_{De} $\mathbf{v_{de}}$) and (λ_{Dv} $\mathbf{v_{dv}}$) be the 2-tuples of the most significant Eigen value and the corresponding unity normalized Eigen vector of the matrices $\mathbf{de}\bullet\mathbf{de}^T$ and $\mathbf{dv}\bullet\mathbf{dv}^T$ respectively.

If the deviation between the most significant eigenvector of $\mathbf{de}\bullet\mathbf{de}^T$ and $\mathbf{dv}\bullet\mathbf{dv}^T$ (similarity score) correlates to the distribution of the instances of **de** and **dv** as classified by being from the same or different biometric source, this provides a basis for a good threshold function. SIPPA-2.0 can then be utilized to provide secure and private derivation on this deviation, without each party revealing their private biometric data to each other.

We will show in theorem 1 below that there is an algebraic relationship between the symmetric matrix representation of the client and the server data in the Eigen vector space; and the algebraic relationship guarantees the existence of a bisector vector that allows each party to use it to determine whether the client and server data are sufficiently similar. Second, the source data can be perfectly reconstructed by the client if a carefully scaled Eigen value of the symmetric matrix representation of the source data is given. In other words, this scaled Eigen value serves as the helper data --- and the only data --- that the server needs to share; thus the privacy of the server side source data is preserved.

Theorem 1: Consider $(\mathbf{de}\bullet\mathbf{de}^T + \mathbf{dv}\bullet\mathbf{dv}^T)x = \lambda_{de}\,\mathbf{v}_{de} + \lambda_{dv}\,\mathbf{v}_{dv}$, the solution x = v satisfying $(\mathbf{de}\bullet\mathbf{de}^T + \mathbf{dv}\bullet\mathbf{dv}^T)\mathbf{v} = \lambda_{de}\,\mathbf{v}_{de} + \lambda_{dv}\,\mathbf{v_{dv}}$ has a unity scalar projection onto the unity normalized $\mathbf{v_{de}}$ and $\mathbf{v_{dv}}$, and is a bisector for the interior angle between $\mathbf{v_{de}}$ and $\mathbf{v_{dv}}$.

Proof: By the definition of Eigen vectors and values, $\mathbf{de}\bullet\mathbf{de}^{T}\bullet\mathbf{v_{de}} = \lambda_{de}\,\mathbf{v_{de}}$. Since $\mathbf{de}^{T}\bullet\mathbf{v_{de}}$ is a scalar, **de** and $\mathbf{v_{de}}$ has the same directionality. Furthermore, $\mathbf{de}/|\mathbf{de}| = \mathbf{v_{de}}$ because $\mathbf{v_{de}}$ is a unity normalized vector. Similarly, $\mathbf{dv}/|\mathbf{dv}| = \mathbf{v_{dv}}$, and the following results can be established:

$$\mathbf{de}/|\mathbf{de}| = \mathbf{v_{de}}\mathbf{de}\bullet\mathbf{de}^{T}\bullet\mathbf{v_{de}} = \lambda_{de}\mathbf{v_{de}} \;\blacksquare\; (\mathbf{de}/|\mathbf{de}|)\bullet(|\mathbf{de}|\bullet\mathbf{de}^{T}\bullet\mathbf{v_{de}}) = (\mathbf{v_{de}})(\lambda_{de}) \;\blacksquare\; \lambda_{de} = \mathbf{de}^{T}\bullet\mathbf{de}$$

$$\mathbf{dv}/|\mathbf{dv}| = \mathbf{v_{dv}}\mathbf{dv}\bullet\mathbf{dv}^{T}\bullet\mathbf{v_{dv}} = \lambda_{dv}\mathbf{v_{dv}} \;\blacksquare\; (\mathbf{dv}/|\mathbf{dv}|)\bullet(|\mathbf{dv}|\bullet\mathbf{dv}^{T}\bullet\mathbf{v_{dv}}) = (\mathbf{v_{dv}})(\lambda_{dv}) \;\blacksquare\; \lambda_{dv} = \mathbf{dv}^{T}\bullet\mathbf{dv}$$

To prove theorem 1, we need to prove that (1) **v** has a unity scalar projection onto the unity normalized **de** and **dv**, and (2) **v** is a bisector.

To prove **v** has a unity scalar projection onto the unity normalized $\mathbf{v_{de}}$ and $\mathbf{v_{dv}}$, it is sufficient to show $\mathbf{v_{de}}\bullet\,\mathbf{v} = \mathbf{v_{dv}}\bullet\mathbf{v} = 1$, or $(\mathbf{de}/|\mathbf{de}|)\bullet\mathbf{v} = (\mathbf{dv}/|\mathbf{dv}|)\bullet\mathbf{v} = 1$. Since **v** is a solution to $(\mathbf{de}\bullet\mathbf{de}^{T} + \mathbf{dv}\bullet\mathbf{dv}^{T})\mathbf{x} = \lambda_{de}\,\mathbf{v_{de}} + \lambda_{dv}\,\mathbf{v_{dv}}$, we re-write the RHS and the LHS as below:

$$\text{LHS} = (\mathbf{de}\bullet\mathbf{de}^{T} + \mathbf{dv}\bullet\mathbf{dv}^{T})\mathbf{v} = \mathbf{de}\bullet(\mathbf{de}^{T}\bullet\mathbf{v}) + \mathbf{dv}\bullet(\mathbf{dv}^{T}\bullet\mathbf{v})$$
$$= |\mathbf{de}|\bullet\mathbf{de}\bullet(\mathbf{de}^{T}\bullet\mathbf{v}/|\mathbf{de}|) + |\mathbf{dv}|\bullet\mathbf{dv}\bullet(\mathbf{dv}^{T}\bullet\mathbf{v}/|\mathbf{dv}|)$$

$$\text{RHS} = \lambda_{de}\,\mathbf{v_{de}} + \lambda_{dv}\,\mathbf{v_{dv}} = \mathbf{de}^{T}\bullet\mathbf{de}\bullet(\mathbf{de}/|\mathbf{de}|) + \mathbf{dv}^{T}\bullet\mathbf{dv}\bullet(\mathbf{dv}/|\mathbf{dv}|)$$

$= |\mathbf{de}|\bullet\mathbf{de} + |\mathbf{dv}|\bullet\mathbf{dv}$ because $\mathbf{de}^{T}\bullet\mathbf{de} = |\mathbf{de}|^{2}$ and $\mathbf{dv}^{T}\bullet\mathbf{dv} = |\mathbf{dv}|^{2}$

Comparing the terms on the RHS and LHS, when de and dv are linearly independent, $\mathbf{de}^{T}\bullet\mathbf{v}/|\mathbf{de}| = 1 \;\blacksquare\; (\mathbf{de}/|\mathbf{de}|)\bullet\mathbf{v} = \mathbf{v_{de}}\bullet\mathbf{v} = 1$ and $\mathbf{dv}^{T}\bullet\mathbf{v}/|\mathbf{dv}| = 1 \;\blacksquare\; (\mathbf{dv}/|\mathbf{dv}|)\bullet\mathbf{v} = \mathbf{v_{dv}}\bullet\mathbf{v} = 1$. Therefore, v has a unity scalar projection onto the unity normalized **de** and **dv**. This completes the proof for (1).

The scalar projection of **v** onto $\mathbf{v_{de}}$ is one, and so as the scalar projection of **v** onto $\mathbf{v_{dv}}$. By the theorem of bisector, v is the bisector of the interior angle of $\mathbf{v_{de}}$ and $\mathbf{v_{dv}}$. This completes the proof for (2).

Theorem 2: Consider $(\mathbf{de}\bullet\mathbf{de}^{T} + \mathbf{dv}\bullet\mathbf{dv}^{T})\mathbf{x} = \lambda_{de}\,\mathbf{v_{de}} + \lambda_{dv}\,\mathbf{v_{dv}}$, **de** can be efficiently reconstructed – with an accuracy proportional to the closeness between $\mathbf{v_{de}}$ and $\mathbf{v_{dv}}$ – by a party with **dv**, λ_{dv},, and $\mathbf{v_{dv}}$ when (i) the interior angle between $\mathbf{v_{de}}$ and $\mathbf{v_{dv}}$ is less than 90 degree and (ii) the party is given **x** and $\lambda_{de}/\,\mathbf{de}^{T}\bullet\mathbf{x}$. Specifically, $\mathbf{de} = (\mathbf{est\_v_{de}}/|\,\mathbf{est\_v_{de}}|)(\lambda_{de}/\,\mathbf{de}^{T}\,\mathbf{x})$; where

$$\mathbf{est\_v_{de}} = \mathbf{v_{dv}} + [|\mathbf{v_{dv}}|\bullet\tan(2\cos^{-1}(\mathbf{v_{dv}}\bullet\mathbf{x}/(|\mathbf{v_{dv}}|\bullet|\mathbf{x}|)))]\bullet[(\mathbf{x}-\mathbf{v_{dv}})/|\mathbf{x}-\mathbf{v_{dv}}|]$$

Proof: Let $\mathbf{x} = \mathbf{v_{de}} + \mathbf{e1}$ and $\mathbf{x} = \mathbf{v_{dv}} + \mathbf{e2}$. We can derive the length of **te** (as shown in Fig. 2), which is a vector with the same directionality as that of the vector **e2** when the interior angle between $\mathbf{v_{de}}$ and $\mathbf{v_{dv}}$ is less than 90 degree. Specifically, $\mathbf{v_{dv}}$ and **e2** are orthogonal (i.e., they are perpendicular of each other). The length of $\mathbf{te}=|\mathbf{te}|=[|\mathbf{v_{dv}}|\bullet\tan(2\cos^{-1}(\mathbf{v_{dv}}\bullet\mathbf{x}/(|\mathbf{v_{dv}}|\bullet|\mathbf{x}|)))]$ because $\mathbf{e1} = \mathbf{e2}$ and the angle between $\mathbf{v_{dv}}$ and $(\mathbf{v_{dv}} + \mathbf{te})$ is twice the angle between $\mathbf{v_{dv}}$ and **x** (theorem 1). Therefore, $\mathbf{te}=|\mathbf{te}|\bullet[\mathbf{e2}/|\mathbf{e2}|]=[|\mathbf{v_{dv}}|\bullet\tan(2\cos^{-1}(\mathbf{v_{dv}}\bullet\mathbf{x}/(|\mathbf{v_{dv}}|\bullet|\mathbf{x}|)))]\bullet[\mathbf{e2}/|\mathbf{e2}|]$. Since $\mathbf{v_{dv}} + \mathbf{te}$ (=$\mathbf{est\_v_{de}}$) produces a vector with the same directionality as $\mathbf{v_{de}}$, and $\mathbf{v_{de}}$ is a unity normalized vector, we can conveniently derive $\mathbf{v_{de}}$ by normalizing $\mathbf{est\_v_{de}}$; i.e., $\mathbf{v_{de}} = \mathbf{est\_v_{de}}/|\,\mathbf{est\_v_{de}}|$. Finally, since $\mathbf{de}\bullet\mathbf{de}^{T}\mathbf{x} \approx \lambda_{de}\,\mathbf{v_{de}}$, we can derive **de** from $(\lambda_{de}/\,\mathbf{de}^{T}\bullet\mathbf{x})\bullet\mathbf{v_{de}}$ or $(\lambda_{de}/\,\mathbf{de}^{T}\bullet\mathbf{x})\bullet(\mathbf{est\_v_{de}}/|\mathbf{est\_v_{de}}|)$ with an approximation error proportional to the closeness between $\mathbf{v_{de}}$ and $\mathbf{v_{dv}}$. Q.E.D.

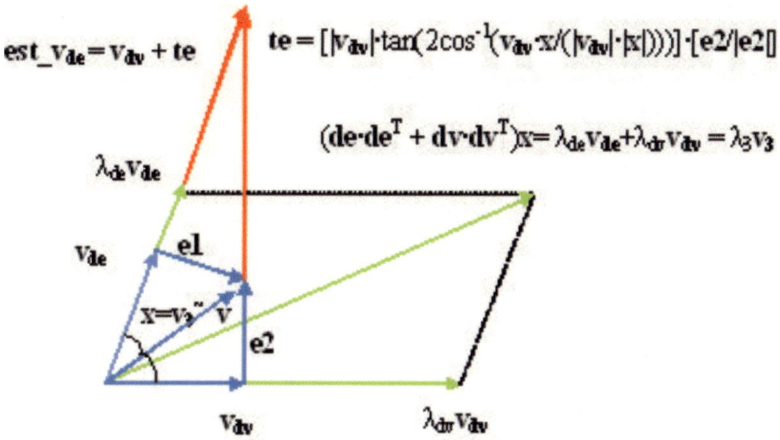

Figure 2. Geometric relationship between x and eigenvector of data.

3.1. Secure Computation of Angular Deviation

In SIPPA-2.0, private reconstruction of the server source data by a client relies on the helper data. The server provides the helper data only if the target data of the client is sufficiently close to the source data. But how could the server determine the closeness between the target data and the source data while the client can keep the target data private? As shown in figure3, v_{de}, v_{dv} and x all converge to each other when **de** and **dv** converge to each other. In addition, the matrices $\mathbf{de} \bullet \mathbf{de}^T$ and $\mathbf{dv} \bullet \mathbf{dv}^T$ can be thought of as the mapping functions for the eigenvectors and x. The difference between **de** and **dv** proportionality affects the difference in the mapping functions, which subsequently introduces an angular deviation on the angle between the unity normalized Eigen vectors as well as the magnitude deviation as measured by the Euclidean distance between the two Eigen vectors scaled by the corresponding Eigen values. Therefore, angular deviation and magnitude deviation between the client and server Eigen vectors can be used to obtain the information about the closeness between the target and the source data.

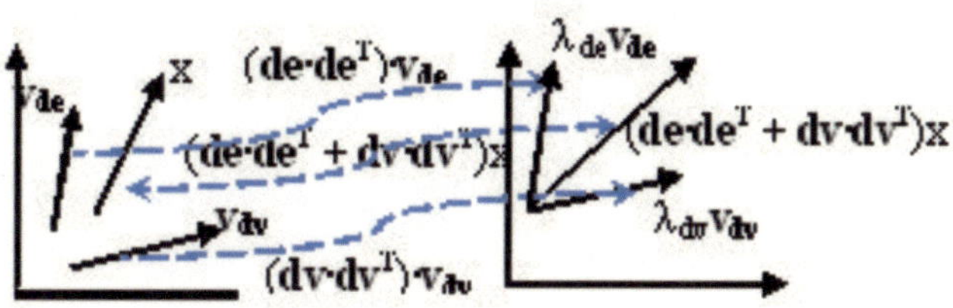

Figure 3. Relationship between source and target data in Eigen space.

In SIPPA-2.0, if angular deviation is used as the metric to determine closeness, then both the server and the client can privately and precisely determine whether the data of the other party is sufficiently similar without revealing one's own private data. Recall from theorem 2 the angular deviation can be derived from $2\cos^{-1}(\mathbf{v_{dv}} \bullet \mathbf{x} / (|\mathbf{v_{dv}}| \bullet |\mathbf{x}|))$ or $2\cos^{-1}(\mathbf{v_{de}} \bullet \mathbf{x} / (|\mathbf{v_{de}}| \bullet |\mathbf{x}|))$. If x is known, each party with one's own Eigen vector can derive the angular deviation.

Therefore, a key aspect to realize SIPPA-2.0 is a 2-party secure computation protocol through which the client and the server can collaborate to solve for x in the algebraic system $(\mathbf{de}\bullet\mathbf{de}^{T} + \mathbf{dv}\bullet\mathbf{dv}^{T})\mathbf{x} = \lambda_{de}\,\mathbf{v_{de}} + \lambda_{dv}\,\mathbf{v_{dv}}$ while each party will keep one's data, Eigen value and Eigen vector private. Furthermore, the security and privacy of SIPPA-2.0 will defer to the security and privacy of the 2-party secure computation protocol for solving the algebraic system. In this research we show one such protocol, referred to as SLSSP (Secure Linear System Solution Protocol), that we developed. As formulated in section 3, SLSSP is a novel and general two-party secure computation protocol to solve for x in (A1+ A2)x = (b1 + b2) without each party revealing their private data (Ai, bi) to each other.

There are two noteworthy points about SLSSP. First SLSSP is readily available to realize SIPPA-2.0 with (A1, b1) and (A2, b2) being $(\mathbf{de}\bullet\mathbf{de}^{T}, \lambda_{de}\,\mathbf{v_{de}})$ and $(\mathbf{dv}\bullet\mathbf{dv}^{T}, \lambda_{dv}\,\mathbf{v_{dv}})$ respectively. Second, SLSSP has the same problem formulation as that of PPCSC (Privacy Preserving Collaborative Scientific Computation). Our focus on SLSSP is to also achieve desirable security properties so that SLSSP is secure and private under realistic and reasonable assumptions discussed in section 3.

4. Procotol design for SLSSP and SIPPA

4.1. SIPPA2.0 Protocol

There are three major aspects of SIPPA-2.0: (1) derivation of the eigenvalues and the corresponding unity normalized eigenvectors of the symmetric matrix representation of the data; (2) derivation of a vector x which provides for the two parties to determine the deviation between their respective eigenvectors, which is formulated as a two-party secure computation SLSSP [28]; and if required: (3) reconstruction of the source data based on *helper data* composed of a scalar eigenvalue combined with a scalar derived from the vector product between the transpose of the linearized source data vector and the vector x. The steps for the SIPPA2.0 protocol are detailed below using the notation introduced in the previous section:

Step 1: Derive, by the respective party, the most significant eigenvalue and its corresponding unity-normalized eigenvector of $\mathbf{de}\bullet\mathbf{de}^{T}$ and $\mathbf{dv}\bullet\mathbf{dv}^{T}$. This step yields $(\lambda_{de}\,\mathbf{v_{de}})$ for SIPPA2.0 server and $(\lambda_{dv}\,\mathbf{v_{dv}})$ for SIPPA2.0 client.

Step 2: Compute $\mathbf{x}$ such that $(\mathbf{de}\bullet\mathbf{de}^{T} + \mathbf{dv}\bullet\mathbf{dv}^{T})\mathbf{x} = \lambda_{de}\,\mathbf{v_{de}} + \lambda_{dv}\,\mathbf{v_{dv}}$ utilizing SLSSP. The vector x is known to both parties following SLSSP. The details on SLSSP will be presented later in this section.

Step 3: The party that wishes to determine the deviation between its eigenvector and the other party's eigenvector can do so utilizing x (derived in step 2). Suppose that the party with $\mathbf{v_{de}}$ wishes to determine the angular deviation between $\mathbf{v_{de}}$ and $\mathbf{v_{dv}}$, this can be done by obtaining the angle between $\mathbf{v_{de}}$ and x. i.e. $\cos^{-1}(\mathbf{v_{de}}\bullet\mathbf{x}/(|\mathbf{v_{de}}|\bullet|\mathbf{x}|))$. The angular deviation between $\mathbf{v_{de}}$ and $\mathbf{v_{dv}}$ is then

$2\cos^{-1}(\mathbf{v_{de}}\bullet\mathbf{x}/(|\mathbf{v_{de}}|\bullet|\mathbf{x}|))$.

Step 4: If **de** and **dv** are sufficiently similar as determined by either the angular distance or the Euclidean distance between vectors $\mathbf{v_{de}}$ and $\mathbf{v_{dv}}$ as measured by some pre-defined threshold, proceed to send the following helper data: $\lambda_{de}/\mathbf{de}^{T}\bullet x$.

Remark: We can also only send $(\lambda_{de})^{0.5}$ as the helper data to allow perfect reconstruction of $\mathbf{de}=(\mathbf{est\_v_{de}}/|\mathbf{est\_v_{de}}|)(\lambda_{de})^{0.5}$ because (1) $\lambda_{de}=\mathbf{de}^{T}\bullet\mathbf{de}=|\mathbf{de}|^2$ (from Theorem 1), (2) $\mathbf{de}/|\mathbf{de}|=\mathbf{v_{de}}$ or $\mathbf{de}=|\mathbf{de}|\bullet\mathbf{v_{de}}$, (from Theorem 1) and (3)$\mathbf{est\_v_{de}}/|\mathbf{est\_v_{de}}|=\mathbf{v_{de}}$ (from Theorem 2) if we are to realize unconditional source data reconstruction.

Step 5: Derive estimated $\mathbf{v_{de}}$- $\mathbf{est\_v_{de}}$ as stated in theorem 2, and then derive $\mathbf{de}=(\mathbf{est\_v_{de}}/|\mathbf{est\_v_{de}}|)(\lambda_{de}/\mathbf{de}^{T}x)$.

SIPPA-2.0 relies on the protocol SLSSP to solve for x in step 2. To provide semantic security, Pailler encryption is adopted in the protocol design for SLSSP. Pailler encryption is operated over Integer domain on scalar values. Yet SIPPA-2.0 deals with Real Number domain and matrix operations. Therefore, prior to presenting the details on the protocol for SLSSP, we will first discuss two related issues: (i) homomorphic matrix addition and multiplication with encrypted matrices, and (ii) the fixed point representation of real numbers.

4.2. Homomorphic Matrix addition and Multiplication with Encrypted Matrices.

All matrix operations described in this section require knowledge of only the Pailler public-key pair(g, n). Encrypted matrices and vectors are denoted$[[M]]^{P(g,n)}$, $[[v]]^{P(g,n)}$respectively, where each element of the matrix or vector is an element encrypted utilizing the Paillier public-key pair (g, n). Specifically, the decryption of any element $[[M]]_{i,j}^{P(g,n)}$ equals $M_{i,j}$ i.e. $M_{i,j}=PD\left([[M]]_{i,j}^{P(g,n)}\right)$. The operator "[+]" denotes homomorphic addition of matrices or vectors; whereas the operator "[X]" represents multiplication of matrices, where one of the two matrices are encrypted.

4.2.1. Paillier Cryptosystem:

The Paillier encryption scheme is a probabilistic, asymmetric, public-key cryptosystem whose security is based on the hypothetical intractability of the Decisional Composite Residuosity Assumption (DCRA). The Paillier encryption function PE(m, r), a bijection $\left(Z_n x Z_n^* \to Z_{n^2}^*\right)$ encrypts a message mby raising a basis gto the power m, then multiplying g^m with a random $r^n$and reducing the product $\left(g^m.r^n\right)$ modulo $n^2$where nis the public modulus. An important consequence of this approach is that the Paillier Cryptosystem is additively homomorphic, specifically the following properties hold:

1. $\left(\left(PE(m_1, r_1) \,.\, PE(m_2, r_2)\right) \bmod n^2\right) = PE(m_1 + m_2,\ r_1 . r_2)$

2. $\left(\left(PE(m_1, r_1) \,.\, g^{m2}\right) \bmod n^2\right) = PE(m_1 + m_2,\ r_1)$

3. $\left(\left(PE(m_1, r_1)^{m2}\right) \bmod n^2\right) = PE(m_1 . m_2,\ r_1)$

Paillier Key Generation:

1. Choose a modulus $n = p \cdot q$. The modulus is chosen in accordance with the RSAES-OAEP [2] specification, where $n$has the properties of a well-chosen RSA modulus.
2. Choose a random $g \in Z_{n^2}^*$ensure that the order of $g$in modulo $n^2$is a multiple of$n$, if not choose another$g$ until the requirement is met.
3. Compute $\lambda = \lambda(n) = \text{lcm}((p-1), (q-1))$, where $\lambda(n)$ is the Carmichael function.
4. Let$L(u) = \frac{(u-1)}{n}$, compute $\mu = (L(g^{\lambda} \bmod n^2))^{-1} \bmod n$.
5. The Paillier public-key pair is (g, n).
6. The Paillier private-key pair is (λ, μ).

The Paillier Encryption function PE(m, r):

Given a Paillier public-key pair, choose a message to be encrypted $m \in Z_n$, and a random$r$ chosen uniformly fromZ_n^*, then the Paillier encryption function is defined as $PE(m, r) = (g^m \cdot r^n) \bmod n^2$.$PE(m, r)$is a bijection $(Z_n x Z_n^* \to Z_{n^2}^*)$which produces a ciphertext $(c \in Z_{n^2}^*)$.

The Paillier decryption function PD(c):

Given a Paillier public-key, private –key pair and a Paillier ciphertext $c \in Z_{n^2}^*$, then the Paillier decryption function is defined as:

$$PD(c) = (L(c^{\lambda} mod\ n^2).\mu)\ mod\ n \tag{1}$$

4.2.2. Homomorphic addition of two matrices:

1. Given two encrypted mXnmatrices $[[A]]^{P(g,n)}$ and$[[B]]^{P(g,n)}$, their homomorphic addition $([[A]]^{P(g,n)}[+][[B]]^{P(g,n)}) = [[A+B]]^{P(g,n)} = [[C]]^{P(g,n)})$ is carried out by multiplying each element of $A$with its matching element in Bi.e.

$$[[C]]_{i,j}^{P(g,n)} = ([[A]]_{i,j}^{P(g,n)} \cdot [[B]]_{i,j}^{P(g,n)})\ mod\ n^2 \tag{2}$$

4.2.3. Multiplication with encrypted matrices.

1. Given an encrypted mXbmatrix $[[A]]^{P(g,n)}$ and a bXnplain-text matrix$B$, $([[A]]^{P(g,n)}[X]B) = [[AB]]^{P(g,n)} = [[C]]^{P(g,n)}$, where $[[C]]^{P(g,n)}$ is an mXnmatrix, which can be computed in the following manner:

$$[[C]]_{i,j}^{P(g,n)} = \left(\prod_{k=1}^{b} \left([[A]]_{i,k}^{P(g,n)}\right)^{B_{k,j}}\right)\ mod\ n^2 \tag{3}$$

2. Given an plain-text mXbmatrix$A$ and an encrypted bXnmatrix $[[B]]^{P(g,n)}(A[X][[B]]^{P(g,n)}) = [[AB]]^{P(g,n)} = [[C]]^{P(g,n)}$, where $[[C]]^{P(g,n)}$ is an mXnmatrix, which can be computed in the following manner:

$$[[C]]_{i,j}^{P(g,n)} = \left(\prod_{k=1}^{b} \left([[B]]_{i,k}^{P(g,n)}\right)^{A_{k,j}}\right) mod\ n^2 \tag{4}$$

4.3. Fixed Point Representation.

The Paillier cryptosystem operates over a finite field Z_n, we extend the cryptosystem to operate over the reals utilizing a simple Fixed Point representation scheme. Let $s \in \mathsf{Z}$be some exponent of 10, then for every $r \in \mathsf{R}$, $r$is represented as$(\lfloor 10^s r \rfloor) \in \mathsf{Z}$. An approximation of r, can be obtained by$\tilde{r} = \frac{\lfloor 10^s r \rfloor}{10^s} \in \mathsf{R}$, specifically:

1. For any$r \in \mathsf{R}^+$, a Paillier ciphertext is obtained by $PE(\lfloor 10^s r \rfloor, x)$, where $x$is some random and$\tilde{r} = \frac{PD(PE(\lfloor 10^s r \rfloor, x))}{10^s}$.

2. For any$r \in \mathsf{R}^-$, a Paillier ciphertext is obtained by $PE(n + \lfloor 10^s r \rfloor, x)$, where $n$is the Paillier modulus and $\tilde{r} = \frac{PD(PE(n + \lfloor 10^s r \rfloor, x)) - n}{10^s}$

It is to be noted that representing reals with a fixed point representation introduces errors due to truncation, which is directly proportional to the size of $s$chosen. The domain of the encryption function is also truncated from Z_n to$\left\{0,1, \ldots \left\lfloor \frac{n-1}{10^s} \right\rfloor\right\}$, whereas extending the fixed point scheme to include negative reals further reduces the encryption domain to $\left\{0,1, \ldots \left\lfloor \frac{n-1}{2 * 10^s} \right\rfloor\right\}$. Since division operations are not properly defined in Paillier, we hold off on downscaling operations in the encrypted domain. A record of the change in scale is kept after each operation in the encrypted domain; this record is utilized to obtain $\tilde{r}$ upon decryption of the result.

4.4. SLSSP protocol details

Step #	PARTY α Private Data: *mXm* Matrix A1, *mX1* vector b1	Step #	PARTY β Private Data: *mXm* Matrix A2, *mX1* vector b2
α1	Generate a random *mXm* matrix**P1**. Generate a random 1Xn vector $\mathbf{v}^T$. Obtain a Paillier Public Key and Private Key pair i.e. (*g*α,*n*α) and (λα,μα) respectively.	β1	Generate a random *mXm* matrix **P2**. Obtain a Paillier Public Key and Private Key pair i.e. (*g*β,*n*β) and (λβ,μβ) respectively.

α2	Compute and Send $([[A1]]^{P(ga,na)})$ and $([[b1]]^{P(ga,na)})$ to PARTY β.	β2	Receive $([[A1]]^{P(ga,na)})$ and $([[b1]]^{P(ga,na)})$ from PARTY α.
α3	Receive $([[A2]]^{P(g\beta,n\beta)})$ and $([[b2]]^{P(g\beta,n\beta)})$ from PARTY β.	β3	Compute and Send $([[A2]]^{P(g\beta,n\beta)})$ and $([[b2]]^{P(g\beta,n\beta)})$ to PARTY α.
α4	Compute and send to PARTY β: $([[P1(A1+A2)]]^{P(g\beta,n\beta)})$	β4	Receive and decrypt matrix obtained from step α4 to obtain a mXm matrix: $(P1(A1+A2))$
α5	Compute $([[(P1(b1+b2)v^{T})]]^{P(g\beta,n\beta)})$	β5	Compute the Moore–Penrose Pseudoinverse of $((P1(A1+A2)))$ to obtain $R=((P1(A1+A2)))^{-1}$
α6	Send the following to party β: $[[Y]]^{P(g\beta,n\beta)}=([[((P1(b1+b2)v^{T}))]]^{P(g\beta,n\beta)})$	β6	Receive from PARTY α (Step α6), and decrypt to obtain $Y=P1(b1+b2)v^{T}$
α7	Send $([[[v^{-1}]]^{P(ga,na)})$ to PARTY β, where v^{-1} is the conjugate transpose of v divided by its magnitude squared.	β7	Receive $[[[v^{-1}]]^{P(ga,na)}$ from step α7 and compute $X1$, utilizing **Y.** Send $X1$ to PARTY α. $X1=[[\mathbf{R^{*}(Y)}]]^{P(g\beta,n\beta)}$
α8	Receive $X1$ from party β, (step β7) and compute the solution $[[x]]^{P(g\beta,n\beta)}$ by homomorphically multiplying v^{-1} to $X1$	β8	Compute the solution $[[x]]^{P(ga,na)}$ by homomorphically multiplying **(R*Y)** to $([[[v^{-1}]]^{P(ga,na)})$
α9	Send $[[x]]^{P(g\beta,n\beta)}$ to PARTY β	β9	Receive $[[x]]^{P(g\beta,n\beta)}$ from PARTY α and decrypt to Obtain the solution x
α10	Receive $[[x]]^{P(ga,na)}$ from PARTY β and decrypt to Obtain the solution x	β10	Send $[[x]]^{P(ga,na)}$ to PARTY α.
VERIFICATION PHASE:			
α10	Compute the mx1 vector using the information obtained in step α3: $\mathbf{c\alpha}=([[((A1+A2)x)-(b1+b2)]]^{P(g\beta,n\beta)})$	β10	Compute the mx1 vector using the information obtained in step β2: $\mathbf{c\beta}=([[((A1+A2)x)-(b1+b2)]]^{P(ga,na)})$
α11	For each element in $\mathbf{c\alpha}_{i,1}$, utilizing the zero-knowledge proof protocol specified in the appendix, verify with party β that $\mathbf{c\alpha}_{i,1}$ is an encryption of some element within a set γ, where the set γ contains a finite list of fixed point elements close to zero. For each verification request from PARTY β, require that one PARTY α's verification request is processed reciprocally. Abort at any $\mathbf{c\alpha}_{i,1}$ if PARTY β is unable to prove that the decryption of $\mathbf{c\alpha}_{i,1}\in\gamma$	β11	For each element in $\mathbf{c\beta}_{i,1}$, utilizing the zero-knowledge proof protocol specified in the appendix, verify with party α that $\mathbf{c\beta}_{i,1}$ is an encryption of some element within a set γ, where the set γ contains a finite list of fixed point elements close to zero. For each verification request from PARTY α, require that one PARTY β's verification request is processed reciprocally. Abort at any $\mathbf{c\beta}_{i,1}$ if PARTY α is unable to prove that the decryption of $\mathbf{c\beta}_{i,1}\in\gamma$

Table 1. SLSSP protocol details

http://dx.doi.org/10.5772/51372

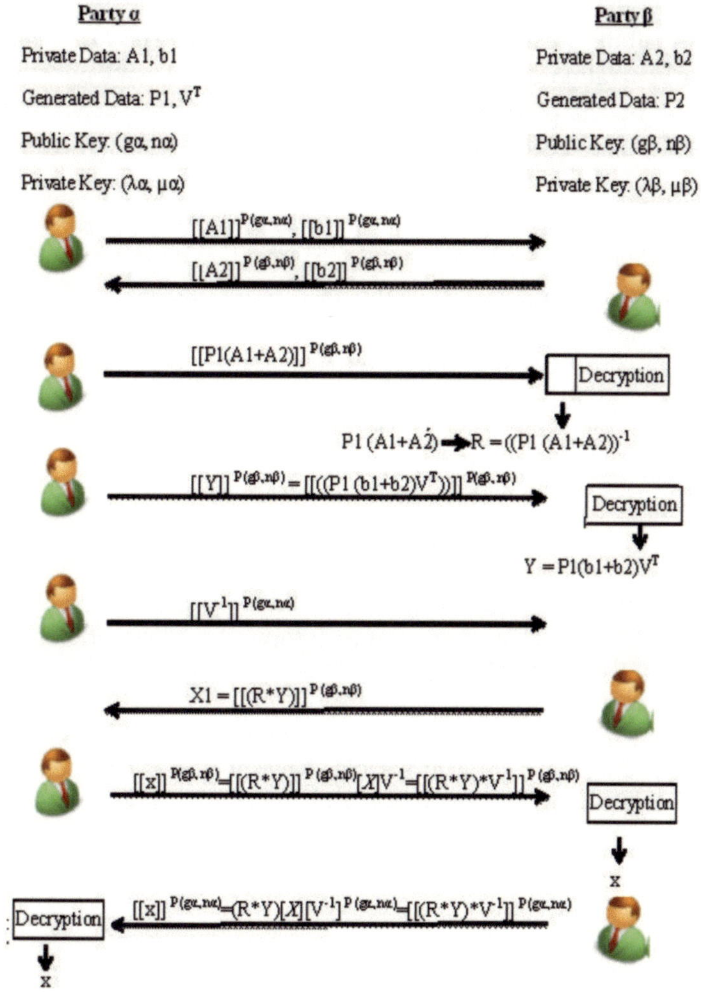

Figure 4. SLSSP protocol illustration.

5. Biometric Crypto Key Experiment & Application Showcase

5.1. Generation and retrieval of cryptographic keys from fingerprints

A modified finger-code approach is used to represent a fingerprint as an *attribute* vector. Several concentric circles are extended from a chosen core point; these concentric circles are further divided into sectors. Each of the sectors forms the boundary of one coding region representing the fingerprint. The Euclidean distance of the farthest and closest minutia points within each coding region in relation to the core point is normalized to a value between 0 and 255. These values make up the above described *attribute* vector. The length of the attribute vector; i.e., the number and area of each coding region is a variable chosen for optimal performance.

In this proposed method, generation of a cryptographic *Key* utilizable with strong symmetric encryption algorithms such as AES256 is straightforward. The *Key* generation phase essentially involves generation of a vector called the *k-vector,* whose length exactly equals the *attribute* vector. The *k-vector* consists of a series of random integers between 0 and 255. A fingerprint template attribute vector (T) is obtained to lock the *k-vector* (K); elementary addition of the two vectors (K + T) produces the locked vector (K_L). The unlocking process begins by deriving an error laden version of K. This is done by procuring a fingerprint sample attribute vector (S), and elementary subtraction (K_L - S) to obtain an error laden k-vector (K_E). K_E typically is not exactly identical to K. It cannot be directly utilized for the decryption of data encrypted with K. Measuring any physical object produces an error between measurements. Hence it is unlikely that matching minutia points in T and S will completely cancel each other during the locking and unlocking process. Our secure computation protocol, SIPPA is utilized to determine the deviation between K_E and K. If the party with K_E deems sufficient similar, it will send *helper data* (as described in the SIPPA section 6) which allows the party with K_E to derive K.

A perfect copy of K is retained at a 3rd party called the SIPPA server, and the SIPPA client engages with the SIPPA server utilizing K_E to obtain a reconstruction of K, if the server deems similarity. SIPPA also guarantees that no information that each of the parties possesses will leak to the other party in the case where T & S are dissimilar.

Figure 5 details the exact parameters utilized by us in our Key generation and retrieval algorithm, A Futronic FS88 [28] fingerprint scanner was utilized to capture fingerprints and a commercial algorithm (Neurotechnology's Verifinger v6.3 [29]) was used to extract minutia and core point coordinates from fingerprints.

5.2. Secure Computation of Angular Deviation

In order to assess SIPPA-2.0's usability in privacy preserving fingerprint biometrics, we conducted our performance analysis with the publicly availalble CASIA-FingerprintV5 database [38]. The database contains five diffrent digital impressions of each finger from 500 subjects. Each of these fingerprint images were converted to our custom fingercode format (as described in figure 8), which yields a 320x1 vector. NEUROtechnology's Verifinger SDK was utilized to orient and extract minutia, corepoints from the fingerprint images.For each session, a random key of size 320x1 of integers in the range 0 and 255 (i.e., 320x256=81920 bits) was generated (R), to which the fingercode vector (T) is added to obtain the vector (R +T). Party A possesses the key vector (R), whereas Party B possesses the vector (R+T). An impostor session is generated by subtracting the fingercode vector of a finger other than (T) from (R+T) to yield (IM), whreas a true user session is generated by subtracting the fingercode vector of a diffrent impression of (T) to yield (TU). SIPPA-2.0 is utilized as the matching function which compares [(R) vs (IM)] or [(R) vs (TU)] where the similarity score can either be the angle between the securely computed vector (X) (vector X is the final output of SIPPA-2.0) and (R), or the euclidean distance between the vector (X) and (R).

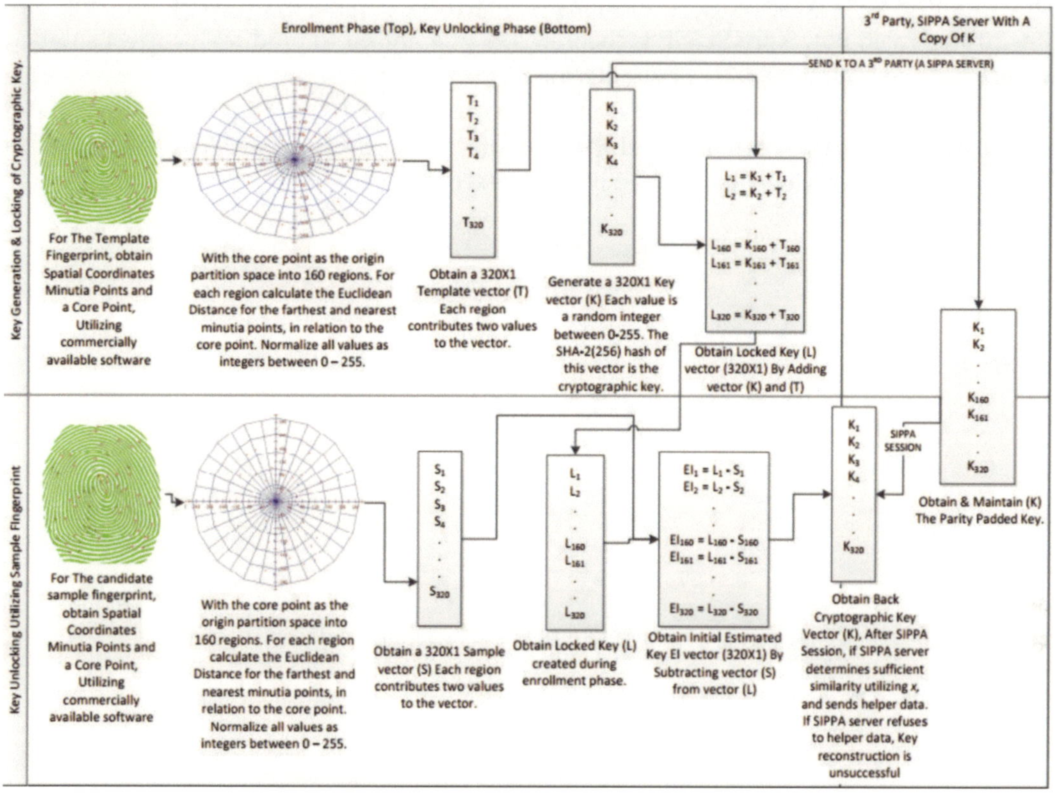

Figure 5. Cryptographic locking and unlocking illustration.

Because of the overheads involved in the matrix encryption and decryption process within our secure computation protocol (SLSSP), it becomes impractical to directly engage in SIPPA-2.0 with a 320x1 vector. An experiment was conducted to determine the performance of SIPPA-2.0 with various vector sizes, i.e., the 320x1 vector was split into 10x1, 16x1 and 20x1 vectors. Each of these splits yields a vector X_i, 100 such experiments were conducted (dual-core 3Ghz machine with 4Gb RAM) with actual fingerprint data at each split size(10,16,20). The average time to process the 320x1 vector at each of the three diffrent split parameters is reported in figure 6.

SIPPA Split Dimension	Average # of seconds
10x1	450
16x1	700
20x1	1120

Figure 6. SIPPA-2.0 complexity performance.

Due to SIPPA-2.0's complexity constraints, an extensive experiment directly utilizing SIPPA-2.0 was ruled out. Since SLSSP is theoretically guaranteed to produce a correct solution x, we conducted our experiment by replacing SLSSP with a standard linear algebra package (EJML) to solve for $x$in the algebraic system $(\mathbf{de}\bullet\mathbf{de}^{T} + \mathbf{dv}\bullet\mathbf{dv}^{T})x = \lambda_{de}\,\mathbf{v}_{de} + \lambda_{dv}\,\mathbf{v}_{dv}$. The error between SLSSP's solution x, and the solution produced EJML was determined experimentally to be always less than 4.77E-8 in over 6800 trials.

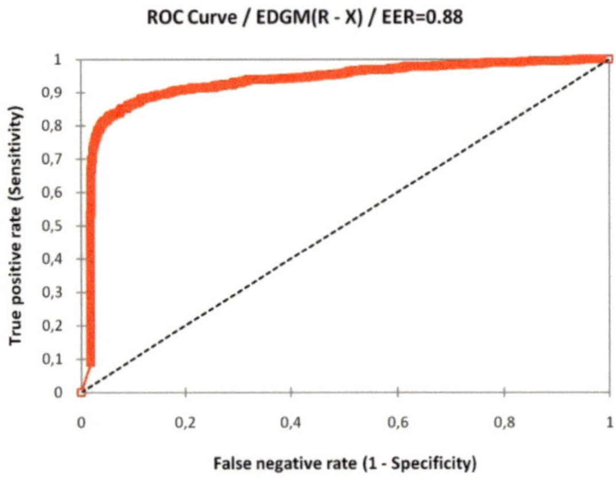

Figure 7. SIPPA-2.0 Performance (Split 10x1), ED(R vs. X).

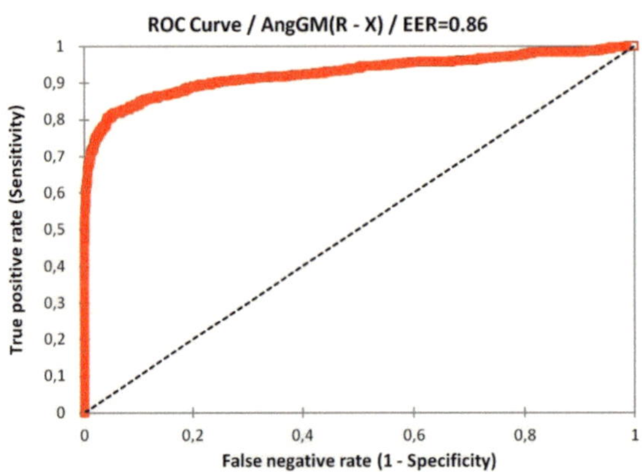

Figure 8. SIPPA-2.0 Performance (Split 10x1), Ang(R vs. X).

To assess SIPPA-2.0's ability to securely distinguish between True Users and Impostors we obtained over 20,000 unique True User sessions (20k-TU) and 20,000 unique Impostor sessions (20k-IM) from the extensive CASIA-FingerprintV5 database as described in the previous paragraphs. The ROC plot for (20k-TU) with (20k-IM) is provided in figure 7, a SIPPA-2.0 split dimension of 10X1 was utilized, and the 32 Euclidean distance (ED) scores (ED(R vs. x)) per session was aggregated into one similarity score by obtaining their Geometric Mean. The ROC plot (20k-TU) with (20k-IM) where a SIPPA-2.0 split dimension of 10X1 was utilized, and the 32 dot product(Ang) scores(Ang(R vs. x)) per session was aggregated into one similarity score by obtaining their Geometric Mean is provided in figure 8. Experiments were also conducted at other split dimensions i.e. 15, 20; however they produced inferior or similar results with an exponentially increased processing times. No obvious methods (addition, scaling etc.) of combining the ED and Ang scores yielded better results suggesting possible dependency (between the two) that will deserve further research. Of the over 50,000 instances where helper data was sent to reconstruct the random key R, R was always reconstructed successfully except 6 instances out of the over 50,000 instances. We postulate that this is due to the sensitivities in finite precision arithmetic. In these 6 instances, the number of errors in the 320 integers constituting the random key R ranges between one and four. To safeguard against this remote possibility, R can be encoded in error correction codes, allowing for correcting R when the reconstruction fails due to a few errors.

5.3. Android app prototype for emergency health data retrieval

For proof of concept, we show a use case of SIPPA-2.0 for emergency health data management on an Android device. The diagram in figure 9 shows a scenario on an emergency responder using his/her Android phone to retrieve the emergency health data from the Android phone of an unconscious individual. In the enrolment process, the emergency health data of the individual is first encrypted and stored in the Shared Preference of his/her Android device. Furthermore, the fingerprint of the individual, together with a random noise vector generated by a third party, are used to encode the decryption key, and the encoded decryption key is also stored in the Shared Preference.

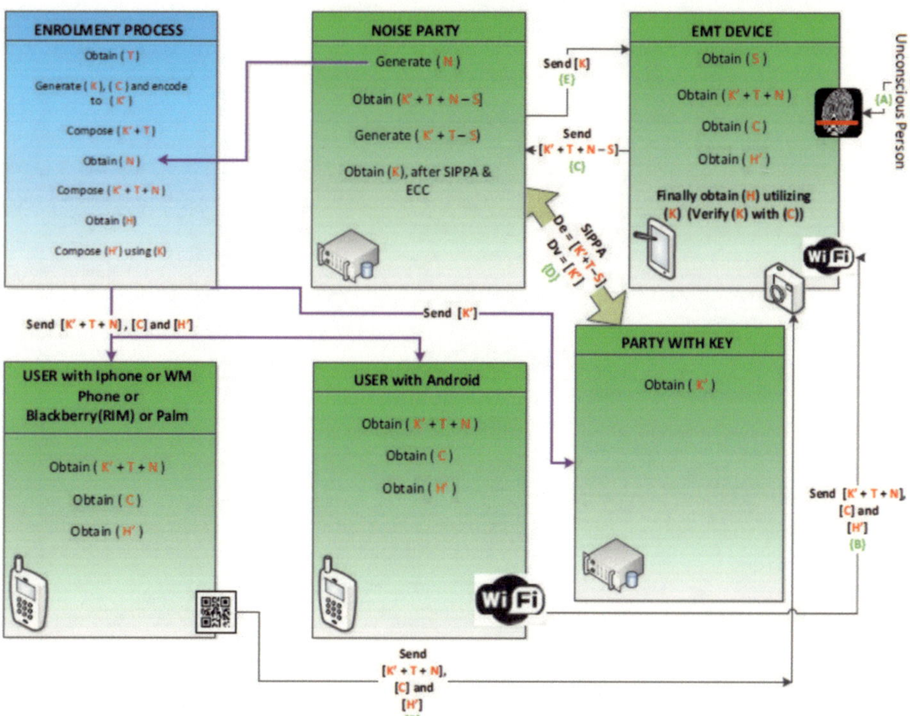

Figure 9. Use Case on applying SIPPA for emergency health data on an Andriod device.

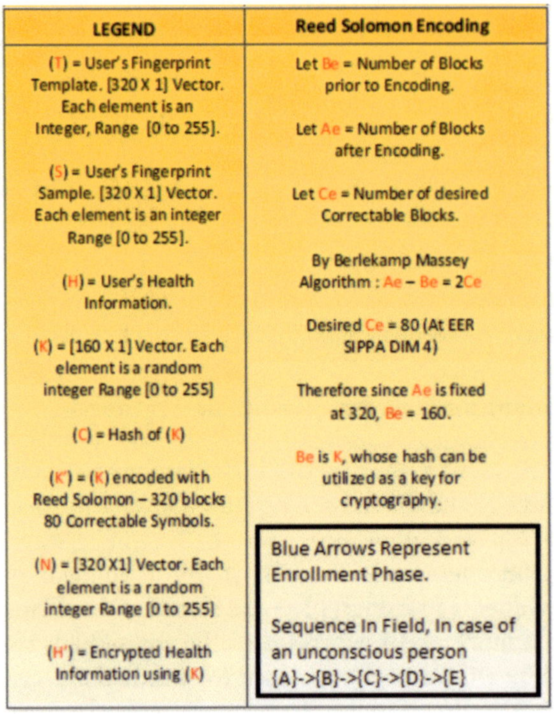

LEGEND

(T) = User's Fingerprint Template. [320 X 1] Vector. Each element is an Integer, Range [0 to 255].

(S) = User's Fingerprint Sample. [320 X 1] Vector. Each element is an integer Range [0 to 255].

(H) = User's Health Information.

(K) = [160 X 1] Vector. Each element is a random integer Range [0 to 255]

(C) = Hash of (K)

(K') = (K) encoded with Reed Solomon – 320 blocks 80 Correctable Symbols.

(N) = [320 X1] Vector. Each element is a random integer Range [0 to 255]

(H') = Encrypted Health Information using (K)

Reed Solomon Encoding

Let Be = Number of Blocks prior to Encoding.

Let Ae = Number of Blocks after Encoding.

Let Ce = Number of desired Correctable Blocks.

By Berlekamp Massey Algorithm : Ae – Be = 2Ce

Desired Ce = 80 (At EER SIPPA DIM 4)

Therefore since Ae is fixed at 320, Be = 160.

Be is K, whose hash can be utilized as a key for cryptography.

Blue Arrows Represent Enrollment Phase.

Sequence In Field, In case of an unconscious person {A}->{B}->{C}->{D}->{E}

Figure 9.1. Figure 9 Legend.

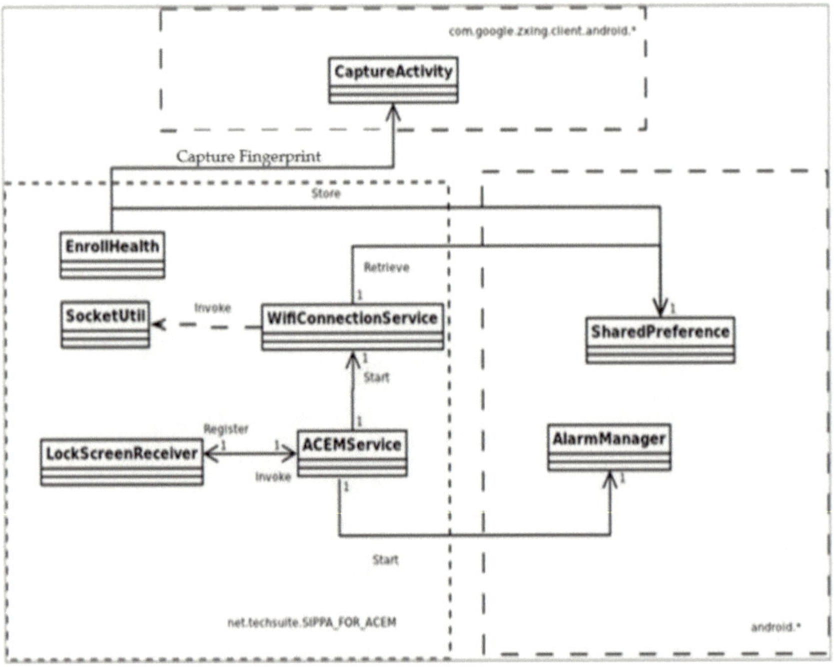

Figure 10. UML class diagram of the overall structural design.

During the retrieval process, the emergency responder will first establish a WiFi connection with the individual's Android device and retrieve the encrypted personal emergency health data and the encoded decryption key. The emergency responder will then use a built-in or wireless bluetooth fingerprint scanner to capture the indvidual's fingerpint for decoding the decryption key. The decoded fingerprint is then transmitted to the third party for noise removal to arrive at a sufficently close decrpytion key. The third party then acts as a SIPPA-2.0 client to interact with the SIPPA-2.0 server, and reconstruct the orginal decryption key based on the helper data provided by the SIPPA-2.0 server. The reconstrcted original key is sent back to the emergency responder for decrypting the personal emergency health data. The UML class diagram in figure 10 illustrates the overall structural design.

6. Conclusion

In this book chapter we present a novel mechanism for generating and retrieving cryptographic *keys* from fingerprints. Our approach brings together the worlds of biometrics and cryptography bytackling the problem of generating revocable repeatable keys (binary strings) from biometric channels which are by their nature noisy. Our scheme efficiently generates strong keys (256 bits) from fingerprint biometrics where there is no direct mapping of a key to the fingerprint from which it was generated. The entire key space is utilized where different keys can be produced from the same fingerprint for varying applications. Our scheme makes possible various new applications where there is a requirement for the strong coupling of an identity to cryptographic applications. For instance, data can be encrypted utilizing biometrics such as fingerprints where the key is linked to a person's physiology, oran individual's identity can be verified without the need for a central database of fingerprints.Such approaches allow for users to retain complete control of their data. It is not necessary for them to store their private data at a third party, thus alleviating privacy concerns. A use case utilizing our cryptographic key generation protocol is also presented; where health data is encrypted with a user's fingerprint and privately stored in a user's smartphone for secure retrieval during emergency scenarios. We also present our newly developed secure computation protocol called SIPPA-2.0, which is central to the cryptographic key generation protocol.Additionally, SIPPA-2.0 is shown to be provably correct, with an included security analysis proving SIPPA-2.0 to be secure under the semi-honest and semi-malicious models. Experiments revealing acceptable computational performance including ROC's indicating usability in practical scenarios are also presented.

Our future plans for this research include exploiting the parallelizability of our protocol to increase performance through a parallel architecture, and exploring recent non-minutia based fingerprint representation/comparison developments to improve segregation performance.

7. Appendix: Security Analysis

We approach the security analysis of SLSSP through the following steps. We first define the notion of perfect secrecy. We then analyze the cryptographic primitives employed by SLSSP and the protocol itself using the notion of perfect secrecy. To show that SLSSP is secure under semi-honest and semi-malicious models, we adopt a zero-knowledge proof protocol that can verify a given cipher text in SLSSP is indeed a Paillier encryption of its corresponding message; thus providing a mechanism to detect malicious behavior and to guarantee correctness with perfect secrecy.

7.1. General Assumptions

Throughout this section the security analysis is carried out in the Random Oracle model [36]; i.e., every party is assumed to have access to a Random Oracle where ideal hash functions and true random generators are available.

Perfect Secrecy:

Given a Cryptosystem, Plaintext (**M**), a Key (**K**) and Ciphertext (**C**); *Perfect Secrecy* [30] or *Information Theoretic Security* is an attribute assigned to Cryptosystems where knowledge of the Ciphertext provides no additional information about the original Plaintext independent of the computational power of an adversary. More specifically, a Cryptosystem has *Perfect Secrecy* if uncertainty within the Plaintext equals uncertainty within the Plaintext given the Ciphertext; i.e. utilizing Shannon Entropy, *Perfect Secrecy* can be defined as $H(M \mid C)=H(M)$.

7.2. Security Analysis of cryptographic primitives in SLSSP

Multiplication of candidate matrix with a random matrix.

At time $\mathbf{t_1}$, Alice wants to securely send an **nXn** matrix $A \in GL_n(\mathbb{Z}_p)$ (p is a prime)[31] to Bob over an authenticated channel [32], where Eve can intercept and store any messages over the channel. Eve is assumed to possess unbounded computational power. Alice wants to be assured that the matrix A is being sent with *Perfect Secrecy;* i.e., Eve should not be able to obtain any information about A due to knowledge of data sent over the channel.

Alice also has access at some time $\mathbf{t_0}$ ($\mathbf{t_0} < \mathbf{t_1}$) to a secure channel [32] with Bob. Alice shares a random nXn matrix R chosen uniformly from $GL_n(\mathbb{Z}_p)$ with Bob. At time $\mathbf{t_1}$, through the authenticated channel Alice sends $C=(A*R)$ to Bob. To decrypt and obtain matrix A, Bob calculates $A=(C*R^{-1})$. Alice and Bob, discard R and do not use it to encrypt any other messages. Assuming that Eve only has knowledge of C, to prove *Perfect Secrecy* it will be sufficient to show that $H(A \mid C)=H(A)$. Let $(\mathbf{A} \in GL_n(\mathbb{Z}_p))$, be the set of possible plaintexts, i.e, the sample space for A. Let $(\mathbf{C} \in GL_n(\mathbb{Z}_p))$, be the set of possible ciphertexts, i.e. the sample space for$C$. Let $(\mathbf{R} \in GL_n(Z_p))$, be the set of possible keys, i.e., the sample space for$R$. Note that $s = |GL_n(Z_p)| = \prod_{i=0}^{i=n-1}(p^n - p^i)$[33].

1. Let $(k \in \mathbf{R})$be a possible key, then $P_R(k) = 1/s$

2. Let $(l \in \mathbf{C})$be a possible ciphertext, and given the independence of $A$and Rthen:

$$P_C(l) = \sum_{\substack{m \in A,\ k \in R \\ l = (m^*k)}} P_A(m) P_R(k) \tag{5}$$

3. Since

$$P_R(k) = 1/s: \tag{6}$$

$$P_C(l) = 1/s * \left(\sum_{\substack{m \in A, k \in \mathcal{R} \\ l = (m^*k)}} P_A(m) \right) \tag{7}$$

4. Because$l$, $m$uniquely determine k(given $l$and$m$ there exists exactly one $k$that satisfies the encryption equation $(l = (m^*k))$, every $m \in \mathbf{A}$occurs exactly once in the above summation; therefore $P_C(l) = 1/s$

5. Since $P_C(l) = P_R(k)$ for all $l$and$k$, $H(C) = H(R)$

6. Since knowledge of (A, R) or(A, C) is sufficient to completely know (A, C, R), $H(A, R, C) = H(A, R) = H(A, C)$

7. Since $M$and $K$are independent, $H(A, R) = H(A) + H(R)$

8. By the chain rule for conditional entropy, $H(A, C) = H(A | C) + H(C)$

9. From (5),(7),(8) we obtain$H(A | C) = H(A)$; Proving *Perfect Secrecy.*

7.3. Security Analysis of the SLSSP protocol:

In an ideal Secure Computation protocol, where there are no assumptions made about maliciousness or computational capabilities of the parties involved; no participant learns anything about any other's private input(s) apart from any advantage obtained from the malleability of a legitimate output. In the semi-honest model[37], the parties involved are limited to PP [34] complexity, are assumed to follow the defined protocol honestly but are allowed to retain a transcript of all communication, which they can utilize to obtain information about other party's private input(s). In the semi-malicious model[37], parties are still restricted to PP complexity, whereas they are allowed to manipulate the secure computation protocol, retain a transcript of all communication, which they can utilize to influence the outcome of the protocol and to obtain information about other party's private input(s). It is assumed in all these models that secure channels are utilized for inter-party communication.

The SLSSP protocol is secure under the semi-honest model, since through the entire protocol, each party only observes encrypted versions of each other's private input(s). The encryption primitives utilized in SLSSP have been shown in this section to be at least IND-CPA. Even though both parties have access to the encryption oracle, and SLSSP is a multi-step protocol, they do not gain any advantage by observing multiple versions of each other's encrypted private input(s). The SLSSP protocol can further be made secure under the semi-malicious model by utilizing the following Zero-Knowledge protocol (ZKP) which guarantees correctness of SLSSP's output.

Zero-Knowledge proof that a Paillier encrypted message encrypts a particular plaintext:

The Paillier encryption function $P(m, r)$is a Bijection$\left(Z_n x Z_n^* \rightarrow Z_{n^2}^*\right)$, which maps every plaintext $(m \in Z_n)$, random $\left(r \in Z_n^*\right)$ pair to a unique Ciphertext$\left(c \in Z_{n^2}^*\right)$. The prover **P** could therefore send $r$toa verifier **V**, which would be sufficient to establish that$c$ encrypts a particular message$m$. Revealing$r$ may however jeopardize certain desirable qualities of the Paillier Cryptosystemincluding its indistinguishability under a chosen plain text attack (IND-CPA). However, since Paillier encryption is semantically secure (IND-CPA), the verifier V will not be able to tell whether a given cipher text c is indeed the encryption of a message m. To solve this problem without leaking additional information, we adapt from [35] an honest verifier Zero-Knowledge protocol which can be formulated as below:

The honest Verifier **V** knows **m** and **possesses** a Paillier Ciphertext$c = g^{m'} . r^n \ mod\ n^2$, and knows only the Paillier public-key pair (g, n). **V**, not knowing $\boldsymbol{r}$ or the corresponding private-key pair(λ, μ), would like to verify that$c$ is the encryption of a particular message$m$, where the prover **P** possesses (g, n) and random$r$.

1. **V** homomorphically subtracts $m$from$c$; i.e., computes z as an encryption of $(\boldsymbol{m'}\text{-}\boldsymbol{m}) \leftrightarrow z = \left(c.g^{-m}\right) mod\ n^2)$. Note that if$m' = m$, then $z$is an encryption of Zero; i.e.,$z = r^n \ mod\ n^2$

Remark: This step may require using the fixed point representation discussed in section 6.3 to compute$z = \left(c.g^{-m}\right) mod\ n^2)$.

2. **P** chooses a random$q \in Z_n^*$ and computes an encryption of zero:$h = g^0 . q^n \ mod\ n^2$. **P** sends h to **V**.

3. **V** chooses a random e $\left(e \neq an, \ \ a \in Z\right) \in Z$and sends $e$to **P**. (This step stages a commitment from **P** through his chosen q that defines an encrypted zero so that **V** can tie it to a random **e** to verify the **r** used in encrypting **m**.)

4. **P** computes$k = qr^e \ mod\ n$. **P** sends $k$to V.

Remark: Even V knows h and n, q cannot be derived under DCRA (Decisional Composite Residuosity Assumption).

5. **V** checks and accepts that $m'=m$ if

$\gcd(h, n)=1$, $\gcd(k, n)=1$ and $(g^0 . k^n \bmod n^2)=(h . z^e \bmod n^2)$ i.e., $(g^0 . k^n \bmod n^2)= (q^n r^{en}) \bmod n^2$

*Completeness –Prover **P** and verifier **V** are assumed to be honest:*

1. Assume that $m'=m$, then z as computed by **V** in Step-1 of the Zero-Knowledge protocol is an encryption of zero, i.e. $z=r^n \bmod n^2$.

2. $(g^0 . k^n \bmod n^2)$, from the verification in Step-5 of the protocol can be rewritten as $(q^n . r^{en} \bmod n^2)$.

3. Due to assumption in (1), $(h . z^e \bmod n^2)$, from the verification in Step-5 can be rewritten as $(q^n . r^{en} \bmod n^2)$.

4. From (1),(2),(3), we get that, $if\ (m'=m),\ then\ ((g^0 . k^n \bmod n^2)=(h . z^e \bmod n^2))$

5. Assume that $m'\neq m$, then z as computed by **V** in Step-1 of the protocol equals $(g^{m'-m} . r^n \bmod n^2)$ where $(g^{m'-m} \neq 1)$.

6. $(g^0 . k^n \bmod n^2)$, from the verification in Step-5 of the protocol can be rewritten as $(q^n . r^{en} \bmod n^2)$.

7. Due to assumption in (5) $(h . z^e \bmod n^2)$, from the verification in Step-5 can be rewritten as $(q^n . (g^{m'-m} . r^n)^e \bmod n^2)$.

8. From (5), (6), (7) we get that: $if\ (\neg(m'=m)),\ then\ (\neg((g^0 . k^n \bmod n^2)=(h . z^e \bmod n^2)))$.

9. Since the verifier **V**, checks the equality in Step-5 of the protocol as a condition for acceptance, from (4), (8), it is shown that the verifier **V** is correct in his conviction i.e. it is indeed true that: $(m'=m)$ *if and only if* $((g^0 . k^n \bmod n^2)=(h . z^e \bmod n^2))$.

*Soundness – Assuming a cheating prover **P*** and honest verifier **V**:*

1. Assume that a cheating prover **P*** is trying to convince **V** that $m'=m$, where in actuality, $(m'-m)\neq 0$. Therefore **P*** would try to show that $(g^0 . k^n \bmod n^2)=(h . z^e \bmod n^2)$, where **P*** has control over k and h and no knowledge of z since $(m'-m)\neq 0$.

2. Any choice of k sent by party **P*** in Step-4 of the protocol will yield the **n** th power of k in modulo n^2 for the left hand side of the verification equation $(g^0 . k^n \bmod n^2)$.

3. Since the **P*** has to show that $(g^0 . k^n \bmod n^2)=(h . z^e \bmod n^2)$ and has no control over z^e; either h must equal $(k^n . z^{-e} \bmod n^2)$ or k^n must equal $(h . z^e)$.

4. (3) presumes knowledge of z and e. It is to be noted that h must be committed before **V** sends e to **P***. Hence **P*** can at best guess **z** and **e**, then computes and sends $h = k^n . z^{-e} \bmod n^2$, before knowledge of e.

5. When computing$k$, **P*** has knowledge of$e$, and no knowledge of z.Since $(m^{'} \neq m)$, $z = (g^{m^{'} - m} . r^{n} \; mod \; n^{2})$ where $(g^{m^{'} - m} \neq 1)$, $(h . z^{e})$contains a term $((g^{m^{'} - m})^{e})$ which is not a power of$n$, $(g^{(m^{'} - m)})$cannot be a power of $n$because of domain restrictions).

6. From (4),(5) **P*** cannot successfully convince **V** that$m' = m$, when in actuality$m' \neq m$.

Acknowledgements

This work was supported in part by a grant from PSC-CUNY Collaborative Research Award and a NSF DUE Award.

Author details

Bon K. Sy and Arun P. Kumara Krishnan*

*Address all correspondence to: bon@bunny.cs.qc.cuny.edu

Computer Science Dept., Queens College/CUNY, Flushing NY, USA

References

[1] Tian, Yingli, & Tsui, Hungtat. (1995). Estimating Shape and Reflectance of Surfaces by Color Image Analysis. *Lecture Notes in Computer Science 1024, "Image Analysis Applications and Computer graphics"*, 266-273.

[2] Belkin, Mikhail, & Niyogi, Partha. (2003). Laplacian Eigenmaps for Dimensionality Reduction and Data Representation. *Neural Computation*, MIT Press, June, 15(6), 1373-1396.

[3] Turk, M., & Pentland, A. (1991a). Eigenfaces for recognition. *Journal of Cognitive Neuroscience*, 3(1).

[4] Sy, Bon K. (1911). Secure Computation for Biometric Data Security Application to Speaker Verification. *IEEE Systems Journal*, 3(4).

[5] Katz, J., & Lindell, Y. (2007). Introduction to Modern Cryptography: Principles and Protocols, Chapman & Hall.

[6] http://en.wikipedia.org/wiki/Advanced_Encryption_Standard.

[7] Kumara Krishnan, Arun P., Ramirez, Adam, & Sy, Bon K. (2011). Parallel Secure Computation Scheme for Biometric Security and Privacy in Standard-Based BioAPI Framework. *Biometrics*, INTECH 2011, http://www.intechopen.com/source/pdfs/14648/InTech-Parallel_secure_computation_scheme_for_biometric_security_and_privacy_in_standard_based_bioapi_framework.pdf.

[8] http://en.wikipedia.org/wiki/Reed%E2%80%93Solomon_error_correction.

[9] Hao, F., Anderson, R., & Daugman, J. (2005). Combining cryptography with biometrics effectively. University of Cambridge, Tech. Rep. UCAMCL-TR-640.

[10] Barni, M., Bianchi, T., Catalano, D., Raimondo, M. D., Labati, R. D., & Faillia, P. (2010). Privacy-preserving finger code authentication. In MM&Sec', Roma, Italy. ACM.

[11] Clancy, T. C., Kiyavash, N., & Lin, D. J. (2003). Secure smart card-based finger print authentication. *Proc. ACMSIGMM 2003 Multimedia, Biometrics Methods and Applications Workshop*, 45-52.

[12] Lalithamani, N., & Soman, K. P. (2009). Irrevocable Cryptographic Key Generation from Cancelable Fingerprint Templates: An Enhanced and Effective Scheme. *European Journal of Scientific Research*, 31(3), 372-387.

[13] http://en.wikipedia.org/wiki/Secure_computation.

[14] Du, W., & Atallah, M. (2001). Privacy-Preserving Statistical Analysis, in ACSAC.

[15] Yao, A. C. (1982). Protocols for secure computations. *Proceeding of 23rd IEEE Sym. On Foundations of Computer Science.*

[16] Goldreich, O., Micali, S., & Wigderson, A. (1987). How to play ANY mental game. *Proceedings of the nineteenth annual ACM symposium on Theory of computing*, 218-229, January, New York.

[17] Goldwasser, S. (1987). Multi party computations: past and present. *Proceedings of the sixteenth annual ACM symposium on Principles of distributed computing*, 1-6, August 21-24, 1997, California.

[18] Goldwasser, S., & Micali, S. (1984). Probabilistic Encryption. *Journal of Computer and System Sciences*, 28(2), 270-299.

[19] Paillier, P. (1999). Public-Key Cryptosystems Based on Composite Degree Residuosity Classes, in EUROCRYPT.

[20] Elgamal, T. (1985). A public key cryptosystem and a signature scheme based on discrete logarithms. *IEEE Transactions on Information Theory*, 31(4), 469-472.

[21] Goldwasser, S., & Micali, S. (1984). Probabilistic Encryption. *Journal of Computer and System Sciences*, 28(2), 270-299.

[22] Gentry, C. (2009). Fully Homomorphic Encryption Using Ideal Lattices. *41st ACM Symposium on Theory of Computing.*

[23] Cooney, M. (2009). IBM touts encryption innovation. *Computerworld*, 25 June 2009. [Online]. Available, http://www.computerworld.com/s/article/9134823/IBM_touts_encryption_innovation, Accessed 15.03.2012.

[24] Goethals, B., Laur, S., Lipmaa, H., & Mielikainen, T. (2004). On Private Scalar Product Computation for Privacy-Preserving Data Mining. *ICISC*.

[25] Erkin, Z., Franz, M., Guajardo, J., Katzenbeisser, S., Lagendijk, I., & Toft, T. (2009). Privacy-Preserving Face Recognition. *Privacy Enhancing Technologies*, Springer Berlin / Heidelberg, 235-253.

[26] Osadchy, M., Pinkas, B., Jarrous, A., & Moskovich, B. (2010). SCiFI- A System for Secure Face Identification. *IEEE Symposium on Security Privacy*.

[27] Kumara Krishnan, Arun P., & Sy, Bon K. (2012). SIPPA-2.0- Secure Information Processing with Privacy Assurance (version 2.0). *Proceeding of the PST 2012*, Paris, France.

[28] http://www.futronic-tech.com/product_fs88.html.

[29] http://www.neurotechnology.com/verifinger.html.

[30] Shannon, C. (1949). Communication Theory of Secrecy Systems. *Bell System Technical Journal*, 28(4), 656-715.

[31] "Wikipedia," [Online]. Available: http://en.wikipedia.org/wiki/General_linear_group. [Accessed 16 3 2012].

[32] "Wikipedia," [Online]. Available: http://en.wikipedia.org/wiki/Secure_channel. [Accessed 16 3 2012].

[33] Overbey, J., Traves, W., & Wojdylo, J. (2005). On the Keyspace of the Hill Cipher. *Cryptologia*, 29(1), 59-72.

[34] "Wikipedia PP Complexity," Wikipedia, [Online]. Available: http://en.wikipedia.org/wiki/PP_(complexity). [Accessed 20 3 2012].

[35] Damgard, M. Jurik, & Nielsen, J. (2010). A generalization of Paillier's public-key system with applications to electronic voting. *International Journal of Information Security*, 9(6), 1615-5262.

[36] Fiat & Shamir, A. (1986). How to Prove Yourself: Practical Solutions to Identification and Signature Problems. *CRYPTO*.

[37] Katz, J., & Lindell, Y. (2007). Introduction to Modern Cryptography, Chapman & Hall.

[38] http://biometrics.idealtest.org/downloadDB.do?id=7 [Accessed 30 3 2012].

[39] Yang, J. C. (2011). Non-minutiae based fingerprint descriptor. book chapter, *Biometrics*, Intech, Vienna, Austria, June, 978-9-53307-618-8.

[40] Yang, J. C., & Park, D. S. (2008). A Fingerprint Verification Algorithm Using Tessellated Invariant Moment Features. *Neurocomputing*, 71(10-12), 1939-1946.

Section 4

Others

Chapter 10

An AFIS Candidate List Centric Fingerprint Likelihood Ratio Model Based on Morphometric and Spatial Analyses (MSA)

Joshua Abraham, Paul Kwan, Christophe Champod,
Chris Lennard and Claude Roux

Additional information is available at the end of the chapter

http://dx.doi.org/10.5772/51184

1. Introduction

The use of fingerprints for identification purposes boasts worldwide adoption for a large variety of applications, from governance centric applications such as border control to personalised uses such as electronic device authentication. In addition to being an inexpensive and widely used form of biometric for authentication systems, fingerprints are also recognised as an invaluable biometric for forensic identification purposes such as law enforcement and disaster victim identification. Since the very first forensic applications, fingerprints have been utilised as one of the most commonly used form of forensic evidence worldwide.

Applications of fingerprint identification are founded on the intrinsic characteristics of the friction ridge arrangement present at the fingertips, which can be generally classified at different levels or resolutions of detail (Figure 1). Generally speaking, fingerprint patterns can be described as numerous curved lines alternated as ridges and valleys that are largely regular in terms orientation and flow, with relatively few key locations being of exception (singularities). A closer examination reveals a more detail rich feature set allowing for greater discriminatory analysis. In addition, analysis of local textural detail such as ridge shape, orientation, and frequency, have been used successfully in fingerprint matching algorithms as primary features [1] [2] or in conjunction with other landmark-based features [3].

Both biometric and forensic fingerprint identification applications rely on premises that such fingerprint characteristics are highly discriminatory and immutable amongst the general population. However, the collectability of such fingerprint characteristics from biometric scanners, ink rolled impressions, and especially, latent marks, are susceptible to adverse factors such as partiality of contact, variation in detail location and appearance due to skin elasticity (specifically for level 2 and 3 features) and applied force, environmental noises such

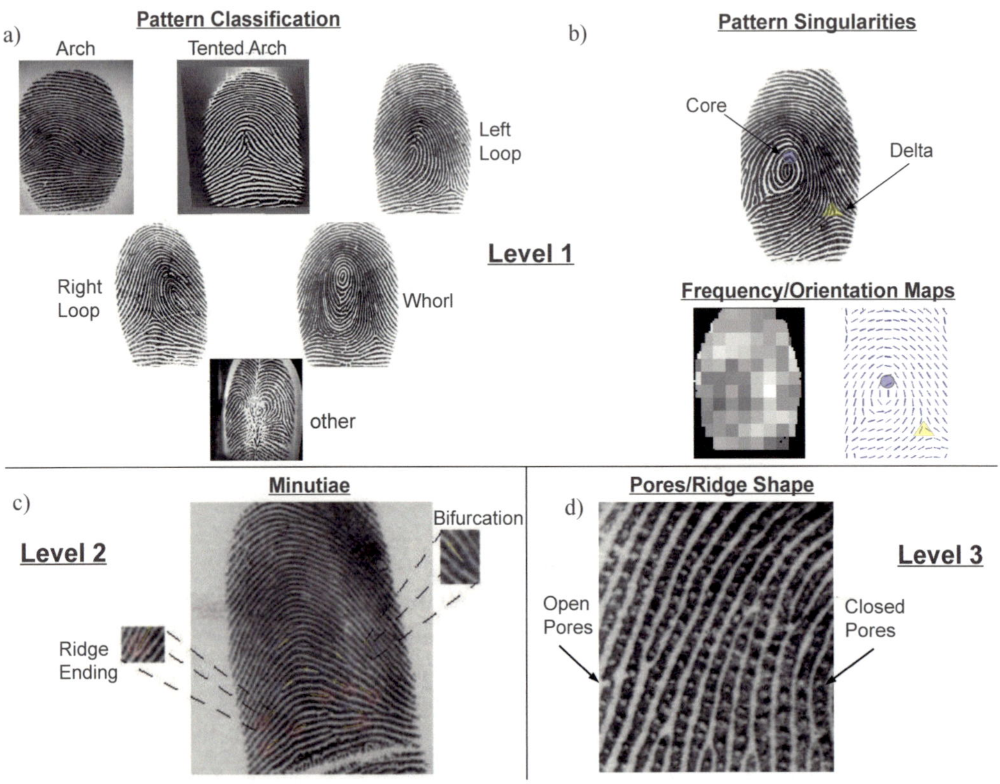

Figure 1. Level 1 features include features such as pattern class (a), singularity points and ridge frequency (b). Level 2 features (c) include minutiae with primitive types ridge endings and bifurcations. Level 3 features (d) include pores (open/closed) and ridge shape. These fingerprints were sourced from the FVC2002 [47], NIST4 [46], and NIST24 [48] databases

as moisture, dirt, slippage, and skin conditions such as dryness, scarring, warts, creases, and general ageing. Such influences generally act as a hindrance for identification, reducing both the quality and confidence of assessing matching features between impressions (Figure 2).

In this chapter, we will firstly discuss the current state of forensic fingerprint identification and how models play an important role for the future, followed by a brief introduction and review into relevant statistical models. Next, we will introduce a Likelihood Ratio (LR) model based on Support Vector Machines (SVMs) trained with features discovered via the morphometric and other spatial analyses of matching minutiae for both genuine and close imposter (or match and close non-match) populations typically recovered from Automated Fingerprint Identification System (AFIS) candidate lists. Lastly, experimentation performed on a set of over 60,000 publicly available fingerprint images (mostly sourced from NIST and FVC databases) and a distortion set of 6,000 images will be presented, illustrating that the proposed LR model is reliably guiding towards the right proposition in the identification assessment for both genuine and high ranking imposter populations, based on the discovered distortion characteristic differences of each population.

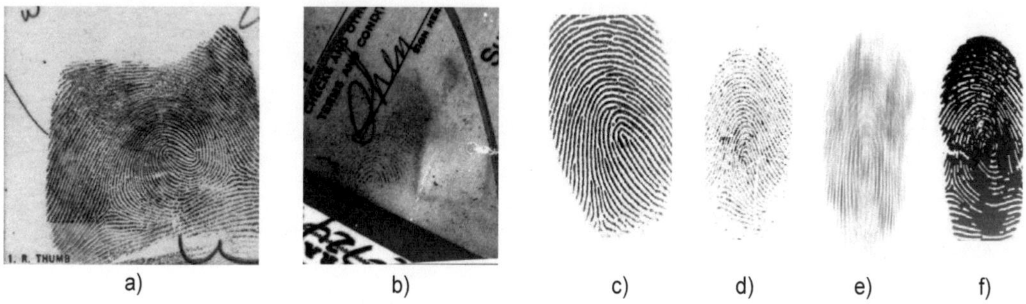

Figure 2. Examples of different fingerprint impressions, including an ink rolled print (a), latent mark (b), scanned fingerprint flats of ideal quality (c), dry skin (d), slippage (e), and over saturation (f). Fingerprints are sourced from the NIST 27 [48], FVC2004 [51], and our own databases.

1.1. Forensic fingerprint identification

Historically, the forensic identification of fingerprints has had near unanimous acceptance as a gold standard of forensic evidence, where the scientific foundations of such testimonies were rarely challenged in court proceedings. In addition, fingerprint experts have generally been regarded as expert witnesses with adequate training, scientific knowledge, relevant experience, and following a methodical process for identification, ultimately giving credibility to their expert witness testimonies.

Fingerprint experts largely follow a friction ridge identification process called ACE-V (Analysis, Comparison, Evaluation, and Verification) [5] to compare an unknown fingermark with known fingerprint exemplars. The ACE-V acronym also details the ordering of the identification process (Figure 3). In the analysis stage, all visible ridge characteristics (level 1, 2, and 3) are noted and assessed for reliability, while taking into account variations caused by pressure, distortion, contact medium, and development techniques used in the laboratory. The comparison stage involves comparing features between the latent mark and either the top n fingerprint exemplars return from an AFIS search, or specific pre-selected exemplars. If a positive identification is declared, all corresponding features are charted, along with any differences considered to be caused by environmental influence. The Evaluation stage consists of an expert making an inferential decision based on the comparison stage observations. The possible outcomes [6] are:

- exclusion: a discrepancy of features are discovered so it precludes the possibility of a common source,
- identification: a significant correspondence of features are discovered that is considered to be sufficient in itself to conclude to a common source, and
- inconclusive: not enough evidence is found for either an exclusion or identification.

The Verification stage consists of a peer review of the prior stages. Any discrepancies in evaluations are handled by a conflict resolution procedure.

Identification evaluation conclusions [7] made by fingerprint experts have historical influence from Edmond Locard's *tripartite rule* [8]. The tripartite rule is defined as follows:

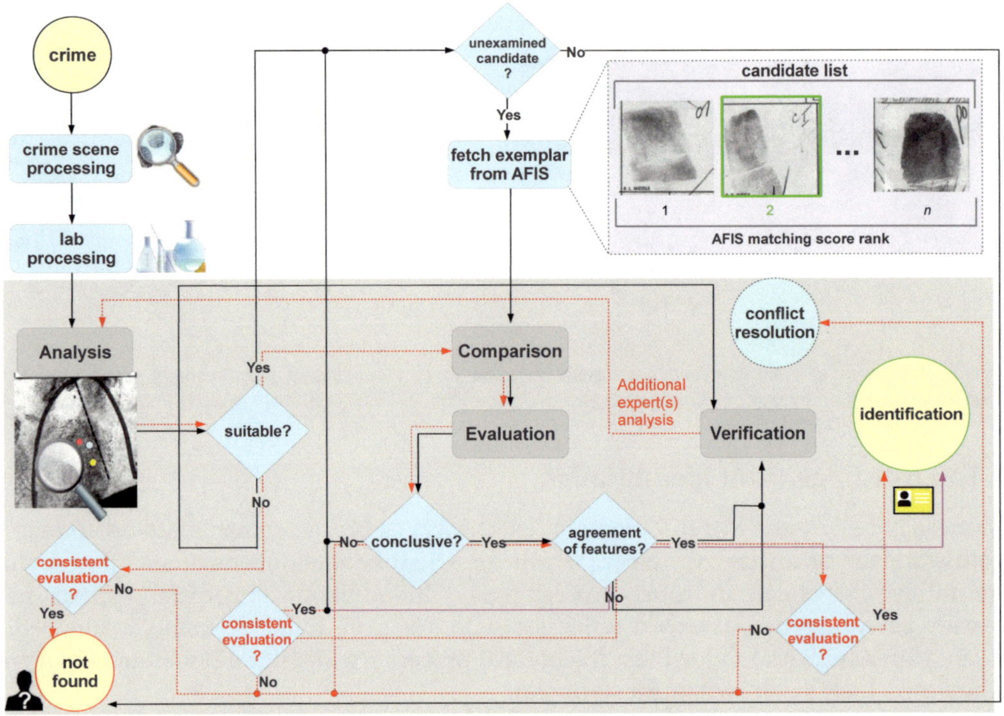

Figure 3. Flowchart of modern ACE-V process used in conjunction with AFIS. The iterative comparison of each exemplar fingerprint in the AFIS candidate list is performed until identification occurs or no more exemplars are left. The red flow lines indicate the process for the verification stage analysis. The purple flow line from the agreement of features test shows the ACE process that skips the evaluation stage.

- Positive identifications are possible when there are more than 12 minutiae within sharp quality fingermarks.
- If 8 to 12 minutiae are involved, then the case is borderline. Certainty of identity will depend on additional information such as finger mark quality, rarity of pattern, presence of the core, delta(s), and pores, and ridge shape characteristics, along with agreement by at least 2 experts.
- If a limited number of minutiae are present, the fingermarks cannot provide certainty for an identification, but only a presumption of strength proportional to the number of minutiae.

Holistically, the tripartite rule can be viewed as a probabilistic framework, where the successful applications of the first and second rules are analogous to a statement with 100% certainty that the mark and the print share the same source, whereas the third rule covers the probability range between 0% to 100%. While some jurisdictions only apply the first rule to set a numerical standard within the ACE-V framework, other jurisdictions (such as Australia, UK, and USA [9]) adopt a holistic approach, where no strict numerical standard or feature combination is prescribed. Nevertheless, current fingerprint expert testimony is largely restricted to conclusions that convey a statement of certainty, ignoring the third rule's probabilistic outcome.

http://dx.doi.org/10.5772/51184

1.2. Daubert and criticisms

Recently, there has been a number of voiced criticisms on the scientific validity of forensic fingerprint identification [10] [11] [12] [13] [14] [15]. Questions with regards to the scientific validity of forensic fingerprint identification began shortly after the *Daubert* case [17]. In the 1993 case of Daubert v. Merrell Dow Pharmaceuticals [18] the US Supreme Court outlined criteria concerning the admissibility of scientific expert testimony. The criteria for a valid scientific method given were as follows:

- must be based on testable and falsifiable theories/techniques,
- must be subjected to peer-review and publication,
- must have known or predictable error rates,
- must have standards and controls concerning its applications, and
- must be generally accepted by a relevant scientific community.

The objections which followed [13] [14] [15] from a number of academic and legal commentators were:

- the contextual bias of experts for decisions made within the ACE-V (Analysis, Comparison, Evaluation, and Verification) framework used in fingerprint identification
- the unfounded and unfalsifiable theoretical foundations of fingerprint feature discriminability, and
- the 'unscientific' absolute conclusions of identification in testimonies (i.e., either match, non-match, or inconclusive).

There have been a number of studies [16] over the last 5 years concerning contextual bias and the associated error rates of ACE-V evaluations in practice. The experiments reported by [19] led to conclusions that experts appear more susceptible to bias assessments of 'inconclusive' and 'exclusion', while false positive rates are reasonably low within simulation of the ACE-V framework. It has also been suggested from results in [20] and [21] that not all stages of ACE-V are equally vulnerable to contextual bias, with primary effects occurring in the analysis stage, with proposals on how to mediate such variability found in [22]. While contextual bias is solely concerned with the influence of the expert, the remaining criticisms can be summarised as the non-existence of a scientifically sound probabilistic framework for fingerprint evidential assessment, that has the consensual approval from the forensic science community.

The theoretical foundations of fingerprint identification primarily rest on rudimentary observational science, where a high discriminability of feature characteristics exists. However, there is a lack of consensus regarding quantifiable error rates for a given pair of 'corresponding' feature configurations [23]. Some critics have invoked a more traditional interpretation for discriminability [24] [25], claiming that an assumption of 'uniqueness' is used. This clearly violates the falsifiable requirement of Daubert. However, it has been argued that modern day experts do not necessarily associate discriminability with uniqueness [26]. Nevertheless, a consensus framework for calculating accurate error rates for corresponding fingerprint features needs to be established.

1.3. Role of statistical models

While a probabilistic framework for fingerprint comparisons has not been historically popular and was even previously banned by professional bodies [8], a more favourable treatment within the forensic community is given in recent times. For example, the IAI have recently rescinded their ban on reporting possible, probable, or likely conclusions [27] and support the future use of valid statistical models (provided that they are accepted as valid by the scientific community) to aid the practitioner in identification assessments. It has also been suggested in [28] that a probabilistic framework is based on strong scientific principles unlike the traditional numerical standards.

Statistical models for fingerprint identification provide a probabilistic framework that can be applied to forensic fingerprint identification to create a framework for evaluations, that do not account for the inherent uncertainties of fingerprint evidence. Moreover, the use of such statistical models as an identification framework helps answer the criticisms of scientific reliability and error rate knowledge raised by some commentators. For instance, statistical models can be used to describe the discriminatory power of a given fingerprint feature configuration, which in hand can be used to predict and estimate error rates associated with the identification of specific fingerprint features found in any given latent mark.

Statistical models could potentially act as a tool for fingerprint practitioners with evaluations made within the ACE-V framework, specifically when the confidence in identification or exclusion is not overtly clear. However, such applications require statistical models to be accurate and robust to real work scenarios.

2. Likelihood Ratio models

A *likelihood ratio* (LR) is a simple yet powerful statistic when applied to a variety of forensic science applications, including inference of identity of source for evidences such as DNA [29], ear-prints [30], glass fragments [31], and fingerprints [32] [33] [34] [35]. An LR is defined as the ratio of two likelihoods of a specific *event* occurring, each of which follow a different prior hypothesis, and thus, empirical distribution. In the forensic identification context, an event, E, may represent the recovered evidence in question, while the prior hypotheses considered for calculating the two likelihoods of E occurring are:

- H_0: E comes from a specific known source, P, and
- H_A: E has an alternative origin to P.

Noting any additional relevant prior information collected from the crime scene as I_{cs}, the LR can be expressed as

$$LR = \frac{P(E|H_0, I_{cs})}{P(E|H_A, I_{cs})} \tag{1}$$

where $P(E|H_0, I_{cs})$ is the likelihood of the observations on the mark given that the mark was produced by the same finger as the print P, while $P(E|H_A, I_{cs})$ is the likelihood of the observations on the mark given that the mark was *not* produced by the same finger as P. The LR value can be interpreted as follows:

- $LR < 1$: the evidence has more support for hypothesis H_A,

- $LR = 1$: the evidence has equal support from both hypotheses, and
- $LR > 1$: the evidence has more support for hypothesis H_0.

The general LR form of equation (1) can be restated specifically for fingerprint identification evaluations. Given an unknown query impression, y, (e.g., unknown latent mark) with m' marked features (denoted as $y^{(m')}$), and a known impression, x, (e.g., known AFIS candidate or latent mark) with m marked features (denoted as $x^{(m)}$), the LR is defined as

$$LR_{finger} = \frac{P(y^{(m')}|x^{(m)}, H_0, I_{cs})}{P(y^{(m')}|x^{(m)}, H_A, I_{cs})} \tag{2}$$

where the value $P(y^{(m')}|x^{(m)}, H_0, I_{cs})$ represents the probability that impressions x and y agree given that the marks were produced by the same finger, while $P(y^{(m')}|x^{(m)}, H_A, I_{cs})$ is the probability that x and y agree given that the marks were *not* produced by the same finger, using the *closest* q corresponding features between $x^{(m)}$ and $y^{(m')}$ with $q \leq \min(m, m')$. Thus, hypotheses used to calculate the LR numerator and denominator probabilities are defined as:

- H_0: x and y were produced by the same finger, and
- H_A: x and y were produced by different fingers.

The addendum crime scene information, I_{cs}, may include detail of surrounding fingermarks, surficial characteristics of the contacted medium, or a latent mark quality/confidence assessment. In order to measure the within-finger and between-finger variability of landmark based feature configurations required to derive values for $P(y^{(m')}|x^{(m)}, H_0, I_{cs})$ and $P(y^{(m')}|x^{(m)}, H_A, I_{cs})$, models either use statistical distributions of dissimilarity metrics (used as a proxy for direct assessment) derived from either the analysis of spatial properties [33] [34] [35], or analysis of similarity score distributions produced by the AFIS [36] [37] [38].

2.1. AFIS score based LR models

AFIS score based LR models use estimates of the genuine and imposter similarity score distributions from fingerprint matching algorithm(s) within AFIS, in order to derive a LR measure. In a practical application, a given mark and exemplar may have an AFIS similarity score of s, from which the conditional probability of the score can be calculated (Figure 4) to give an LR of

$$LR = \frac{P(s|H_0)}{P(s|H_A)}. \tag{3}$$

2.1.1. *Parametric Based Models*

In order to estimate the score distributions used in equation (3), the authors of [36] proposed using the Weibull $W(\lambda, \beta)$ and Log-Normal $\ln \mathcal{N}(\mu, \sigma^2)$ distributions with scale/shape parameters tuned to estimate the genuine and imposter AFIS score distributions, respectively. Given query and template fingermarks with an AFIS similarity score, s, the LR is

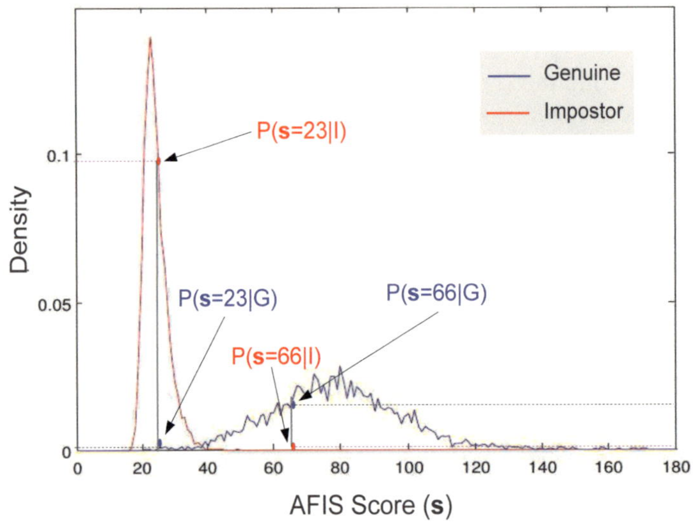

Figure 4. Typical AFIS imposter and genuine score distributions. The LR can be directly calculated for a given similarity score using the densities from these distributions.

$$LR = \frac{f_W(s|\lambda,\beta)}{f_{\ln\mathcal{N}}(s|\mu,\sigma^2)} \tag{4}$$

using the proposed probability density functions of the estimated AFIS genuine and imposter score distributions.

An updated variant can be found in [37], where imposter and genuine score distributions are modelled per minutiae configuration. This allows the rarity of the configuration to be accounted for.

2.1.2. Non-Match Probability Based Model

The authors of [38] proposed a model based on AFIS score distributions, using LR and Non-Match Probability (NMP) calculations. The NMP can be written mathematically as

$$NMP = P(H_A|s) = \frac{P(s|H_A)P(H_A)}{P(s|H_A)P(H_A) + P(s|H_0)P(H_0)}, \tag{5}$$

which is simply the complement of the probability that the null hypothesis (i.e., x and y come from the same known source) is true, given prior conditions x, y, and I_{cs} (i.e., background information).

Three main methods for modelling the AFIS score distributions where tested, being (i) histogram based, (ii) Gaussian kernel density based, and (iii) parametric density based estimation using the proposed distributions found in [36]. Given an AFIS score, s, the NMP and LR were calculated by setting $P(H_A) = P(H_0)$, while estimating both $P(s|H_A)$ and

$P(s|H_0)$ either by normalised bin (method (i)) or probability density (methods (ii) and (iii)) values for respective distributions. Experimentation revealed that the parametric method was biased. In addition, the authors suggest that the kernel density method is the most ideal, as it does not suffer from bias while it can be used to extrapolate NMP scores where no match has been observed, unlike the histogram based representation.

2.1.3. Practicality of AFIS based LR Models

AFIS score based LR models provide a framework that is both practically based and simple to implement in conjunction with the AFIS architecture. However, model performance is dependent on the matching algorithm of the AFIS. In fact, LR models presented will usually reflect the exact information contained in a candidate list of an AFIS query. A more complex construction, for instance, multiple AFIS matching algorithms with a mixture-of-experts statistical model would be more ideal and avoid LR values that are strictly algorithm dependent.

The scores produced from matching algorithms in AFIS detail pairwise similarity between two impressions (i.e., mark and exemplar). However, the methods used in [36] [38], which generalise the distributions for all minutiae configurations, do not allow evidential aspects such as the rarity of a given configuration to be considered. A more sound approach would be to base LR calculations on methods that do not have primary focus on only pairwise similarities, but consider statistical characteristics of features within a given population. For instance, the LR for a rare minutiae configuration should be weighted to reflect its significance. This is achieved in the method described in [37] by focusing distribution estimates of scores for each minutiae configuration.

2.2. Feature Vector based LR models

Feature Vector (FV) based LR models are based on FVs constructed from landmark (i.e., minutiae) feature analyses. A dissimilarity metric is defined that is based on the resulting FV. The distributions of such vector dissimilarity metrics are then analysed for both genuine and imposter comparisons, from which an LR is derived.

2.2.1. Delauney Triangulation FV Model

The first FV based LR model proposed in the literature can be found in [33]. FVs are derived from Delaunay triangulation (Figure 5 **left**) for different regions of the fingerprint. Each FV was constructed as follows:

$$x = [GP_x, R_x, Nt_x, \{A_{1x}, L_{1x-2x}\}, \{A_{2x}, L_{2x-3x}\}, \{A_{3x}, L_{3x-1x}\}] \tag{6}$$

where GP_x is the pattern of the mark, R_x is the region of the fingerprint, Nt_x is the number of minutiae that are ridge endings in the triangle (with $Nt_x \in \{0,1,2,3\}$), A_{ix} is the angle of the ith minutia, and $L_{ix-((i+1) \mod 3)x}$ is the length in pixels between the ith and the $((i+1) \mod 3)^{th}$ minutiae, for a given query fingerprint. Likewise, these structures are created for candidate fingerprint(s):

$$y = \left[GP_y, R_y, Nt_y, \{A_{1y}, L_{1y-2y}\}, \{A_{2y}, L_{2y-3y}\}, \{A_{3y}, L_{3y-1y}\}\right]. \tag{7}$$

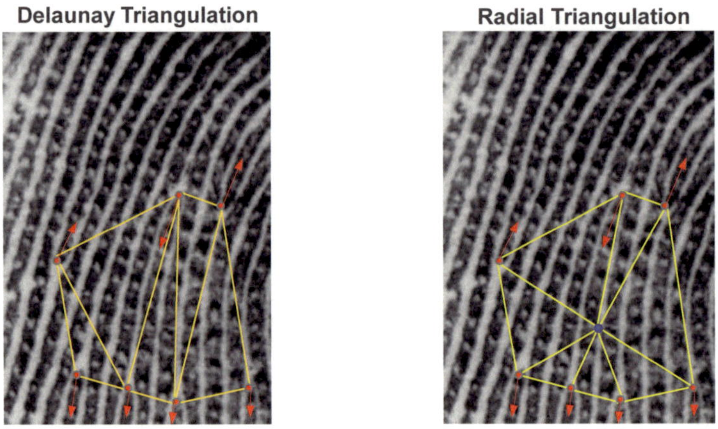

Figure 5. Delaunay triangulation (**left**) and radial triangulation (**right**) differences for a configuration of 7 minutiae. The blue point for the radial triangulation illustration represents the centroid (i.e., arithmetic mean of minutiae x-y coordinates).

The FVs can be decomposed into *continuous* and *discrete* components, representing the measurement based and count/categorical features, respectively. Thus, the likelihood ratio is rewritten as:

$$LR = \underbrace{\frac{P(x_c, y_c|x_d, y_d, H_0, I_{cs})}{P(x_c, y_c|x_d, y_d, H_A, I_{cs})}}_{LR_{c|d}} \cdot \underbrace{\frac{P(x_d, y_d|H_0, I_{cs})}{P(x_d, y_d|H_A, I_{cs})}}_{LR_d} = LR_{c|d}.LR_d \tag{8}$$

where LR_d is formed as a prior likelihood ratio with discrete FVs $x_d = [GP_x, R_x, Nt_x]$ and $y_d = [GP_y, R_y, Nt_y]$, while continuous FVs x_c and y_c contain then remaining features in x and y, respectively. The discrete likelihood numerator takes the value of 1, while the denominator was calculated using frequencies for general patterns multiplied by region and minutia-type combination probabilities observed from large datasets.

A dissimilarity metric, $d(x_c, y_c)$, was created for comparing the continuous FV defined as:

$$d(x_c, y_c) = \Delta^2 A_1 + \Delta^2 L_{1-2} + \Delta^2 A_2 + \Delta^2 L_{2-3} + \Delta^2 A_3 + \Delta^2 L_{3-1} \tag{9}$$

with Δ^2 as the squared difference of corresponding variables from x_c and y_c. This was used to calculate the continuous likelihood value, with:

$$LR_{c|d} = \frac{P(d(x_c, y_c)|x_d, y_d, H_0, I_{cs})}{P(d(x_c, y_c)|x_d, y_d, H_A, I_{cs})}. \tag{10}$$

Finger/Region	LR True < 1	LR False > 1
Index/All	2.94 %	1.99 %
Middle/All	1.99 %	1.84 %
Thumbs/All	3.27 %	3.24 %
Index/Core	4.19 %	1.36 %
Middle/Core	3.65 %	1.37 %
Thumbs/Core	3.74 %	2.43 %
Index/Delta	1.95 %	2.62 %
Middle/Delta	2.96 %	2.58 %
Thumbs/Delta	2.39 %	5.20 %

Table 1. Some likelihood ratio error rate results for different finger/region combinations.

Density functions of both $P(d(x_c, y_c)|x_d, y_d, H_0, I_{cs})$ and $P(d(x_c, y_c)|x_d, y_d, H_A, I_{cs})$ were estimated using a kernel smoothing method. All LR numerator and denominator likelihood calculations were derived from these distribution estimates.

Two experiments were configured in order to evaluate within-finger (i.e., genuine) and between-finger (i.e., imposter) LRs. Ideally, LRs for within-finger comparisons should be larger than all between-finger ratios. The within-finger experiment used 216 fingerprints from 4 different fingers under various different distortion levels. The between-finger datasets included the same 818 fingerprints used in the minutia-type probability calculations. Delaunay triangulation had to be manually adjusted in some cases due to different triangulation results occurring under high distortion levels. Error rates for LRs greater than 1 for false comparisons (i.e., between-finger) and LRs less than 1 for true comparisons (i.e., within-finger) for index, middle, and thumbs, are given in Table 1. These errors rates indicate the power that 3 minutiae (in each triangle) have in creating an LR value dichotomy between within and between finger comparisons.

2.2.2. Radial Triangulation FV Model: I

Although the triangular structures of [33] performed reasonably well in producing higher LRs for within-finger comparisons against between-finger comparisons, there are issues with the proposed FV structure's robustness towards distortion. In addition, LRs could potentially have increased dichotomy between imposter and genuine comparisons by including more minutiae in the FV structures, rather than restricting each FV to only have three minutiae.

The authors of [34] defined *radial triangulation* FVs based on n minutiae $x = [GP_x, x_s]$ with:

$$x^{(n)} = [\{T_{x,1}, RA_{x,1}, R_{x,1}, L_{x,1,2}, S_{x,1}\}, \{T_{x,2}, RA_{x,2}, R_{x,2}, L_{x,2,3}, S_{x,2}\}, \\ \ldots, \{T_{x,n}, RA_{x,n}, R_{x,n}, L_{x,n,1}, S_{x,n}\}], \tag{11}$$

(and similarly for y and $y^{(n)}$), where GP denotes the general pattern, T_k is the minutia type, RA_k is the direction of minutia k relative to the image, R_k is the radius from the kth minutia to the centroid (Figure 5 **right**), $L_{k,k+1}$ is the length of the polygon side from minutia k to $k+1$, and S_k is the area of the triangle defined by minutia k, $(k+1) \mod n$, and the centroid.

The LR was then calculated as

$$LR = \underbrace{\frac{P(x^{(n)}, y^{(n)}|GP_x, GP_y, H_0, I_{cs})}{P(x^{(n)}, y^{(n)}|GP_x, GP_y, H_A, I_{cs})}}_{LR_{n|g}} \cdot \underbrace{\frac{P(GP_x, GP_y|H_0, I_{cs})}{P(GP_x, GP_y|H_A, I_{cs})}}_{LR_g} = LR_{n|g}.LR_g \tag{12}$$

The component LR_g is formed as a prior likelihood with $P(GP_x, GP_y|H_0, I_{cs}) = 1$ and $P(GP_x, GP_y|H_A, I_{cs})$ equal to the FBI pattern frequency data. Noting that the centroid FVs can be arranged in n different ways (accounting for clockwise rotation):

$$\begin{aligned} y_j^{(n)} = (\{&T_{y,k}, RA_{y,k}, R_{y,k}, L_{y,k,(k+1) \bmod n}, S_{y,k}\}, \\ &k = j, (j+1) \bmod n, \ldots, (j-1) \bmod n), \end{aligned}$$

for $j = 1, 2, \ldots, n$, $LR_{n|g}$ was defined as

$$LR_{n|g} = \frac{P(d(x^{(n)}, y^{(n)})|GP_x, GP_y, H_0, I_{cs})}{P(d(x^{(n)}, y^{(n)})|GP_x, GP_y, H_A, I_{cs})} \tag{13}$$

where the dissimilarity metric is

$$d(x^{(n)}, y^{(n)}) = \min_{i=1,\ldots,n} d(x^{(n)}, y_i^{(n)}). \tag{14}$$

The calculation of each of the $d(x^{(n)}, y_i^{(n)})$ is the Euclidean distance of respective FVs which are normalised to take a similar range of values. The two conditional probability density functions of $P(d(x^{(n)}, y^{(n)})|GP_x, GP_y, H_0, I_{cs})$ and $P(d(x^{(n)}, y^{(n)})|GP_x, GP_y, H_A, I_{cs})$ were estimated using mixture models of normal distributions with a mixture of three and four distributions, respectfully, using the EM algorithm to estimate distributions for each finger and number of minutiae used.

This method modelled within and between finger variability more accurately in comparison to the earlier related work in [33], due to the flexibility of the centroid structures containing more than three minutiae. For example, the addition of one extra minutia halved the LR error rate for some fingerprint patterns. In addition, the prior likelihood is more flexible in real life applications as it is not dependent on identifying the specific fingerprint region (which is more robust for real life fingermark-to-exemplar comparisons).

2.2.3. Radial Triangulation FV Model: II

The authors of [35] proposed a FV based LR model using radial triangulation structures. In addition, they tuned the model using distortion and examination influence models. The radial triangulation FVs used were based on the structures defined in [34], where five features are stored per minutia, giving

http://dx.doi.org/10.5772/51184

$$y_i^{(n)} = (\{\delta_j, \sigma_j, \theta_j, \alpha_j, \tau_j\}, i = j, (j+1) \bmod n, \ldots, (j-1) \bmod n),$$

for a configuration $y^{(n)}$ starting from the ith minutia, for $i = 1, 2, \ldots, n$, where δ_j is the distance between the jth minutia and the centroid point, σ_j is the distance between the jth minutia and the next contiguous minutia (in a clockwise direction), θ_j is the angle between the direction of a minutia and the line from the centroid point, α_j is the area of the triangle constituted by the jth minutia, the next contiguous minutia and the centre of the polygon, and τ_j is the type of the jth minutia (ridge ending, bifurcation, unknown).

The distance between configurations $x^{(n)}$ and $y^{(n)}$, each representing n minutiae, is

$$d(x^{(n)}, y^{(n)}) = \min_{i=1,\ldots,n} d_c(x^{(n)}, y_i^{(n)}) \tag{15}$$

where

$$d_c(x^{(n)}, y_i^{(n)}) = \sum_{j=1}^{n} \Delta_j \tag{16}$$

with

$$\begin{aligned} \Delta_j = {} & q_\delta.(x^{(n)}(\delta_j) - y_i^{(n)}(\delta_j))^2 + q_\sigma.(x^{(n)}(\sigma_j) - y_i^{(n)}(\sigma_j))^2 \\ & + q_\theta.d_\theta(x^{(n)}(\theta_j), y_i^{(n)}(\theta_j))^2 + q_\alpha.(x^{(n)}(\alpha_j) - y_i^{(n)}(\alpha_j))^2 \\ & + q_\tau.d_T(x^{(n)}(\tau_j), y_i^{(n)}(\tau_j))^2 \end{aligned} \tag{17}$$

where $x^{(n)}(\delta_j)$ (and $y_i^{(n)}(\delta_j)$) is the normalised value for δ for the jth minutiae, and likewise for all other normalised vector components σ, θ, α, and τ, while d_θ is the angular difference and d_T is the defined minutiae type difference metric. The multipliers (i.e., q_δ, q_σ, q_θ, q_α, and q_τ) are tuned via a heuristic based procedure.

The proposed LR calculation makes use of:

- distortion model: based on the Thin Plate Spline (TPS) bending energy matrices representing the non-affine differences of minutiae spatial detail trained from a dataset focused on finger variability,
- examiner influence model: created to represent the variability of examiners when labelling minutiae in fingerprint images.

Let $y^{(k)}$ be the configuration of a fingermark, $x_{\min}^{(k)}$ the closest k configuration found, and $z_{i,\min}^{(k)}$ the closest configuration for the ith member of a reference database containing N impressions. Synthetic FVs can be generated from minute modifications to minutiae locations represented by a given FV, via Monte-Carlo simulation of both distortion and examiner influence models. A set of M synthetic FVs are created for $x^{(k)}_{\text{min}}$ $(\{\zeta^{(k)}_1, \ldots, \zeta^{(k)}_M\})$ and for each $z^{(k)}_{i,\text{min}}$ $(\{\zeta^{(k)}_{i,1}, \ldots, \zeta^{(k)}_{i,M}\})$, from which the LR is given as

$$LR = \frac{N \sum_{i=1}^{M} \psi\left(d(y^{(k)}, \zeta^{(k)}_i)\right)}{\sum_{i=1}^{N} \sum_{j=1}^{M} \psi\left(d(y^{(k)}, \zeta^{(k)}_{i,j})\right)} \tag{18}$$

where ψ is defined as

$$\psi(d(y^{(k)}, \bullet)) = \exp\left(\frac{-\lambda_1 d(y^{(k)}, \bullet)}{T^{(k)}}\right) + \frac{B(d(y^{(k)}, \bullet), \lambda_2 k)}{B(d_0, \lambda_2 k)} \tag{19}$$

which is a mixture of Exponential and Beta functions with tuned parameters λ_1 and λ_2, while d_0 is the smallest value into which distances were binned, and $T^{(k)}$ is the 95th percentile of simulated scores from the examiner influence model applied on $y^{(k)}$. Experimental results from a large validation dataset showed that the proposed LR model can generally distinguish within and between finger comparisons with high accuracy, while an increased dichotomy arose from increasing the configuration size.

2.2.4. Practicality of FV based LR Models

Generally speaking, to implement robust FV based statistical models for forensic applications, the following must be considered:

- Any quantitative measures used should be based on the data driven discovery of statistical relationships of features. Thus, a rich dataset for both within and between finger data is essential.
- Effects of skin distortion must be considered in models. Latent marks can be highly distorted from skin elasticity and applied pressure. For instance, differences in both minutiae location (relative to other features) and type (also known as type transfer) can occur when different distortion exists.
- Features used in models must be robust to noisy environmental factors, whilst maintaining a high level of discriminatory power. For instance, level 1 features such as classification may not be available due to partiality. In addition, level 2 sub-features such as ridge count between minutiae, minutiae type, and level 3 features such as pores, may not be available in a latent mark due to the material properties of the contacted medium or other environmental noise that regularly exist in latent mark occurrences.
- The model should be robust towards reasonable variations in feature markings from practitioners in the analysis phase of ACE-V. For instance, minutiae locations can vary slightly depending on where a particular practitioner marks a given minutia.

The LR models proposed in [33] and [34] use dissimilarity measures of FVs (equations (9) and (14)) which are potentially erroneous as minutiae types can change, particularly in distorted impressions. While the method in [35] has clearly improved the dissimilarity function by introducing tuned multipliers, squared differences in angle, area, and distance based measures are ultimately not probabilistically based. A joint probabilistic based metric for each FV component using distributions for both imposter and genuine populations would be more consistent with the overall LR framework.

With regards to skin distortion, the radial triangulation FV structures of [34] [35] are robust, unlike the Delaunay triangulation structure of [33]. Furthermore, the model proposed in [35] models realistic skin distortion encountered on flat surfaces by measuring the bending energy matrix for a specialised distortion set. However, this only accounts for the non-affine variation. Affine transformations such as shear and uniform compression/dilation are not accounted for. Such information can be particularly significant for comparisons of small minutiae configurations encountered in latent marks. For instance, a direct downward application of force may have prominent shear and scale variations (in addition to non-affine differences) for minutiae configurations, in comparison to the corresponding configurations of another impression from the same finger having no notable downward force applied.

3. Proposed method: Morphometric and Spatial Analyses (MSA) based Likelihood Ratio model

In this section, we present a newly formulated FV based LR model that focuses on the important sub-population of close non-matches (i.e., highly similar imposters), with intended practicality for fingermark-to-exemplar identification scenarios where only sparse minutiae triplet information may be available for comparisons. First we discuss relevant background material concerning morphometric and spatial measures to be used in the FVs of the proposed model. The proposed model is presented, which is based on a novel machine learning framework, followed by a proposed LR calculation that focuses on the candidate list population of an AFIS match query (i.e., containing close non-match exemplars and/or a matching exemplar). Finally, an experimental framework centred around the simulation of fingermark-to-exemplar close non-match discovery is introduced, followed by experimental results.

3.1. Morphometric and spatial metrics

The foundations of the morphometric and spatial analyses used in the proposed FV based LR model are presented. This includes a non-parametric multidimensional goodness-of-fit statistic, along with several other morphometrical measures that describe and contrast shape characteristics between two given configurations. In addition, a method for finding close non-match minutiae configurations is presented.

3.1.1. Multidimensional Kolmogorov-Smirnov Statistic for Landmarks

A general multidimensional Kolmogorov-Smirnov (KS) statistic for two empirical distributions has been proposed in [39] with properties of high efficiency, high statistical power, and distributional freeness. Like the classic one dimensional KS test, the multidimensional variant looks for the largest absolute difference between the empirical and cumulative distribution functions, as a measure of fit. Without losing generality, let two sets with m and n points in $\mathbb{R}^3$ be denoted as $X = \{(x_1, y_1, z_1), \ldots, (x_m, y_m, z_m)\}$ and $Y = \{(x'_1, y'_1, z'_1), \ldots, (x'_n, y'_n, z'_n)\}$, respectively. For each point $(x_i, y_i, z_i) \in X$ we can divide the plane into eight defined regions

$$\begin{aligned} q_{i,1} &= \{(x,y,z) | x < x_i, y < y_i, z < z_i\}, \\ q_{i,2} &= \{(x,y,z) | x < x_i, y < y_i, z > z_i\}, \\ &\vdots \\ q_{i,8} &= \{(x,y,z) | x \geq x_i, y \geq y_i, z \geq z_i\}, \end{aligned}$$

and similarly for each $(x'_j, y'_j, z'_j) \in Y$,

$$\begin{aligned} q'_{j,1} &= \{(x,y,z) | x < x'_i, y < y'_i, z < z'_i\}, \\ q'_{j,2} &= \{(x,y,z) | x < x'_i, y < y'_i, z > z'_i\}, \\ &\vdots \\ q'_{j,8} &= \{(x,y,z) | x \geq x'_j, y \geq y'_j, z \geq z'_j\}. \end{aligned}$$

Further defining

$$D_m = \max_{\substack{i=1,\ldots,m \\ s=1,\ldots,8}} \left| |X \cap q_{i,s}| - |Y \cap q_{i,s}| \right| \tag{20}$$

which is the maximum pairwise difference of point tallies for X and Y within each of the eight defined regions centred and evaluated at each point in X, and likewise,

$$D_n = \max_{\substack{j=1,\ldots,n \\ s=1,\ldots,8}} \left| |X \cap q'_{j,s}| - |Y \cap q'_{j,s}| \right| \tag{21}$$

which is the maximum pairwise difference of point tallies for the eight defined regions centred and evaluated at each point in Y, the three dimensional KS statistic is

$$Z_{m,n,3D} = \sqrt{n.m/(n+m)}.\left(\frac{D_m + D_n}{2}\right). \tag{22}$$

The three dimensional KS statistic can be specific to the minutiae triplet space where each minutia spatial and directional detail is represented as a three dimensional point, (x, y, θ). Given $m = n$ matching minutiae correspondences from two configurations X and Y, alignment is performed prior to calculating the statistic, in order to ensure that minutiae correspondences are close together both spatially and directionally. However, direction has a circular nature that must be handled differently from the spatial detail. Instead of raw angular values, we use the orientation difference defined as

$$z = z(\theta, \theta_0) = \frac{\pi}{2} - \min(2\pi - |\theta - \theta_0|, |\theta - \theta_0|) \tag{23}$$

where $z \in [-\frac{\pi}{2}, \frac{\pi}{2}]$. Each minutia, (x, y, θ), is then transformed to $(x, y, z(\theta, \theta_0))$ if the centred minutia used to create the eight regions has a direction of θ_0, while region borders are defined in the third dimension by $z \geq 0$ and $z < 0$.

3.1.2. Thin Plate Spline and Derived Measures

The Thin Plate Spline (TPS) [40] is based on the algebraic expression of physical bending energy of an infinitely thin metal plate on point constraints after finding the optimal affine transformations for the accurate modelling of surfaces that undergo *natural warping* (i.e., where a diffeomorphism exists). Two sets of landmarks from each surface are paired in order to provide an interpolation map on $\mathbb{R}^2 \rightarrow \mathbb{R}^2$. TPS decomposes the interpolation into an affine transform that can be considered as the transformation that expresses the global geometric dependence of the point sets, and a non-affine transform that fine tunes the interpolation of the point sets. The inclusion of the affine transform component allows TPS to be invariant under both rotation and scale.

Given n control points

$$\{\mathbf{p}_1 = (x_1, y_1), \mathbf{p}_2 = (x_2, y_2), \ldots, \mathbf{p}_n = (x_n, y_n)\}$$

from an input image in $\mathbb{R}^2$ and control points

$$\{\mathbf{p'}_1 = (x'_1, y'_1), \mathbf{p'}_2 = (x'_2, y'_2), \ldots, \mathbf{p'}_n = (x'_n, y'_n)\}$$

from a target image $\mathbb{R}^2$, the following matrices are defined in TPS:

$$\mathbf{K} = \begin{bmatrix} 0 & u(r_{12}) & \ldots & u(r_{1n}) \\ u(r_{21}) & 0 & \ldots & u(r_{2n}) \\ \ldots & \ldots & \ldots & \ldots \\ u(r_{n1}) & u(r_{n2}) & \ldots & 0 \end{bmatrix},$$

where $u(r) = r^2 \log r^2$ with r as the Euclidean distance, $r_{ij} = \|p_i - p_j\|$,

$$\mathbf{P} = \begin{bmatrix} 1 & x_1 & y_1 \\ 1 & x_2 & y_2 \\ \ldots & \ldots & \ldots \\ 1 & x_n & y_n \end{bmatrix}, \ \mathbf{V} = \begin{bmatrix} x'_1 & x'_2 & \ldots & x'_n \\ y'_1 & y'_2 & \ldots & y'_n \end{bmatrix}, \mathbf{Y} = \begin{bmatrix} \mathbf{V} & \mathbf{0}_{2\times 3} \end{bmatrix}^T, \ \mathbf{L} = \begin{bmatrix} \mathbf{K} & \mathbf{P} \\ \mathbf{P}^\mathbf{T} & \mathbf{0}_{3\times 3} \end{bmatrix},$$

where **K**, **P**, **V**, **Y**, **L** have dimensions $n \times n$, $3 \times n$, $2 \times n$, $(n+3) \times 2$, and $(n+3) \times (n+3)$, respectively. The vector $W = (w_1, w_2, \ldots, w_n)$ and the coefficients a_1, a_x, a_y, can be calculated by the equation

$$\mathbf{L}^{-1}\mathbf{Y} = (\mathbf{W}| \ a_1 \ a_x \ a_y)^T. \tag{24}$$

The elements of $\mathbf{L}^{-1}\mathbf{Y}$ are used to define the TPS interpolation function

$$f(x,y) = \left[f_x(x,y), f_y(x,y)\right], \tag{25}$$

with the coordinates compiled from the first column of $\mathbf{L}^{-1}\mathbf{Y}$ giving

$$f_x(x,y) = a_{1,x} + a_{x,x}x + a_{y,x}y + \sum_{i=1}^{n} w_{i,x}U(\|\mathbf{p}_i - (x,y)\|) \tag{26}$$

where $\left[a_{1,x}\ a_{x,x}\ a_{y,x}\right]^T$ is the affine transform component for x, and likewise for the second column, where

$$f_y(x,y) = a_{1,y} + a_{x,y}x + a_{y,y}y + \sum_{i=1}^{n} w_{i,y}U(\|\mathbf{p}_i - (x,y)\|) \tag{27}$$

with $\left[a_{1,y}\ a_{x,y}\ a_{y,y}\right]^T$ as the affine component for y. Each point (or minutia location in our application) can now be updated as

$$(x_{new}, y_{new}) = (f_x(x,y), f_y(x,y)). \tag{28}$$

It can be shown that the function $f(x,y)$ is the interpolation that minimises

$$I_f \propto \mathbf{WKW}^T = \mathbf{V}(\mathbf{L_n^{-1}KL_n^{-1}})\mathbf{V}^T, \tag{29}$$

where I_f is the *bending energy* measure

$$I_f = \int\int_{\mathbb{R}^2} \left(\frac{\partial^2 z}{\partial x^2}\right)^2 + 2\left(\frac{\partial^2 z}{\partial x \partial y}\right)^2 + \left(\frac{\partial^2 z}{\partial y^2}\right)^2 dxdy \tag{30}$$

and $\mathbf{L_n}$ is the $n \times n$ sub-matrix of $\mathbf{L}$. Affine transform based metrics relating to shear, rotation, and scale (i.e., compression and dilation) can be calculated straight from Singular Value Decomposition (SVD) of the affine matrix

$$\mathbf{USV}^T = SVD\left(\begin{bmatrix} a_{x,x} & a_{x,y} \\ a_{y,x} & a_{y,y} \end{bmatrix}\right). \tag{31}$$

From this decomposition, we define an angle cost

$$d_\theta = \min(\theta, 2\pi - \theta) \tag{32}$$

http://dx.doi.org/10.5772/51184

with $\theta = |(\arctan(\mathbf{V}_{1,2}, \mathbf{V}_{1,1}) - \arctan(\mathbf{U}_{1,2}, \mathbf{U}_{1,1})|$, a shear cost

$$d_{shear} = \log(\mathbf{S}_{1,1}/\mathbf{S}_{2,2}), \tag{33}$$

and a scale cost

$$d_{scale} = \log\left(\max\left(\mathbf{S}_{1,1}, \mathbf{S}_{2,2}, \frac{1}{\mathbf{S}_{1,1}}, \frac{1}{\mathbf{S}_{2,2}}\right)\right). \tag{34}$$

3.1.3. Shape Size and Difference Measures

Shape size measures are useful metrics for comparing general shape characteristics. Given a matrix $\mathbf{X}$ of dimensions $k \times m$, representing a set of k m-dimensional points, the *centroid size* [41] is defined as

$$S(\mathbf{X}) = \sqrt{\sum_{i=1}^{k} \|(\mathbf{X})_i - \bar{\mathbf{X}}\|^2}, \tag{35}$$

where $(\mathbf{X})_i$ is the ith row of $\mathbf{X}$ and $\bar{\mathbf{X}}$ is the arithmetic mean of the points in $\mathbf{X}$ (i.e., centroid point). Given a second landmark configuration $\mathbf{Y}$ also with k m-dimensional points, we define the shape size difference as

$$d_S = |S(\mathbf{X}) - S(\mathbf{Y})|. \tag{36}$$

Another useful shape metric is derived from the partial Procrustes method [41], which finds the optimal superimposition of one set of landmarks, $\mathbf{X}$, onto another, $\mathbf{Y}$, using translation and rotation affine operators:

$$\min_{\Gamma,\gamma} \|\mathbf{Y} - \mathbf{X}\Gamma - 1_k\gamma^T\|^2 \tag{37}$$

where 1_k is a $(k \times 1)$ vector of ones, Γ is a $m \times m$ rotation matrix and γ is the $(m \times 1)$ translation offset vector. Using centred landmarks, $\mathbf{X}_c = C\mathbf{X}$ and $\mathbf{Y}_c = C\mathbf{Y}$ where $C = \mathbf{I}_k - \frac{1}{k}1_k1_k^T$, the ordinary partial Procrustes sum of squares is

$$OSS_p(\mathbf{X}_c, \mathbf{Y}_c) = \text{trace}\left(\mathbf{X}_c^T\mathbf{X}_c\right) + \text{trace}\left(\mathbf{Y}_c^T\mathbf{Y}_c\right) - 2\|\mathbf{X}_c\|\|\mathbf{Y}_c\|\cos\rho\left(\mathbf{X}_c, \mathbf{Y}_c\right) \tag{38}$$

with $\rho\left(\mathbf{X}_c, \mathbf{Y}_c\right)$ as the Procrustes distance defined as

$$\rho\left(\mathbf{X}_c, \mathbf{Y}_c\right) = \arccos\left(\sum_{i=1}^{m} \lambda_i\right) \tag{39}$$

where $\lambda_1, \ldots, \lambda_m$ are the square roots of the eigenvalues of $Z_X^T Z_Y Z_Y^T Z_X$ with $Z_X = H\mathbf{X}/\|H\mathbf{X}\|$ and $Z_Y = H\mathbf{Y}/\|H\mathbf{Y}\|$ for the Helmert sub-matrix, H, with dimension $k \times k$.

3.1.4. Close Non-Match Discovery and Alignment

In order to reproduce the process of an examiner querying a minutiae configuration marked on fingermark with an AFIS, a method for finding close configurations was developed. To find close non-matches for a particular minutiae configuration, we employed a simple search algorithm based solely on minutiae triplet features, in order to maintain robustness towards such fingermark-to-exemplar match scenarios. The minutiae triplet features are extracted in a fully automated manner using the NIST mindtct tool [49] without particular attention to spurious results, besides minimum quality requirements as rated by the mindtct algorithm.

Algorithm 1 *findCloseTripletConfigs*: Find all close triplet configurations to **X**

```
Require: A minutiae triplet set X and a dataset of exemplars D.
  candidateList = null
  for all minutiae configurations Y ∈ D with |X| = |Y| do
    for all minutiae (x_Y, y_Y, θ_Y) ∈ Y do
      found ← false
      for all minutiae (x_X, y_X, θ_X) ∈ X do
        Y' ← Y
        rotate Y' by (θ_X − θ_Y) {This includes rotating minutiae angles.}
        translate Y' by offset (x_X − x_Y, y_X − y_Y)
        if Y' is close to X then
          found = true
          goto finished:
        end if
      end for
    end for
    finished:
    if found = true then
      Y' ← PartialProcrustes(X, Y') {Translate/Rotate Y' using partial Procrustes}
      TPS(X, Y') {non-affine registration by TPS}
      if I_f < I_max then
        add Y' to candidateList {Add if bending energy < limit (equation (29))}
      end if
    end if
  end for
  return candidateList
```

Once feature extraction is complete, the close match search algorithm (Algorithm 1) finds all equally sized close minutiae configurations in a given dataset of exemplars to a specified minutiae set configuration (i.e., potentially marked from a latent) in an iterative manner by assessing all possible minutiae triplet pairs via a crude affine transform based alignment on configuration structures. Recorded close minutiae configurations are then re-aligned using the partial Procrustes method using the discovered minutiae pairings. Unlike the Procrustes method, the partial Procrustes method does not alter scale of either landmarks. For the application of fingerprint alignment, ignoring scale provides a more accurate comparison of landmarks since all minutiae structures are already normalised by the resolution and dimensions of the digital image. The TPS registration is then applied for a non-affine transformation. If the bending energy is higher than a defined threshold, we ignore the potential match due to the likely *unnatural* distortion encountered. Finally, a candidate list with all close minutiae configurations is produced for analysis.

3.2. Proposed model

We now propose an LR model based on what is found in [4], developed specifically to aid AFIS candidate list assessments, using the intrinsic differences of morphometric and spatial analyses (which we label as MSA) between match and close non-match comparisons, learnt from a two-class probabilistic machine learning framework.

3.2.1. Feature Vector Definition

Given two matching configurations X and Y (discovered from the procedure described in Section 3.1.4) a FV based on the previously discussed morphometric and spatial analyses is defined as:

$$\mathbf{x}_i = \{Z_{m,n,3D}, I_f, d_\theta, d_{shear}, d_{scale}, S(\mathbf{X}), d_S, OSS_p(\mathbf{X}_c, \mathbf{Y}_c), d_{mc}\} \tag{40}$$

where $Z_{m,n,3D}$ is the three dimensional KS statistic of equation (22) using the transformed triplet points, I_f, d_θ, d_{shear}, and d_{scale} are the defined measures of equations (29) and (32-34) resulting from registering $\mathbf{X}$ onto $\mathbf{Y}$ via TPS, $S(\mathbf{X})$ and d_S are the shape size and difference metric of equations (35-36), $OSS_p(\mathbf{X}_c, \mathbf{Y}_c)$ is the ordinary partial Procrustes sum of squares of equation (38), and d_{mc} is the difference of the number of interior minutiae within the convex hulls of $\mathbf{X}$ and $\mathbf{Y}$. The d_{mc} measure is an optional component to the FV dependent on the clarity of a fingermark's detail within the given minutiae configuration. For the experiments presented later in this chapter, we will exclude this measure.

The compulsory measures used in the proposed feature vector rely solely on features that are robust to the adverse environmental conditions of latent marks, all of which are based on minutiae triplet detail. The FV structures are categorised by genuine/imposter (or match/close non-match) classes, number of minutiae in the matching configurations, and configuration area (categorised as small, medium, and large).

3.2.2. Machine Learning of Feature Vectors

Using the categories prescribed for the defined FVs, a probabilistic machine learning framework is applied for finding the probabilities for match and close non-match classes. The probabilistic framework employed [42] is based on Support Vector Machines (SVMs) with unthresholded output, defined as

$$f(\mathbf{x}) = h(\mathbf{x}) + b \tag{41}$$

with

$$h(\mathbf{x}) = \sum_i y_i \alpha_i k(\mathbf{x}_i, \mathbf{x}) \tag{42}$$

where $k(\bullet, \bullet)$ is the kernel function, and the target output $y_i \in \{-1, 1\}$ represents the two classes (i.e., 'close non-match' and 'match', respectively). We use the radial basis function

$$k(\mathbf{x}_i, \mathbf{x}) = \exp(-\gamma \|\mathbf{x}_i - \mathbf{x}\|^2) \tag{43}$$

due to the observed non-linear relationships of the proposed FV. Training the SVM minimises the error function

$$C \sum_i (1 - y_i f(\mathbf{x}_i))_+ + \frac{1}{2} \|h\|_{\mathcal{F}} \tag{44}$$

where C is the soft margin parameter (i.e., regularisation term which provides a way to control overfitting) and $\mathcal{F}$ is the Reproducing Kernel Hilbert Space (RKHS) induced by the kernel k. Thus, the norm of h is penalised in addition to the approximate training misclassification rate. By transforming the target values with

$$t_i = \frac{y_i + 1}{2}, \tag{45}$$

the posterior probabilities $P(y_i = 1 | f(\mathbf{x}_i))$ and $P(y_i = -1 | f(\mathbf{x}_i))$ which represents the probabilities that $\mathbf{x}_i$ is of classes 'match' and 'close non-match', respectively, can now be estimated by fitting a sigmoid function after the SVM output with

$$P(\mathbf{x}_i \text{ is a match} | f(\mathbf{x}_i)) = P(y_i = 1 | f(\mathbf{x}_i)) = \frac{1}{1 + \exp(Af(\mathbf{x}_i) + B)} \tag{46}$$

and

$$P(\mathbf{x}_i \text{ is a close non-match} | f(\mathbf{x}_i)) = P(y_i = -1 | f(\mathbf{x}_i)) = 1 - \frac{1}{1 + \exp(Af(\mathbf{x}_i) + B)}. \tag{47}$$

The parameters A and B are found by minimising the negative log-likelihood of the training data:

$$\arg\min_{A,B} \left[- \left(\sum_i t_i \log \left(\frac{1}{1+\exp(Af(\mathbf{x}_i)+B)} \right) + (1 - t_i) \log \left(1 - \frac{1}{1+\exp(Af(\mathbf{x}_i)+B)} \right) \right) \right] \tag{48}$$

using any optimisation algorithm, such as the Levenberg-Marquardt algorithm [43].

3.2.3. Likelihood Ratio Calculation

The probability distributions of equations (47-48) are posterior probabilities. Nevertheless, for simplicity of the initial application, we assume uniform distributions for $P(f(\mathbf{x}_i)) = z$ for some constant, z, whereas $P(\mathbf{x}_i \text{ is a match}) = a$ and $P(\mathbf{x}_i \text{ is a close non-match}) = 1 - a$

where a reflects the proportion of close minutiae configuration comparisons that are ground truth matches. Thus, the LR is equivalent to the posterior ratio (PR)

$$LR = \left(\frac{1-a}{a}\right).PR = \left(\frac{1-a}{a}\right).\frac{P(\mathbf{x}_i \text{ is a match}|f(\mathbf{x}_i))}{P(\mathbf{x}_i \text{ is a close non-match}|f(\mathbf{x}_i))}. \quad (49)$$

For future consideration, the probabilities $P(\mathbf{x}_i \text{ is a match})$ and $P(\mathbf{x}_i \text{ is a close non-match})$ can be adaptively based on Cumulative Match Characteristic (CMC) curve [44] statistics of a given AFIS system or any other relevant background information.

As already noted, the LR formulas are based on different distributions specified per FV categories of minutiae count and the area of the given configuration. This allows the LR models to capture any spatial and morphometric relational differences between such defined categories. Unlike previous LR methods that are based on the distributions of a dissimilarity metric, the proposed method is based on class predictions based on a number of measures, some of which do not implicitly or explicitly rate or score a configuration's dissimilarity (e.g. centroid size, $S(\mathbf{X}_i)$). Instead, statistical relationships of the FV measures and classes are learnt by SVMs in a supervised manner, only for class predictions.

In its current proposed form, the LR of equation (49) is not an evidential weight for the entire population, but rather, an evidential weight specifically for a given candidate list.

3.3. Experimentation

3.3.1. Experimental Databases

Without access to large scale AFISs, a sparse number of fingermark-to-exemplar datasets exists in the public domain (i.e., NIST27 is the only known dataset with only 258 sets). Thus, to study the within-finger characteristics, a distortion set was built.

We follow a methodology similar to that of [35] where live scanned fingerprints have eleven directions applied, eight of which are linear directions, two torsional, and central application of force. Using a readily available live scan device (Suprema Inc. Realscan-D: 500ppi with rolls, single and dual finger flats), we follow a similar methodology, described as follows:

- sixteen different linear directions of force,
- four torsion directions of force,
- central direction of force,
- all directions described above have at least three levels of force applied,
- at least five rolled acquisitions are collected,
- finally, numerous impressions with emphasis on partiality and high distortion are obtained by recording fifteen frames per second, while each finger manoeuvres about the scan area in a freestyle manner for a minimum of sixty seconds.

This gave a minimum total of 968 impressions per finger. A total of 6,000 impressions from six different fingers (from five individuals) were obtained for our within-finger dataset, most of which are partial impressions from the freestyle methodology. For the between-finger comparisons, we use the within-finger set in addition to the public databases of NIST 14 [45] (27000 $\times$ 2 impressions), NIST 4 [46] (2000 $\times$ 2 impressions), FVC 2002 [47] (3 $\times$ 110 $\times$ 8 flat scan/swipe impressions), and the NIST 27 database [48] (258 exemplars + 258 latents), providing over 60,000 additional impressions.

3.3.2. SVM Training Procedure

A simple training/evaluation methodology was used in the experiments. After finding all FVs for similar configurations, a random selection of 50% of the FVs were used to train each respective SVM by the previously defined categories (i.e., minutiae configuration count and area). The remaining 50% of FVs were used to evaluate the LR model accuracy. The process was then repeated by swapping the training and test sets (i.e., two-fold cross-validation). Due to the large size of the within-finger database, a substantially larger number of within-finger candidates are returned. To alleviate this, we randomly sampled the within-finger candidates to be of equal number to the between-finger counterparts (i.e., $a = 0.5$ in equation (49)). All individual features within each FV were scaled to have a range of $[0, 1]$, using pre-defined maximum and minimum values specific to each feature component.

A naive approach was used to find the parameters for the SVMs. The radial basis kernel parameter, γ, and the soft learning parameter, C, of equations (43) and (44), respectively, were selected using a grid based search, using the cross-validation framework to measure the test accuracy for each parameter combination, (γ, C). The parameter combination with the highest test accuracy was selected for each constructed SVM.

3.3.3. Experimental Results

Experiments were conducted for minutiae configurations of sizes of 6, 7, and 8 (Figure 6) from the within-finger dataset, using configurations marked manually by an iterative circular growth around a first minutiae until the desired configuration sizes were met. From the configuration sizes, a total of 12144, 4500, and 1492 candidates were used, respectively, from both the within (50%) and between (50%) finger datasets. The focus on these configuration settings were due to three reasons: firstly, the high computational overhead involved in the candidate list retrieval for the prescribed datasets, secondly, configurations of such sizes perform poorly in modern day AFIS systems [50], and finally, such configuration sizes are traditionally contentious in terms of Locard's tripartite rule, where a probabilistic approach is prescribed to be used.

The area sizes used for categorising the minutiae configurations were calculated by adding up the individual areas of triangular regions created using Delaunay triangulation. Small, medium, and large configuration area categories were defined as $0 < A < 4.2mm^2$, $4.2mm^2 \leq A < 6.25mm^2$, and $A \geq 6.25mm^2$, respectively.

The results clearly indicate a stronger dichotomy of match and close non-match populations when the number of minutiae was increased. In addition, the dichotomy was marginally stronger for larger configuration areas with six minutiae. Overall, the majority of FV's of class 'match' derive significantly large LR values.

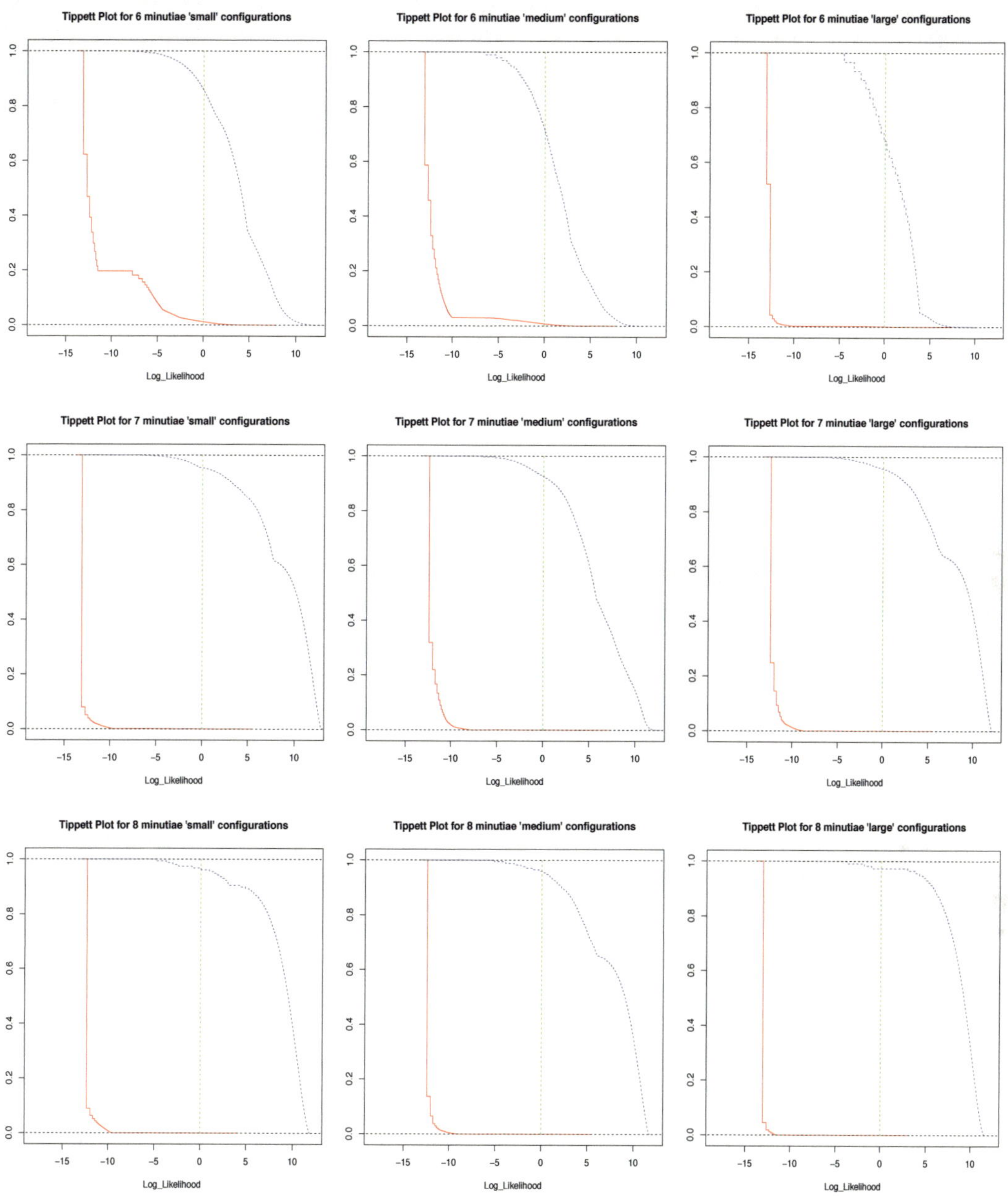

Figure 6. Tippett plots for minutiae configurations of 6 (top row), 7 (middle row), and 8 (bottom row) minutiae with small, medium, and large area categories (left to right, respectively), calculated from $P(\mathbf{x}_i \text{ is a match}|f(\mathbf{x}_i))$ and $P(\mathbf{x}_i \text{ is a close non-match}|f(\mathbf{x}_i))$ distributions. The x-axes represents the logarithm (base 2) of the LR values in equation (49) for match (blue line) and close non-match (red line) populations, while the y-axes represents proportion of such values being greater than x. The green vertical dotted line at $x = 0$ signifies a marker for $LR = 1$ (i.e., $x = log_2 1 = 0$).

4. Summary

A new FV based LR model using morphometric and spatial analysis (MSA) with SVMs, while focusing on candidate list results of AFIS, has been proposed. This is the first LR model known to the authors that use machine learning as a core component to learn spatial feature relationships of close non-match and match populations. For robust applications for fingermark-to-exemplar comparisons, only minutiae triplet information were used to train the SVMs. Experimental results illustrate the effectiveness of the proposed method in distinguishing match and close non-match configurations.

The proposed model is a preliminary proposal and is not focused on evidential value for judicial purposes. However, minor modifications can potentially allow the model to also be used for evidential assessments. For future research, we hope to evaluate the model with commercial AFIS environments containing a large set of exemplars.

Author details

Joshua Abraham[1,⋆], Paul Kwan[2], Christophe Champod[3],
Chris Lennard[4] and Claude Roux[1]

⋆ Address all correspondence to: joshua.abraham@uts.edu.au

1 Centre for Forensic Science, University of Technology, Sydney, Australia
2 School of Science and Technology, University of New England, Australia
3 Institute of Forensic Science, University of Lausanne, Switzerland
4 National Centre for Forensic Studies, University of Canberra, Australia

References

[1] J.C. Yang (2008), D.S. Park. A Fingerprint Verification Algorithm Using Tessellated Invariant Moment Features, *Neurocomputing, Vol. 71, No. 10-12*, pages 1939-1946.

[2] J.C. Yang (2011). Non-minutiae based fingerprint descriptor, in *Biometrics, Jucheng Yang (Ed.), ISBN: 978-953-307-618-8, InTech*, pages 79-98.

[3] J. Abraham (2011), P. Kwan, J. Gao. Fingerprint Matching using a Hybrid Shape and Orientation Descriptor, in *State of the art in Biometrics, Jucheng Yang and Loris Nanni (Eds.), ISBN: 978-953-307-489-4, InTech*, pages 25-56.

[4] J. Abraham (2012), C. Champod, C. Lennard, C. Roux. Spatial Analysis of Corresponding Fingerprint Features from Match and Close Non-Match Populations, *Forensic Science International*, DOI: 10.1016/j.forsciint.2012.10.034

[5] C. Champod (2004), C. J. Lennard, P. Margot, M. Stoilovic. Fingerprints and Other Ridge Skin Impressions, *CRC Press*. 2004.

[6] C. Champod (2000). Fingerprints (Dactyloscopy): Standard of Proof, in *Encyclopedia of Forensic Sciences, J. Siegel, P. Saukko and G. Knupfer (Eds.), London: Academic Press*, pages 884-890.

[7] C. Champod (2009). Friction Ridge Examination (Fingerprints): Interpretation Of, *in Wiley Encyclopedia of Forensic Science (Vol. 3), A. Moenssens and A. Jamieson (Eds.), Chichester, UK: John Wiley & Sons*, pages 1277-1282.

[8] C. Champod (1995). Edmond Locard–numerical standards and "probable" identifications, *J. Forensic Ident., Vol. 45*, pages 136-163.

[9] J. Polski (2011), R. Smith, R. Garrett, et.al. The Report of the International Association for Identification, Standardization II Committee,*Grant no. 2006-DN-BX-K249 awarded by the U.S. Department of Justice, Washington, DC, March 2011.*

[10] M. Saks (2010). Forensic identification: From a faith-based "Science" to a scientific science, *Forensic Science International Vol. 201*, pages 14-17.

[11] S. A. Cole (2008). The 'Opinionization' of Fingerprint Evidence, *BioSocieties, Vol. 3*, pages 105-113.

[12] J. J. Koehler (2010), M. J. Saks. Individualization Claims in Forensic Science: Still Unwarranted, *75 Brook. L. Rev. 1187-1208.*

[13] L. Haber (2008), R. N. Haber. Scientific validation of fingerprint evidence under Daubert Law, *Probability and Risk Vol. 7, No. 2*, pages 87-109.

[14] S. A. Cole (2007). Toward Evidence-Based Evidence: Supporting Forensic Knowledge Claims in the Post-Daubert Era, *Tulsa Law Review, Vol 43*, pages 263-283.

[15] S. A. Cole (2009). Forensics without Uniqueness, Conclusions without Individualization: The New Epistemology of Forensic Identification, *Law Probability and Risk, Vol. 8*, pages 233-255.

[16] I. E. Dror (2010), S. A. Cole. The Vision in 'Blind' Justice: Expert Perception, Judgement, and Visual Cognition in Forensic Pattern Recognition, *Psychonomic Bulletin & Review, Vol. 17*, pages 161-167.

[17] M. Page (2011), J. Taylor, M. Blenkin. Forensic Identification Science Evidence Since Daubert: Part I-A Quantitative Analysis of the Exclusion of Forensic Identification Science Evidence, *Journal of Forensic Sciences, Vol. 56, No. 5*, pages 1180-1184.

[18] Daubert v. Merrel Dow Pharmaceuticals (1993), *113 S. Ct. 2786.*

[19] G. Langenburg (2009), C. Champod, P. Wertheim. Testing for Potential Contextual Bias Effects During the Verification Stage of the ACE-V Methodology when Conducting Fingerprint Comparisons, *Journal of Forensic Sciences, Vol. 54, No. 3*, pages 571-582.

[20] L. J. Hall (2008), E. Player. Will the introduction of an emotional context affect fingerprint analysis and decision-making?, *Forensic Science International, Vol. 181*, pages 36-39.

[21] B. Schiffer (2007), C. Champod. The potential (negative) influence of observational biases at the analysis stage of fingermark individualisation, *Forensic Science International, Vol. 167*, pages 116-120.

[22] I. E. Dror (2011), C. Champod, G. Langenburg, D. Charlton, H. Hunt. Cognitive issues in fingerprint analysis: Inter- and intra-expert consistency and the effect of a 'target' comparison, *Forensic Science International, Vol. 208*, pages 10-17.

[23] J.J. Koehler (2008). Fingerprint Error Rates and Proficiency Tests: What They are and Why They Matter. *Hastings Law Journal, Vol. 59, No. 5*, pages 1077.

[24] M. J. Saks (2008), J. J. Koehler. The Individualization Fallacy in Forensic Science Evidence, *Vanderbilt Law Rev., Vol 61*, pages 199-219.

[25] S. A. Cole (2006). Is Fingerprint Identification Valid? Rhetorics of Reliability in Fingerprint Proponents' Discourse, *Law & Policy*, pages 109-135.

[26] D. H. Kaye (2010). Probability, Individualization, and Uniqueness in Forensic Science Evidence: Listening to the Academies. *Brooklyn Law Review, Vol. 75, No. 4*, pages 1163-1185.

[27] IAI (2010) Resolution 2010-18, *International Association For Identification*, http://www.theiai.org

[28] C. Champod (2001), I. W. Evett. A Probabilistic Approach to Fingerprint Evidence, *J. Forensic Ident., Vol. 51, No. 2*, pages 101-122.

[29] A. Collins (1994), N. E. Morton. Likelihood ratios for DNA identification, *Proc Natl Acad Sci U S A., Vol. 91, No. 13*, pages 6007-6011.

[30] C. Champod (2001), I. W. Evett, B. Kuchler. Earmarks as evidence: a critical review, *J Forensic Sci., Vol. 46, No. 6*, pages 1275-1284.

[31] G. Zadora (2009). Evaluation of evidence value of glass fragments by likelihood ratio and Bayesian Network approaches, *Anal Chim Acta., Vol. 642, No. 1-2*, pages 279-290.

[32] D. A. Stoney (1985). Quantitative Assessment of Fingerprint Individuality, *D. Crim. Dissertation, University of California, Graduate Division of the University of California.*

[33] C. Neumann (2006), C. Champod, R. Puch-Solis, N. Egli, A. Anthonioz, D. Meuwly, A. Bromage-Griffiths. Computation of Likelihood Ratios in Fingerprint Identification for Configurations of Three Minutiae, *Journal of Forensic Sciences, Vol. 51, No. 6*, pages 1255-1266.

[34] C. Neumann (2007), C. Champod, R. Puch-Solis, N. Egli, A. Anthonioz. Computation of likelihood ratios in fingerprint identification for configurations of any number of minutiae, *Journal of Forensic Sciences, Vol. 52, No. 1*, pages 54-64.

[35] C. Neumann (2012), C. Champod, R. Puch-Solis, N. Egli, Quantifying the weight of evidence from a forensic fingerprint comparison: a new paradigm, *Journal of the Royal Statistical Society: Series A (Statistics in Society), Vol. 175, No. 2*, pages 371-415.

[36] N. M. Egli (2007), C. Champod, P. Margot. Evidence evaluation in fingerprint comparison and automated fingerprint identification systems–modelling within finger variability, *Forensic Science International, Vol. 167, No. 2-3*, pages 189-195.

[37] N. M. Egli (2009). Interpretation of Partial Fingermarks Using an Automated Fingerprint Identification System, *PhD Thesis, Uiversity of Lausanne*

[38] Heeseung Choi (2011), A. Nagar, A. K. Jain. On the Evidential Value of Fingerprints, *in Biometrics (IJCB), 2011 International Joint Conference on*, pages 1-8.

[39] G. Fasano (1987), A. Franceschini. A multidimensional version of the Kolmogorov-Smirnov test, *Mon. Not. R. astr. Soc., Vol. 225*, pages 155-170.

[40] F. Bookstein (1989). Principal Warps: Thin-Plate Splines and the Decomposition of Deformations., *IEEE Trans. Pattern Anal. Mach. Intell., Vol. 11, No. 6*, pages 567-585.

[41] I. Dryden (1998) and K. Mardia. Statistical Shape Analysis, *John Wiley & Sons*.

[42] J. Platt (1999). Probabilistic outputs for support vector machines and comparison to regularized likelihood methods, *In: A. Smola, P. Bartlett, B. Scholkopf, and D. Schuurmans (Eds.): Advances in Large Margin Classifiers. Cambridge, MA, MIT Press.*

[43] C. Kelley (1999). Iterative Methods for Optimization, *SIAM Frontiers in Applied Mathematics, No. 18*.

[44] H. Moon (2001), P. Phillips. Computational and performance aspects of pca-based face-recognition algorithms, *In Perception, Vol. 30, No. 3*, pages 303-321.

[45] C. I. Watson (1993), NIST Special Database 14, NIST Mated Fingerprint Card Pairs 2 (MFCP2), http://www.nist.gov/srd/nistsd14.cfm

[46] C. I. Watson (1992), *NIST Special Database 4, NIST 8-bit Gray Scale Images of Fingerprint Image Groups (FIGS)*, http://www.nist.gov/srd/nistsd4.cfm

[47] D. Maio (2002), D. Maltoni, R. Cappelli, J.L. Wayman, A. K. Jain. FVC2002: Second Fingerprint Verification Competition, *In Proceedings of 16th International Conference on Pattern Recognition (ICPR2002)*, pages 811-814.

[48] M. D. Garris (2000), R. M. McCabe, NIST Special Database 27, Fingerprint Minutiae from Latent and Matching Tenprint Images, http://www.nist.gov/srd/nistsd27.cfm

[49] NIST Biometric Image Software (2012), http://www.nist.gov/itl/iad/ig/nbis.cfm

[50] M. Indovina (2012), V. Dvornychenko, R. A. Hicklin, G. I. Kiebuzinski, ELFT-EFS Evaluation of Latent Fingerprint Technologies: Extended Feature Sets [Evaluation #2], *NISTIR 7859*, http://dx.doi.org/10.6028/NIST.IR.7859

[51] D. Maio (2004), D. Maltoni, R. Cappelli, J. L. Wayman, A. K. Jain, FVC2004: Third Fingerprint Verification Competition, *Proc. International Conference on Biometric Authentication (ICBA)*, pages 1-7.

Chapter 11

Physiological Signal Based Biometrics for Securing Body Sensor Network

Fen Miao, Shu-Di Bao and Ye Li

Additional information is available at the end of the chapter

http://dx.doi.org/10.5772/51856

1. Introduction

Nowadays, the constraints in the healthcare of developing countries, including high population growth, a high burden of disease prevalence, low health care workforce, large numbers of rural inhabitants, and limited financial resources to support healthcare infrastructure and health information systems, accompanied with the improvement of potential of lowering information and transaction costs in healthcare delivery due to the explosively access of mobile phones to all segments of a country, has motivated the development of mobile health or m-health field. M-health is known as the practice of medical and public health supported by mobile devices such as mobile phones and PDAs for delivering medical and healthcare services. Thus, the popularity of m-health can be subjected to the development of wearable medical devices and wireless communication technology. In order to fully utilize wireless technology between the wearable medical devices, the concept of body sensor network (BSN), which is a kind of wireless sensor network around human body, was proposed in 2002.

1.1. Body sensor network

BSN, which has great potential in being the main front-end platform of telemedicine and mobile health systems, is currently being heavily developed to keep pace with the continuously rising demand for personalized healthcare. Comprised of sensors attached to the human body for collecting and transmitting vital signs, BSN is able to facilitate the joint processing of spatially and temporally collected medical data from different parts of the body for resource optimization and systematic health monitoring. In a typical BSN, each sensor node collects various physiological signals in order to monitor the patient's health status no matter their location and then instantly transmit all information in real time to the medical server or the doctors. When an emergency is detected, the physicians will immediately inform the patient through the computer system by providing appropriate messages or alarms. By this way, BSN is preferred in monitoring patients in environments lack of medical doctors, such as home and workplaces. Fig.1 presents a simplified example of a BSN application scenario in a mobile health system. Sensor nodes on or inside the human body and a Master Node (MN), are connected to form a BSN. Medical information collected by different sensors in a BSN will be sent to the MN for data fusion and then to personal server for pre-processing before being forwarded to a central server for further analysis or the physicians for care giving via various forms of communications such as wireless personal area network (WPAN), wireless local area network (WLAN) and wide area network (WAN).

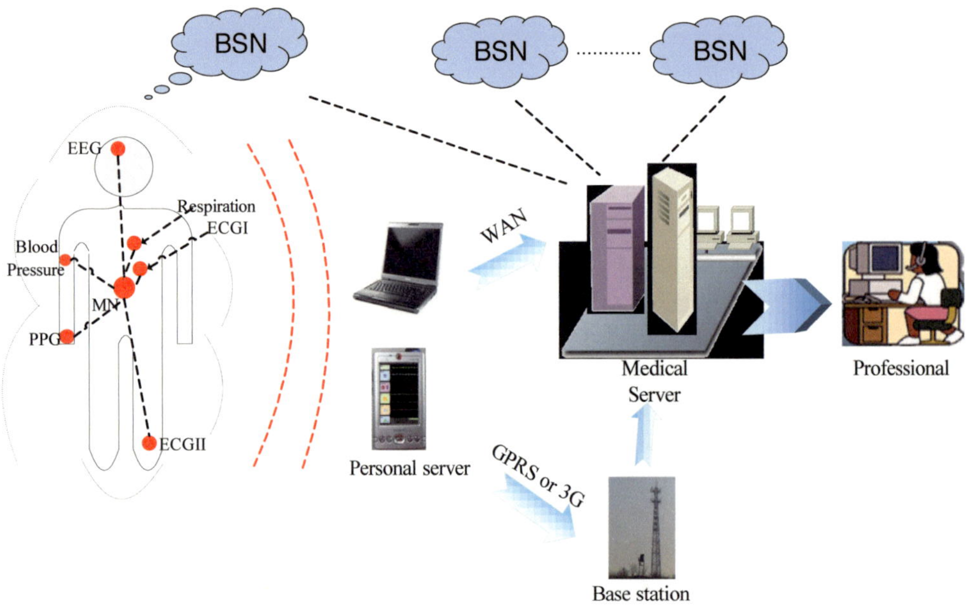

Figure 1. An application scenario of BSN

1.2. Security challenge in BSN

As mandated by privacy laws and regulations, such as the Health Information and Portability Accountability Act (HIPAA) (Bowen et al, 2005) and the European Union Directive 2002/58/EC (2002), wireless standards with medical applications have to have a high level of reliability to guarantee the security of patients' information and the privacy of healthcare history. To ensure the security of the overall mobile health system, BSN as an important end, should be protected from different attacks such as eavesdropping, injection and modification. However, it is a nontrivial task due to stringently limited processing capability, memory, and energy, as well as lack of user interface, unskilled users, longevity of devices, and global roaming for most sensor nodes.

Symmetric cryptography, in which communication parties must possess a shared secret key via an invulnerable key distribution solution prior to any encryption process, is a promising approach to relieve the stringent resource constraints in BSN. Existing key distribution techniques for large-scale sensor networks, such as random-key pre-distribution protocols (Gligor et al, 2002; Perrig et al, 2003) and polynomial pool-based key distribution (Ning et al, 2003), require some form of pre-deployment. However, given the progressively increasing deployments of BSN, these approaches may potentially involve considerable latency during network initialization or any subsequent adjustments, due to their need for pre-deployment. In addition, it obviously discourages people, such as family members, to share sensors between themselves because whenever there is need to add or change a body sensor, the user has to configure a new initial key to ensure that the new sensor can securely communicate with the existing ones. Therefore, a new series of key distribution solutions without any form of initial deployment to provide plug and play security is desirable for BSNs.

1.3. Novel biometrics for BSN security

As well known, the human body physiologically and biologically consists of its own transmission systems such as the blood circulation system, thus, how to make use of these secured communication pathways available specifically in BSN to secure it is a good idea (Poon et al, 2006). It is undoubtedly practical in securing BSN with a telemedicine or m-health application, as nodes of these BSN would already comprise biosensors for collecting medical data, which could be physiological characteristics uniquely representing an individual. If these intrinsic characteristics can be used to verify whether two sensors belong to the same individual, the use of physiological signals to identify individuals and secure encryption key transmission with resources-saving is feasible. Building upon this initial idea, a family of lightweight and resource-efficient biometrics-based security solutions, which are based on time-variant physiological signals, has been proposed for the emerging BSN with a dual purpose of individual identification and key transmission. It is different from traditional biometrics, where the physiological or behavioural characteristics are static and merely used to automatic identify or verify an individual. The utilized biometric traits in traditional biometric systems should have the characteristics of universality, distinctiveness, permanence, effectiveness, invulnerability and so on, while the physiological characteristics should be dynamic at different times to ensure the security of key transmission in BSN.

As depicted in Fig.2, in biometrics solution the physiological signals of human body, such as electrocardiograph (ECG) and photoplethysmograph (PPG), were used to generate the entity identifier (EI) of each node for identifying nodes and then protecting the transmission of keying materials by a key hiding/un-hiding process. It is based on the fact that EIs generated simultaneously from the same subject are with high similarity, while those generated non-simultaneously or from different subjects are with significant differentiation.

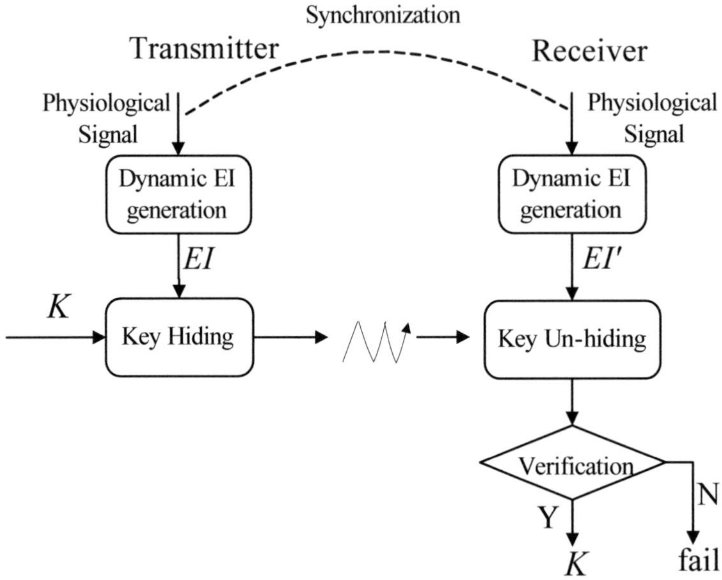

Figure 2. Workflow of biometrics-based security solution

1.3.1. Dynamic EI generation

The timing information of heartbeats was demonstrated by Bao et al (2005) to be a possible biometric characteristic to be used in proposed entity authentication scheme due to its chaotic nature, which can ensure the dynamic random performance of the generated EIs and then the security performance for BSN. Thus, the authors proposed to use Inter-Pulse-Interval (IPI) to generate EIs for securing the distribution of keying materials. A rigorously information-theoretic secure extraction scheme to properly extract the randomness of ECG signal, mainly from the IPI information, was proposed by Xu et al (2011). It was demonstrated that there are two advantages of using IPI to secure BSN. Firstly, it can be derived from multiple physiological signals such as electrocardiograph (ECG) and photoplethysmograph (PPG) by measuring the time difference between peaks in the signals. Secondly, it has been demonstrated that EIs generated from a series of IPI values passed the selected randomness tests from the National Institute of Standards and Technology (NIST) standards, and thus show an acceptable degree of randomness. However, an R-wave detection process is required before IPI measurement, which not only increases the computational complexity, but also leads to the uncertain performance because the accuracy of R-wave detection seriously affects the performance of IPI-based security system. In addition, 32 IPIs need to be utilized to generate a 128-bit EI, which means about 30 seconds of ECG/PPG measurements are required before cryptographic keys can be securely distributed. To overcome these problems, the frequency-domain characteristics of physiological signals (FDPS), was proposed by Gupta et al (2010) to be a promising biometric characteristic due to its real-time performance, where 5 seconds measurement is enough to generate EIs. Also, there is no need of R-wave detection in FDPS-based EI generation scheme. However, the poor randomness and recognition rate performance are the bottlenecks of using FDPS to generate EIs and need to be broken through to ensure the security performance of BSN.

1.3.2. Fuzzy method based key distribution solution

Since intrinsic characteristics captured simultaneously at different parts of the same subject have slight differences, fuzzy methods should be deployed on the transmitter/receiver for an increased tolerance in acceptable differences to protect the transmission of keying materials using generated EIs. Fuzzy commitment scheme proposed by Juels (2002), which works effectively in the case that the generated EIs are all sequential and with the same length, is employed in BSN security due to its low computational complexity, low memory occupied, as well as convenience to be implemented. However, Fuzzy commitment scheme is not appropriate while the feature points in EIs are un-ordered or with missing values due to its requirement for correspondence of features in terms of order. To address this issue, Juels and Sudan (2006) proposed the fuzzy vault scheme, which offers attractive properties in terms of security, changeable key, and flexibility, and thus has been a good candidate for biometrics based cryptographic systems. It has been applied in different traditional biometric systems, for example, fingerprint, face, and Iris biometric systems for better performance than fuzzy commitment. Though fuzzy vault scheme was also adopted in biometrics based BSN security in more and more studies, it is noted that (Miao et al, 2010) the scheme is not good enough to achieve stable performance if the generated EIs are with dynamic random patterns in bit difference. Also, fuzzy vault has its drawbacks of low recognition rate due to not considering the inequality of the number of features in EIs generated from the two communication parties.

This chapter will describe the aspects of this kind of new biometrics with focus on the state-of-the-art biometric solutions for BSN security. In Section 2, the schemes of generating EIs from physiological signals based on both time-domain and frequency-domain information will be presented, followed by the performance evaluation as being a dynamic individual identifier to differentiate different subjects. Secondly, the usage of such generated EIs for securing BSN, i.e. key transmission schemes, will be detailed with a performance comparison of different schemes designed according to EIs' specific characteristics in Section 3. In Section 4, we conclude this chapter with an illustration of different biometric solutions in BSN security, where some issues need to be further studied will be emphasized.

2. Entity identifier generation schemes

EI generation scheme is the most important issue should be addressed in the biometrics solutions because the security of BSN depends heavily on the characteristics of EIs generated. As described in Section 1, the state-of-the-art EI generation schemes are mainly classified into two categories, one is based on the time-domain information of physiological signals (TDPS) and the other is based on the frequency-domain information (FDPS). In this section, we will illustrate the two schemes separately with a detail performance evaluation on their advantages and disadvantages.

2.1. TDPS-based EI generation scheme

IPI is the most commonly used timing information in TDPS-based EI generation scheme. Fig.3 presents the experimental protocol of IPI-based EI generation scheme and the application of EIs for node identification. In IPI-based EI generation scheme, each node extracts the time-domain information by calculating a series of IPIs from its own recorded cardiovascular signal such as ECG and PPG based on a synchronization signal initiated by the master node, which can be denoted as $\{IPI_i \mid 1 \le i \le N\}$. IPI-based EI generation process is then deployed on the series of IPIs of each end to generate its own EI. The EIs generated simultaneously from the transmitter and the receiver are with high similarity for the same subject, while high dissimilarity for different subjects or generated non-simultaneously, and thus can be used to identify nodes by comparing the Hamming distance between two EIs.

As depicted in Fig.3, given a sequence of IPI values, the IPI-based EI generation process for the transmitter/receiver is comprised of the following three processes: accumulation & modulo, contraction mapping and Gray coding. Give N consecutive individual IPIs, a series of multi-IPIs can be obtained as follows:

$$\left\{ mIPI_i = \sum_{n=1}^{i} IPI_n \;\middle|\; 1 \le i \le N \right\} \tag{1}$$

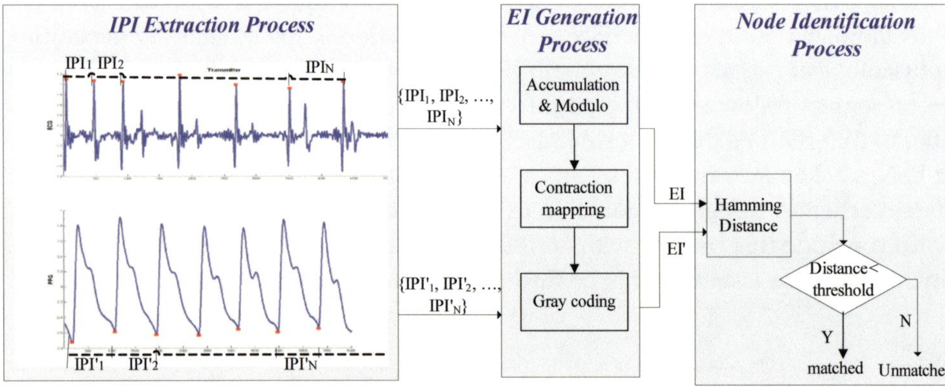

Figure 3. Experimental Protocol of TDPS-based EI generation scheme and node identification

To randomize the monotonically increasing multi-IPIs, a modulo operation is further introduced, i.e. $(mIPI_i)\text{mod}(2^L)$, where L is a positive integer referred to as the modulo parameter. To compensate measurement differences among different BSN nodes, the modulo result is further transformed into a small integer q by a contraction mapping $\hat{f}: [0, 2^L) \to [0, 2^q)$, i.e.,

http://dx.doi.org/10.5772/51856

$$\hat{f}(m) = \left\lfloor \frac{m}{2^{(L-q)}} \right\rfloor \tag{2}$$

where $L > q$ and $\lfloor . \rfloor$ returns the largest integer less than or equal to $m / 2^{(L-q)}$. Finally, to increase the noise margin of measurements, the Gray code scheme is employed to get binary EIs. The generated EI can be expressed as $EI = I_1 || I_2 \cdots || I_{L-1} || I_N$, where I_i is generated from a corresponding $mIPI_i$ with the bit length of q. Such generated EIs have a bit length of $N \times q$.

2.2. FDPS-based EI generation scheme

Fig.4 presents a demonstration of the experimental protocol of FDPS-based EI generation scheme and the application of EIs for node identification with PPG as the physiological signal. In state-of-the-art FDPS-based EI generation schemes, nodes in the same BSN obtained independently the same physiological signal in a loosely synchronized manner, at a specific sampling rate for a fixed duration. An EI generation process is then deployed on the signal acquired from each end to generate its own EI. In order to realize node identification and the security of keying materials, the EIs generated simultaneously from the transmitter and the receiver should be with high similarity for the same subject, while high dissimilarity for different subjects or generated non-simultaneously. Therefore, the EIs can be used to identify nodes by comparing the distance between two EIs. Different from TDPS-based EI generation scheme, the distance of EIs measured here cannot be Hamming distance, the reason of which will be explained in Section 2.3.

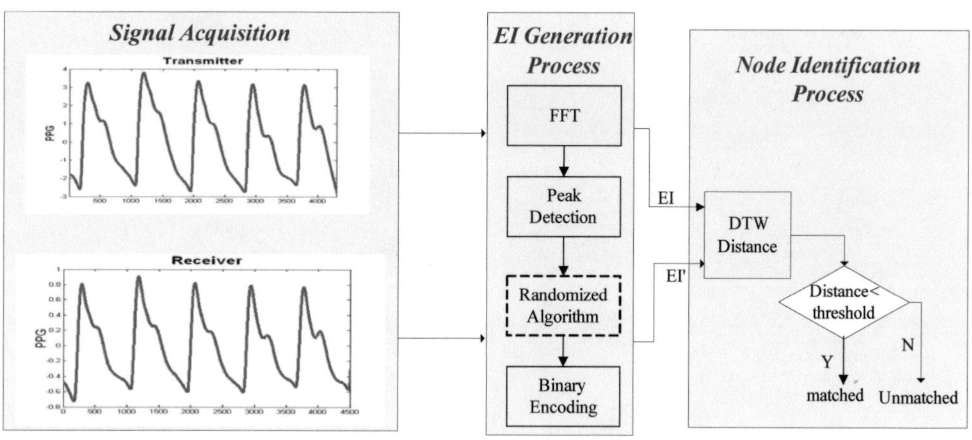

Figure 4. Experimental Protocol of FDPS-based EI generation scheme and node identification

As depicted in Fig.4, an entire FDPS-based EI generation process is comprised of a Fast Fourier Transform (FFT) process, a peak detection process, a randomized algorithm in some situations and a binary encoding process. In the previous FDPS-based EI generation process proposed by Gupta *et al* (2010), the samples collected are divided into several windows and a FFT is performed on each of these parts, denoted as Multi-Windows generation scheme. A combination with the form of $<K_x^i, K_y^i>$ is derived through the peak detection process deployed on the FFT coefficients, where K_x^i is the FFT point at which peak is observed, K_y^i is the corresponding FFT coefficient values, and i is the index of the peaks. Each of the peak-index and peak-value are quantized and converted into a binary string and concatenated to form an EI, which can be denoted as $EI = \{f^1, f^2, \cdots f^N\}$, where $f^i = [K_x^i, K_y^i]$, $1 \leq i \leq N$, N is the number of indexes where peaks are observed, which varies upon situation. However, based on what we learned from experimental analysis, K_y^i is not a good resource to generate EIs because the amplitudes of physiological signals can be easily affected by a lot of measurement factors, such as the degree of skin exposure to sensor nodes.

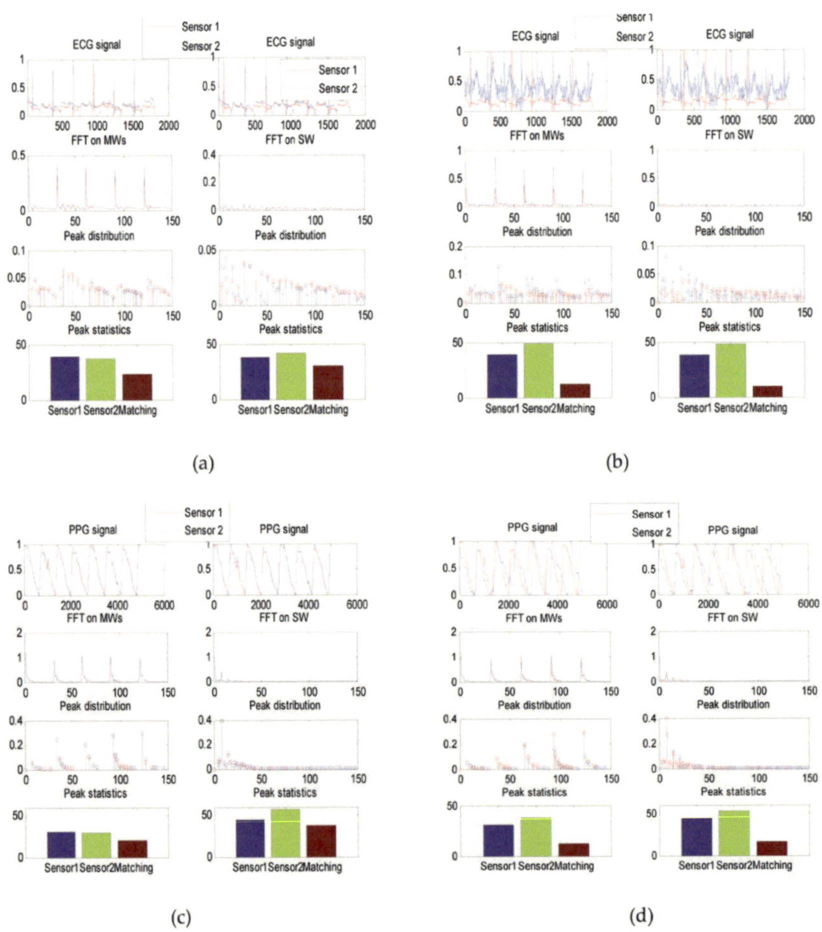

Figure 5. Multi-Windows versus Single-Window feature points generation process: (a) Same subject with ECG; (b) Different subjects with ECG; (c) Same subject with PPG; (d) Different subjects with PPG

Therefore, a Single-Window (SW) method to generate EIs was proposed by Miao *et al* (2011) aiming for a significant improvement in recognition performance and increase in randomness performance. Firstly, FFT is directly performed on the physiological signal in a loosely synchronized manner, at a specific sampling rate for a fixed duration, such as 5 seconds. Then, each peak-index, i.e. $<K_x^i>$, of the first M points of FFT coefficients is selected and concatenated to form a set of feature points $F=\{K_x^1,\ K_x^2,\ \cdots K_x^N\}$, where N is the number of indexes where peaks are observed, which varies upon situation. Before binary encoding process, a randomized algorithm is designed to overcome the bottleneck of randomness performance. Fig.5(a) and Fig.5(b) indicate an example of the differences between Multi-Windows (MWs) and Single-Window (SW) methods before randominzed algorithm with ECG signals collected by two nodes on one single subject and from two different subjects, respectively, while Fig.5(c) and Fig.5(d) indicate an example of the differences with PPG signals. It can be seen from Fig.5 that the number of peaks generated from nodes on the same subject has a higher number of matchings in terms of peak-index compared to those from different subjects; however, there is no such findings with FFT coefficients. In addtion, compared with MWs method, the SW method presents a larger matching rate, which is defined as the rate between the number of matched peaks and the number of the detected peaks, for the same subject and smaller matching rate for different subjects, no matter what kind of physiological signal is.

Obviously, all of the integer values of feature points are ascending and within a certain scale, which would bring about the bottleneck of the randomness performance and security weakness. Therefore, a randomized algorithm similar to Linear Congruential Generator (LCG), which is a kind of pseudorandom number generator, is deployed to randomize F and form a new set F', i.e.,

$$\begin{aligned} F' &= \{(bK_x^1+c)\bmod 2^p,\ (bK_x^2+c)\bmod 2^p,\ \cdots (bK_x^N+c)\bmod 2^p\} \\ &= \{f_1,\ f_2 \cdots,\ f_N\} \end{aligned} \tag{3}$$

where 2^p is the "modulus" and p is a positive integer referred to as modulo parameter, $b \geq 0$ is the "multiplier", $0 \leq c < 2^p$ is the "increment". The selection of $b,\ c,\ p$ is directly related to the randomness performance of F. In the randomized algorithm, it is recommended that the most optimal relationship between $b,\ c,\ p$ is as followings:

$$\begin{cases} b = \lfloor 2^{p/2} \rfloor + 1 \\ c = 2\beta + 1,\ c \big/ 2^p = (1\big/2 - \sqrt{3}\big/6) \end{cases} \tag{4}$$

where $\beta \geq 0$, $\lfloor x \rfloor$ returns the largest integer less than or equal to x. Then, a permuted feature points set is generated with the form of $F'' = RandomPermute(f_1,\ f_2,\ \cdots,\ f_N) = (f'_1,\ f'_2,\ \cdots f'_N)$ by randomly permuting the order of each point f_i. The generated EI can be expressed as $EI = I_1 || I_2 \cdots || I_{N-1} || I_N$, where $||$ is a concatenation operation. Each block of EI, i.e., I_i is the binary result of a corresponding f_i'. The bit length of I_i is p, and thus, the bit length of EI is $N \times p$.

2.3. Performance evaluation

To demonstrate the performance of different EI generation scheme, we conduct the performance evaluation in terms of randomness performance and group similarity. The performance comparison will be given to systematically illustrate the advantages and disadvantages of different schemes with two experiments. In the first experiment (Exp. I), the experimental data to be used for performance evaluation include ECG and PPG from 14 healthy subjects, where ECG was captured from the three fingers of each subjects and two channels of PPG were captured from the index fingers of the two hands, respectively. For each subject, the three channels of signals were captured simultaneously for 2-3min. All the three channels of signals were used to generate TDPS-based EIs, while two channels of PPG were used to generate FDPS-based EIs. In the second experiment (Exp. II), there were in total 85 clinical subjects from the hospital and two channels of physiological signals (including one-channel ECG and one-channel PPG) with a duration of 40 seconds were simultaneously recorded from each subject on three or four days within two-month period.

2.3.1. Randomness performance analysis

The randomness performance of binary sequences can be evaluated using a variety of randomness tests. Beacause of the length limitation in the generated binary EIs from each subject, several tests from the National Institute of Standards and Technology (NIST) standards were selected, including frequency (monobit) test, frequency test within a block, cumulative sums test, runs test, and approximate entropy test with the decision rule of 1% level.

Test	Pass rate	
	FDPS-based EIs $b=23$, $c=109$, $p=9$	TDPS-based EIs
Frequency Test	99.219%	100%
Frequency Test within a Block (M=10)	100%	100%
Runs Test	99.219%	100%
Cumulative Sums Test	100%	100%
Approximate Entropy Test	99.219%	100%

Table 1. Randomness test results

Table 1 shows the randomness test results of TDPS-based EIs and FDPS-based EIs, where the randomizing parameters in FDPS-based EI generation scheme were set as b=23, c=109, p=9. It can be seen that all bit streams generated based on TDPS and most of

FDPS-based EIs passed the selected tests, and TDPS-based EIs show a better randomness performance than FDPS-based EIs.

2.3.2. *Group similarity analysis*

The similarity between any pair of TDPS-based EIs generated simultaneously by sensors on the same individual can be analyzed with the Hamming distance. Fig.6 depicts the Hamming distance distribution of EIs with L =8, N =16, q=3. It can be seen that more than 95% of the Hamming distances between TDPS-based EIs are less than 10, and thus shows a good group similarity performance with the two experiments. Therefore, the proposed scheme is applicable in both healthy people and clinical subjects.

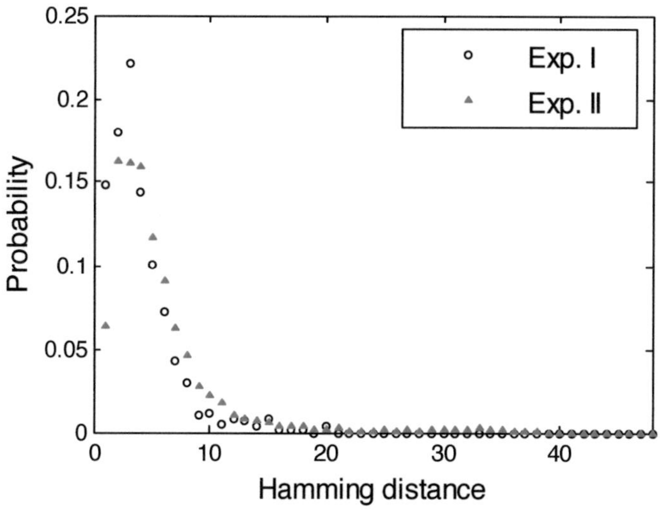

Figure 6. Similarity analysis with the Hamming distance (L =8, N =16, q=3)

Different from TDPS-based EIs, FDPS-based EIs cannot be analyzed with the Hamming distance due to the unequal length of generated EIs and matching points at different orders. As shown in Fig.7, the feature sets generated at the transmitter/receiver of the same subject after randomized algorithm have some common points, such as 174, 225, 156 at different orders, and thus direct Hamming distance in sequence can not reflect the real matching performance.

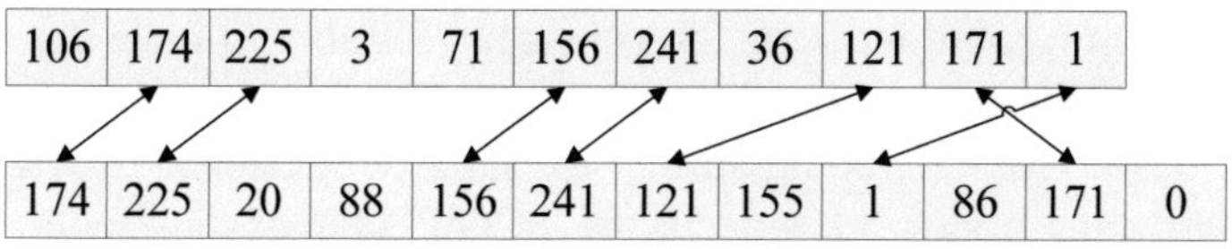

Figure 7. Feature points set generated at the transmitter/receiver of the same subject

Therefore, dynamic time warping (DTW) distance was selected to measure the group similarity between any pair of EIs generated from the same subject. DTW is an algorithm for measuring similarity between two sequences that vary in time or speed, which meets the characteristics of the EIs generated from FDPS. It is able to find an optimal match between two given sequences with certain restrictions. The sequences are "warped" non-linearly in the time dimension to determine a measure of their similarity independent of certain non-linear variations in the time dimension. Let s_1 and s_2 be two vectors with lengths of m and n. The goal of DTW is to find a mapping path $\{(p_1, q_1), (p_2, q_2), \cdots, (p_k, q_k)\}$ such that the distance on this mapping path $\sum_{i=1}^{k} | s_1(p_i) - s_2(q_i) |$ is minimal.

Fig.8 depicts the DTW distance distribution of EIs generated from the true pairs, i.e., two nodes on the same individual, with the SW and MWs methods on PPG data, respectively. It can be seen that with the SW EI generation scheme, 98% of the DTW distance between true pairs are less than 90, compared with 82% with the MWs, and thus exhibit a better performance of group similarity than those with MWs.

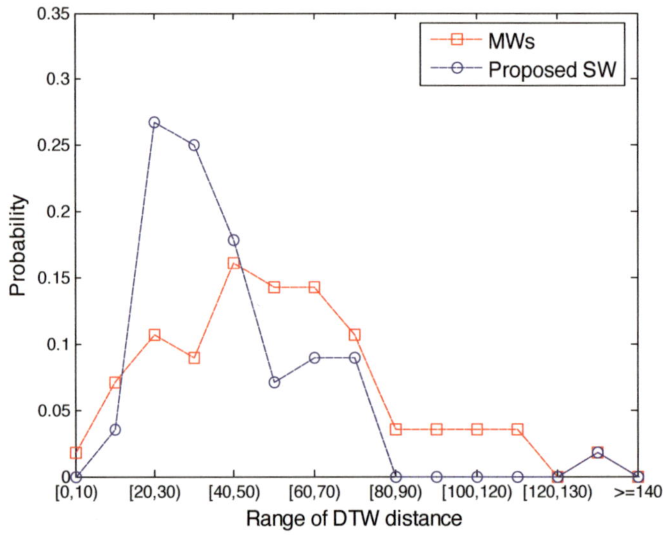

Figure 8. DTW distance distribution of FDPS-based EIs of the true pairs.

2.3.3. Performance comparison between two EI generation schemes

In order to realize high recognition rate, the generated EIs should have the characteristics of effectiveness (being able to be generated fast and easily), robustness (resistance to uncertainty), randomness, distinctiveness (being similar for same subjects and differentiate for different subjects). Firstly, as about 30 seconds of ECG/PPG measurements are required to generate a 128-bit EI based on TDPS while only 5 seconds based on FDPS, and an R-wave detection is needed in TDPS-based EI generation scheme for the IPI measurement, which increases the computational complexity, the FDPS-based EIs shows a better effectiveness performance than TDPS. Secondly, the accuracy of R-wave detection affects the recognition performance of TDPS-based EIs heavily. For example, once a negative R-wave is detected or a positive R-wave is missed in one end, the EIs from true pairs will be dissimilar. Therefore, there would be a requirement for the given TDPS-based EI generation scheme that, the physiological signals shall be with an acceptable quality for peak detection. Though FDPS-based EI generation may also require a good signal quality, there is no evidence that the requirement is more constrict while compared to the TDPS-based one. Thirdly, from both the randomness performance and group similarity analysis, TDPS-based EIs shows a better performance than FDPS-based. In conclusion, TDPS-based EIs is superior in randomness and distinctiveness performance, while FDPS-based EIs is superior in effectiveness and robustness performance.

3. Key distribution solution

As presented in the workflow of the biometrics security in Section 1.3, the EIs can not only be used to identify individuals, but also be used to protect the transmission of keying materials. The key distribution process in biometrics security model works as follows: one of the two sensors, called transmitter, hides the random symmetric key generated by its own using an EI obtained from the physiological signal. This hidden key is sent over to another sensor, called receiver, which uses its own version of EI to recover the random key after compensating for the differences between its EI and the one used by the transmitter. The most common fuzzy methods used in biometrics security solution until now are fuzzy commitment and fuzzy vault, dependent on the characteristics of the EI generated. In this section, the two fuzzy methods application will be detailed with a discussion of the specific fuzzy method to be adopted for TDPS-based EIs and FDPS-based EIs according to their characteristics.

3.1. Fuzzy commitment scheme applied in BSN security

The block diagram of key distribution solution between communication parties based on the fuzzy commitment scheme is presented in Fig.9. Let $K \in \{0,1\}^k$ and $\hat{K} \in \{0,1\}^n$ represent the cryptographic key need to be protected and its corresponding error-correction codeword, respectively, $EI \in \{0,1\}^n$ represent the EI value at the transmitter used to protect keying materials, and $h:\{0,1\}^n \rightarrow \{0, 1\}^l$ be a one-way hash function. The fuzzy commitment scheme is defined as $F(\hat{K}, EI)=(h(K), \hat{K} \oplus EI)$, where $\oplus$ is the bitwise XOR operation. To decommit $F(\hat{K}, EI)$ using a witness EI' at its own end, the receiver computes $K'=f(EI' \oplus (\hat{K} \oplus EI))=f(\hat{K} \oplus (EI' \oplus EI))$, where f is the relevant error-correction decoding process. If $h(K')=h(K)$, then the decommitment is successful and K' is the correct key K. Otherwise, EI' is an incorrect witness that is not close enough to the original encrypting witness EI. It is obvious that the EI used in such a security model must be sequential and with the same length. In fact, in order to realize high-level security performance, EI used in fuzzy commitment must have the performance of distinctiveness and time-variance to ensure the invulnerability.

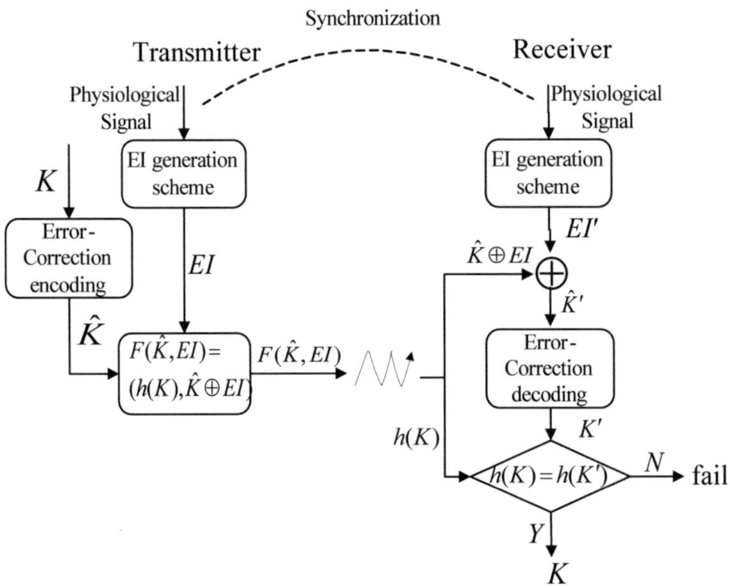

Figure 9. Key distribution solution based on fuzzy commitment scheme

3.2. Fuzzy vault scheme applied in BSN

Fig.10 gives the block diagram of key distribution solution between communication parties based on the fuzzy vault scheme applied in BSN security. In fuzzy vault based key distribution scheme, let $K \in \{0,1\}^n$ represent the cryptographic key need to be protected, $a_i \in \{0, 1\}^k$, $i=1 \cdots M$ represent the binary biometric features derived from the generated EI used to protect keying materials. A polynomial $P(x)=c_m x^m + c_{m-1}x^{m-1} + c_{m-2}x^{m-2} + \cdots c_1 x + c_0$ is created for binding of K and $a_i \in \{0, 1\}^k$, $i=1 \cdots M$ by segmenting K as its coefficients with the form of $K = c_m \,||\, c_{m-1} \,||\, c_{m-2} \,||\, \cdots \,||\, c_0$, where m is the degree of the polynomial. The polynomial $P(x)$ is then evaluated on each of the feature points X_i, where X_i is an integer number corresponds to binary feature a_i. The generated pairs $\{(X_i, P(X_i)), i=1 \cdots M\}$ are termed the genuine set G. Then the transmitter generates the chaff points set $C=\{(u_j, v_j), j=1 \cdots N_c\}$, where $N_c \gg M$, $u_j \neq X_i$ and each pair does not lie on the polynomial, i.e. $v_j \neq f(u_j)$. The final vault is constructed by taking the union of the two sets, i.e. $G \cup C$, combined with the message authentication code (e.g. MD5, SHA1)of K, denoted as $MAC(K)$, and pass through a scrambler so that it is not clear which are the feature points and which are the chaff points. The receiver decodes the fuzzy vault using binary biometric features $a'_i \in \{0, 1\}^k$, $i=1 \cdots M$ derived from the EI generated by itself by searching for the matchings in the fuzzy vault. All the candidate points are identified together with their pair values in the vault to form a set S. Let U denotes the number of pairs in S. To reconstruct the polynomial with m degree, all possible combinations of $m+1$ points are identified, with a total number of $\binom{U}{m+1}$ combinations. Each of the possible combinations is used to recover the polynomial using Lagrange interpolating technique. The coefficients in the generated polynomial is mapped back and concatenated in the same order as encoding to generate an n-bit code K'. The cryptographic key K can be retrieved while the message authentication code of K' equals to $MAC(K)$ if the two EIs generated at both ends are with high similarity.

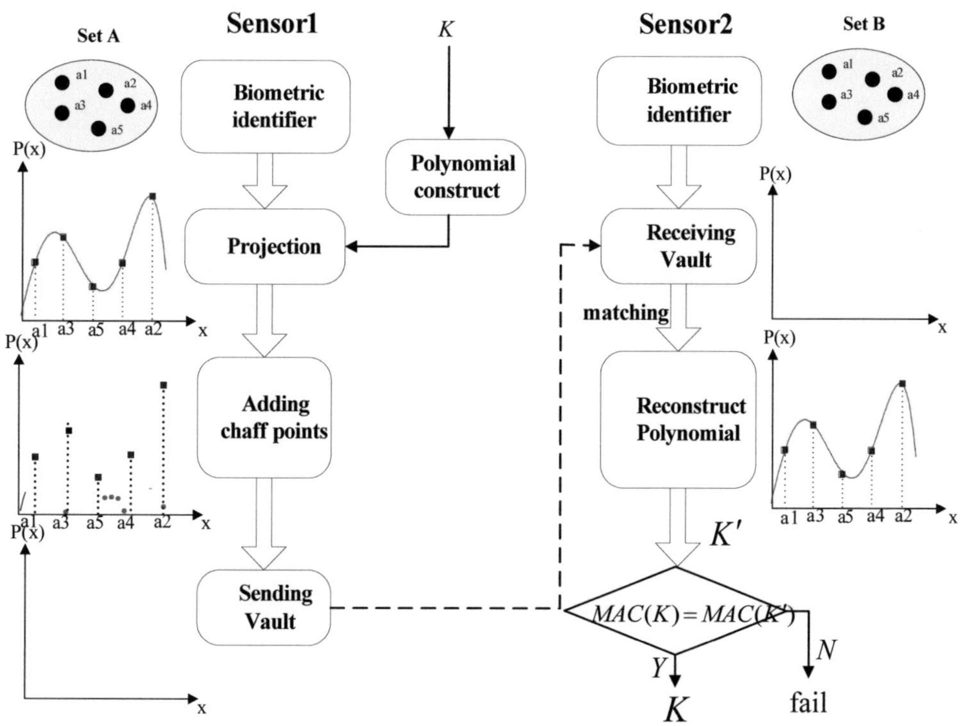

Figure 10. Key distribution solution based on fuzzy vault scheme

3.3. Performance comparison between different application scenarios

In order to realize high recognition performance and security, a suitable key distribution solution should be selected based on the specific characteristics of EIs generated based on TDPS and FDPS. In this section, we conduct a series of experiments to evaluate the performance of different key distribution solutions. Firstly, a detailed recognition performance in terms of False Accept Rate (FAR)/False Reject Rate (FRR) is conducted for different EI generation scheme with different key distribution solution to demonstrate the suitable key distribution solution for different EIs generated. Then, the security performance of different fuzzy methods are presented. At last, the computational complexity performances are conducted for different key distribution solutions with the appropriate EI generation scheme.

3.3.1. FAR/FRR performance

FAR and FRR are two important indexes to evaluate the recognition rate performance of a biometric system, where FAR is the probability that a system incorrectly matches the input pattern from false pairs, FRR is the probability that a system fails to detect a match between the true pairs. The most suitable fuzzy method for different EIs should achieve a minumum half total error rate (HTER) that equals (FAR+FRR)/2.

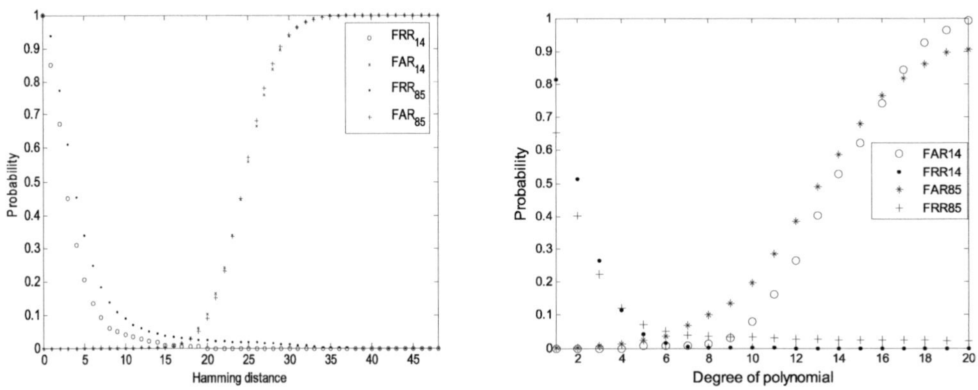

(a) (b)

Figure 11. FAR/FRR curves with TDPS-based EIs. (a) Fuzzy commitment scheme; (b) Fuzzy vault scheme

For TDPS-based EIs, we conduct our performance evaluation based on data from two experiments described in Section 2.3. In Exp.I, i.e. there were in total 14 healthy subjects and three channels of physiological signals (including 1-channel ECG and 2-channel PPG) with a duration of 2-3 minutes were simultaneously recorded from each subject. In Exp.II, there were in total 85 clinical subjects and two channels of physiological signals (including one-channel ECG and one-channel PPG) with a duration of 40 seconds were simultaneously recorded from each subject on three or four days within a two-month period. Data from the both experiments are with 12-bit A/D resolution and at a sampling rate of 1000 Hz. Fig.11(a) depicts the FAR/FRR curves with fuzzy commitment scheme, where FRR is the rate at which the two EIs generated from the same subject during the same period are unmatched, i.e. Hamming distance is larger than a specific threshold, FAR is the rate at which the two EIs generated from the different subjects or during different periods are matched, i.e. Hamming distance is larger than a specific threshold. Fig.11(b) depicts the FAR/FRR curves with fuzzy vault scheme, where FRR is the rate at which the two EIs generated from the same subject during the same period are unmatched, i.e. matching number is smaller than a predefined degree of polynomial, FAR is the rate at which the two EIs generated from the different subjects or during different periods are matched, i.e. matching number is smaller than a predefined degree of polynomial. It can be seen that the fuzzy commitment scheme shows a better recognition performance with a minumum HTER of less than 1.46% and 3.19% on 14 and 85 subjects, compared to 3.4% and 5.6% with fuzzy vault scheme. The results indicate that the fuzzy commitment scheme is superior to fuzzy vault scheme in different settings, such as the lab and the clinical setting, for TDPS-based EIs.

As presented in Section 2.3.2, the two feature sets generated based on FDPS from the transmitter and receiver are with different numbers of points and it is common to have matching points at different orders of the two sets, thus fuzzy commitment scheme is not suitable for FDPS-based EIs due to its requirement for correspondence of features in terms of order. Therefore, fuzzy vault scheme is probably the only approriate solution to protect the transmmission of keying materials with FDPS-based EIs. The data we used for performance evaluation include ECG data of 20 subjects from the physioBank database (http://www.physionet.org/physiobank), including 10 healthy people and 10 people with different kinds of diseases, which were simultaneously collected from two leads on each subject at a sampling rate of 360 Hz, and two-channel PPG data at a sampling rate of 1000 Hz from 14 subjects in Exp.I Fig.12 depicts the FAR/FRR curves with fuzzy vault scheme. It can be seen that fuzzy vault shows an recognition performance with a minumum HTER of 5.2% and 8.9% on ECG and PPG, respectively.

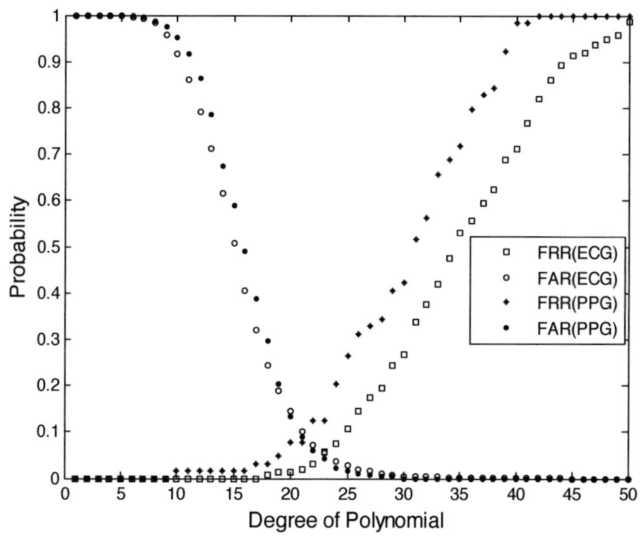

Figure 12. FAR/FRR curves with FDPS-based EIs based on fuzzy vault scheme

From the above analysis we can see, fuzzy commitment scheme is suitable for TDPS-based EIs while fuzzy vault scheme for FDPS-based EIs. In addition, TDPS-based solution shows a better recognition rate performance than FDPS-based one.

3.3.2. Security analysis

Suppose the EIs generated are random enough, the security issues in the proposed key distribution solution primarily exist during its package exchange process by brute-forcing the key (K) or EI directly. Therefore, to ensure the security of the key distribution protocol, the information contained in EI must be larger than that in K.

For fuzzy commitment scheme, an eavesdropper can try out each bit of K by brute-force attack. Also, he can try out most of bits in EI to reconstruct the same K. Suppose the length of K is l, the computation requirement of directly attack on K in terms of its equivalence to brute-forcing a key of a particular length (bits) is l. The number of attempts by attacking EI depends on the length of K and the ability of its corresponding error-correction. Take Reed-Solomon as the error-correction code for example, a redundancy code of $2\times t$ bits should be attached to correct t-bit errors, thus the length of EI should be equal to$l+2\times t$. As the error-correction code can correct t-bit errors, an attempt of $l+2\times t-t=l+t$ bits can reconstruct K successfully. In conclusion, the computation requirement in terms of its equivalence to brute-forcing a key of a particular length (bits) is $\min(l,\ l+t)=l$. In another word, the security of fuzzy commitment depends on the security of K directly.

For fuzzy vault scheme, except for brute-forcing K directly, an eavesdropper can record the vault and try to construct the hidden polynomial from it. As described above, the computation requirement of directly attack on K is l. Suppose the degree of the polynomial is m, as the feature points are hidden among a much larger number of chaff points, whose values are randomly distributed in the same range in some situation, an adversary is able to try out each group of $m+1$ points in the vault to get the correct polynomial, the average attempts are $\binom{L}{m+1}\Big/2$, where L is the vault size and $L\le 2^p$. Thus, the security of vault is a balance act between the vault size L and the degree of the polynomial m, but subject to p and l. In conclusion, the computation requirement in terms of its equivalence to brute-forcing a key of a particular length (bits) is $\min(\log_2^{\binom{L}{m+1}},\ l)$. The security of the vault for different values of m and different number of vault size in the condition $l=128$ and $p=9$ is presented in Fig.13. For ease of understanding, we represent this computation requirement in terms of its equivalence to brute-forcing a key of a particular length (bits). As expected, increasing the number of chaff points increases the security provided by the vault, but the security is subject to p and l. Higher the order of the polynomial means higher security, where more common feature points shall be hold by two ends.

3.3.3. Computational complexity

As described in Section 3.3.1, the suitable fuzzy method for TDPS-based EIs is fuzzy commitment while fuzzy vault for FDPS-based EIs. We estimate the cost performance of proposed key distribution solutions in terms of computational complexity, including time complexity and space complexity.

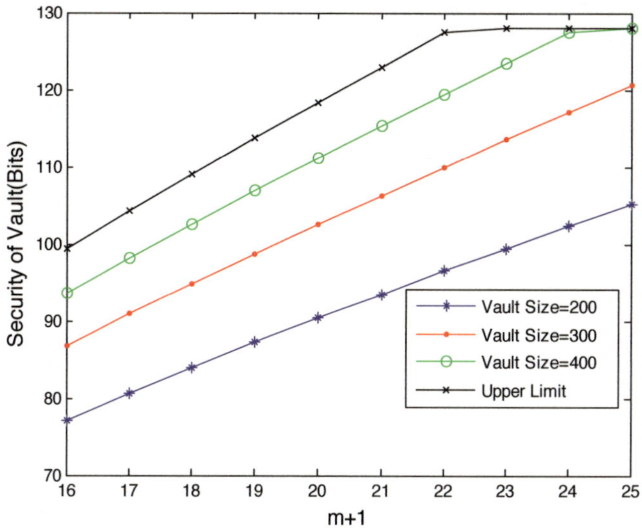

Figure 13. Security of fuzzy vault scheme

The time complexity involved in TDPS-based key distribution solution requires the following tasks: 1)R-wave detection; 2) IPI-based EI generation process; 3) Error-correction encoding process; 4) Error-correction decoding process. From the FAR/FRR performance analysis we can see, the Hamming distance to achieve minimum HTER is about 18. Thus, from the security analysis, in order to ensure the security of 128 bits, an EI of 164 bits should be generated. Take $q=4$ for example, 41 IPIs should be calculated, which means 42 R-waves should be detected. Take difference threshold algorithm for example, which has the minimum computational complexity in R-wave detection algorithms, the time complexity of R-wave detection process on n points is $O(n)$. It was demonstrated by Bao et al (2009) that the time complexity for IPI-based EI generation process is $O(N^2)$, where N is the number of IPIs used. Take Reed-Solomon as the error-correction code, the time complexity for the encoding process is $O(N.q)$, and for the decoding process based on Berlekamp–Massey algorithm the time complexity is $O((N.q)^2)$. As q is a fixed number, the time complexity of proposed solution can be expressed as $O(n+N^2)$. The space complexity is estimated in terms of memory required for implementing proposed schemes. Excluding the dynamic occupied memory due to R-wave detection process and error-correction encoding/decoding process, the primary static components in the transmitter is $F(\hat{K}, EI)$ while $F(\hat{K}, EI)$ and EI' in the receiver, and the overall memory required is 84 bytes.

The time complexity involved in FDPS-based key distribution solution requires the following tasks: 1) FFT computation; 2) Peak detection; 3) EI generation; 4) Key hiding (polynomial evaluation); 5) Key un-hiding (Lagrange interpolation). For the FFT computation process performed on n points, the time complexity is $O(n\log n)$. As M points of FFT coefficients that are selected to perform a peak detection process, the time complexity for peak detection is

M, where $M=150$ in our experiment. EI generation scheme includes an addition operation and a modulo operation on each feature point. The number of feature points depends on peak indexes detected, the time complexity of EI generation process is $O(\beta M)$, where β is the rate between peaks detected and the FFT coefficients selected and thus $0<\beta<1$. The polynomial evaluation in key hiding process would require $48\times m(m+1)/2$ operations, so the time complexity of key hiding process is $48\times m(m+1)/2$. It is demonstrated by J.P. Berrut that the improved Lagrange interpolation, i.e., Barycentric interpolation, requires only $O(m)$ operations as opposed to $O(m^2)$ for evaluating the Lagrange basis individually. Therefore, the time complexity of key un-hiding process is reduced to $O(\binom{N_2}{m+1}m)=O(m)$, where N_2 is the number of feature points generated at the receiver. As m and M are fixed numbers, the time complexity of proposed solution can be expressed as $O(n\log n)$. From the FAR/FRR performance analysis we can see, the degree of polynomial to achieve minimum HTER is about 23. Thus, in order to realize the security of 128 bits, the vault size should be larger than 400. Excluding the dynamic occupied memory due to FFT process and randomized process, the primary static components of the memory required are the physiological features (9 bit values, about 48 for PPG and ECG for example) and their polynomial projects (12 bit values), chaff points (400 for example to realize the security of 128 bits, 9 bit x-values and 12 bit y-values). The overall memory required is 4.854KB.

Table 2 gives the detailed computational complexity of the TDPS-based and FDPS-based key distribution solution, separately. It can be seen that TDPS-based key distribution solution is superior in space complexity with only 84B of memory required, compared to 4.854KB for FDPS-based solution.

Computational complexity			Task	Value
TDPS-based with fuzzy commitment	Time complexity $O(n+N^2)$	Transmitter $O(n+N^2)$	R-wave detection	$O(n)$
			IPI_based EI generation process	$O(N^2)$
			Error correction encoding	$O(N.q)$
		Receiver $O(N^2)$	Error correction decoding	$O((N.q)^2)$
	Static space complexity (84B)	Transmitter (34B)	$\hat{K}\oplus EI$	18B
			hash(K)	16B
		Receiver (50B)	$F(\hat{K}, EI)$	34B
			EI'	16B

http://dx.doi.org/10.5772/51856

Computational complexity			Task	Value
FDPS-based with fuzzy vault	Time complexity $O(n\log n)$ Static space complexity (4.854KB)	Transmitter $O(n\log n)$	FFT computation	$O(n\log n)$
			Peak detection	$M = 150$
			Randomized process	$O(\beta M)$
			Key hiding	$48 \times m(m+1)/2$
		Receiver $O(m)$	Key un-hiding (Polynomial reconstruction)	$O(\binom{N_2}{m+1}m) = O(m)$
		Transmitter (2.302KB)	Chaff points (i.e. 400)	2.05KB
			Feature points (i.e. 48)	252B
		Receiver (2.552KB)	Vault (i.e. 448)	2.302KB
			Feature points (i.e. 48)	252B

Table 2. Computational complexity

4. Conclusion

In the biometrics solution for BSN security, physiological signals within human body are used to generate dynamic EIs, which is not only used to realize node identification, but also protect the transmission of keying materials. In this chapter, the procedures of biometric solutions for securing BSN, including the EI generation scheme and relevant key distribution solution, have been described. From the experimental results we can see that, TDPS-based EI generation scheme is superior in randomness and recognition performance, while FDPS-based scheme has advantage on its real-time performance and robustness. The two common used fuzzy methods, including fuzzy commitment scheme and fuzzy vault scheme, also have their own advantages and disadvantages. Fuzzy commitment can achieve low computation complexity and low memory occupied, but it is not suitable for EIs that are un-ordered or with different length. Fuzzy vault scheme can be suitable to most of cases, but with a high computation complexity and memory occupied. To realize high recognition performance, fuzzy commitment should be selected for TDPS-based EIs, called TDPS-based solution, while fuzzy vault for FDPS-based EIs, called FDPS-based solution. There are a lot of issues need to be further studied to make it applicable into practical BSN platforms.

The challenges of TDPS-based solution primary exist in the EI generation process, where a signal of about 30s is needed to generate a 128-bit EI. Firstly, how to increase the positive detection rate of R-wave with lower computational complexity or design a more robust EI generation scheme being little influenced by the precision of R-wave should be studied to increase the robustness performance of the solution. Secondly, a faster EI generation scheme based on minimum number of IPIs should be addressed to increase its real-time performance.

For FDPS-based solution, the randomness performance of generated EIs, the computational complexity and the recognition rate pose great challenges to its application. Because the less satisfying randomness performance of EIs would bring about the security issue to the overall solution, how to make generated EIs as random as possible while not affecting its recognition rate is an issue should be addressed. In addition, the high computational complexity especially the space complexity brought by large amount of chaff points should be decreased to satisfy the stringent restriction of processing power, memory and energy for most sensor nodes. And what is the most important is that the recognition rate shall be significantly increased to make the solution applicable.

In some cases, not all of the physiological sensors that need to communicate with each other can obtain the needed information, such as IPI or same kind of physiological signals. Thus, how to extract a common feature from other kinds of physiological signal, such as respiration and blood pressure, might be further studied.

Author details

Fen Miao, Shu-Di Bao and Ye Li

Key Laboratory for Biomedical Informatics and Health Engineering, Shenzhen Institutes of Advanced Technology, Chinese Academy of Sciences, Shenzhen, China

References

[1] J. Hash, P. Bowen, A. Johnson, C. D. Smith, and D. I. Steinberg (2005). *An introductory resource guide for implementing the health insurance portability and accountability act (HIPAA) security rule,* Nat. Inst Stand. Technol., NIST Spec. Publ. 800-66, Gaithersburg, MD.

[2] The European Parliament and the council of The European Union (Jul. 2002). *Directive 2002/58/EC concerning the processing of personal data and the protection of privacy in the electronic communications sector,* Official J. Eur. Communities, pp. L201/37-47.

[3] L. Eschenauer and V. Gligor (2002). *A key-management scheme for distributed sensor networks,* Proceedings of the 9th ACM Conf. on Computer and Communication Security, pp.41–47.

[4] H. Chan, A. Perrig, D. Song (2003). *Random key predistribution schemes for sensor networks,* in: proceedings of the 2003 IEEE Symposium on security and privacy, May 11-15, pp. 197-213.

http://dx.doi.org/10.5772/51856

[5] D. Liu, P. Ning (2003). *Establishing pariwise keys in distributed sensor networks*, proceedings of the 10th ACM Conference on Computer and Communication, pp. 42-51.

[6] S. Cherukuri, K. K. Venkatasubramanian, S. K. S. Gupta (2003). *BioSec: a biometric based approach for securing communication in wireless networks of biosensors implanted in the human body*, Proc. IEEE International Conference Parallel Processing Workshop, pp.432–439.

[7] S. D. Bao, Y. T. Zhang, and L. F. Shen (2005). *Physiological Signal Based Entity Authentication for Body Area Sensor Networks and Mobile Healthcare Systems*, Proc. 27th IEEE Int'l. Conf. Eng. Med. and Bio. Soc., Shanghai, China.

[8] S. D. Bao, C. C. Y. Poon, Y. T. Zhang, and L. F. Shen (2008). *Using the timing information of heartbeats as an entity identifier to secure body sensor network*, IEEE transactions on information technology in biomedicine, Vol. 12, no. 6, pp. 772-779.

[9] Fengyuan Xu, Zhengrui Qin et al, *IMDGuard: Securing Implantable Medical Devices with the External Wearable Guardian*, IEEE INFOCOM 2011.

[10] C. C. Y. Poon, Y. T. Zhang, S. D. Bao (2006). *A Novel Biometrics Method to Secure Wireless Body Area Sensor Networks for Telemedicine and M-Health*, IEEE Communication Magazine, pp.73-81.

[11] K. K. Venkatasubramanian, A. Banerjee, S. K. S. Gupta (2008). *Plenthysmogram-based secure inter-sensor communication in body sensor networks*, Proc. of IEEE Military Communiations, pp.1–7.

[12] K. K. Venkatasubramanian, A. Banerjee, S. K. S. Gupta (2010). *PSKA: usable and secure key agreement scheme for body area networks*, IEEE Transactions on Information Technology in Biomedicine, Vol. 14, no. 1, pp.60-68.

[13] F. Miao, L. Jiang, Y. Li, Y. T. Zhang (2009). *Biometrics based novel key distribution solution for body sensor networks*, Proc. Annual Conference of IEEE-EMBS, pp.2458–2461.

[14] A. Juels, M. Wattenberg (1999). *A fuzzy commitment scheme*, Proceedings of 6th ACM conference on Computer and Communication Security.

[15] A. Juels, M. Sudan (2006). *A fuzzy vault scheme*, Design Codes and Cryptography, Vol. 38, no. 2, pp. 237-257.

[16] U. Uludag, S. Pankanti, A. K. Jain (2005). *Fuzzy vault for fingerprints*, In: Kanade T, Jai AK, Ratha NK. Proc. of the 5th Int'l Conf. on AVBPA. Berlin: Springer-Verlag, pp. 310–319

[17] Y. Wang, K. Plataniotis (2007). *Fuzzy vault for face based cryptographic key generation*, In: Proc. of the Biometrics Symp. Berlin: Springer-Verlag, pp. 1–6.

[18] Y. Lee, K. Bae, S. Lee, K. Park, J. Kim (2007). *Biometric key binding: fuzzy vault based on iris images*, In: Lee SW, Li SZ eds. Proc. of the ICB 2007. LNCS 4642, Berlin: Springer-Verlag, pp.800–808.

[19] F. Miao, S. D. Bao, Y. Li (2010). *A Modified Fuzzy Vault Scheme for Biometrics-based Body Sensor Networks Security,* IEEE Globecom.

[20] S. D. Bao and Y. T. Zhang (2005). *A new symmetric cryptosystem of body area sensor networks for telemedicine,* in 6th Asian–Pacific Conference on Medical and Biological Engineering.

[21] Miao, F., Bao, S. D., & Li, Y. A Novel Biometric Key Distribution Solution with Energy Distribution Information of Physiological Signals for Body Sensor Networks Security. IET Information Security. Accepted.

[22] J.P. Berrut, L. Trefethen. *Barycentric Lagrange Interpolation.* SIAM Review 46 (3): 501–517,2004.

[23] Lin Yao, Bing Liu, Guowei Wu et al. *A Biometric Key Establishment Protocol for Body Area Networks, International Journal of Distributed Sensor Networks,* 2011.

Chapter 12

Influence of Skin Diseases on Fingerprint Quality and Recognition

Michal Dolezel, Martin Drahansky,
Jaroslav Urbanek, Eva Brezinova and Tai-hoon Kim

Additional information is available at the end of the chapter

http://dx.doi.org/10.5772/51992

1. Introduction

Fingerprint recognition belongs to one of the most often used biometric technologies worldwide. It is believed that fingerprints could be used for the recognition of a person in nearly any case; however there exist many cases, where the fingerprint recognition could not be used. There exist some influencing factors [1] that have an impact to the process of fingerprint recognition, e.g. the environmental influences, dirtiness on finger or the sensor, electromagnetic radiation or diseases. This chapter deals with the circumstances which influence the quality of fingerprints – we are limited on skin diseases here, further we explain how we can evaluate the quality of the acquired fingerprint.

The fingerprint recognition consists of five main steps (see Fig. 1) [2, 3, 4]:

- *Fingerprint acquirement* – the fingerprint is scanned using a sensor (for sensor technologies see [1]), i.e. the physical human biometric attribute is digitized and transferred to the computer.
- *Image enhancement* – this step is very important for further processing, because the quality of the fingerprint image could be enhanced here. There are several methods used for image quality enhancement – edge filters, filtering in frequency spectrum (after Fast Fourier Transform), Gabor filter, etc.
- *Thresholding* – the image is normally acquired with 256 gray levels, but we need a binary representation. Using various thresholding schemes (e.g. adaptive thresholding or regional average thresholding), it is possible to separate papillary lines (ridges) from background (valleys).

- *Thinning* or *Skeletization* – the papillary lines from the previous step have varying thickness. To make the algorithm for minutiae extraction as simple as possible, we prefer the thickness of all papillary lines in all parts having only one pixel.
- *Minutiae extraction* – this algorithm detects and extracts all minutiae found in the fingerprint. We distinguish between minutiae in verification systems (here are generally used 2 minutiae – ridge ending and bifurcation [2]) and identification (dactyloscopic) systems [5], where many special minutiae are used.

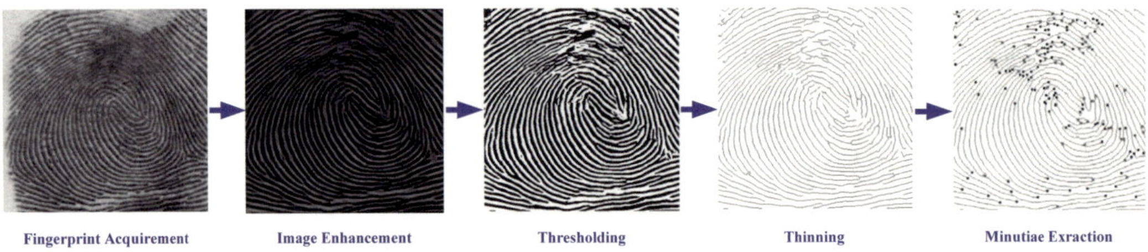

Figure 1. An overview of the fingerprint recognition.

The fingerprint recognition technology is well accepted in our society [6]. Fingerprints could be used not only for the known user verification / identification tasks, but also e.g. for cryptographic key generation [7, 8, 9, 10], computerized patient record [11] or for use with credit cards [12] etc. Anyway, the influence of skin diseases to fingerprint recognition in biometric systems has not been discussed sufficiently till today, therefore we hope that this chapter brings you closer information to this topic.

In the chapter 2, the categorization into three groups of skin diseases is done and the most important diseases in each group are briefly described. The chapter 3 describes how these skin diseases could influence the process of automatic fingerprint recognition. Chapters 4 and 5 deal with fingerprint image enhancement and estimation of their quality.

2. Skin diseases

Skin diseases represent very important, but often neglected factor of the fingerprint acquirement. It is impossible to say in general how many people suffer from skin diseases, because there are so many various skin diseases [4]. In a general medical practice about 20-25% of patients with skin complaints are referred. When discussing whether the fingerprint recognition technology is a perfect solution capable to resolve all our security problems, we should always keep in mind those potential users who suffer from some skin disease.

In the following text, several skin diseases, which attack hand palms and fingertips, are introduced from the medical point of view.

The situation after successful recovery of a potential user from such skin diseases is, however, very important for the possible further use of fingerprint recognition devices. If the dis-

http://dx.doi.org/10.5772/51992

ease has attacked and destroyed the structure of papillary lines in the epidermis and underlying dermis (top two layers of the skin), the papillary lines will not grow in the same form as before (if at all) and therefore such user could be restricted in their future life by being excluded from the use of fingerprint recognition systems, though their fingers do not have any symptoms of the skin disease anymore.

Skin makes up to 12-15% of an adult's body weight. Each square centimeter has 6 million cells, 5,000 sensory points, 100 sweat glands and 15 sebaceous glands. It consists of three layers [18]: *epidermis* (the outer layer), *dermis* and *subcutaneous* (fat) layer.

Skin is constantly being regenerated. A keratinocyte („skin cell") starts its life at the lower layer of epidermis (the basal layer), which is nourished by blood vessels and is supplied with nerve endings from dermis. The cell migrates upward from basal layer to stratum corneum (the outermost skin layer). During four weeks the cell undergoes a series of changes, gradually flattening out and moving toward the surface. Then it dies and is shed. The epidermis is not supplied with blood vessels, but has nerve endings. The shape of dermoepidermal junction basically forms the structure of papillary lines.

There are several skin functions [19]:

- *Sensation* – the nerve endings in the skin identify touch, heat, cold, pain and light pressure.
- *Heat regulation* – the skin helps to regulate the body temperature by sweating to cool the body down when it overheats and by shivering creating "goose bumps" when it is cold. Shivering closes the pores. The tiny hair that stands on end traps warm air and thus helps keep the body warm.
- *Absorption* – absorption of ultraviolet rays from the sun helps to form vitamin D in the body, which is vital for bone formation. Some creams, essential oils and medicines (e.g. anti-smoking patches) can also be absorbed through the skin into the blood stream.
- *Protection* – the skin protects the body from ultraviolet light – too much of it is harmful to the body – by producing a pigment called melanin. It also protects us from the invasion of bacteria and germs by forming an acid mantle (formed by the skin sebum and sweat). This barrier also prevents moisture loss.
- *Excretion* – waste products and toxins are eliminated from the body through the sweat glands. It is a very important function which helps to keep the body "clean".
- *Secretion* – sebum and sweat are secreted onto the skin surface. The sebum keeps the skin lubricated and soft, and the sweat combines with the sebum to form an acid mantle which creates the right pH-balance for the skin to fight off infection.

There are a lot of skin diseases, which can affect palms and fingers. We find plenty of skin diseases including description of their influence on the structure and color of the skin in specialized medical literature, e.g. [16]. In the following subchapters we describe some of these diseases together with photographs. These clearly show that these diseases may cause many problems in automatic biometric systems.

The fingerprint recognition systems are usually used only for adults. There is almost no information from appropriate tests with children. Although we know that papillary lines emerge on infant's fingers already in the mother's uterus [24], i.e. we might be able to recognize the fingerprints of infants, the common fingerprint recognition systems are suitable for adults only (due to the area and resolution of fingerprint sensors, etc.). It should not be forgotten that a skin disease in early childhood could have an influence on the skin in adult years (example is *incontinentia pigmenti* [25] on a small child hand), i.e. there could be some problems with fingerprint acquirement caused by such skin disease in a young age.

The subcategory of skin diseases affecting only the skin color are the least dangerous for the quality of the fingerprint image. In fact, only one fingerprint technology can be considered as sensitive to such diseases – the optical technology [26], but if FTIR-based optical sensors are used, the change of skin color may have no influence on the quality of the resulting images. The case of the other two subcategories (influence of skin structure and combination of influence of skin color and structure) is different. If the structure of papillary lines has changed, it is often impossible to recognize the original curvatures of papillary lines and therefore it is impossible to decide whether the claimed identity is the user's identity. Unfortunately, there are many such skin diseases which attack papillary line structure. Nearly all sensor technologies, namely optical, capacitive, e-field, electro-optical, pressure sensitive and thermal are exposed to such risk [26]. Only one sensor technology is missing here – the ultrasound technology. This technology has an advantage: the ultrasound waves can penetrate under the upper skin layer to the curvatures in dermoepidermal junction forming the papillary lines structures and therefore it might be possible to reconstruct the real fingerprint image, but only if the disease has not attacked this underlying structure. If yes, there is no chance to get an original papillary lines structure.

The situation after successful recovery of a potential user from such skin diseases is, however, very important for the possible further use of fingerprint recognition devices. If the disease has attacked and destroyed the structure of papillary lines in dermoepidermal junction, the papillary lines will not grow in the same form as before (if at all) and therefore such user could be restricted in his/her future life by being excluded from the use of fingerprint recognition systems, though his fingers don't have any symptoms of a skin disease any more.

2.1. Diseases causing histopathological changes of epidermis and dermis

These diseases may cause problems for the most types of sensors, because color of the skin and structure of epidermis and dermis are influenced.

Hand eczema [17] is an inflammatory non-infectious long-lasting disease with relapsing course. It is one of the most common problems encountered by the dermatologist. Hand dermatitis causes discomfort and embarrassment and, because of its locations, interferes significantly with normal daily activities. Hand dermatitis is common in industrial occupations. The prevalence of hand eczema was approximately 5.4% and was twice as common in females as in males. The most common type of hand eczema was irritant contact dermatitis (35%), followed by atopic eczema (22%), and allergic contact dermatitis (19%). The most common contact allergies were to nickel, cobalt, fragnance mix, balsam of Peru, and colophony. Hand eczema was more common among people reporting occupational exposure. The most harmful exposure was to chemicals, water and detergents, dust, and dry dirt.

Fingertip eczema [17] is very dry, chronic form of eczema of the palmar surface of the fingertips, it may be result of an allergic reaction or may occur in children and adults as an isolated phenomenon of unknown cause. One finger or several fingers may be involved. Initially the skin may be moist and then become dry, cracked, and scaly. The skin peels from the fingertips distally, exposing a very dry, red, cracked, fissured, tender, or painful surface without skin lines – see Figure 2.

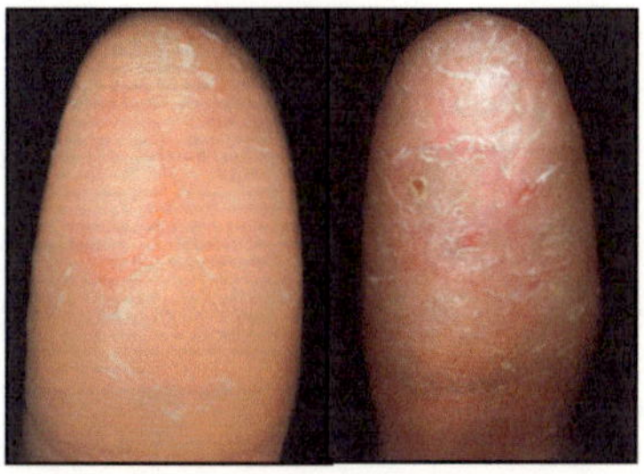

Figure 2. Fingertip eczema [17].

Pomfolyx (dishydrosis) [16] is a distinctive reaction pattern of unknown etiology presenting as symmetric vesicular hand and foot dermatitis. Itching precedes the appearance of vesicles on the palms and sides of the fingers. The skin may be red and wet. The vesicles slowly resolve and are replaced by rings of scale. Chronic eczematous changes with erythema, scaling, and lichenification may follow.

Tinea of the palm [17] is dry, diffuse, keratotic form of tinea. The dry keratotic form may be asymptomatic and the patient may be unaware of the infection, attributing the dry, thick, scaly surface to hard physical labor. It is frequently seen in association with tineapedis which prevalence is 10 to 30%.

Pyoderma [22] is a sign of bacterial infection of the skin. It is caused by *Staphylococcus aureus* and *Streptococcus pyogenes*. Some people are more susceptible to these diseases (such as diabetics, alcoholics, etc.) – see Figure 3.

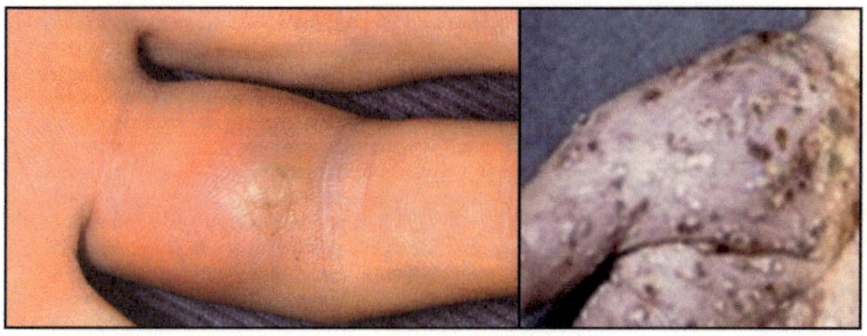

Figure 3. Abscess on finger of patient with diabetes [16] and pyoderma [23].

Pitted keratolysis [17] is a disease mimicking tinea, especially for people who swelter and wear rubber gloves in the hot, humid environment. Hyperhydrosis is the most frequently observed symptom. The disease is bacterial in origin, characterized by many circular or longitudinal, punched out depressions in the skin surface. The eruption is limited to the stratum corneum.

Keratolysis exfoliativa [17] is a common, chronic, asymptomatic, non-inflamatory, bilateral peeling of the palms of the hands. Its cause is unknown. The eruption is most common during the summer months and is often associated with sweaty palms and soles. It is characterized by scaling and peeling, the central area becomes slightly red and tender.

Lichen planus [22] is quite common, unique inflammatory cutaneous and mucous membrane reaction pattern of unknown etiology. LP of the palm and soles generally occurs as an isolated phenomenon. The lesions are papules aggregated into semitranslucent plaques with globular waxy surface, ulceration may occur.

Acanthosis nigricans [16] is non-specific reaction pattern that may accompany obesity, diabetes, tumors. AN is classified into benign and malignant forms. In all cases the disease presents with symmetric, brown thickening of the skin. During the process there is papillary hypertrophy, hyperkeratosis, and increased number of melanocytes in the epidermis.

Pyogenic granuloma [17] is a benign acquired vascular lesion of the skin that is common in children and young adults. It often appears as a response to an injury or hormonal factors. Lesions are small rapidly growing, yellow-to-bright red, dome-shaped.

Systemic sclerosis [20] is a chronic autoimmune disease characterized by sclerosis of the skin or other organs. Emergence of acrosclerosis is decisive for fingerprinting. Initially the skin is infused with edema mainly affecting hands. With the progressive edema stiff skin appears and necrosis of fingers may form. The disease leads to sclerodactyly with contractures of the fingers. For more than 90% of patients is typical Raynaud's phenomenon (see below). The typical patient is a woman over 50 years of age.

Raynaud's phenomenon[17] represents an episodic vasoconstriction of the digital arteries and arterioles that is precipitated by cold and stress. It is much more common in women. There are three stages during a single episode: pallor (white), cyanosis (blue), and hyperemia (red).

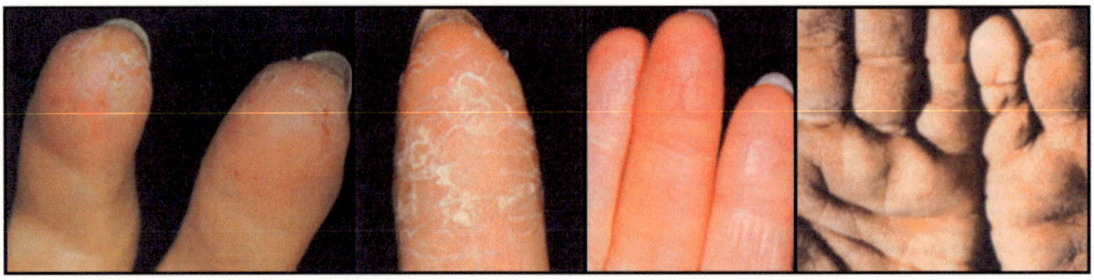

Figure 4. Different types of eczema [17] (3x left) and acanthosis nigricans [16] (right).

http://dx.doi.org/10.5772/51992

Drug induced skin reactions [17] are among the most common adverse drug reactions. They occur in many forms and can mimic virtually any dermatosis. Occur in 2-3% of hospitalized patients. Sulfonamides, NSAIDs and anticonvulsants are most often applied in the etiology.

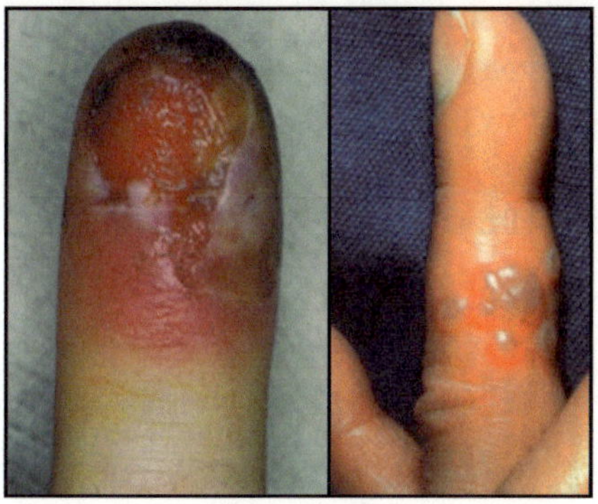

Figure 5. Herpes simplex virus:patient with HIV (left) [20]; deepseated blisters (right) [16].

Herpes simplex virus [16] in the host with systemic immune-compromise may cause chronic ulcerations as you can see by patient with advanced HIV disease in Figure 5 (left).

Herpetic infection may uncommonly occur on the fingers or periungually. Lesions begin with tenderness and erythema and deepseated blisters develop 24 to 48 hours after symptoms begin (see Figure 5, right).

Scabies [21] is highly contagious disease caused by the mite *Sarcoptes scabiei*. It is characterized by red papules, vesicles and crusts located usually on the areas with tender skin, palms and soles especially in infants.

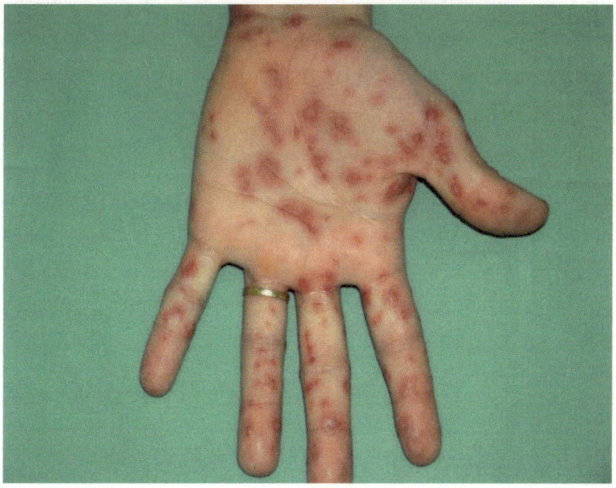

Figure 6. Erythmea multiforme.

Erythema multiforme [22] is quite common skin disorder with multifactorial cause (see Figure 6). The most common triggering agents are infections (in the first place herpes virus) and drugs. Minor and major variant of this disease is described. Both forms are characterized by erythematous target-shaped lesions with a center with hemorrhage, blistering, necrosis or crust. When the trigger is herpetic infection, frequent recurrences come.

Dermatitis artifacta [25] are changes of skin due to the manipulation by patient. Patients often have psychosomatic, psychiatric or drug abuse problems.

2.2. Diseases causing skin discoloration

Hand, foot, and mouth disease (HFMD) [16] is contagious enteroviral infection occurring primarily in children and characterized by a vesicular palmoplantar eruption. The skin lesions begin as red macules that rapidly become pale, white, oval vesicles with red areola.

Xantomas [17] are lipid deposits in the skin and tendons that occur secondary to a lipid abnormality. These localized deposits are yellow and are frequently very firm.

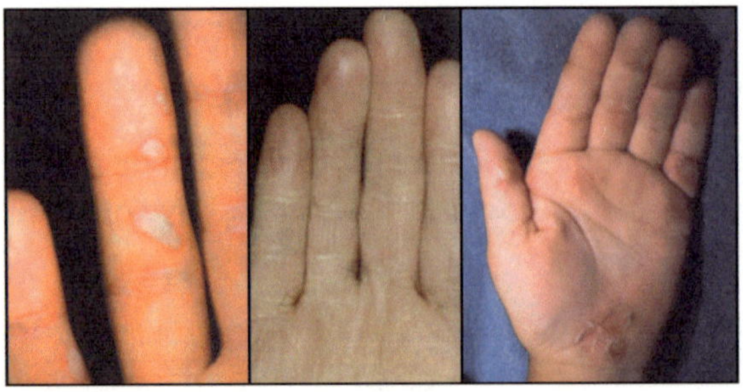

Figure 7. Hand, foot and mouth syndrome[16]; xantomas [20]; epidermolysis bullosa [21].

Scarlet fever (scarlatina) [17] is contagious disease produced by streptococcal, erythrogenic toxin. It is most common in children (ages 1 to 10 years). In the ending stages of the disease large sheats of epidermis may be shed from the palms in glovelike cast, exposing new tender and red epidermis beneath.

Kawasaki's disease [20] is an acute febrile illness of infants and children, characterized by cutaneous and mucosal erythema and edema with subsequent desquamation, cervical lymphadenitis, and complicated by coronary artery aneurysms (20%). Most cases of Kawasaki's disease in adults represent toxic shock syndrome. Erytematous macules appear 1 to 3 days after onset of fever, enlarge and become more numerous, then desquamation beginning on tips of fingers is highly characteristic.

Secondary syphilis [20]is characterized by mucocutaneous lesions, which may assume a variety of shapes, including round, elliptic, or annular. The color is characteristic, resembling a „clean-cut ham" or having a copery tint.

Carotenosis [16] is yellowish discoloration of the skin, especially of the palms and soles that is sometimes seen in diabetic patients.

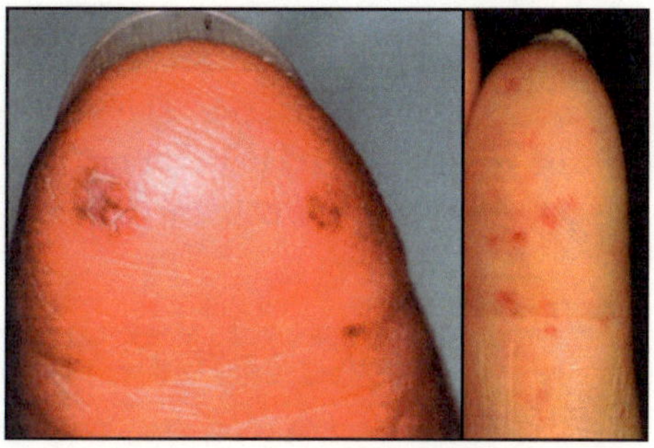

Figure 8. Hereditary hemorrhagic teleangiectasia [16].

Hereditary hemorrhagic teleangiectasia [20] is an autosomal dominant condition affecting blood vessels, especially in the mucous membranes of the mouth and the gastrointestinal tract. The diagnostic lesions are small, pulsating, macular and papular, usually punctuate. Teleangiectases are present on different parts of the body, palms and soles including (see Figure 8).

2.3. Diseases causing histopathological changes in junction of epidermis and dermis

These diseases are focused mainly on ultrasonic sensors, which detect the base of papillary lines on the border of epidermis and dermis. The diagnoses also belong to the first group.

Hand eczema – particularly chronic forms (see above).

Warts (verruca vulgaris) [22] are benign epidermal neoplasms that are caused by human papilloma viruses (HPVs). Warts commonly appear at sites of trauma, on the hand, in periungual regions. HPVs induce hyperplasia and hyperkeratosis.

Psoriasis [20] is characterized by scaly papules and plaques. It occurs in 1% to 3% of the population. The disease is transmitted genetically; environmental factors are needed to precipitate the disease. The disease is lifelong and characterized by chronic, recurrent exacerbations and remissions that are emotionally and physically debilitating. Psoriasis of the palms and fingertips is characterized by red plaques with thick brown scale and may be indistinguishable from chronic eczema.

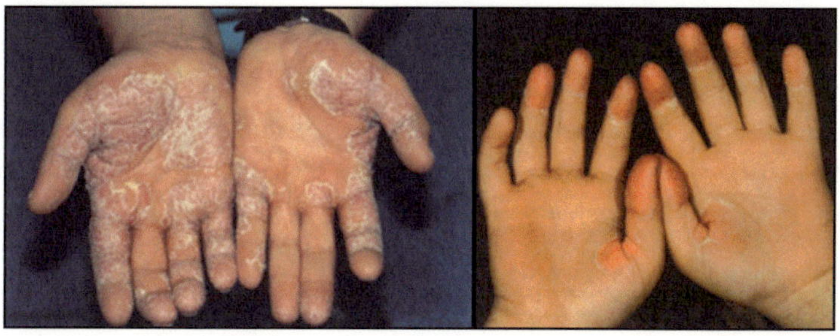

Figure 9. Psoriasis (left) [21]; scarlet fever (right) [17].

Systemic lupus erytematosus (SLE) [17] is a multisystem disease of unknown origin characterized by production of numerous diverse of antibodies that cause several combinations of clinical signs, symptoms and laboratory abnormalities. The prevalence of LE in North America and northern Europe is about 40 per 100,000 population. In the case of acute cutaneous LE indurated erythematous lesions may be presented on palms.

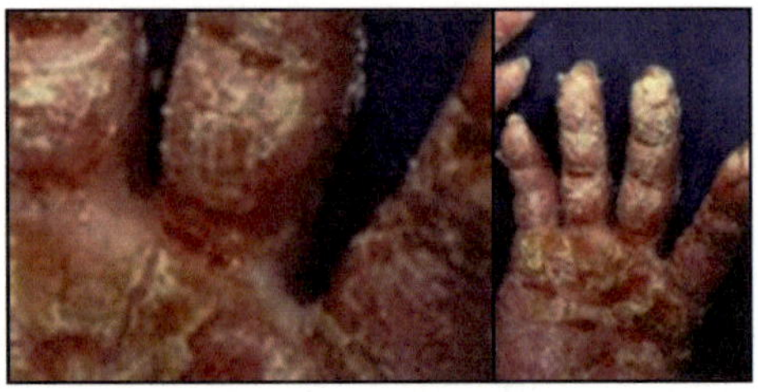

Figure 10. Psoriasis vulgaris [23].

Epidermolysis bullosa [20] is a term given to groups of genetic diseases in which minor trauma causes non-inflammatory blistering (mechanobullosus diseases). Repetitive trauma may lead to a mitten-like deformity with digits encased in an epidermal „cocoon". These diseases are classified as scarring and non-scarring and histologically by the level of blister formation. Approximately 50 epidermolysis cases occur per million live births in the United States.

3. Influence of skin diseases to fingerprint pattern

The process of analysis and further elimination of influence of dermatologic diseases to fingerprint recognition process begins with analysis of influence to the fingerprint pattern. Image of fingerprint pattern can be obtained either by classic manual way using dactyloscopic card and special ink or using the electronic sensors. Both ways have their advantages and disadvantages and both of them could have been influenced by skin diseases in different ways. It will be necessary to analyze the influence on both of these capturing methods.

3.1. Ability of fingerprint scanners to scan a finger distorted by skin disease

For acquiring the digital image of a fingerprint pattern in the most cases the so called fingerprint scanners are used. These scanners are called "live-scan" fingerprint capture devices [28]. This term reflexes the fact that these sensors cannot be used for latent fingerprint scanning and for the scanning the live finger is needed. These scanners can be divided into several groups upon their sensing technology [4, 27, 28] – see the following subchapters

3.1.1. Optical fingerprint scanners

Basic principle of optical fingerprint scanners works in the following way: finger is placed on the sensor platen and it's illuminated by a light source. The pattern of fingerprint papillary lines is then captured by an integrated CCD or CMOS camera. The oldest and most commonly used type of optical fingerprint scanner is the type which uses the Frustrated Total Internal Reflection (FTIR) for the fingerprint image acquisition.

There also exist models which use another image acquisition techniques like FTIR technique with sheet prism made of a number of prismlets adjacent to each other instead of a single large prism or a model which uses optical fibers [28].

3.1.2. Capacitive fingerprint scanners

Fingerprint scanners based on a capacitive sensing technology are also very common type of fingerprint scanners. The sensor itself is a two-dimensional array of conductive plates. By placing the finger on sensor surface, each small plate and the corresponding part of skin over it start behave like a micro-capacitor. By measuring the small electrical charges between plates and finger, it is possible to reconstruct the profile of papillary lines ridges and valleys and thus to reconstruct the fingerprint image.

3.1.3. Thermal fingerprint scanners

Thermal fingerprint scanners contain special, so called pyro-electric cell which detects the thermal changes and converts them into an electrical charge. The main idea is that fingerprint papillary line ridges produce a higher temperature differential to the valleys. The temperature difference produces an image when a contact occurs, but this image soon disappears because the thermal equilibrium is quickly reached and the pixel temperature is stabilized [28]. Therefore the thermal sensors are usually made in sweep variant in which this disappearing problem does not occur.

3.1.4. Pressure fingerprint scanners

Pressure fingerprint scanners are made from two parallel electro-conductive layers with non/conductive gel between them. Ridges of papillary lines unlike the valleys by pressing the first flexible conductive layer create the contact of these two conductive layers. The conductive layers are in contact only in sensor parts where papillary line ridges are. By measuring the electrical charge between connected layers, it is possible to reconstruct the original fingerprint image.

3.1.5. Electro-optical fingerprint scanners

Electro-optical scanners contain two layers. First layer is made from a special polymer, which emits light when connected to the proper voltage [28]. Proper voltage can be obtained by contact with finger skin, which is conductive enough. Only the ridges are touching the polymer so on the other side of the polymer we could see light pattern of the fingerprint. The light pattern is than captured by the second layer, which is composed of an array of photodiodes.

3.1.6. E-field fingerprint scanners

The sensor consists of a drive ring that generates an RF (radio frequency) sinusoidal signal and a matrix of active antennas that receives a very small amplitude signal transmitted by the drive ring and modulated by the derma structure (subsurface of the finger skin) [28]. By analyzing the signal response received by antennas array, the reconstruction of fingerprint image is performed. The fingerprint pattern is acquired by simply measuring the electric field in subsurface of finger skin.

3.1.7. Ultrasonic fingerprint scanners

Ultrasonic scanners are based on sending acoustic signals toward the fingertip and capturing the response. The received response is analyzed and the fingerprint is reconstructed.

3.2. Creation of station for diseased fingerprint capturing

For analyzing the influence of skin diseases on the process of fingerprint recognition it will be necessary for the capturing station to contain as much dactyloscopic sensors as possible, ideally each of them based on different scanning technology. It is also presumable that some very invasive skin disease deforms the fingerprint pattern in a way that no connected sensor will be able to scan this fingerprint. For these situations the capturing station has to be equipped with tools for manual dactyloscopic fingerprinting. Another significant and inseparable part of capturing station creation process is creation of capturing application. This capturing application has to be able to communicate with all connected sensors and to fast fingerprint capturing of all patient's fingers. The capturing station should also contain some device for affected finger photo-documentation like camera, video-camera or digital microscope. This device should also be controllable by the capturing application.

The final version of capturing station consists of the following components:

- laptop and its accessories
- capturing application installed on laptop
- set of electronic dactyloscopic sensors
- dactyloscopic card and special ink
- digital microscope
- laboratory stand with boss and clamp for microscope

Due to available financial, technological and implementation resources the following dactyloscopic scanners were chosen: **Sagem MSO 300** (optical touch), **UPEK EikonTouch 500** (capacitive touch), **UPEK Eikon II Fingerprint Reader** (capacitive sweep), **TBS 3D Enroll Series 2011** (touchless optical multispectral) and the **digital microscope DinoLite Pro.**

After obtaining all necessary hardware the next step was to design and implement the capturing application. During the design and implementation process the following requirements had to be considered:

- application has to be able to communicate with all connected sensors and with connected digital microscope,
- application has to contain united and practical interface for easy and fast capturing of multiple samples of each patients of the affected finger by each dactyloscopic sensor,
- application has to contain controls for entering the patients diagnosis by a doctor.

The newest version of capturing application also contains full multi-language support including runtime dynamic language switching. At the moment, the application supports Czech, English and German languages.

The first created station is installed in Faculty Hospital in Olomouc in the Czech Republic. The capturing is performed by a medical specialist from the Dermatologic and Venerologic Clinic at the Palacky University and Faculty Hospital in Olomouc. In the nearest future the process of the second station creation will be finished and the second station (see Fig. 11) will be installed at a dermatologist in Darmstadt, Germany.

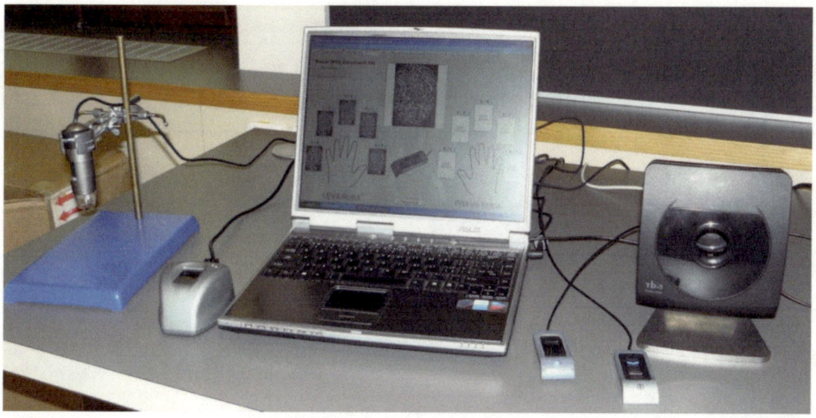

Figure 11. Second version of the capturing station.

3.3. Creation of suitable database of diseased fingerprints

Very significant and inseparable part of skin diseases influence analysis plays the process of suitable testing data acquirement. By these data it is meant a database of fingerprints affected and influenced by at least one of various dermatologic diseases. Having done the database acquirement it will be possible to analyze the influence of specific skin diseases and/or test the designed and implemented correction algorithms.

Obtaining a high quality biometric database usually is a long time consuming task which demands a big amount of patience. Biometric algorithms cannot be tested only on few samples from a small group of individuals of similar age and employment like research colleagues. High quality biometric database has to contain samples from wide spectrum of individuals categorized by all factors which may have influence on reason for which the database is acquired. Also there has to be enough samples in each of such category. For example the ideal database of fingerprints has to contain enough fingerprints of men and women of all age groups and such database should also contain so called critical samples, i.e. samples from individuals whose job or hobby affects their fingerprint pattern like mountain climbers or people working with chemicals.

For our developing and testing purposes it is necessary to create a database of fingerprints affected by a dermatologic disease. In the presence there exists no such special database so it will be necessary to create a new and first one. The most promising and reliable sources of such data are dermatological departments in hospital. It is also necessary to agree cooperation with dermatological specialists from such departments which will be willing to scan theirs patient's fingerprints and to provide reliable diagnosis of the scanned disease. For the purpose of database categorization the following factors are considered and recorded: age, gender, job and kind of dermatologic disease.

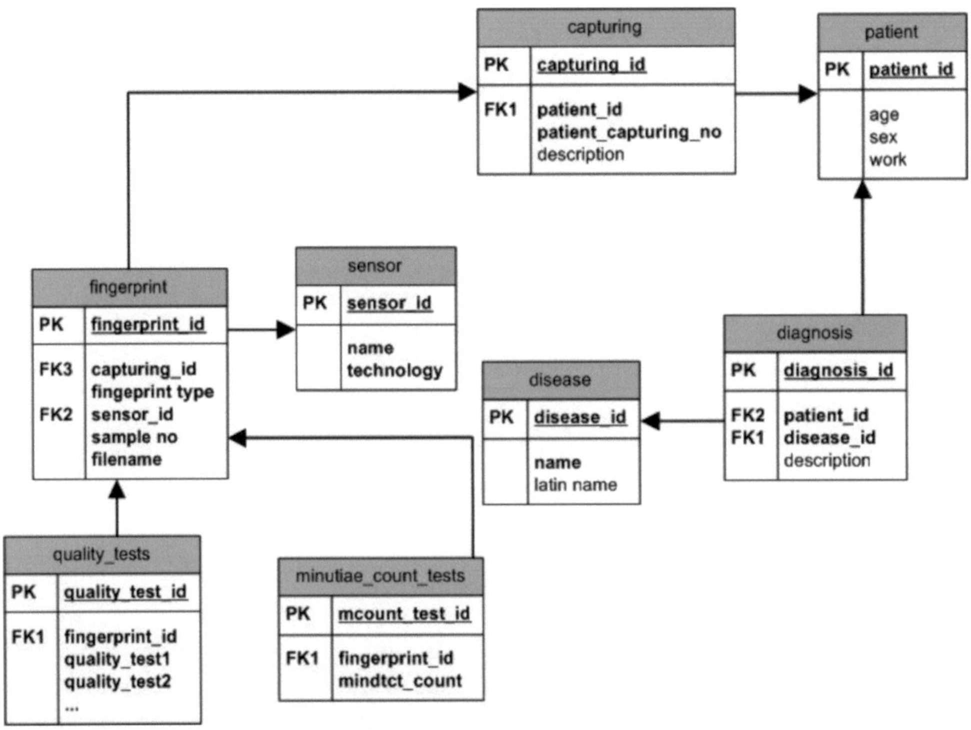

Figure 12. ER diagram of current diseased fingerprint database.

Current version of the database contains 594 fingerprints of 19 different patients. These amounts are from the first acquired set from the hospital in Olomouc. There are two more sets of fingerprints but they were not processed yet. The real number of fingerprints in our database is two or three times higher. In Figure 12 you can see the entity relationship diagram of actual version of database. The database contains fingerprints of eleven different dermatologic diseases. The most common and typical that are present in the database are: light atopic eczema, advanced atopic eczema, verruca vulgaris, psoriasis and cut wound. The last sample does not belong to the dermatologic diseases it is related to them because it can negatively affect the process of fingerprint recognition.

In Figures 13 to 17 we show several samples of acquired fingerprints. Each set of fingerprints begins with photography of the affected finger from the digital microscope and fingerprints made manually by using the dactyloscopic card and ink. After them there are fingerprints from electronic sensors if the sensor capturing was successful.

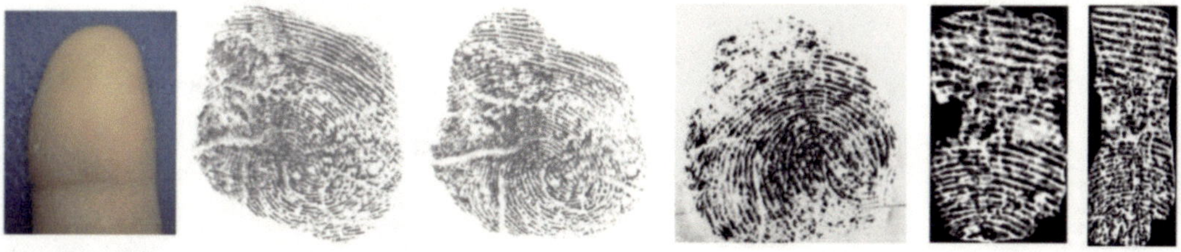

Figure 13. Light atopic eczema – influence on fingerprints.

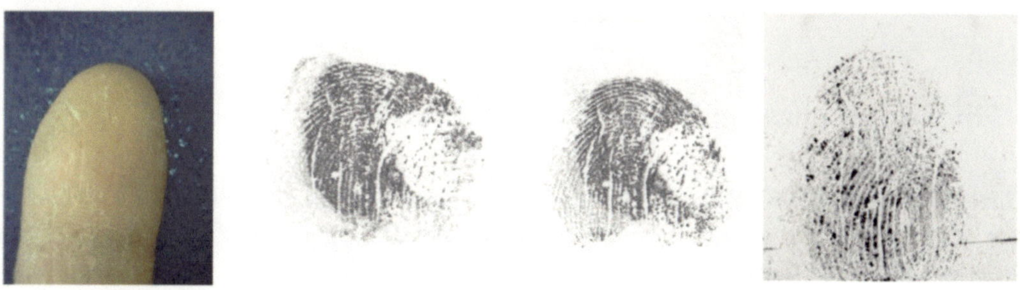

Figure 14. Advanced atopic eczema – influence on fingerprints.

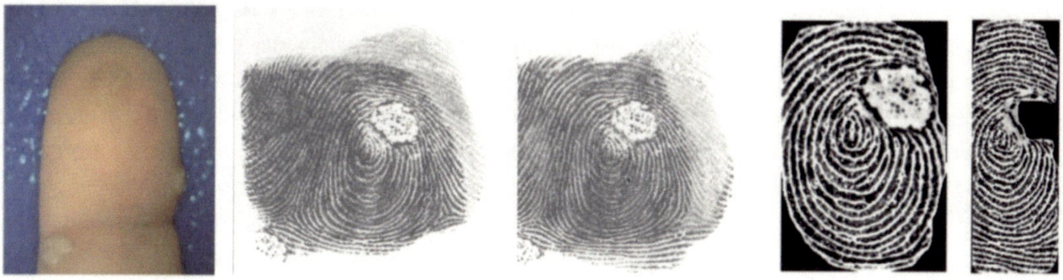

Figure 15. Verruca vulgaris – influence on fingerprints.

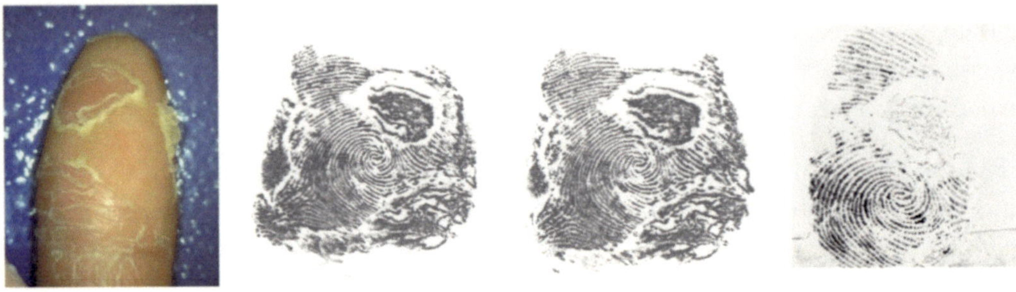

Figure 16. Psoriasis – influence on fingerprints.

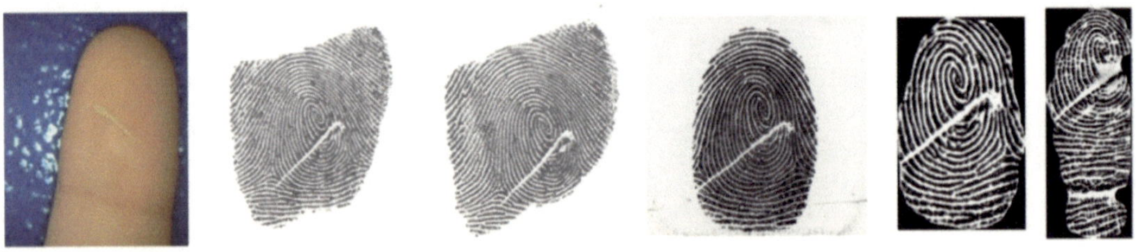

Figure 17. Cut wound – influence on fingerprints.

4. Fingerprint image enhancement algorithm

Currently the most widely used and the most accurate automatic fingerprint verification/ identification techniques use minutiae-based automatic fingerprint matching algorithms. Reliably extracting minutiae from the input fingerprint images is critical to fingerprint matching. The performance of current minutiae extraction algorithms depends heavily on the quality of input fingerprint images [29]. In an ideal fingerprint image, ridges and valleys alternate and flow in a locally constant direction and minutiae are anomalies of ridges. In practice, due to variations in impression conditions, ridge configurations, skin conditions (dryness, moist finger, aberrant formations in epidermal ridges of fingerprints, postnatal marks, occupational marks, skin diseases), acquisition devices, and non-cooperative attitudes of subjects, etc., a significant percentage of acquired fingerprint images (approximately 10% according to [29]) is of a poor quality. The ridge structures in poor-quality fingerprint images are not always well defined and hence they cannot be always correctly detected. This could result in failures of minutiae extraction algorithms; a significant number of spurious minutiae may be created, a large percentage of genuine minutiae may be undetected, and a significant amount of error in position and orientation may be introduced.

To ensure that the performance of the minutiae extraction algorithms is robust with respect to the quality of input fingerprint images, an *enhancement algorithm* [42], which can improve the quality of the ridge structures of input fingerprint images, is thus necessary. Generally, for a given fingerprint image, fingerprint regions can be assigned to one of the following three categories (Fig. 18) [29]:

- *Well-defined regions,* in which ridges and furrows are clearly visible for a minutia extraction algorithm to operate reliably.
- *Recoverable corrupted regions,* in which ridges and furrows are corrupted by a small amount of creases, smudges, etc. But they can still be correctly recovered by an enhancement algorithm.
- *Unrecoverable corrupted regions,* in which ridges and furrows are corrupted by such a severe amount of noise and distortion that it is impossible to recover them.

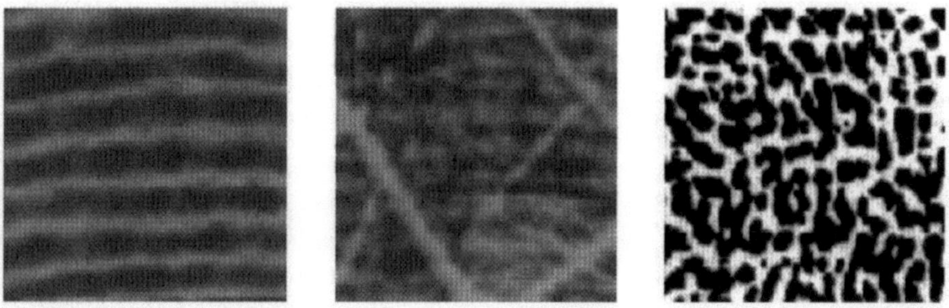

Figure 18. Examples of fingerprint regions [29]: a) Well-defined region (left); b) Recoverable region (middle); c) Unrecoverable region (right).

The interoperability among sensors from different vendors, or using different sensing technologies, plays a relevant role. The resulting images from different technologies vary very much in the representation of the grayscale levels, sharpness of valleys and ridges and resolution. Fortunately, it is often possible to compensate these factors to achieve a good interoperability among such sensors, e.g. see [30].

Based on filtering domains, most fingerprint enhancement schemes can be roughly classified using two major approaches [31]: *spatial-domain and frequency-domain*. The filtering in a spatial-domain applies a convolution directly to the fingerprint image. On the other hand, the filtering in a frequency-domain needs the Fourier analysis and synthesis. Thus a fingerprint image is transformed than multiplied by filter coefficients and in the end inverse-transformed by Fourier coefficients back to an enhanced fingerprint image. In fact, if the employed filters are the same, enhancement results from both domains should be exactly the same according to the signal processing theorem. However, in a practical implementation, these two approaches are different in terms of enhancement quality and computational complexity of algorithms.

In the following subchapters, some important and often used fingerprint enhancement methods will be introduced. Nevertheless, the list of such methods cannot be complete, as the amount of such methods exceeds the scope and possibilities of this chapter.

4.1.1. Spatial domain filtering algorithm

The *spatial domain filtering algorithm* [29] adaptively enhances the clarity of ridge and valley structures using a bank of Gabor filters (see below) that are tuned to the local ridge orientation and ridge frequency. The local ridge orientation and ridge frequency are estimated directly from input images in the spatial domain.

A 2D Gabor filter [32] can be thought of as a complex plane wave modulated by a 2D Gaussian envelope [33]. These filters optimally capture both the local orientation and frequency information and their development has been initiated by observing the linear response of the receptive field in simple striate cortex cells. By tuning a Gabor filter to a specific frequency and direction, the local frequency and orientation information can be obtained. Thus, they are well suited for extracting the texture information from images.

An even symmetric Gabor filter has the following general form in the spatial domain [33]:

$$G_{\theta,f}(x,y) = e^{-\frac{1}{2}\left[\frac{x'^2}{\delta_x^2}+\frac{y'^2}{\delta_y^2}\right]}\cos(2\pi f x') \tag{1}$$

$$\text{and } x' = x\sin\theta + y\cos\theta,\ y' = x\cos\theta - y\sin\theta \tag{2}$$

where f is the frequency of the sinusoidal plane wave at the angle θ with the x-axis, and δ_x and δ_y are the standard deviations of the Gaussian envelope along the x and y axes, respectively.

The main steps of the enhancement algorithm are shown in Fig. 19 and are listed below [29]:

- *Normalization.* An input image needs to be normalized so that it has a pre-specified mean and variance. The normalization is a pixel-wise operation, in which an output pixel value depends only on the corresponding input pixel. It does not change the clarity of the ridge and valley structures. The main purpose of normalization is to reduce the variations in gray-level values along ridges and valleys what facilitates the subsequent steps.

- *Local ridge orientation estimation.* The local orientation indicates the major ridge orientation tendency in a local neighborhood. It represents an intrinsic property of a fingerprint image and defines an invariant coordinate for ridges and valleys in a local neighborhood. In neighboring ridges, the local ridge orientation changes slowly. Therefore, it is usually a specified block-wise property. In addition, there is no difference between a local ridge orientation of 90° and 270°, since the ridges oriented at 90° and the ridges oriented at 270° in a local neighborhood cannot be differentiated from each other.

- *Local ridge frequency estimation.* Local ridge frequency is the frequency of the ridge and valley structures in a local neighborhood along a direction normal to the local ridge orientation. The ridge and valley structures in a local neighborhood, where minutiae or singular points appear, do not form a well-defined sinusoidal-shaped wave. In such situations, the frequency is defined as the average frequency in the neighborhood. The local ridge frequency represents another intrinsic property of a fingerprint image.

- *Estimation of region mask.* The region mask is used to indicate the category of pixels. A pixel could be either a non-ridge-and-valley (unrecoverable) pixel or a ridge-and-valley (recoverable) pixel. A pixel (or a block of pixels) in an input fingerprint image could be either in a recoverable region or in an unrecoverable region. The classification of pixels into recoverable and unrecoverable categories can be performed based on the assessment of the shape of the wave formed by local ridges and valleys.
- Filtering. A bank of Gabor filters tuned to the local ridge orientation and ridge frequency is applied to the ridge-and-valley pixels in the normalized input fingerprint image to obtain an enhanced fingerprint image.

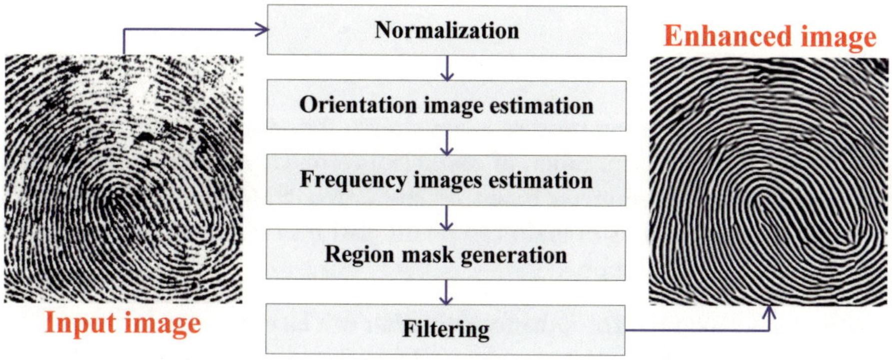

Figure 19. The flowchart of the spatial domain fingerprint enhancement algorithm [34].

4.1.2. Frequency domain filtering algorithm

The fingerprint enhancement approach in a frequency domain introduced in [31] consists of four concatenated processes: discrete cosine transform of sub-blocks of partitioning fingerprint, ridge orientation and frequency parameters estimation, filtering in DCT (*Discrete Cosine Transform*) domain and inverse discrete cosine transform of sub-blocks. The advantages of the proposed approach are as follows [31]:

- Fingerprint ridges form a natural sinusoid image – its spectrums are packed or localized in a frequency domain. Hence these spectrums can be easily shaped or filtered in this domain. Moreover, a filter can be specially designed in order to handle high curvature ridge area such as singular points. This is a great advantage over the spatial-domain filtering approach.
- When comparing with the discrete Fourier transform, the discrete cosine transform performs better in terms of energy compaction. Moreover, DCT coefficients are real numbers in comparison with complex numbers of discrete Fourier transform (DFT) coefficients. Therefore, we can handle DCT coefficients easier than DFT coefficients. Besides, the fast

DCT requires less computational complexity and less memory usage when comparing with the fast Fourier transform (FFT).

- By partitioning a fingerprint into sub-blocks, the proposed approach utilizes the spatially contextual information including the instantaneous frequency and orientation. Intrinsic features such as ridge frequency, ridge orientation, and angular bandwidth can be simply analyzed directly from DCT coefficients.

Conventional fingerprint enhancement schemes, when applied with non-overlapping blocks of partitioning fingerprint, often encounter blocking artifacts such as ridge discontinuities and spurious minutiae [31]. To preserve the ridge continuity and eliminate blocking artifacts, an overlapping block is applied to both DCT decomposition and reconstruction procedures. However, there is no need to apply any smooth spectral window for DCT because the overlapping area is large enough to prevent any blocking effects, corresponding with its energy compaction property.

4.1.3. Enhancement filtering in DCT domain

In the DCT domain, the filtering process is not simply the same as in the DFT domain [31] which required only the multiplication of coefficients. The Gabor filter is modified in order to cooperate with the DCT domain based on the Cartesian-form representation. The enhancement filtering in the DCT domain can be divided into two arithmetic manipulations, i.e. multiplication and convolution.

Filtering by Multiplication [31]: The enhancement filter can be expressed in terms of the product of separable Gaussian functions what is similar to the frequency-domain filtering technique [31]:

$$F_{fd}(\rho,\varphi) = F(\rho,\varphi)H_f(\rho)H_d(\varphi) \tag{3}$$

where $F(\varrho,\phi)$ are DCT coefficients in polar-form representation, directly related to DCT coefficients $F(u,v)$ in rectangular-form representation. $F_{fd}(\varrho,\phi)$ are DCT coefficients of the filtering output. The $H_f(\varrho)$ filter, which performs the ridge frequency filtering in Gaussian shape, is given by [31]:

$$H_f(\rho \mid \rho_0, \sigma_\rho, Z) = e^{-\frac{(\rho-\rho_0)^2}{2\sigma_\rho^2}}, \rho_0 = \sqrt{u_0^2 + v_0^2}, \quad \rho_{\min} \le \rho_0 \le \rho_{\max} \tag{4}$$

where ϱ_0 and σ_ϱ are the center of the high-peak frequency group and the filtering bandwidth parameter, respectively. The ϱ_{min} and ϱ_{max} parameters are minimum and maximum cut-off frequency constraints which suppress the effects of lower and higher frequencies such as ink, sweat gland holes or scratches in the fingerprint. Z is a filtering normalization factor depending on the filtering energy result.

The $H_d(\phi)$ filter, which performs the ridge orientation filtering, is given by [31]:

$$H_d(\varphi|\varphi_0,\sigma_\varphi,\varphi_{BW}) = \begin{cases} e^{-\frac{(\varphi-\varphi_0)^2}{2\sigma_\varphi^2}} & |\varphi-\varphi_0| \geq \varphi_{BW} \\ 1 & otherwise \end{cases} \quad (5)$$

where ϕ_0 is the peak orientation for the bandpass filter, σ_ϕ is the directional bandwidth parameter, and ϕ_{BW} is the angular bandwidth.

Filtering by Convolution [31]: Since θ and π-θ ridge orientation coefficients are projected into the same DCT domain region, both directional coefficients still remain from the previous filtering. In order to truncate inappropriate directional coefficients, two diagonal Gabor filters are exploited by the convolution operation. The finally enhanced DCT coefficients are given by [31]:

$$F_{enh}(u,v) = F_{fd}(u,v) * H_q(u,v) \quad (6)$$

where $F_{enh}(u,v)$ are enhanced DCT coefficients in rectangular-form, $F_{fd}(u,v)$ is the previous result of enhanced DCT coefficients in rectangular-form converted from $F_{fd}(\varrho,\phi)$ in polar-form. The quadrant correction filter, $H_q(u,v)$, is given by [31]:

$$H_q(u,v) = \begin{cases} \cos\left[\frac{(u+v)\pi}{2}\right] \cdot e^{-\frac{(u+v)^2}{2\sigma_q^2}} & \theta \geq \pi/2 \\ \cos\left[\frac{(u-v)\pi}{2}\right] \cdot e^{-\frac{(u-v)^2}{2\sigma_q^2}} & otherwise \end{cases} \quad (7)$$

where σ_q is the quadratic parameter and $\cos(n\pi/2)$ can attain only one of the three following values: -1, 0 or 1. Indeed, this convolution operation requires less computing because most of bandpass filtered coefficients are truncated to zero from the previous operation. In case of highly curved ridges, the transformed coefficients are projected into widely curved sub-band of the DCT domain as shown in Fig. 20.

From Fig. 20, we can approximate the orientation range from θ_1 to θ_2 by a non-coherence factor from Eq. (2). The curved sub-band can be classified as one of two regions, either the principal region (R_1) or the reflection region (R_2). The principal region R_1 contains only one diagonal component (45° or 135°) as mentioned before. The 45° or 135° diagonal components correspond to the phase pattern of the oriented ridges in the range of 0° to 90° or 90° to 180°, respectively. The reflection region R_2 is composed of both 45° and 135° diagonal components from the reflection property of DCT coefficients. Then the convolution is applied only in the principal region.

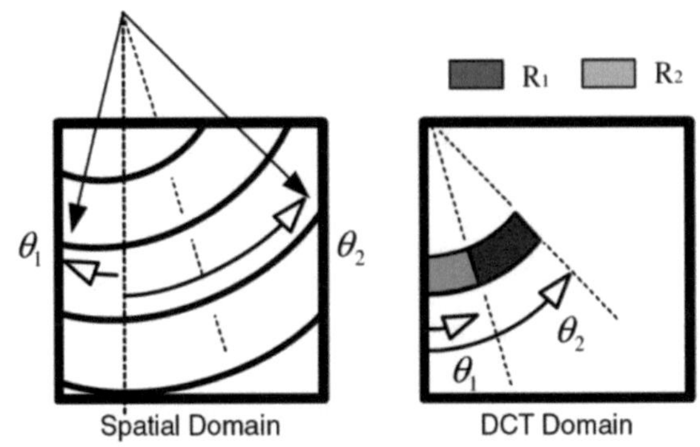

Figure 20. Highly curved ridges in spatial and frequency (DCT) domain. The signal is localized in a widely curved subband which can be classified as either the principal region (R_1) or the reflection region (R_2) [31].

It is then possible to compute a quality index of the fingerprint in the frequency domain [35] which gives us the information about the fingerprint image quality.

5. Fingerprint quality estimation

Quality of fingerprint image has a strong influence on biometric system performance. There exist several factors on which the final fingerprint quality depends: skin conditions, sensor quality and conditions, user cooperation and proper use of sensing device [36]. For the skin conditions the most influencing factors are dryness, presence of dirt and smudge and mainly the presence of skin disease. By the quality of the fingerprint image usually the "clarity" of ridge and valley pattern is meant. Because of existence of different fingerprint quality measures and indexes the standardization of fingerprint image quality as a precisely defined unit was needed. Fingerprint image quality according the international standard ISO/IEC 19794-4:2005 is defined as an integer from interval <0, 100>, where 0 corresponds to the lowest possible fingerprint image quality and 100 corresponds to the best possible fingerprint image quality. Transformation of values from other quality indexes can be performed by, for example, normalization.

The process of fingerprint image quality estimation is very important part of fingerprint recognition system, because it enables for example:

- to reject fingerprints with very low quality during the enrolment process and force the user to perform a new attempt to enroll a quality fingerprint,
- to reject fingerprints with very low quality during the comparison process – for the non-forensic applications it is better way than false accept decision,
- appropriate choosing the comparing algorithm in systems having different algorithms for differently quality fingerprints,

- to attach weights for each minutiae according the quality of fingerprint area in which they are located so during the minutiae based comparison process the weights of each minutiae are considered as well.

According to the source [28] the methods for fingerprint quality estimation can be divided into two categories: approaches based on local features extraction and approaches based on global features extraction.

Generally the process of fingerprint quality estimation consists of three phases:

1. Fingerprint area segmentation
2. Fingerprint foreground feature extraction (local or global)
3. Quality value estimation

Fingerprint area segmentation, sometimes also known as fingerprint foreground / background detection, is complex and difficult task.

5.1. Fingerprint area segmentation

The human finger and its fingerprint have a typical rounded shape. Fingerprint images from electronic dactyloscopic scanners are usually rectangles containing the rounded-shape fingerprint and of course a background. For the fingerprint processing purposes, mainly for the quality estimation process based on local feature extraction it is important to exclude the fingerprint background from the process. This needs to be done not only for speeding up the calculation time but also for making the estimation process more precise. Therefore, the main fingerprint foreground feature extraction is needed before the fingerprint area segmentation.

Generally the segmentation is a process of dividing the input image into several non-overlapping parts where usually the individual objects and the background are meant by the parts. If there is only one object in the image the segmentation can be called foreground/background detection. The fingerprint area segmentation is a process of detection which part of an image belongs to the fingerprint and which part of the image belongs to the background.

For our research we decided to test the following fingerprint area segmentation techniques: block grayscale variance method [37], *directional method* [37] and the *Gabor filter method* [38]. The block grayscale variance method computes variance of pixel intensity in each block and by using a set up threshold the decision logic marks each block as a background block or as a foreground (fingerprint) block. The block grayscale variance method is based on the idea that image blocks which contain fingerprint pattern have a high pixel intensity variance and the blocks with background have a low pixel intensity variance. The directional method described in [37] makes a foreground/background decision based on the block nominal direction computed from pixel nominal direction. This approach is based on the idea that the block with fingerprint has a high value of the block nominal direction and the others have a low value of the block nominal direction. The third method (Gabor filter method) [38] uses eight different oriented Gabor filters for computing the vector of eight Gabor features. The standard deviation of these features can be used as a threshold for the foreground/background decision.

5.2. Local feature extraction based methods

Local feature extraction methods divide the input image into rectangular blocks of a specific size. Next step is to estimate fingerprint quality value for each block and by using these values to compute the fingerprint quality value for the whole image. The final fingerprint image quality value is usually computed as a rate of count of blocks with high fingerprint quality value divided by the count of all blocks. These blocks may also contain information about their weight. The weight of each block then corresponds to its quality.

In the presence we have the following implementations of the local feature based quality estimation algorithms: *directional contrast method, directional method, Gabor filter method and the check ratio method*. These methods work with blocks and compute a feature which characterizes the block and works as a quality index. The directional contrast method [39] computes the directional contrast of a local ridge flow orientation. The directional method uses the block nominal direction value and the Gabor filter method makes the quality value estimation by using the standard deviation of several different orientated Gabor filter responses. The check ratio method [40] is very simple and not precise method which presumes that the high quality fingerprints have a higher rate of foreground block count to the background block count. The success of the basic check ratio method mainly depends on the quality of the previous fingerprint image segmentation. However the check ratio method has a much better utilization because it can be used for weighting the result of previous three fingerprint quality estimation algorithms in order to make the quality estimation result more precise.

5.3. Methods on global feature extraction

The methods based on global feature extraction estimate the fingerprint quality value from the features extracted from the whole fingerprint image, not only some image block. The most important representative of this group is the method developed by the US National Institute of Standards and Technology (NIST) and its name is NFIQ *(NIST Fingerprint Image Quality)* rate. The NFIQ rate divides the fingerprint images into five categories according to their estimated quality. NFIQ defines the quality of an input image as a prediction of a comparison performance [28]. The fingerprints with a high quality will probably achieve a high comparison score. The NFIQ implementation uses a special vector of features for fingerprint quality estimation, created by the fingerprint quality map and statistics of its internal algorithm for minutiae extraction. These feature vectors are then used as an input for the multilayer perceptron neural network [41] which decides about the resulting fingerprint quality.

5.4. Creation of batch fingerprint quality estimation tool

One of the crucial tasks for the mapping the influence of dermatologic diseases on the fingerprint image quality was to design and implement an application for automatic batch fin-

http://dx.doi.org/10.5772/51992

gerprint image quality estimation. The main requirements were capability of batch fingerprint image batch processing using different processing algorithms and reusable extendable code design. During the design process the whole task was split into two important sub-tasks: the fingerprint quality estimation library and the batch processing tool graphical user interface.

The fingerprint quality estimation library was implemented in C++ programming language with the use of OpenCV 2.1 library for some image processing operation. The library provides three fingerprint segmentation algorithms (variance, directional and Gabor filter) and four fingerprint quality estimation algorithms (check ratio, directional contrast, directional and Gabor filter).

The graphical user interface was implemented in C++ programming language with the use of Qt 4.6 framework. The application observes the Model-View-Controller design model. The application uses the cooperating library algorithms for fingerprint segmentation and fingerprint quality estimation and due to fact that the check ratio quality estimation algorithm can be used as add-on for other quality estimation methods the application can batch process the all fingerprint images in specified directory by 21 different fingerprint quality estimation pipelines. Results of the fingerprint quality estimation are then normalized into 0 – 100 interval according the standard and can be exported into .csv or .xml file format.

5.5. Diseased fingerprints quality testing

The created database of fingerprints with a skin disease has been tested for the quality in the closest past. For the testing the implemented tool with all 21 local feature extraction based methods and the global NFIQ method were used. The results were normalized into interval from 0 to 100 where 100 means the best possible fingerprint quality. The example of obtained results of the most promising methods can be seen in Table 1.

Quality estimation method	*Cut wound*	*Verruca vulgaris*	*Atopic eczema*	*Psoriasis*
NFIQ	61	45	5	7
Variance method segmentation + Gabor filter quality estimation + Check ratio	48	53	41	37
Variance method segmentation + Directional quality estimation	10	11	10	13
Directional method segmentation + Directional contrast quality + Check ratio	48	52	51	48

Table 1. Example of results of diseased fingerprint quality testing.

6. Conclusion and future challenges

The dermatologic diseases have a strong negative influence on the process of fingerprint recognition and are causing problems to people who are suffering from them. These people are discriminated because they cannot use the fingerprint recognition systems which are very common these days. Currently there exists no usable database of fingerprints affected by a skin disease. As a first step in this wide and complex research we designed and developed a special diseased fingerprints capturing station. With this station the medical experts captured the first version of this special fingerprint database. A special algorithm for fingerprint image enhancement has been designed and fingerprint batch processing tool has been implemented. The first diseased fingerprint quality testing has been realized. Our greatest challenge in the nearest future is to develop an algorithm for distinguishing diseased fingerprints from the other fingerprints with a low quality.

In the nearest future the several challenges will be needed to face. First,the global analysis of the results of testing of the quality estimation algorithms has to be done. We will try to find out why some quality estimation algorithm failed and why some did not fail. The biggest challenge for us will now be to design and implement an algorithm for dermatologic disease presence detection. This algorithm should be able to detect whether the fingerprint with a low quality is diseased or if it is not and the low quality is caused for example by dirt, dry skin, mud etc.

Acknowledgement

This research has been realized under the support of the following grants: "*Security-Oriented Research in Information Technology*" – *MSM0021630528 (CZ), "Information Technology in Biomedical Engineering"* – GD102/09/H083 (CZ), "*Advanced secured, reliable and adaptive IT*" – FIT-S-11-1 (CZ) and "*The IT4Innovations Centre of Excellence*" – IT4I-CZ 1.05/1.1.00/02.0070 (CZ).

Authors of this research thank to the student Bc. Tomas Korec who created the implementation of batch fingerprint image quality estimation application for us.

Author details

Michal Dolezel[1], Martin Drahansky[1], Jaroslav Urbanek[2], Eva Brezinova[3] and Tai-hoon Kim[4]

1 Faculty of Information Technology, Brno University of Technology, Brno, Czech Republic

2 Faculty of Medicine and Dentistry, Palacky University and Faculty Hospital, Olomouc, Czech Republic

3 Faculty of Medicine, Masaryk University, Brno, Czech Republic

4 Department of Multimedia Engineering, Hannam University, Deadeok-gu, South Korea

References

[1] *Fingerprint Recognition Technology - Related Topics*. LAP, 2011, p. 172, ISBN 978-3-8443-3007-6.

[2] Maltoni D., Maio D., Jain A.K., Prabhakar S. *Handbook of Fingerprint Recognition*. Springer-Verlag, 1st Edition, 2005, p. 348, ISBN 978-03-879-5431-8.

[3] Bhanu, B. Tan, X. *Computational Algorithms for Fingerprint Recognition*. Kluwer Academic Publishers, 2004, p. 188, ISBN 1-4020-7651-7.

[4] Jain A.K., Flynn P., Ross A.A. *Handbook of Biometrics*. Springer-Verlag, 2008, p. 556, ISBN 978-0-387-71040-2.

[5] Straus, J. *Kriminalistická daktyloskopie* (*Criminalistic Dactyloscopy*). Kriminalistický ústav Praha Policie ČR, Prague, 2005, p. 285, ISBN 80-7251-192-0.

[6] Petermann T., Scherz C., Sauter A. *Biometrie und Ausweisdokumente*. TAB – Büro für Technikfolgen-Abschätzung beim Deutschen Bundestag, AB No. 93, 2003, p. 168.

[7] Drahanský M., Orság F., Zbořil F.V.: *Biometrics in Security Applications*. In: Proceedings of 38th International Conference MOSIS'04, Ostrava, MARQ, 2004, pp. 201-206, ISBN 80-85988-98-4.

[8] Hao F., Anderson R., Daugman J. *Combining Cryptography with Biometric Effectivity*. Technical Report, University of Cambridge, 2005, p. 17, ISSN 1476-2986.

[9] Uludag U. *Secure Biometric Systems*. Dissertation Thesis, Michigan State University, 2006, p. 171.

[10] Müller R. *Fingerprint Verification with Microprocessor Security Tokens*. Ph.D. Thesis, Technical University Munich, Germany, 2001, p. 151.

[11] Ling Q., Bardzimashvili T. *Biometrics in Computerized Patient Record*. Presentation, 2005, p. 33.

[12] Murray L., Park U. *Biometrics in Credit Cards: A New Way to Pay*. CSE891, 2005, p. 31.

[13] Jain A.K., Pankanti S. *A Touch of Money*. IEEE Spectrum, 2006, pp. 14-19, www.spectrum.ieee.org.

[14] *Evaluation of Fingerprint Recognition Technologies – BioFinger*. Public Final Report, version 1.1, Bundesamt für Sicherheit in der Informationstechnik, p. 122, 2004.

[15] Bolle R. M., Connell J. H., Pankanti S., Ratha N. K., Senior A. W. *Guide to Biometrics*. Springer-Verlag, 2004, p. 364, ISBN 0-387-40089-3.

[16] James W. D., Berger T. G., Elston D. M. *Andrew's Diseases of the Skin – Clinical Dermatology*. 10th Edition, Saunders Elsevier, 2006, p. 961, ISBN 0-8089-2351-X.

[17] Habif T. P. *Clinical Dermatology*. 4th Edition, Mosby, China, 2004, p. 1004, ISBN 978-0-323-01319-2.

[18] Iyad J. and Hao Y. *New algorithms for contrast enhancement in grayscale images based on the variational definition of histogram equalization*. Integrated Computer-Aided Engineering, Vol. 15, No. 2, pp. 131-147.

[19] *The Science of the Skin* [online]. [cit. 2012-05-30]. Available at: <http://www.naturalrussia.com/natural/skin/structure.html>.

[20] Wolff K., Johnson R. A., Suurmond D. *Fitzpatrick's Color Atlas and Synopsis of Clinical Dermatology*. 5th Edition, McGraw-Hill, 2005, p. 1085, ISBN 0-07-144019-4.

[21] Weston W. L., Lane A. T., Morelli J. G. *Color Textbook of Pediatric Dermatology*. Mosby Elsevier, 2007, p. 446, ISBN 978-03-23049-09-2.

[22] Štork J., et al. *Dermatovenerologie*. Galén, Prague, 2008, p. 502, ISBN 978-80-7262-371-6.

[23] Niedner R., Adler Y.: *Kožní choroby – kapesní obrazový atlas*. Triton, Prague, 2005, p. 359, ISBN 80-7254-734-8.

[24] Web page: http://www.rodina.cz/scripts/detail.asp?id=1966.

[25] Benáková N. (Ed.) et al. *Dermatovenerologie, dětstká dermatologie a korektivní dermatologie (Dermatovenerology, Pediatric Dermatology and Corrective Dermatology)*. Triton, Prague, CZ, 2006, p. 294, ISBN 80-7254-855-7.

[26] Drahanský M. *Fingerprint Recognition Technology – Liveness Detection*. Image Quality and Skin Diseases, FIT-BUT, 2009, p. 153.

[27] Ratha N. K., Govindaraju V. *Advances in Biometrics: Sensors, Algorithms and Systems*. London, Springer, 2008, p. 503, ISBN 978-1-84628-920-0.

[28] Maltoni D., Maio D., Jain A.K., Prabhakar S. *Handbook of Fingerprint Recognition*. Springer-Verlag, 2nd Edition, 2009, p. 494, ISBN 978-1-84882-253-5.

[29] Ratha N., Bolle R. *Automatic Fingerprint Recognition Systems*. Springer-Verlag, 2004, p. 458, ISBN 0-387-95593-3.

[30] Jang J., Elliott S.J., Kim H. *On Improving Interoperability of Fingerprint Recognition Using Resolution Compensation Based on Sensor Evaluation*. In: S.-W. Lee and S.Z. Li (Eds.): ICB 2007, LNCS 4642, 2007, pp. 455-463, Springer-Verlag Berlin Heidelberg, 2007, ISSN 0302-9743.

[31] Jirachaweng S., Areekul V. *Fingerprint Enhancement Based on Discrete Cosine Transform*. In: Proceedings of ICB 2007, LNCS 4642, Springer-Verlag Berlin Heidelberg, 2007, pp. 96-105, ISBN 978-3-540-74548-8.

[32] Bauer N. *Handbuch zur Industriellen Bildverarbeitung*. Fraunhofer IRB Verlag, Stuttgart, Germany, 2007, p. 513, ISBN 978-3-8167-7386-3.

[33] Ross A. *Information Fusion in Fingerprint Authentication*. Michigan State University, USA, 2003, p. 187.

[34] Jain A.K. *Fingerprint Enhancement*. Presentation, Michigan State University, p. 16, 2005.

[35] Chen Y., Dass S., Jain A.K. *Fingerprint Quality Indices for Predicting Authentication Performance*. In: Proceedings of AVBPA2005, USA, p. 10, ISBN 3-540-27887-7, 2005.

[36] Boulgouris N. V., Plataniotis K. N., Micheli-Tzanakou E. *Biometrics: Theory, Methods and Applications*. Hoboken, N.J.: Wiley, 2010, p. 745, ISBN 978-0470-24782-2.

[37] Mehtre B., Chatterjee B. *Segmentation of Fingerprint images – A composite method*. In: Pattern Recognition, 1989, pp. 381 - 385, ISSN 0031-3203.

[38] Shen L., Kot A., Koo W. *Quality Measures of Fingerprint Images*. In: Audio- and Video-Based Biometric Person Authentication. Springer Berlin / Heidelberg, 2001, p.266, ISBN 978-3-540-42216-7.

[39] Wu C., Tulyakov S., Govindaraju V. *Image Quality Measures for Fingerprint Image Enhancement*. In: Multimedia Content Representation, Classification and Security, Springer Berlin / Heidelberg, 2006, p. 215. ISBN 978-3-540-39392-4.

[40] Joun S., Kim H., Chung Y. et al. *An Experimental Study on Measuring Image Quality of Infant Fingerprints*. In: Knowledge-Based Intelligent Information and Engineering Systems, Springer Berlin / Heidelberg, 2003, p. 1261, ISBN 978-3-540-40804-8.

[41] Noriega L. *Multilayer Perceptron Tutorial*, tutorial, School of Computing, Staffordshire University, UK, 2005, p. 12.

[42] Yang J.C., Xiong N., Vasilakos A.V. *Two-stage Enhancement Scheme for Low-quality Fingerprint Images by Learning from the Image*. IEEE Transactions on Systems, Man, and Cybernetics, Part C, 2012.

Chapter 13

Algorithms for Processing Biometric Data Oriented to Privacy Protection and Preservation of Significant Parameters

Vladimir B. Balakirsky and A. J. Han Vinck

Additional information is available at the end of the chapter

http://dx.doi.org/10.5772/51800

1. Introduction

We address a general theory of transformations of biometric data, independently on particular biometric features taken into the processing. An application assumes representation of data in the specified format and the use of the proposed technique.

The content of a biometric database can be used for different purposes, and their complete list is usually unknown in advance. These purposes include different variants of processing noisy data, such as authentication and identification of a person on the basis of his biometric observations, detection of certain features, etc. General requirements to data processing schemes in any of these applications contain the design of a verification scheme consisting of the enrollment and the verification stages. At the enrollment stage, the input data should be converted to the data stored in the database under the identifier of the person. At the verification stage, the presented data have to be analyzed to make the decision whether they belong to the chosen person or not. Privacy protection of the data includes protection against attackers of three types:

- a blind attacker, who wants to guess the content of the database using his knowledge about the probability distribution over input biometric data;
- an attacker, who has access to the database and wants to find the input biometric vector processed at the enrollment stage;
- an attacker, who has access to the database and wants to generate artificial data to pass through the verification stage with the acceptance decision.

We will present the class of transformations having the following features.

- If input data are represented by the vector whose components are generated by a stationary memoryless source having the known probability distribution, then they can be converted to the vector $\boldsymbol{x}$ whose components are uniformly distributed over the $(-1,+1)$ interval. Therefore, the scheme has a perfect protection against blind attackers. A generalized version of the procedure brings the same property for non-stationary sources. Moreover, if the source has memory or the input probability distribution is unknown, an approximate uniform distribution can be created.
- The enrollment can be organized in such a way that the constructed vector $\boldsymbol{x}$ is encrypted and mapped to the vector $\hat{\boldsymbol{x}}$, which is stored in the database. The encryption is understood as replacement of certain components of the vector $\boldsymbol{x}$ by randomly chosen components. As a result, the input biometric data cannot be reconstructed from the vector $\hat{\boldsymbol{x}}$. We show that the encryption can be organized in such a way that the properties of the constructed uniform distribution are conserved, but the union of $(-1,-a)$ and $(+a,+1)$ intervals replaces the $(-1,+1)$ interval. The value of parameter $a \in (0,1)$ controls the trade-off between privacy protection and the verification performance, and it has be assigned in advance. As a result, the scheme becomes protected against attackers, who have access to the database and want to guess the input vector by reading the corresponding vector stored in the database.
- The case, when biometrics of the same person is measured at the enrollment and the verification stages, is simulated as transmission of outcomes of the enrollment stage measurements over an observation channel. We create another channel between results of transformations of these outcomes. It turns out that this channel has the property that the level of noise essentially depends on the magnitude of the transmitted component, and it is very low when the magnitude is large. Since a large magnitude at the output of the transformer is obtained when the input magnitude is large, we talk about the preservation of significant parameters under the noise, provided that these parameters are represented in a vector of outcomes of biometric measurements by components having large magnitudes. We present a verification algorithm designed on the basis of these properties.

Verification algorithms are considered in the most of publications, related to biometrics (see, in particular [1]–[4]), and they are usually introduced as algorithms of combinatorial matching of the outcomes of observations received at the enrollment and at the verification stages. However, secrecy requirements to a biometric system to be designed do not allow storage of the outcomes received at the enrollment stage, and lead to the schemes where only relatively few outcomes characterizing the person are taken into account. In the present chapter, these outcomes are referred to as significant components. The algorithms with similar understanding are presented in [6]–[8] where significance is determined by the values of the probability distribution function computed at the observed values. This approach follows the lines of information theory when data processing is represented as secret sharing [9]–[12]. Some part of the secret is published, while another part is hidden by the so–called one-way hash function [13] and it has to be decoded after a noisy version of the observation data is available. The transformation of the outcomes, received at the enrollment stage, to a published part of the secret is also viewed as wrapping in a number of applications where the unwrapping is possible only when outcomes, received at the verification stage, are close to the wrapped data [14]. The use of possibly non-stationary probability distributions also allows us to include multi–biometric measurements (see, for example [15], [16]) into the

http://dx.doi.org/10.5772/51800

processing. Furthermore, the addressed issues are relevant to constructing fault–tolerant passwords from biometric data [17]–[19]. The cited list of publications is certainly far from being complete, but we only indicated directions that are relevant to the material of the chapter. We also understand that specific applications of the presented results need research on probability distributions of the measured biometric data. In particular, the approaches can be fruitful for the schemes where different lengths are processed (for example, distances between certain points on the face or hand).

The chapter is organized as follows. We begin with the introduction and the notation sections and then introduce the F-transformation for the input data and their noisy observations in Sections 3,4. A possible implementation of the verification scheme, constructed using the derived properties, is presented in Section 5. Some general conclusions are included in Section 6.

Suppose that outcomes of biometric measurements of a person, received at the enrollment stage, are represented by a float–valued vector $\boldsymbol{r} = (r_1, \ldots, r_n) \in \mathsf{R}^n$. The t-th component of the vector $\boldsymbol{r}$ has the sign, which is understood as

$$\text{sgn}(r_t) = \begin{cases} 1, \text{ if } r_t \geq 0 \\ 0, \text{ if } r_t < 0 \end{cases} \tag{1}$$

and the magnitude

$$|r_t| = \begin{cases} +r_t, \text{ if } r_t \geq 0 \\ -r_t, \text{ if } r_t < 0 \end{cases} \tag{2}$$

Thus, the specification of the component r_t is equivalent to the specification of the pair $(\text{sgn}(r_t), |r_t|)$. Such a representation is introduced, because we assume that $\text{sgn}(r_t)$ and $|r_t|$ are independent parameters: if one knows the sign, then he has no information about the magnitude; if one knows the magnitude, then he has no information about the sign. Furthermore, we will assume that the magnitude $|r_t|$ characterizes "significance" of the t-th component: for example, if r_t is defined as the difference between the value of the measured parameter and the average or the expected value, then $|r_t|$ determines the deviation of the t-th parameter for the particular person.

We will analyze the scheme where one of results of the processing of the vector $\boldsymbol{r}$ at the enrollment stage is expressed by a float–valued vector $\tilde{\boldsymbol{x}} = (\tilde{x}_1, \ldots, \tilde{x}_n) \in \mathsf{F}^n$ whose components have magnitudes less than 1, i.e.,

$$\mathsf{F} = \Big\{ x \in \mathsf{R} : |x| < 1 \Big\} \tag{3}$$

The vector $\tilde{\boldsymbol{x}}$ is stored in the database under the identifier of the person, associated with the vector $\boldsymbol{r}$. We call it the wrapped version of the input data. The transformation $\boldsymbol{r} \to \tilde{\boldsymbol{x}}$ is not a one-to-one mapping, and some data are lost. This transformation is divided into two steps. We first introduce a one-to-one mapping $\boldsymbol{r} \leftrightarrow \boldsymbol{x}$, where $\boldsymbol{x} = (x_1, \ldots, x_n) \in \mathsf{F}^n$, and

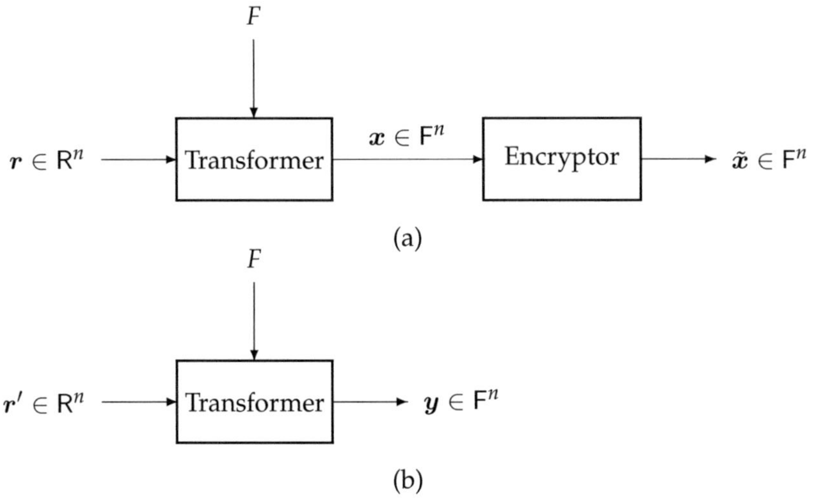

Figure 1. (a) Transformations of the vector $\boldsymbol{r}$ to the vector $\tilde{\boldsymbol{x}}$ stored in the database under the identifier of the person. (b) Transformation of the vector $\boldsymbol{r}'$ to the vector $\boldsymbol{y}$ at the verification stage for its comparison with the vector $\tilde{\boldsymbol{x}}$ and investigation of the closeness of the vectors $\boldsymbol{r}$ and $\boldsymbol{r}'$.

then encrypt the vector $\boldsymbol{x}$ in such a way that the change of the t-th component x_t is possible only if $|r_t|$ is small.

At the verification stage, the verifier observes a vector $\boldsymbol{r}' = (r_1', \ldots, r_n') \in \mathsf{R}^n$. This vector is mapped to the vector $\boldsymbol{y}$ in the same way as $\boldsymbol{r}$ was mapped to $\boldsymbol{x}$, and there should be an algorithm that analyzes the pair $(\boldsymbol{y}, \tilde{\boldsymbol{x}})$ to find the closeness of the vector $\boldsymbol{r}'$ and some vector $\boldsymbol{r}$ that could be used as an origin of the vector $\tilde{\boldsymbol{x}}$. If the verifier decides that these vectors are close enough, then components of the vector $\boldsymbol{r}'$ are considered as possible outcomes of biometric measurements of the person whose identifier corresponds to the vector $\tilde{\boldsymbol{x}}$.

The procedures above describe a general structure of the verification scheme under constraints that the transformation $\boldsymbol{r} \to \tilde{\boldsymbol{x}}$ is divided into two steps and that components of the constructed vectors belong to the set F. These procedures are illustrated in Figure 1 where we use some additional notation. Namely, we parameterize the mappings $\boldsymbol{r} \leftrightarrow \boldsymbol{x}$ and $\boldsymbol{r}' \leftrightarrow \boldsymbol{y}$ by a monotone increasing function $F(r), r \in \mathsf{R}$, approaching 0 when $r \to -\infty$ and $r \to +\infty$, respectively. Formally,

$$\frac{d}{dr} F(r) > 0, \quad r \in \mathsf{R} \tag{4}$$

and

$$(F(-\infty), F(+\infty)) = (0, 1) \tag{5}$$

By (4), (5), the function F has a uniquely determined inverse function F^{-1}, and we can simulate the data received at the verification stage, as the result of transmission of the vector $\boldsymbol{x}$ over a channel consisting of the deterministic F^{-1}-transformation $\boldsymbol{x} \to \boldsymbol{r}$, the stochastic mapping $\boldsymbol{r} \to \boldsymbol{r}'$ introduced by a physical V^n channel, and the deterministic F-transformation $\boldsymbol{r}' \to \boldsymbol{y}$ (see Figure 2a). As the verifier also has access to the vector $\tilde{\boldsymbol{x}}$

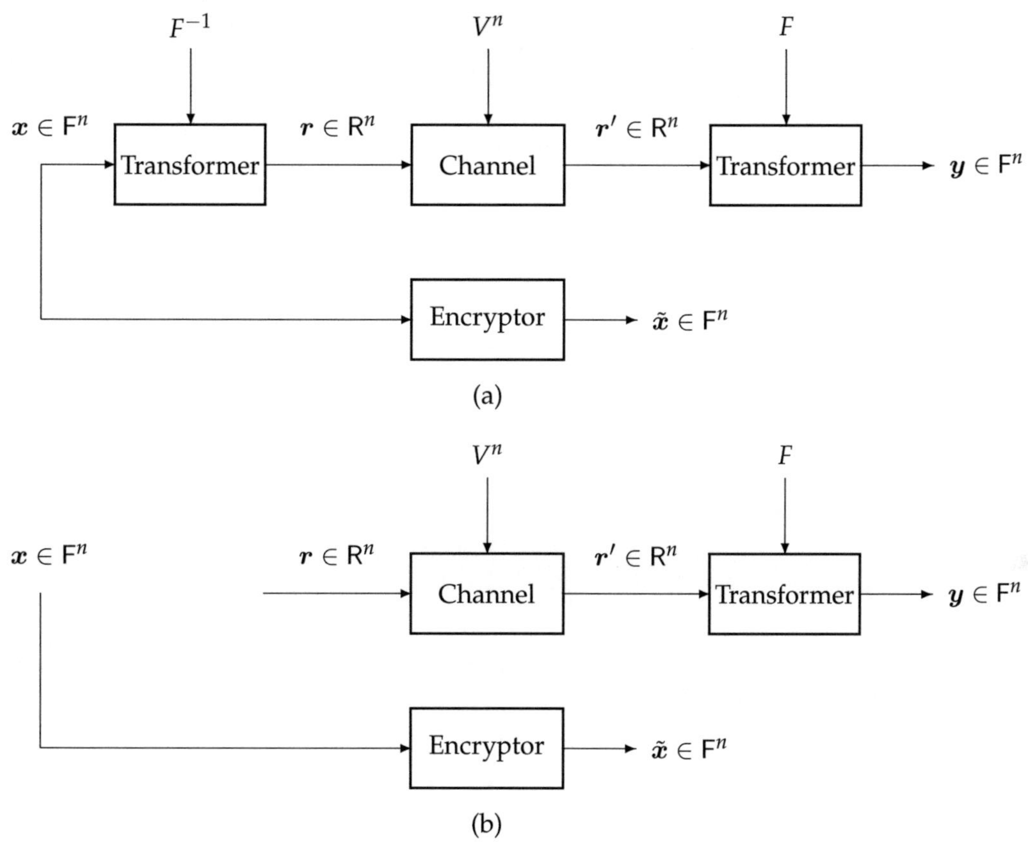

Figure 2. Schemes for transmission of the vector $\boldsymbol{x}$ to the verifier: (a) Legitimate case. (b) Attack.

constructed as an encrypted version of the vector $\boldsymbol{x}$, we get the situation, when the vector $\boldsymbol{x}$ is sent to the verifier over two parallel channels. If the level of noise in the physical channel is not high, then the verifier is supposed to make the acceptance decision. As an alternative, there is a possibility that the vector $\boldsymbol{r}$ is generated independently of the vector $\boldsymbol{x}$ (see Figure 2b where we delete the F^{-1}-transformation). In this case, the verifier is supposed to make the rejection decision.

2. Notation

Let R, R', X, Y denote random variables and r, r', x, y denote their values. This notation is also extended to the vectors of random variables $R^n, (R')^n, X^n, Y^n$ and their values $\boldsymbol{r}, \boldsymbol{r}', \boldsymbol{x}, \boldsymbol{y}$.

In the basic model, we assume that the vector $\boldsymbol{r}$ is generated by a stationary memoryless source having the probability distribution (PD) F^* and the probability density function (PDF) P^*,

$$F^* = \Big(F^*(r) = \Pr_{\text{data}} \{R < r\}, r \in \mathsf{R} \Big) \tag{6}$$

$$P^* = \Big(P^*(r) = \frac{d}{dr} F^*(r),\ r \in \mathsf{R} \Big) \tag{7}$$

The value of the PDF, associated with the vector $\boldsymbol{r}$, is expressed as

$$\text{PDF}(\boldsymbol{r}) = \prod_{t=1}^{n} P^*(r_t) \tag{8}$$

We will simulate the stochastic mapping $\boldsymbol{r} \to \boldsymbol{r}'$ as transmission of the vector $\boldsymbol{r}$ over an observation channel, which is introduced as a stationary memoryless channel specified by the collection of the conditional PDs Φ_r and the collection of the conditional PDFs V_r,

$$\Phi_r = \Big(\Phi(r'|r) = \Pr_{\text{noise}} \{R' < r' \,|\, R = r\}, r' \in \mathsf{R} \Big) \tag{9}$$

$$V_r = \Big(V(r'|r) = \frac{d}{dr'} \Phi(r'|r), r' \in \mathsf{R} \Big) \tag{10}$$

for all $r \in \mathsf{R}$. The value of the conditional PDF, associated with the output vector $\boldsymbol{r}'$, given the input vector $\boldsymbol{r}$, is expressed as

$$\text{PDF}(\boldsymbol{r}'|\boldsymbol{r}) = \prod_{t=1}^{n} V(r_t'|r_t) \tag{11}$$

Let

$$\text{FG}_{m,\gamma} = \Big(\text{FG}_{m,\gamma}(r) = \frac{1}{2} + \frac{1}{2}\text{erf}\Big(\frac{r-m}{\gamma\sqrt{2}}\Big), r \in \mathsf{R} \Big) \tag{12}$$

$$\text{G}_{m,\gamma} = \Big(\text{G}_{m,\gamma}(r) = \frac{1}{\gamma\sqrt{2\pi}} \exp\Big\{-\frac{(r-m)^2}{2\gamma^2}\Big\}, r \in \mathsf{R} \Big) \tag{13}$$

where

$$\text{erf}(r) = \frac{2}{\sqrt{\pi}} \int_0^r \exp\{-\tilde{r}^2\}\, d\tilde{r},\ \ r \in \mathsf{R} \tag{14}$$

is the erf-function, denote the Gaussian PD and PDF, when m is the mean and γ^2 is the variance. We will also use the function

$$\psi_c(x) = \frac{1}{2} + \frac{1}{2}\text{erf}\Big(c \cdot \text{erf}^{-1}(x)\Big) \tag{15}$$

http://dx.doi.org/10.5772/51800

3. The F-transformation of the input data

The function F, satisfying (4), (5), is the PD of some random variable R, and we write

$$F = \Big(F(r) = \Pr\{ R < r \}, r \in \mathsf{R} \Big) \tag{16}$$

The corresponding PDF is defined as

$$P = \Big(P(r) = \frac{d}{dr} F(r), r \in \mathsf{R} \Big) \tag{17}$$

Notice that $(F^*, P^*) \neq (F, P)$ in general case and denote

$$f^* = \Big(f^*(x) = \Pr_{\text{data}} \{ 2F(R) - 1 < x \}, x \in \mathsf{F} \Big) \tag{18}$$

$$p^* = \Big(p^*(x) = \frac{d}{dx} f^*(x), x \in \mathsf{F} \Big) \tag{19}$$

Let us fix the function F, satisfying (4), (5), and map an $r \in \mathsf{R}$ to the $x \in \mathsf{F}$ using the rule

$$x = 2F(r) - 1 \tag{20}$$

The function F has a uniquely determined inverse function

$$F^{-1} = \Big(F^{-1}(z), z \in (0,1) \Big) \tag{21}$$

and the equality (20) implies $r = r(x)$, where

$$r(x) = F^{-1}\Big(\frac{x+1}{2} \Big) \tag{22}$$

The F-transformation of the vector $\boldsymbol{r} \in \mathsf{R}^n$ will be understood as the result of n component-wise applications of the mapping (20).

Some values of $r(x)$ for Gaussian data are given in Table 1. Notice that

$$F = FG_{0,\rho} \Rightarrow \frac{1}{2} + \frac{1}{2}\mathrm{erf}\Big(\frac{r(x)}{\rho\sqrt{2}} \Big) = \frac{x+1}{2} \Rightarrow r(x) = \rho\sqrt{2} \cdot \mathrm{erf}^{-1}(x) \tag{23}$$

The data in Table 1 illustrate the point that (20) is a non-linear mapping. In particular, if $\rho = 2$, then the values belonging to the interval $(0, 0.64)$ are mapped to the values between 0 and $0.25, \ldots,$ the values greater than 3.92 are mapped to the values between 0.95 and 1. The mapping $r \leftrightarrow x$ is also illustrated in Figure 3.

x =	0	0.25	0.50	0.75	0.80	0.85	0.90	0.95	1
$\rho = 2$	0	0.64	1.35	2.30	2.56	2.88	3.29	3.92	$+\infty$
$\rho = 1$	0	0.32	0.67	1.15	1.28	1.44	1.64	1.96	$+\infty$
$\rho = 1/2$	0	0.16	0.34	0.58	0.64	0.72	0.82	0.98	$+\infty$

Table 1. Some values of $r(x)$ for the function $F = FG_{0,\rho}$.

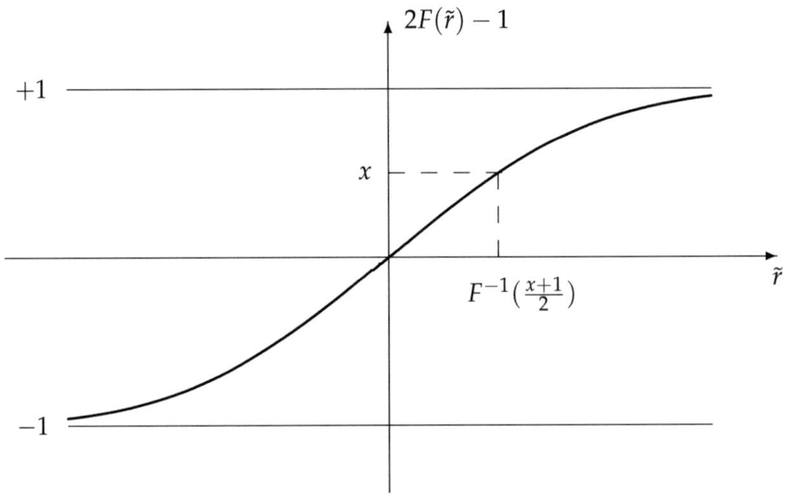

Figure 3. Illustration of the one-to-one mapping $x \leftrightarrow r = r(x)$.

In the following considerations we will restrict ourselves to the class of functions F, satisfying (4), (5) and having additional symmetric properties:

$$r(-x) = -r(+x) \tag{24}$$

and

$$P(r(-x)) = P(r(+x)), \;\; x \in \mathsf{F} \tag{25}$$

The F-transformation of input data can be viewed as an application of the inverse to the well-known construction of pseudorandom generators having a fixed probability distribution F. In this case, an algorithm generates the value z of a random variable "uniformly distributed over the $(0,1)$ interval" and outputs $F^{-1}(z) \in (0,1)$. Our scheme receives an $r \in \mathsf{R}$ and outputs $2F(r) - 1$ where the multiplication by 2 and the subtraction of 1 are introduced because of further processing of the signs and the magnitudes. Notice that a similar approach can be used to generate Gaussian variables having the mean 0 and the fixed variance ρ^2; the transformer has to output $FG_{0,\rho}^{-1}(F(r))$ in this case.

http://dx.doi.org/10.5772/51800

As $2F(R)-1$ is a deterministic function of the random variable R, the value of x is the observation of the random variable $X = 2F(R)-1$ having the PD f^* and the PDF p^*. We write

$$f^*(x) = \Pr_{\text{data}}\{2F(R)-1 < x\} = \Pr_{\text{data}}\left\{F(R) < \frac{x+1}{2}\right\} = \Pr_{\text{data}}\left\{R < F^{-1}\left(\frac{x+1}{2}\right)\right\}$$
$$= F^*\left(F^{-1}\left(\frac{x+1}{2}\right)\right) = F^*(r(x)) \tag{26}$$

and

$$p^*(x) = \frac{d}{dx}f^*(x) = \frac{d}{dx}F^*(r(x))$$
$$= \left(\frac{d}{d\tilde{r}}F^*(\tilde{r})\Big|_{\tilde{r}=r(x)}\right)\cdot\frac{d}{dx}r(x) = P^*(r(x))\cdot\frac{d}{dx}F^{-1}\left(\frac{x+1}{2}\right)$$
$$= P^*(r(x))\cdot\left(\frac{d}{d\tilde{r}}F(\tilde{r})\Big|_{\tilde{r}=r(x)}\right)^{-1}\cdot\frac{d}{dx}\frac{x+1}{2} = \frac{1}{2}\cdot\frac{P^*(r(x))}{P(r(x))} \tag{27}$$

Therefore

$$f^* = \Big(F^*(r(x)),\ x\in\mathsf{F}\Big),\quad p^* = \left(\frac{P^*(r(x))}{2P(r(x))},\ x\in\mathsf{F}\right) \tag{28}$$

By (8) and the fact that the F-transformation is a component-wise mapping, the value of the PDF, associated with the vector $\boldsymbol{x}$, is expressed as

$$\text{PDF}(\boldsymbol{x}) = \prod_{t=1}^{n}\frac{P^*(r(x_t))}{2P(r(x_t))} \tag{29}$$

for all $\boldsymbol{x}\in\mathsf{F}^n$.

If $(F^*,F) = (FG_{0,\rho^*}, FG_{0,\rho})$, then we use (23) and write

$$f^*(x) = FG_{0,\rho^*}(\rho\sqrt{2}\cdot\text{erf}^{-1}(x)) = \frac{1}{2}+\frac{1}{2}\text{erf}\left(\frac{\rho\sqrt{2}\cdot\text{erf}^{-1}(x)}{\rho^*\sqrt{2}}\right) \tag{30}$$

$$p^*(x) = \frac{G_{0,\rho^*}(r(x))}{2G_{0,\rho}(r(x))} = \frac{\rho\sqrt{2\pi}}{2\rho^*\sqrt{2\pi}}\exp\left\{-\frac{r^2(x)}{2(\rho^*)^2}+\frac{r^2(x)}{2\rho^2}\right\} \tag{31}$$

Hence,

$$f^* = \Big(\psi_{\rho/\rho^*}(x),\ x\in\mathsf{F}\Big),\quad p^* = \left(\frac{\rho}{2\rho^*}\exp\left\{-\frac{\rho^2-(\rho^*)^2}{2\rho^2(\rho^*)^2}r^2(x)\right\},\ x\in\mathsf{F}\right) \tag{32}$$

where $\psi_{\rho/\rho^*}(x)$ is defined by (15) with $c=\rho/\rho^*$. Examples of the functions $f^*(x)$ and $p^*(x)$ are given in Figures 4, 5.

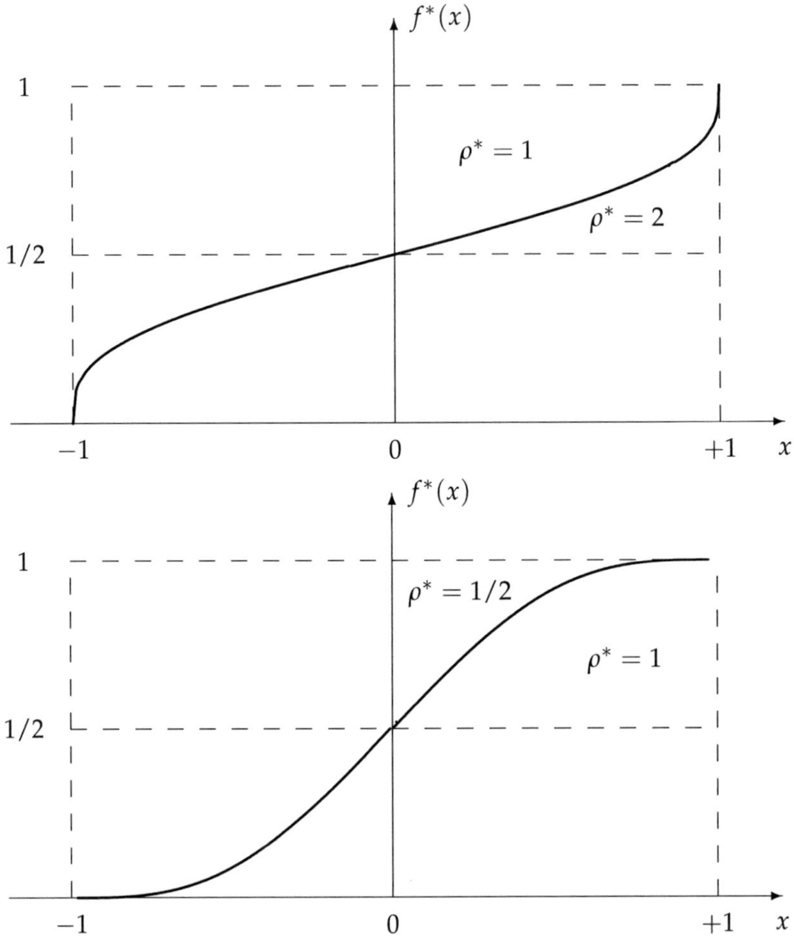

Figure 4. Examples of the PDs f^*, when $(F, F^*) = (FG_{0,1}, FG_{0,\rho^*})$.

Suppose that $F^* = F$. Then

$$f^*(x) = F\Big(F^{-1}\Big(\frac{x+1}{2}\Big)\Big) = \frac{x+1}{2}, \; p^*(x) = \frac{d}{dx}\frac{x+1}{2} = \frac{1}{2} \tag{33}$$

and

$$f^* = \Big(\frac{x+1}{2}, \; x \in \mathsf{F}\Big), \; p^* = \Big(\frac{1}{2}, \; x \in \mathsf{F}\Big) \tag{34}$$

i.e., X is a random variable, uniformly distributed over the set F. If the vector $\boldsymbol{x}$ is stored, then the database is perfectly protected against attackers, who want to guess its content. If $F^* \neq F$, then we get an approximate uniform distribution. However, $\boldsymbol{r} \to \boldsymbol{x}$ is a one-to-one mapping, and the attackers, who have access to the database, can reconstruct the vector $\boldsymbol{r}$.

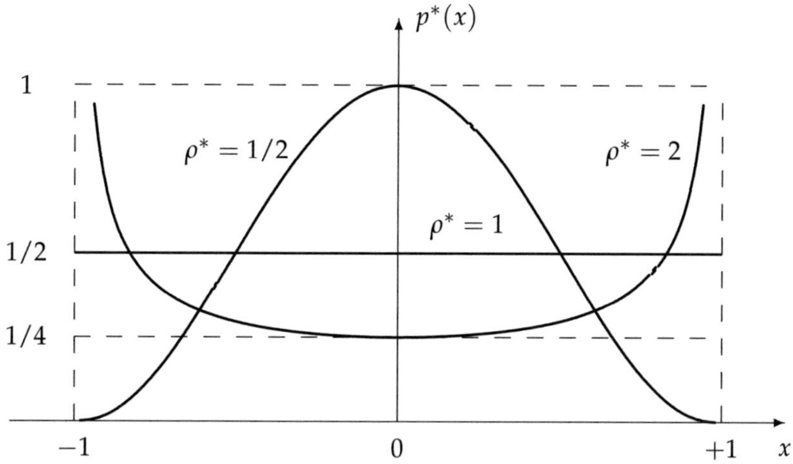

Figure 5. Examples of the PDFs p^*, when $(F, F^*) = (FG_{0,1}, FG_{0,\rho^*})$.

Our assumption that the vector $\boldsymbol{r}$ is generated by a known stationary memoryless source, and the value of the PDF, associated with this vector, is expressed by (8), can contradict to the practice. If the source is non–stationary, and $P_1^*(r_1), \ldots, P_n^*(r_n)$ replace the multipliers at the right-hand side of (8), then considerations above are directly extended by replacing the function F with the functions

$$F_t = \Big(F_t(r) = \Pr\{ R_t < r \}, r \in \mathsf{R} \Big), \quad t = 1, \ldots, n \tag{35}$$

that approximate the PDs of components of the input vector. A more general assignment corresponds to the sources with memory, when the PDs and the PDFs are given as

$$F^*(\boldsymbol{r}_{t-1}) = \Big(F(r|\boldsymbol{r}_{t-1}) = \Pr_{\text{data}} \{ R_t < r \,|\, (R_1, \ldots, R_{t-1}) = \boldsymbol{r}_{t-1} \}, r \in \mathsf{R} \Big) \tag{36}$$

$$P^*(\boldsymbol{r}_{t-1}) = \Big(P(r|\boldsymbol{r}_{t-1}) = \frac{d}{dr} F(r|\boldsymbol{r}_{t-1}), r \in \mathsf{R} \Big) \tag{37}$$

where $\boldsymbol{r}_{t-1} = (r_1, \ldots, r_{t-1})$ and $t = 1, \ldots, n$. Then

$$\text{PDF}(\boldsymbol{r}) = \prod_{t=1}^{n} P^*(r_t|\boldsymbol{r}_{t-1}) \tag{38}$$

Let

$$x_t = 2F_t(r_t) - 1, \; r_t(x_t) = F_t^{-1}\Big(\frac{x_t+1}{2}\Big) \tag{39}$$

and $\boldsymbol{x}_{t-1} = (x_1,\dots,x_{t-1}), r(\boldsymbol{x}_{t-1}) = (r_1(x_1),\dots,r_{t-1}(x_{t-1}))$. We also denote

$$f^*(\boldsymbol{x}_{t-1}) = \Big(f(x|\boldsymbol{x}_{t-1}) = \Pr_{\text{data}}\{X_t < x \,|\, (X_1,\dots,X_{t-1}) = \boldsymbol{x}_{t-1}\},\; x \in \mathsf{F}\Big) \tag{40}$$

$$p^*(\boldsymbol{x}_{t-1}) = \Big(p(x|\boldsymbol{x}_{t-1}) = \frac{d}{dx}f(x|\boldsymbol{x}_{t-1}),\; x \in \mathsf{F}\Big) \tag{41}$$

Then

$$f^*(\boldsymbol{x}_{t-1}) = \Big(F_t^*(r_t(x)|r(\boldsymbol{x}_{t-1})),\; x \in \mathsf{F}\Big) \tag{42}$$

$$p^*(\boldsymbol{x}_{t-1}) = \Big(\frac{P^*(r_t(x)|r(\boldsymbol{x}_{t-1}))}{2P_t(r_t(x))},\; x \in \mathsf{F}\Big) \tag{43}$$

These formulas allow us to extend statistical properties of the F-transformation of the input data to the general case.

4. The F-transformation of noisy observations of the input data

Let us denote

$$\varphi_x = \Big(\varphi(y|x) = \Pr_{\text{noise}}\{2F(R') - 1 < y \,|\, 2F(R) - 1 = x\},\, y \in \mathsf{F}\Big) \tag{44}$$

$$v_x = \Big(v(y|x) = \frac{d}{dy}\varphi(y|x),\, y \in \mathsf{F}\Big) \tag{45}$$

for all $x \in \mathsf{F}$. If $(\Phi_r, V_r) = (F\mathsf{G}_{r,\sigma}, \mathsf{G}_{r,\sigma})$ for all $r \in \mathsf{R}$, then the observation channel is an additive white Gaussian noise channel having the variance of the noise equal to σ^2.

Let us map an $r' \in \mathsf{R}$ to the $y \in \mathsf{F}$ in the same way as an $r \in \mathsf{R}$ was mapped to the $x \in \mathsf{F}$, i.e., $y = 2F(r') - 1$ and $r' = r(y)$, where $r(y) = F^{-1}\big(\frac{y+1}{2}\big)$. Notice that the value of y is the observation of the random variable $Y = 2F(R') - 1$ having the conditional PD φ_x and the conditional PDF v_x, given $X = x$, since $2F(R') - 1$ is a deterministic function of the random variable R'. The result of the F-transformation of the vector $\boldsymbol{r}' \in \mathsf{R}^n$, will be understood is the vector $(2F(r_1') - 1,\dots,2F(r_n') - 1)$.

One can see that the stochastic dependence between random variables R and R' is translated to the stochastic dependence between random variables X and Y in such a way that

$$\begin{aligned}\varphi(y|x) &= \Pr_{\text{noise}}\{Y < y \,|\, X = x\} = \Pr_{\text{noise}}\Big\{2F(R') - 1 < y \,|\, 2F(R) - 1 = x\Big\} \\ &= \Pr_{\text{noise}}\Big\{R' < F^{-1}\Big(\frac{y+1}{2}\Big) \,\Big|\, R = F^{-1}\Big(\frac{x+1}{2}\Big)\Big\} \\ &= \Pr_{\text{noise}}\{R' < r(y) \,|\, R = r(x)\} = \Phi(r(y)|r(x))\end{aligned} \tag{46}$$

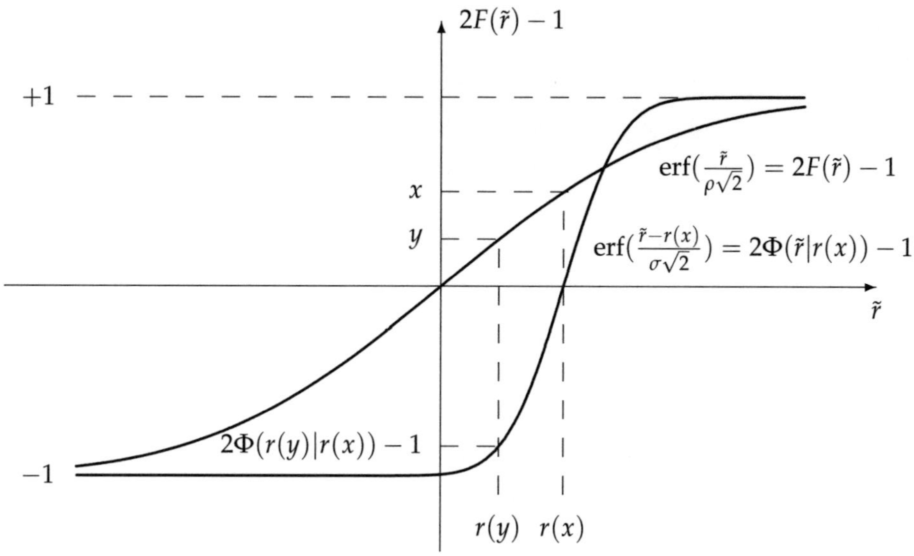

Figure 6. Illustration of the computation of the probability $\Phi(r(y)|r(x))$ for a given pair $(x,y) \in \mathsf{F} \times \mathsf{F}$, when $F = FG_{0,1}$.

and

$$\begin{aligned} v(y|x) &= \frac{d}{dy} \Pr_{\text{noise}} \{ Y < y \,|\, X = x \} = \frac{d}{dy} \Phi(r(y)|r(x)) \\ &= \frac{d}{d\tilde{r}} \Phi(\tilde{r}|r(x)) \Big|_{\tilde{r}=r(y)} \cdot \frac{d}{dy} r(y) = V(r(y)|r(x)) \cdot \frac{d}{dy} F^{-1}\Big(\frac{y+1}{2}\Big) \\ &= V(r(y)|r(x)) \cdot \Big(\frac{d}{d\tilde{r}} F(\tilde{r}) \Big|_{\tilde{r}=r(y)} \Big)^{-1} \cdot \frac{d}{dy} \frac{y+1}{2} = \frac{V(r(y)|r(x))}{2P(r(y))} \end{aligned} \tag{47}$$

Therefore the conditional PDs and the conditional PDFs are specified as

$$\varphi_x = \Big(\Phi(r(y)|r(x)),\, y \in \mathsf{F} \Big), \;\; v_x = \Big(\frac{V(r(y)|r(x))}{2P(r(y))},\, y \in \mathsf{F} \Big) \tag{48}$$

for all $x \in \mathsf{F}$. By (11) and the fact that the F-transformation is a component-wise mapping, the value of the PDF, associated with the vector $\boldsymbol{y}$, given the vector $\boldsymbol{x}$, is expressed as

$$\mathrm{PDF}(\boldsymbol{y}|\boldsymbol{x}) = \prod_{t=1}^{n} \frac{V(r(y_t)|r(x_t))}{2P(r(y_t))} \tag{49}$$

for all $\boldsymbol{x}, \boldsymbol{y} \in \mathsf{F}^n$.

The computation of the PDs φ_x is illustrated in Figure 6 for Gaussian data, and examples of functions constructed using this procedure are given in Figures 7, 8.

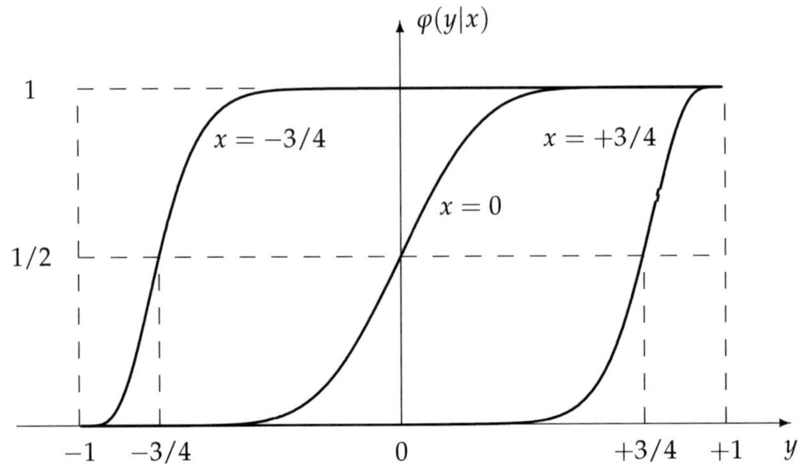

Figure 7. Examples of the conditional PDs φ_x, when $(F, \Phi_r) = (FG_{0,1}, FG_{r,1/4})$.

If the observation channel is an additive channel, then $V(r'|r)$ depends only on the absolute value of the difference $r' - r$. It is also usually assumed that

$$V(r'|r) \text{ is a monotone decreasing function of } |r' - r| \tag{50}$$

and

$$\max_{r' \in \mathsf{R}} V(r'|r) = V(r|r) = \text{Const} \tag{51}$$

In particular, Const $= 1/(\sigma\sqrt{2\pi})$ for additive white Gaussian noise channels having the variance of the noise equal to σ^2.

We include transformations at the input/output of the channel and create another channel $\boldsymbol{x} \to \boldsymbol{y}$ whose conditional PDFs essentially depend on the magnitude of the input symbols. This point is illustrated in Figures 7, 8: the slope of the function $\varphi(x|x)$ increases with $|x|$, and $v(x|x)$ tends to the δ-function, as $x \to \pm 1$. Notice that the behavior of functions under considerations is completely determined by the description of physical channel and the chosen function F, and it is not affected by the PD F^*, which can be unknown.

By (51),

$$\frac{V(r(y)|r(x))}{2P(r(y))}\bigg|_{y=x} = \frac{V(r(x)|r(x))}{2P(r(x))} = \frac{\text{Const}}{2P(r(x))} \tag{52}$$

Suppose that, for any $\varepsilon > 0$, there is an $r_\varepsilon \in \mathsf{R}$ such that $|r| > r_\varepsilon$ implies $P(r) \le \varepsilon$. Then

$$|r(x)| > r_\varepsilon \Rightarrow \frac{V(r(y)|r(x))}{2P(r(y))}\bigg|_{y=x} \ge \frac{\text{Const}}{2\varepsilon} \tag{53}$$

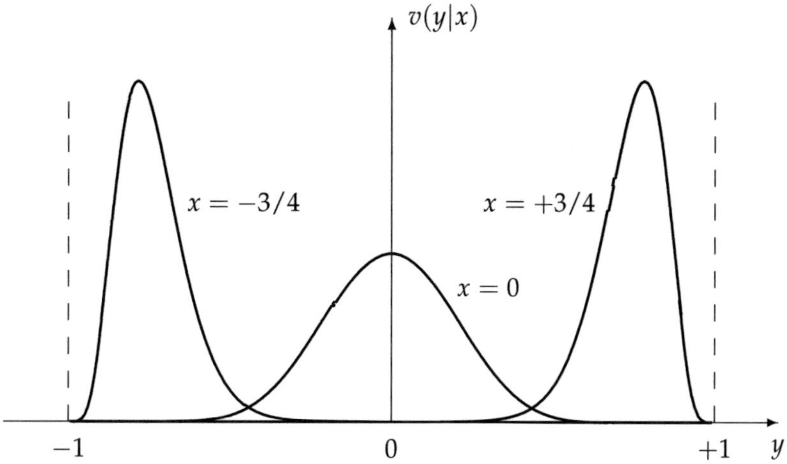

Figure 8. Examples of the conditional PDFs v_x, when $(F, \Phi_r) = (FG_{0,1}, FG_{r,1/4})$.

and the expression at the right-hand side tends to infinity, as $\varepsilon \to 0$, i.e., the created channel becomes noiseless. In other words, we preserve significant components of the vector $\boldsymbol{r}$ in noisy observations for a wide class of observation channels.

If $\Phi_r = FG_{r,\sigma}$, then

$$\varphi(y|x) = \frac{1}{2} + \frac{1}{2}\mathrm{erf}\Big(\frac{r(y) - r(x)}{\sigma\sqrt{2}}\Big), \quad v(y|x) = \frac{1}{2P(r(y))}\mathrm{G}_{r(x),\sigma}(r(y)) \tag{54}$$

and if $F = FG_{0,\rho}$, then these equalities can be continued as

$$\varphi(y|x) = \frac{1}{2} + \frac{1}{2}\mathrm{erf}\Big(\frac{\rho}{\sigma}\Big(\mathrm{erf}^{-1}(y) - \mathrm{erf}^{-1}(x)\Big)\Big) \tag{55}$$

$$v(y|x) = \frac{\rho}{2\sigma}\exp\Big\{-\frac{\rho^2}{\sigma^2}\Big(\mathrm{erf}^{-1}(y) - \mathrm{erf}^{-1}(x)\Big)^2 + \Big(\mathrm{erf}^{-1}(y)\Big)^2\Big\} \tag{56}$$

as it follows from (23). We also write

$$(F, \Phi_r) = (FG_{0,\rho}, FG_{r,\sigma}) \Rightarrow \frac{\mathrm{Const}}{2P(r(x))} = \frac{\rho}{2\sigma}E(x) \tag{57}$$

where

$$E(x) = \exp\Big\{\frac{r^2(x)}{2\rho^2}\Big\} = \exp\Big\{\Big(\mathrm{erf}^{-1}(x)\Big)^2\Big\} \tag{58}$$

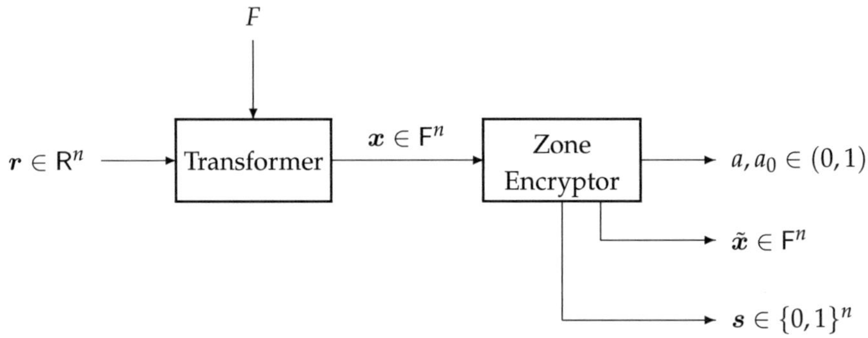

Figure 9. Processing the vector $\boldsymbol{r}$ at the enrollment stage with zone encryption.

does not depend on ρ. By (52), the expression at the right-hand side of (57) specifies the value of $v(x|x)$. The function $E(x)$ is minimized at $x = 0$ and tends to infinity, as $x \to \pm 1$ (see Table 2). Thus, the PDF v_x tends to the δ-function, as $x \to \pm 1$. The speed of convergence is proportional to the ratio $\rho/(2\sigma)$.

The derived formulas will be used in the evaluation of verification performance, but some preliminary estimates can be already presented. Namely, let us fix a $\lambda \in (0,1)$ and, for all $x \in (0,1)$, denote

$$\Delta_x(\lambda) = x - y_\lambda \tag{59}$$

where y_λ is the solution to the equation $\varphi(y_\lambda|x) = \lambda$ and the function $\varphi(y|x)$ is expressed in (55). Furthermore, let

$$\Lambda_x = \Pr_{\text{noise}} \{Y < 0 \,|\, X = x\} = \varphi(0|x) = \psi_{-\rho/\sigma}(x) \tag{60}$$

where the function $\psi(x)$ is defined in (15) for $c = -\rho/\sigma$. By the symmetry properties, Λ_x is the probability that the input symbol, having the magnitude x, changes the sign after the symbol is transmitted over the $X \to Y$ channel. The probability that $Y < x - \Delta_x(\lambda)$ is equal to λ, when $+x$ is transmitted. The probability that $Y > -x + \Delta_x(\lambda)$ is also equal to λ, when $-x$ is transmitted. The numerical illustration is included in Table 2 for $(\rho,\sigma) = (1, 1/4)$. For example, if $x = 0.90$, then $Y < 0$ with the probability $2.4 \cdot 10^{-11}$ and components of the vector $(10^{-2}, 10^{-4}, 10^{-8}, 10^{-16})$ are the probabilities of the events $Y < 0.90 - (0.19, 0.37, 0.71, 1.22) = (+0.71, +0.53, +0.19, -0.32)$. Comparison of parameters above for different x allows us to conclude that the increase of the magnitude of the transmitted symbol leads to essential improvement over the channel having the input alphabet (-1,+1) and the output alphabet {-,+}.

5. Constructing the wrapped versions of input data and verification over noisy observations

We believe that there is a large variety of verification schemes that can be constructed on the basis of statistical properties of the probabilistic ensemble (X, Y). We modify the scheme in

x	E(x)	Λ_x	$\Delta_x(10^{-2})$	$\Delta_x(10^{-4})$	$\Delta_x(10^{-8})$	$\Delta_x(10^{-16})$
0	1.00	0.5	0.44	0.65	0.84	0.96
0.25	1.05	0.1	0.46	0.71	0.97	1.17
0.50	1.25	$3.5 \cdot 10^{-3}$	0.43	0.70	1.03	1.33
0.75	1.94	$2.1 \cdot 10^{-6}$	0.32	0.58	0.95	1.38
0.80	2.22	$1.5 \cdot 10^{-7}$	0.28	0.52	0.90	1.36
0.85	2.82	$4.3 \cdot 10^{-9}$	0.24	0.46	0.82	1.31
0.90	3.87	$2.4 \cdot 10^{-11}$	0.19	0.37	0.71	1.22
0.91	4.21	$5.9 \cdot 10^{-12}$	0.18	0.35	0.68	1.19
0.92	4.63	$1.3 \cdot 10^{-12}$	0.16	0.33	0.65	1.16
0.93	5.16	$2.1 \cdot 10^{-13}$	0.15	0.31	0.61	1.12
0.94	5.86	$2.7 \cdot 10^{-14}$	0.13	0.28	0.57	1.08
0.95	6.82	$2.3 \cdot 10^{-15}$	0.12	0.25	0.53	1.03
0.96	8.24	$< 10^{-15}$	0.10	0.22	0.48	0.96
0.97	10.53	$< 10^{-15}$	0.08	0.18	0.41	0.88
0.98	14.97	$< 10^{-15}$	0.06	0.14	0.34	0.77
0.99	27.59	$< 10^{-15}$	0.04	0.09	0.23	0.59

Table 2. Some values of $E(x)$, Λ_x, and $\Delta_x(\lambda)$ for $(\rho, \sigma) = (1, 1/4)$.

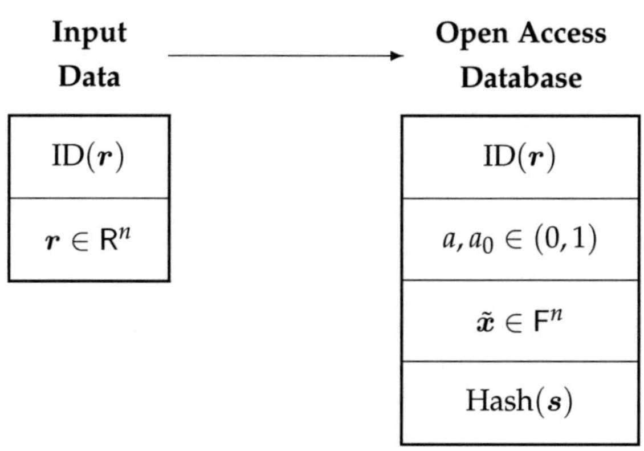

Figure 10. Mapping of the input data to the data stored in an open access database.

Figure 1a and introduce the so–called zone encryption (see Figure 9),

$$\boldsymbol{x} \rightarrow \Big((a, a_0), \tilde{\boldsymbol{x}}, \boldsymbol{s} \Big) \tag{61}$$

where $a, a_0 \in (0,1)$, $a > a_0$; $\tilde{\boldsymbol{x}} = (\tilde{x}_1, \ldots, \tilde{x}_n) \in \mathsf{F}^n$; $\boldsymbol{s} = (s_1, \ldots, s_n) \in \{0,1\}^n$. If $\mathrm{ID}(\boldsymbol{r})$ is the identifier of the person whose data are given by the vector $\boldsymbol{r}$, then the enrollment is represented as the mapping

$$\Big(\mathrm{ID}(\boldsymbol{r}), \boldsymbol{r} \Big) \rightarrow \Big(\mathrm{ID}(\boldsymbol{r}), (a, a_0), \tilde{\boldsymbol{x}}, \mathrm{Hash}(\boldsymbol{s}) \Big) \tag{62}$$

where the function Hash is a cryptographic "one–way" function having the property that one can easily find the value of the function for the given argument, but the inversion (finding the argument for the known value of the function) is practically impossible. The parameters at the right-hand side are stored in an open access database (see Figure 10).

The use of "the zone encryption", is caused by the point that we partition the $(-1,+1)$ interval into 5 zones: Significant$^{+/-}$ zones $(\mathrm{Sg}^+, \mathrm{Sg}^-)$, Buffer $^{+/-}$ zones $(\mathrm{Bf}^+, \mathrm{Bf}^-)$, Zero zone (Zr), where

$$\begin{cases} \mathrm{Sg}^+ = (+a, +1), \mathrm{Sg}^- = (-1, -a) \\ \mathrm{Bf}^+ = (+a_0, +a), \mathrm{Bf}^- = (-a, -a_0) \\ \mathrm{Zr} = (-a_0, +a_0) \end{cases} \tag{63}$$

Let the notation $\tilde{x}_t \sim \mathrm{U}(+a, +1)$ be understood in such a way that the value of $\tilde{x}_t$ is chosen at random using a uniform PD over the $(+a, +1)$ interval. Similarly, if $\tilde{x}_t \sim \mathrm{U}(-1, -a)$, then the value of $\tilde{x}_t$ is chosen at random using a uniform PD over the $(-1, -a)$ interval. If $\boldsymbol{x}$ is the wrapped version of the vector $\boldsymbol{r}$, constructed by the F-transformation, then we set

$$\begin{cases} \tilde{x}_t = x_t, & \text{if } x_t \in \mathrm{Sg}^+ \cup \mathrm{Sg}^- \\ \tilde{x}_t \sim \mathrm{U}(-1, -a), & \text{if } x_t \in \mathrm{Bf}^+ \\ \tilde{x}_t \sim \mathrm{U}(+a, +1), & \text{if } x_t \in \mathrm{Bf}^- \\ \tilde{x}_t = 0, & \text{if } x_t \in \mathrm{Zr} \end{cases} \tag{64}$$

Therefore components of the vector $\boldsymbol{x}$, belonging to the Significant zones, are unchanged and components, belonging to the Zero zone, are set to zero. Components, belonging to the Buffer zones, are changed in such a way that the results belong to the Significant zones with different signs. The presented procedure is illustrated in Figure 11, and the binary vector $\boldsymbol{s}$ having components

$$s_t = \begin{cases} 1, \text{ if } x_t \in \mathrm{Sg}^+ \cup \mathrm{Sg}^- \\ 0, \text{ if } x_t \notin \mathrm{Sg}^+ \cup \mathrm{Sg}^- \end{cases} \tag{65}$$

specifies the Significant zones.

http://dx.doi.org/10.5772/51800

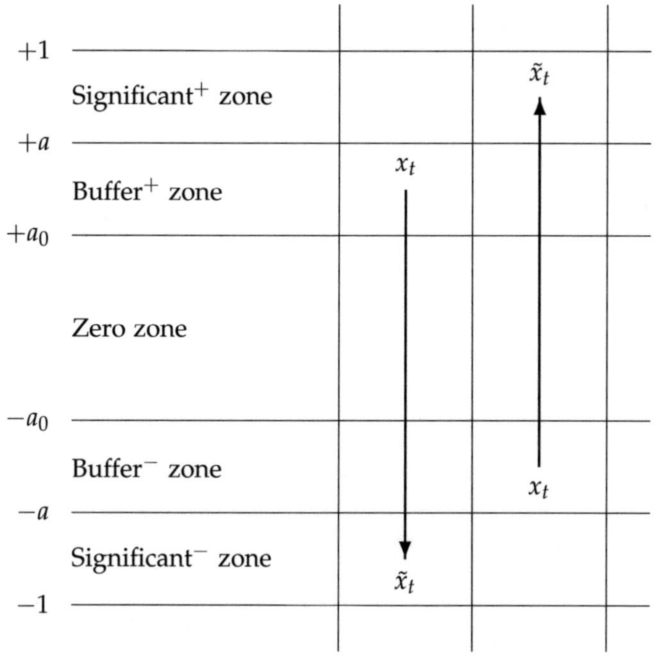

Figure 11. Partitioning of the $(-1, +1)$ interval into zones and illustration of the mapping $x_t \to \tilde{x}_t$, when x_t belongs to the Buffer zones.

The zone encryption can be introduced as representation of the vector $\boldsymbol{x}$ by the sum of three vectors,

$$\boldsymbol{x} = \boldsymbol{x}^{(\mathrm{Sg})} + \boldsymbol{x}^{(\mathrm{Bf})} + \boldsymbol{x}^{(\mathrm{Zr})} \tag{66}$$

constructed as follows: set $x_t^{(\mathrm{Sg})} = x_t^{(\mathrm{Bf})} = x_t^{(\mathrm{Zr})} = 0$ for all $t = 1, \ldots, n$ and use the rules

$$\begin{cases} x_t^{(\mathrm{Sg})} = x_t, \text{ if } x_t \in \mathrm{Sg}^+ \cup \mathrm{Sg}^- \\ x_t^{(\mathrm{Bf})} = x_t, \text{ if } x_t \in \mathrm{Bf}^+ \cup \mathrm{Bf}^- \\ x_t^{(\mathrm{Zr})} = x_t, \text{ if } x_t \in \mathrm{Zr} \end{cases} \tag{67}$$

The vector $\tilde{\boldsymbol{x}}$ can be also represented by the sum of three vectors,

$$\tilde{\boldsymbol{x}} = \tilde{\boldsymbol{x}}^{(\mathrm{Sg})} + \tilde{\boldsymbol{x}}^{(\mathrm{Bf})} + \tilde{\boldsymbol{x}}^{(\mathrm{Zr})} \tag{68}$$

	$(\mathbf{a}, \mathbf{a_0}) = (.88, .76)$							
$\boldsymbol{x}$	$+.68$	$-.77$	$+.91$	$+.24$	$-.98$	$+.08$	$-.52$	$-.81$
$\boldsymbol{x}^{(\text{Sg})}$			$+.91$		$-.98$			
$\boldsymbol{x}^{(\text{Bf})}$		$-.77$						$-.81$
$\boldsymbol{x}^{(\text{Zr})}$	$+.68$			$+.24$		$+.08$	$-.52$	
$\tilde{\boldsymbol{x}}^{(\text{Sg})}$			$+.91$		$-.98$			
$\tilde{\boldsymbol{x}}^{(\text{Bf})}$		$+.90$						$+.95$
$\tilde{\boldsymbol{x}}^{(\text{Zr})}$	0			0		0	0	
$\tilde{\boldsymbol{x}}$	0	$+.90$	$+.91$	0	$-.98$	0	0	$+.95$
$\boldsymbol{s}$	0	0	1	0	1	0	0	0

Table 3. Example of the zone encryption where gaps contain zeroes.

where we first set $\tilde{x}_t^{(\text{Sg})} = \tilde{x}_t^{(\text{Bf})} = \tilde{x}_t^{(\text{Zr})} = 0$ for all $t = 1, \ldots, n$ and then set

$$\begin{cases} \tilde{x}_t^{(\text{Sg})} = x_t^{(\text{Sg})}, & \text{if } x_t \in \text{Sg}^+ \cup \text{Sg}^- \\ \tilde{x}_t^{(\text{Bf})} \sim \text{U}(-1, -a), & \text{if } x_t \in \text{Bf}^+ \\ \tilde{x}_t^{(\text{Bf})} \sim \text{U}(+a, +1), & \text{if } x_t \in \text{Bf}^- \\ \tilde{x}_t^{(\text{Zr})} = 0, & \text{if } x_t \in \text{Zr} \end{cases} \tag{69}$$

Thus, the t-th component of the vector $\tilde{\boldsymbol{x}}$ is either equal to 0, or belongs to the set $\text{Sg}^+ \cup \text{Sg}^-$. Furthermore, $\tilde{x}_t > 0$ implies $\tilde{x}_t \in \text{Sg}^+$, and $\tilde{x}_t < 0$ implies $\tilde{x}_t \in \text{Sg}^-$. Thus, $n = n^{(\text{Sg})}(\tilde{\boldsymbol{x}}) + n^{(\text{Zr})}(\tilde{\boldsymbol{x}})$, where

$$n^{(\text{Sg})}(\tilde{\boldsymbol{x}}) = \Big\{ t \in \{1, \ldots, n\} : \tilde{x}_t \in \text{Sg}^+ \cup \text{Sg}^- \Big\} \tag{70}$$

$$n^{(\text{Zr})}(\tilde{\boldsymbol{x}}) = \Big\{ t \in \{1, \ldots, n\} : \tilde{x}_t = 0 \Big\} \tag{71}$$

Moreover, $n^{(\text{Sg})}(\tilde{\boldsymbol{x}}) = n^{(\text{Sg})}(\boldsymbol{x}) + n^{(\text{Bf})}(\boldsymbol{x})$, where $n^{(\text{Sg})}(\boldsymbol{x}) = |\,\mathcal{T}^{(\text{Sg})}(\boldsymbol{x})\,|$, $n^{(\text{Bf})}(\boldsymbol{x}) = |\,\mathcal{T}^{(\text{Bf})}(\boldsymbol{x})\,|$, and

$$\mathcal{T}^{(\text{Sg})}(\boldsymbol{x}) = \Big\{ t \in \{1, \ldots, n\} : x_t \in \text{Sg}^+ \cup \text{Sg}^- \Big\} \tag{72}$$

$$\mathcal{T}^{(\text{Bf})}(\boldsymbol{x}) = \Big\{ t \in \{1, \ldots, n\} : x_t \in \text{Bf}^+ \cup \text{Bf}^- \Big\} \tag{73}$$

The numerical example of the zone encryption is given in Table 3. Since $|-.77|$, $|-.81| \in (.76, .88) = (a_0, a)$, the 2-nd and the 8-th components of the vector $\boldsymbol{x}$ belong to the Buffer zones. The encryptor replaces these components by numbers chosen at random from the $(+.88,+1)$ interval. For example, $-.77 \to +.90$ and $-.81 \to +.95$. The vector

$$\tilde{\boldsymbol{x}} = (0,+.90,+.91,0,-.98,0,0,+.95) \tag{74}$$

and the hidden version of the vector $\boldsymbol{s} = (0,0,1,0,1,0,0,0)$ are stored in the database.

Similarly to (63), let us introduce the sets

$$\begin{cases} \text{rSg}^+ = (r(+a),r(+1)),\ \text{rSg}^- = (r(-1),r(-a)) \\ \text{rBf}^+ = (r(+a_0),r(+a)),\ \text{rBf}^- = (r(-a),r(-a_0)) \\ \text{rZr} = (r(-a_0),r(+a_0)) \end{cases} \tag{75}$$

where the function $r(x), x \in \mathsf{F}$, is defined in (22). It is important to notice that the same vector $\tilde{\boldsymbol{x}}$ encrypts many vectors $\boldsymbol{r}$ and

$$\tilde{x}_t \in \text{Sg}^+ \Rightarrow r_t \in \text{rSg}^+ \cup \text{rBf}^-,\ \tilde{x}_t \in \text{Sg}^- \Rightarrow r_t \in \text{rSg}^- \cup \text{rBf}^+,\ \tilde{x}_t = 0 \Rightarrow r_t \in \text{rZr} \tag{76}$$

If $\tilde{x}_t \in \text{Sg}^+$, then the conclusion, whether r_t belongs to the sets rSg^+ or rBf^-, is specified by the t-th component of the vector $\boldsymbol{s}$, which is hidden from the attacker. Similarly, if $\tilde{x}_t \in \text{Sg}^-$, then the conclusion, whether r_t belongs to the sets rSg^- or rBf^+, is also specified by the t-th component of the vector $\boldsymbol{s}$. The total number of variants is equal to $2^{n^{(\text{Sg})}(\tilde{\boldsymbol{x}})}$. All of them are presented in Table 4 for the vector $\tilde{\boldsymbol{x}}$, defined in (74). For example, if $F = FG_{0,1}$, then $(r(.88),r(.76)) = (1.55,1.17)$ and $r_2,r_3,r_8 \in (+1.55,+\infty) \cup (-1.55,-1.17)$, $r_5 \in (-\infty,-1.55) \cup (+1.17,+1.55)$, $r_1,r_4,r_6,r_7 \in (-1.17,+1.17)$.

If we construct a uniform probability distribution at the enrolment stage by using the F-transformation, then all variants are equivalent, and the probability of the correct guess of the vector $\boldsymbol{s}$ by an attacker, who knows the vector $\tilde{\boldsymbol{x}}$, is equal to

$$P_{\text{att}}(\tilde{\boldsymbol{x}}) = 2^{-n^{(\text{Sg})}(\tilde{\boldsymbol{x}})} = 2^{-(n^{(\text{Sg})}(\boldsymbol{x})+n^{(\text{Bf})}(\boldsymbol{x}))} \tag{77}$$

and the value of the sum $n^{(\text{Sg})}(\boldsymbol{x}) + n^{(\text{Bf})}(\boldsymbol{x})$ is a function of the vector $\boldsymbol{x}$ and the pair (a,a_0).

Notice that the randomization at the enrollment stage can be replaced by deterministic mappings $\text{Bf}^+ \to \text{Sg}^-$ and $\text{Bf}^- \to \text{Sg}^+$. For example, if the Significant and the Buffer zones have equal sizes, i.e., if $1-a = a-a_0$, then one can follow the rules: if $x_t \in \text{Bf}^+$, then $\tilde{x}_t = -a-(x_t-a_0)$; if $x_t \in \text{Bf}^-$, then $\tilde{x}_t = +a+(a_0-x_t)$.

Let us introduce the decoding as the mapping

$$\Big(\boldsymbol{y},(a,a_0),\tilde{\boldsymbol{x}}\Big) \to \hat{\boldsymbol{s}} \in \{0,1\}^n \tag{78}$$

				$(\mathbf{a}, \mathbf{a_0}) = (.88, .76)$			
s_2	s_3	s_5	s_8	$\tilde{x}_2 = +.90$	$\tilde{x}_3 = +.91$	$\tilde{x}_5 = -.98$	$\tilde{x}_8 = +.95$
0	0	0	0	$r_2 \in \text{rBf}^-$	$r_3 \in \text{rBf}^-$	$r_5 \in \text{rBf}^+$	$r_8 \in \text{rBf}^-$
0	0	0	1	$r_2 \in \text{rBf}^-$	$r_3 \in \text{rBf}^-$	$r_5 \in \text{rBf}^+$	$r_8 \in \text{rSg}^+$
0	0	1	0	$r_2 \in \text{rBf}^-$	$r_3 \in \text{rBf}^-$	$r_5 \in \text{rSg}^-$	$r_8 \in \text{rBf}^-$
0	0	1	1	$r_2 \in \text{rBf}^-$	$r_3 \in \text{rBf}^-$	$r_5 \in \text{rSg}^-$	$r_8 \in \text{rSg}^+$
0	1	0	0	$r_2 \in \text{rBf}^-$	$r_3 \in \text{rSg}^+$	$r_5 \in \text{rBf}^+$	$r_8 \in \text{rBf}^-$
0	1	0	1	$r_2 \in \text{rBf}^-$	$r_3 \in \text{rSg}^+$	$r_5 \in \text{rBf}^+$	$r_8 \in \text{rSg}^+$
0	1	1	0	$r_2 \in \text{rBf}^-$	$r_3 \in \text{rSg}^+$	$r_5 \in \text{rSg}^-$	$r_8 \in \text{rBf}^-$
0	1	1	1	$r_2 \in \text{rBf}^-$	$r_3 \in \text{rSg}^+$	$r_5 \in \text{rSg}^-$	$r_8 \in \text{rSg}^+$
1	0	0	0	$r_2 \in \text{rSg}^+$	$r_3 \in \text{rBf}^-$	$r_5 \in \text{rBf}^+$	$r_8 \in \text{rBf}^-$
1	0	0	1	$r_2 \in \text{rSg}^+$	$r_3 \in \text{rBf}^-$	$r_5 \in \text{rBf}^+$	$r_8 \in \text{rSg}^+$
1	0	1	0	$r_2 \in \text{rSg}^+$	$r_3 \in \text{rBf}^-$	$r_5 \in \text{rSg}^-$	$r_8 \in \text{rBf}^-$
1	0	1	1	$r_2 \in \text{rSg}^+$	$r_3 \in \text{rBf}^-$	$r_5 \in \text{rSg}^-$	$r_8 \in \text{rSg}^+$
1	1	0	0	$r_2 \in \text{rSg}^+$	$r_3 \in \text{rSg}^+$	$r_5 \in \text{rBf}^+$	$r_8 \in \text{rBf}^-$
1	1	0	1	$r_2 \in \text{rSg}^+$	$r_3 \in \text{rSg}^+$	$r_5 \in \text{rBf}^+$	$r_8 \in \text{rSg}^+$
1	1	1	0	$r_2 \in \text{rSg}^+$	$r_3 \in \text{rSg}^+$	$r_5 \in \text{rSg}^-$	$r_8 \in \text{rBf}^-$
1	1	1	1	$r_2 \in \text{rSg}^+$	$r_3 \in \text{rSg}^+$	$r_5 \in \text{rSg}^-$	$r_8 \in \text{rSg}^+$
				$\tilde{x}_1 = \tilde{x}_4 = \tilde{x}_6 = \tilde{x}_7 = 0$			
				$r_1, r_4, r_6, r_7 \in \text{rZr}$			

Table 4. The list of vectors $\boldsymbol{r}$ that are encrypted by the vector $\tilde{\boldsymbol{x}}$, defined in (74).

Let the verifier set $\hat{s}_1 = \cdots = \hat{s}_n = 0$ and, for all $t = 1, \ldots, n$, use the rule:

$$\left.\begin{array}{r} \tilde{x}_t \neq 0 \\ |y_t| > T \\ \text{sgn}(\tilde{x}_t) = \text{sgn}(y_t) \end{array}\right\} \Rightarrow \hat{s}_t = 1 \tag{79}$$

where the value of the threshold T is a function of (a, a_0), which will be specified later. The verifier can then check whether $\text{Hash}(\hat{\boldsymbol{s}})$ is equal to the value of $\text{Hash}(\boldsymbol{s})$, stored in the database, or not. If the answer is positive, then the acceptance decision is made. If the answer is negative, then the rejection decision is made.

Without loss of generality, let us suppose that

http://dx.doi.org/10.5772/51800

$$x_1, \ldots, x_n \in \mathrm{Sg}^+ \cup \mathrm{Bf}^+ \cup \mathrm{Zr} \tag{80}$$

The decoding error in the case, when the vector $\boldsymbol{r}'$ is a noisy version of the vector $\boldsymbol{r}$, occurs in one of two situations (see Figure 12).

E_{10}: $(s_t, \hat{s}_t) = (1,0)$. Then $x_t \in (+a, +1)$, as it follows from (80) and $s_t = 1$. Furthermore, $y_t < +T$, since $\hat{s}_t = 0$ implies that the conditions at the left-hand side of (79) are not satisfied. Hence,

$$x_t - y_t \geq (+a) - (+T) \tag{81}$$

E_{01}: $(s_t, \hat{s}_t) = (0,1)$. Then $x_t \in (+a_0, +a)$, as it follows from (80) and $s_t = 0$, $\hat{s}_t \neq 0$. Furthermore, $y_t < -T$, since $\hat{s}_t = 1$ implies that the conditions at the left-hand side of (79) are satisfied. Hence,

$$x_t - y_t \geq (+a_0) - (-T) \tag{82}$$

If the channel $X_t \to Y_t$ would be an additive channel, then its probabilistic description does not depend on the input to the channel, and the differences at the left-hand sides of (81), (82) specify the magnitudes of the noise. The differences at the right-hand sides give lower bounds on these magnitudes. If $T = (a - a_0)/2$, then these differences are equal. However, as the created channel is not an additive channel, we will use another assignment of T.

The decoding error probability, denoted by $\Lambda(T|\boldsymbol{x})$, can be bounded from above as

$$\Lambda(T|\boldsymbol{x}) \leq \Lambda_{10}(T|\boldsymbol{x}) + \Lambda_{01}(T|\boldsymbol{x}) \tag{83}$$

where

$$\begin{aligned}
\Lambda_{10}(T|\boldsymbol{x}) &= \Pr_{\text{noise}} \{Y_t < +T, \text{ for some } t \in \mathcal{T}^{(\mathrm{Sg})}(\boldsymbol{x}) \,|\, X^n = \boldsymbol{x}\} \\
&= 1 - \Pr_{\text{noise}} \{Y_t \geq +T, \text{ for all } t \in \mathcal{T}^{(\mathrm{Sg})}(\boldsymbol{x}) \,|\, X^n = \boldsymbol{x}\} \\
&= 1 - \prod_{t \in \mathcal{T}^{(\mathrm{Sg})}(\boldsymbol{x})} \Pr_{\text{noise}} \{Y_t \geq +T \,|\, X_t = x_t\} \\
&\leq 1 - \prod_{t \in \mathcal{T}^{(\mathrm{Sg})}(\boldsymbol{x})} \Pr_{\text{noise}} \{Y_t \geq +T \,|\, X_t = +a\} \\
&= 1 - \Big(1 - \varphi(+T \,|\, +a)\Big)^{n^{(\mathrm{Sg})}(\boldsymbol{x})}
\end{aligned} \tag{84}$$

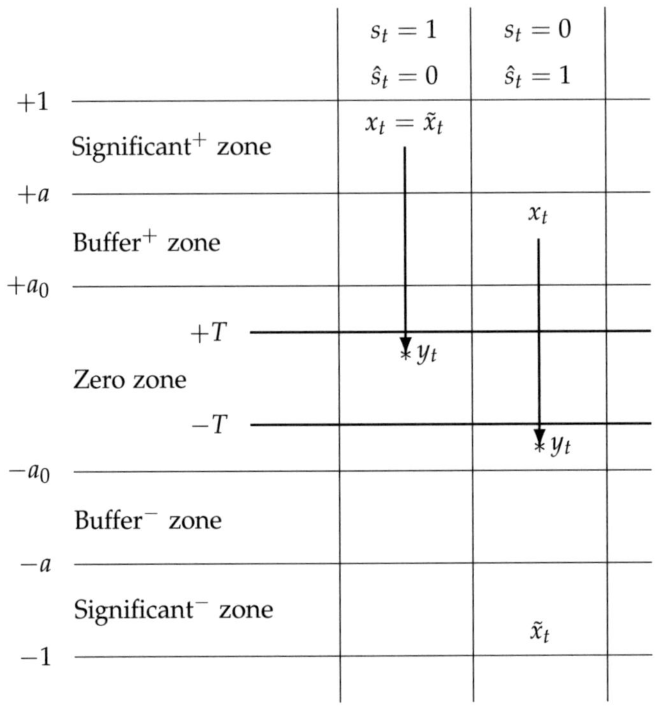

Figure 12. Illustration of the events, when the decoding error occurs and $x_t \in \mathrm{Sg}^+ \cup \mathrm{Bf}^+$.

and

$$\begin{aligned}\Lambda_{01}(T|\boldsymbol{x}) &= \Pr_{\text{noise}}\{Y_t < -T, \text{ for some } t \in \mathcal{T}^{(\mathrm{Bf})}(\boldsymbol{x}) \,|\, X^n = \boldsymbol{x}\} \\ &= 1 - \Pr_{\text{noise}}\{Y_t \geq -T, \text{ for all } t \in \mathcal{T}^{(\mathrm{Bf})}(\boldsymbol{x}) \,|\, X^n = \boldsymbol{x}\} \\ &= 1 - \prod_{t \in \mathcal{T}^{(\mathrm{Bf})}(\boldsymbol{x})} \Pr_{\text{noise}}\{Y_t \geq -T \,|\, X_t = x_t\} \\ &\leq 1 - \prod_{t \in \mathcal{T}^{(\mathrm{Bf})}(\boldsymbol{x})} \Pr_{\text{noise}}\{Y_t \geq -T \,|\, X_t = +a_0\} \\ &= 1 - \Big(1 - \varphi(-T \,|\, +a_0)\Big)^{n^{(\mathrm{Bf})}(\boldsymbol{x})} \end{aligned} \tag{85}$$

The products on t at the right-hand sides are written because the observation channel is memoryless and the inequalities follow from the assumption (50). Notice that, by (55),

$$\varphi(+T|+a) = \frac{1}{2} + \frac{1}{2}\mathrm{erf}\Big(\frac{\rho}{\sigma}\Big(\mathrm{erf}^{-1}(T) - \mathrm{erf}^{-1}(a)\Big)\Big) \tag{86}$$

$$\varphi(-T|+a_0) = \frac{1}{2} - \frac{1}{2}\mathrm{erf}\Big(\frac{\rho}{\sigma}\Big(\mathrm{erf}^{-1}(T) + \mathrm{erf}^{-1}(a_0)\Big)\Big) \tag{87}$$

and assign T in such a way that

$$\Lambda_{10}(T|\boldsymbol{x}) = \Lambda_{01}(T|\boldsymbol{x}) \tag{88}$$

Suppose that there is a blind attacker, who does not have access to the database and wants to pass through the verification stage with the acceptance decision. We also assume that the attacker can fix a small $\delta > 0$ in such a way that $1 - \delta > a$. Let the attacker submit a vector $\boldsymbol{r}'$, which is mapped to the vector $\boldsymbol{y} \in \{-1+\delta, +1-\delta\}^n$, i.e., the t-th component of the vector $\boldsymbol{y}$ is either equal to $-1+\delta$ or $+1-\delta$. Let the decision, whether the t-th component of the vector $\boldsymbol{r}'$ is equal to $r(-1+\delta)$ or $r(+1-\delta)$, be made with probabilities $1/2$. The probability of the acceptance decision is equal to $2^{-n^{(\mathrm{Sg})}(\tilde{\boldsymbol{x}})}$, since the verifier "punctures" $n - n^{(\mathrm{Sg})}(\tilde{\boldsymbol{x}})$ components $\tilde{x}_t$ equal to 0 and sets the t-th component of the binary vector equal to 1 if and only if $\mathrm{sgn}(\tilde{x}_t) = \mathrm{sgn}(y_t)$. By (77), the obtained probability is exactly the same as the probability of success of an attacker, who knows the vector $\tilde{\boldsymbol{x}}$. Thus, we attain the property of a perfect algorithmic secrecy of the designed verification scheme: although the database is open and an attacker may know the vector $\tilde{\boldsymbol{x}}$, he cannot include this information into the guessing strategy.

Suppose that the vector $\boldsymbol{x} \in \mathsf{F}^n$ is generated by a memoryless source according to a uniform probability distribution over the set F. One can see that the probability that there are $i, i_0, n-i-i_0$ components of the vector $\boldsymbol{x}$ whose magnitudes belong to the $(a,1), (a_0,a), (0,a)$ intervals, respectively, is equal to

$$Q_{a,a_0}(i,i_0) = \frac{n!}{i!i_0!(n-i-i_0)!}(1-a)^i(a-a_0)^{i_0}(1-a-a_0)^{n-i-i_0} \tag{89}$$

and

$$\arg \max_{(i,i_0)\in\{0,\ldots,n\},\, i+i_0\le n} Q_{a,a_0}(i,i_0) = \Big(\,(1-a)n,\,(a-a_0)n\,\Big) \tag{90}$$

Hence, the typical distribution of magnitudes under considerations (see Figure 13) is specified as

$$(a,a_0) = \Big(\frac{n-w}{n}, \frac{n-w_0}{n}\Big) \;\Rightarrow\; \Big(\,(1-a)n,\,(a-a_0)n\,\Big) = (w,\, w_0 - w) \tag{91}$$

where $w, w_0 \in \{0,\ldots,n\}$ are integers, fixed in such a way that $w \le w_0$.

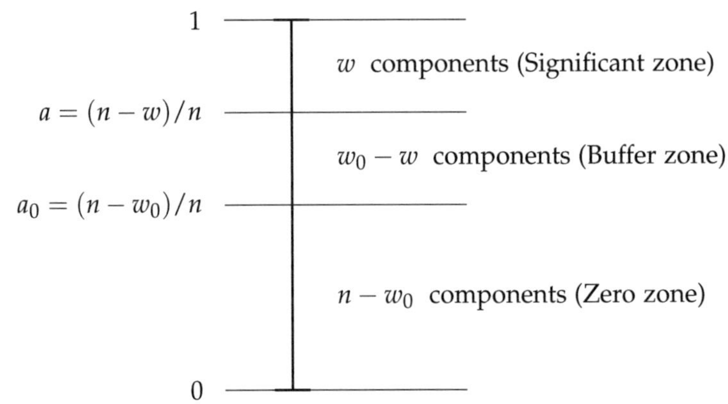

Figure 13. The typical partitioning of the values of magnitudes in three zones.

Let $(w, w_0) = (32, 64)$. Compute (a, a_0) using the expressions at the left-hand side of (91), and consider the typical case when the distribution of magnitudes of components, belonging to the Significant and the Buffer zones, is given by the right-hand side of (91), i.e., there are 32 magnitudes belonging to the Significant zones, $64 - 32 = 32$ magnitudes belonging to the Buffer zones, and $n - 64$ magnitudes belonging to the Zero zone. Thus, the vectors $\boldsymbol{x}$ under consideration are such that $n^{(\mathrm{Sg})}(\boldsymbol{x}) = n^{(\mathrm{Bf})}(\boldsymbol{x}) = 32$. Then (88) is equivalent to the equality $\varphi(+T| + a) = \varphi(-T| + a_0)$. One can see that the equality above implies the assignment

$$\left.\begin{aligned} (F, \Phi_r) = (FG_{0,\rho}, FG_{r,\sigma}) \\ n^{(\mathrm{Sg})}(\boldsymbol{x}) = n^{(\mathrm{Bf})}(\boldsymbol{x}) \end{aligned}\right\} \Rightarrow T = \mathrm{erf}\Big(\frac{\mathrm{erf}^{-1}(a) - \mathrm{erf}^{-1}(a_0)}{2}\Big) \tag{92}$$

independently of ρ and σ. The corresponding vectors $\tilde{\boldsymbol{x}}$ contain $32 + 32 = 64$ non–zero components, and the secrecy of the verification scheme, evaluated by the probability of correct guess of the vector $\boldsymbol{s}$ on the basis of the vector $\tilde{\boldsymbol{x}}$ (see (77)), is equal to 2^{-64}. Notice that if the attacker would know that $n^{(\mathrm{Sg})}(\boldsymbol{x}) = n^{(\mathrm{Bf})}(\boldsymbol{x}) = 32$, then this probability is equal to $\binom{64}{32}^{-1}$. Some numerical results are included in Table 5, and one can see that the decoding error probability is very small even for noisy channels and relatively small lengths.

The presented version of the verification algorithm uses only the signs of components of the vector $\tilde{x}$, and this vector can be transformed further to a ternary vector whose contain either 0 or the sign. An improvement of the performance is attained by using the maximum likelihood decoding rule, when we construct the vector $\hat{\boldsymbol{s}}$ in such a way that

$$\hat{s}_t = \begin{cases} 1, \text{ if } \tilde{x}_t \neq 0,\ v(y_t|\tilde{x}_t) \geq v_{a,a_0}(y_t|\mathrm{sgn}(\tilde{x}_t)) \\ 0, \text{ if } \tilde{x}_t = 0 \text{ or } \tilde{x}_t \neq 0,\ v(y_t|\tilde{x}_t) < v_{a,a_0}(y_t|\mathrm{sgn}(\tilde{x}_t)) \end{cases} \tag{93}$$

http://dx.doi.org/10.5772/51800

				σ				
n	a	a_0	T	1/2	1/3	1/4	1/5	1/6
128	.750	.500	.188	> 1	$1.9 \cdot 10^{-1}$	$8.4 \cdot 10^{-3}$	$1.6 \cdot 10^{-4}$	$1.4 \cdot 10^{-6}$
256	.875	.750	.152	$2.2 \cdot 10^{-1}$	$1.8 \cdot 10^{-3}$	$2.5 \cdot 10^{-6}$	$6.2 \cdot 10^{-10}$	$2.8 \cdot 10^{-14}$
512	.938	.875	.131	$2.2 \cdot 10^{-2}$	$1.1 \cdot 10^{-5}$	$3.5 \cdot 10^{-10}$	$< 10^{-15}$	$< 10^{-15}$
1024	.969	.938	.116	$1.9 \cdot 10^{-3}$	$5.4 \cdot 10^{-8}$	$2.8 \cdot 10^{-14}$	$< 10^{-15}$	$< 10^{-15}$

Table 5. Values of the upper bound on the decoding error probability, when $(w, w_0) = (32, 64)$, (a, a_0) are expressed by the left-hand side of (91), and $(F, \Phi_r) = (FG_{0,1}, FG_{r,\sigma})$.

where

$$\left(v_{a,a_0}(y_t|1), v_{a,a_0}(y_t|0) \right) = \left(\frac{1}{a - a_0} \int_{-a}^{-a_0} v(y_t|x)\, dx, \frac{1}{a - a_0} \int_{+a_0}^{+a} v(y_t|x)\, dx \right) \tag{94}$$

6. Conclusion

We believe that there is a request for general theory of processing biometric data, caused by a large variety of parameters that can be taken into account and their different descriptions. It is usually difficult to find a probabilistic models for biometric observations received both at the enrollment and the verification stages that agree with practical situations. One of the most important features is privacy protection, which makes the reconstruction of outcomes of biometric measurements on the basis of the corresponding record record, stored in the database difficult. Another part of privacy protection should make the generation of artificial outcomes of the measurements that allow an attacker to pass through the verification with the acceptance decision difficult. The algorithms presented above can be considered as candidates for the inclusion into such a theory. We introduce the F-transformation of input data, where F specifies some probability distribution. As a result, the data are mapped into the $(-1, +1)$ interval and, if the actual probability distribution is memoryless and it coincides with the multiplicative extension of F, then we attain a uniform probability distribution over the $(-1, +1)$ interval. Otherwise, a uniform distribution can be approached using a generalized version of the F-transformation. The use of the proposed technique for noisy observations at the verification stage leads to an interesting effect that rare outcomes over the artificial ensemble, defined by the probability distribution F and the corresponding probability density function P, are reliably transmitted over any additive observation channel, since $P(r(y))$ appears in the denominator of the constructed probability density function (see 48). This property allows us to transmit large magnitudes over the constructed $X \to Y$ channel with high reliability. Notice that this claim is not affected by the match of the actual probability distribution of input data and the introduced probability distribution F.

The points above can be translated to different verification strategies. Our verification algorithm can be viewed as a secret sharing scheme where the input vector $\boldsymbol{r}$ is converted to a pair of vectors $(\tilde{\boldsymbol{x}}, \boldsymbol{s})$. The vector $\tilde{\boldsymbol{x}}$ is published, while the vector $\boldsymbol{s}$ is supposed to be decoded on the basis of the vector $\tilde{x}$ and a noisy version of the vector r. An important ingredient of the presented algorithms is the dependence of the threshold T on the pair (a, a_0). This dependence assumes that the verifier assigns this pair depending on the vector x received at the enrollment stage. Some other verification schemes are described in [20].

Author details

Vladimir B. Balakirsky[1] and A. J. Han Vinck[2]

1 Data Security Association "Confident", St-Petersburg, Russia
American University of Armenia, Yerevan, Armenia
2 Institute for Experimental Mathematics, University of Duisburg-Essen, Essen, Germany

References

[1] Bolle, R. M., Connell, J. H., Pankanti S., Ratha, N. K., & Senior A. W. (2004). *Guide to Biometrics.*

[2] Ross, A., Jain, A. K., & Zhang, D. (2006). *Handbook on Multibiometrics.*

[3] Tuyls, P., Scoric, B., & Kavenaar, T. (2007). *Security with Noisy Data: Private Biometrics, Secure Key Storage and Anti–Counterfeiting.*

[4] Bhattacharyya, D., Ranjian, R., Alisherov, F., & Choi, M. (2009). Biometric authentication: A review, *International Journal of u- and e-Service, Science and Technology,* vol. 2, no. 3, pp. 13–28.

[5] Balakirsky, V. B., Ghazaryan, A. R., & Han Vinck, A. J. (2007). Testing the independence of two non–stationary random processes with applications to biometric authentication, *Proceedings of the International Symposium on Information Theory,* France, pp. 2671–2675.

[6] Balakirsky, V. B., & Han Vinck, A. J. (2011). Biometric authentication based on significant parameters, *Lecture Notes in Computer Science: Biometrics and ID management,* vol. 6583, pp. 13–22.

[7] Voloshynovskiy, S., Koval, O., Beekhof, F., Farhadzadeh, F., & Holotyak, T. (2011). Private content identification based on soft fingerprinting, *Proceedings of SPIE Photonics West, Electronic Imaging, Media Forensics and Security XIII.* San Fransisco, U.S.A.

[8] Balakirsky, V. B., Voloshynovskiy, S., Koval, O., & Holotyak, T. (2011). Information–theoretic analysis of privacy protection for noisy identification based on soft fingerprinting, *Proceedings of International Conference "Computer Science and Information Technologies"*, Yerevan, Armenia, pp. 107–110. http://www.csit.am/2011/

[9] Kullback, S. (1968). *Information Theory and Statistics.*

[10] Ahlswede, R., & Csiszár, I. (1993) Common randomness in information theory and cryptography, Part I: Secret sharing, *IEEE Transactions on Information Theory,* vol. 39, pp. 1121–1132.

[11] Han, T. S. & Verdu, S. (1993). Approximation theory of output statistics, *IEEE Transactions on Information Theory*, vol. 39, pp. 752–772.

[12] Ignatenko, T., & Willems, F. M. J. (2008). Privacy leakage in biometric secrecy systems, *Proceedings of the 46th Annual Alerton Conference on Communication, Control and Computing*, U.S.A., pp. 850–857.

[13] Levin, L. A. (2003). The tale of one–way functions, *Problems of Information Transmission*, vol. 39, no. 1, pp. 92–103.

[14] Venugopalan, S., & Savvides, M. (2011). How to generate spoofed irises from an iris code template, *IEEE Transactions on Information Forensics and Security*, vol. 6, no. 2, pp. 385–395.

[15] Puente, L., Poza, M. J., Ruiz, B., & Carrero, D. (2011). Biometrical fusion – input statistical distribution, *Advanced Biometric Technologies*, InTech, pp. 87–108. doi:10.5772/18092.

[16] Boumbarov, O., Velchev, Y., Tonchev K., & Paliy, I. (2011). Face and ECG based multi–model biometric authentication, *Advanced Biometric Technologies*, InTech, pp. 67–86. doi:10.5772/21842.

[17] Inuma, M., Otsuka, A., & Imai, H. (2009). Theoretical framework for constructing matching algorithms in biometric authentication systems, *Lecture Notes in Computer Science: Advances in Biometrics*, vol. 5558, pp. 806–815.

[18] Balakirsky, V. B., Ghazaryan, A. R., & Han Vinck, A. J. (2009b). Mathematical model for constructing passwords from biometrical data, *Security and Communication Networks*, vol. 2, no. 1, pp. 1–9.

[19] Balakirsky, V. B., & Han Vinck, A. J. (2010). A simple scheme for constructing fault–tolerant passwords from biometric data, *EURASIP Journal on Information Security*, vol. 2010. doi:10.1155/2010/819376.

[20] Balakirsky, V. B. (2012). Binary multimedia wrap approaches to verification over noisy data. Submitted to *The Computer Journal*.